THE ETHICAL FOUNDATIONS

OF ECONOMICS

THE ETHICAL FOUNDATIONS OF ECONOMICS

JOHN J. PIDERIT, S.J.

GEORGETOWN UNIVERSITY PRESS / WASHINGTON, D.C.

Georgetown University Press, Washington, D.C.   20057–1079
© 1993 by Georgetown University Press. All rights reserved.
Printed in the United States of America
10 9 8 7 6 5 4 3 2 1   1993
THIS VOLUME IS PRINTED ON ACID-FREE OFFSET BOOK PAPER.

Library of Congress Cataloging-in-Publication Data

Piderit, John J.
      The ethical foundations of economics   /   John J. Piderit.
            p.   cm.
      Includes bibliographical references.
          1. Economics--Moral and ethical aspects.   2. Economics-
-Philosophy.   I. Title.
HB72.P53   1992   330'.01--dc20   92-41288
ISBN 0-87840-535-6

*To Mother and Dad,
who made the tradition come alive*

Contents

Preface

In recent years the discipline of economics in the United States has alienated many—students, practitioners, and ordinary citizens. Its almost mechanical approach to problems is irritating while its purported value neutrality is cloying. Most of all, citizens are disenchanted, not because they are overly familiar with the contents of economics but because the country has experienced the less than overwhelming success of policies recommended by mainstream economists. Faced with lethargic growth and uncomfortably high unemployment rates, people expect the experts to ameliorate the situation. But in the eyes of the populace, who judge both by empirical results and plausibility, economists have lost their touch since many of their policy recommendations are neither effective nor convincing.

In the 1960s and 1970s economists proposed sweeping changes in taxing patterns and levels of government expenditure, and the policies worked—at least for a while. But in the 1980s they encouraged the government to allow greater freedom to individual industries in the expectation that unfettered competition would lead to a dramatic upturn in economic activity. Introduced in democratically haphazard fashion, such alterations often had, at best, a modest beneficial impact. The changes did not make a significant difference in areas central to people's lives: employment, income, safety, health, education, the environment, civility, and even domestic tranquility. Instead, younger people today have to work harder to enjoy a standard of living below the level attained by their parents, while more of their time is spent coping with crime, inadequate health care, rudeness, tension about domestic finances, and uncertainty concerning the stability of their marriages.

Economists belonging to different traditions have tried their respective approaches and the results have not been encouraging. No particular group of economic theorists or practitioners can point to unparalleled successes, though distinct schools of economics remain committed to their respective assumptions. Each school recommends to interested parties more faithful adherence to the tenets of its own doctrine, convinced that systematic application of all its policy prescriptions will generate strong, steady economic growth.

Politicians and ordinary citizens, however, remain skeptical—and for good economic reasons. Economists believe in incremental changes. For them, modest changes in key variables should produce detectable improvements in the economy. But if few of the incremental changes introduced during the past twenty years have made the economy tangibly more vigorous, why, the common people ask, should we dramatically change the system? Is the only way to test whether a particular school of economics has the correct approach to overhaul the entire economy so that it conforms to the assumptions of that school of economics? And, is such experimentation worth the disruption to people's lives that would inevitably ensue in subsequent years?

Thus, the current anemic performance by the economy has occasioned disillusionment among the public and even some economists. But for most economists, including myself, disquiet is not a reason for despair. The economy will inevitably improve when this business cycle ends, as it surely will. The economy will experience a new spurt and put people back to work. Unfortunately, however, the upturn in the economy will mask important shortcomings in economic science as currently practiced.

Economics is much more than formulating policies and forecasting growth rates for particular industries or the entire economy. Like any discipline, economics exists to provide insight into the human endeavor. It should help nations, firms, and individuals to understand their economic past and develop fruitful alternatives for the future. Consequently, although the discipline may occasionally offer errant forecasts and make weak policy recommendations, in principle it should also help explain how a country arrived at its current position or what goals a country or person should strive for in the future.

The real reason for popular impatience with economics is its limited relevance. During the past ten years economists began, with good reason, seriously to restrict the applicability of their theories. Using excessively general mathematical assumptions in the post-World War II era, they gradually perceived that they were forcing reality to fit these assumptions. As economists discovered how complex the reality is that they try to grasp in their models and how austere their assumptions concerning consumer and producer behavior were, they became increasingly aware that any applications to actual situations must be tentative at best.

Policy recommendations that used to be made confidently to the federal government were gradually hedged with a multitude of cautionary provisos. Whether the suggested changes were at the macro or microeconomic level, intellectual honesty required economists to note that a policy will be effective only if particular circumstances are fulfilled. Policies that, because of their broad applicability, once offered insight and hope for legislators and executives are now riddled with caveats, warning legislators that policy prescriptions do not apply unless numerous, unrealistic conditions are fulfilled. Consequently, noneconomists are less inclined to look to economics for assistance in resolving large problems.

Porous, meticulously qualified policies developed by modern economists attract many special interest groups who latch on to one or more of the provisos, which they use for their own advantage. With so many groups pulling proposed laws in different directions, any policy initiative becomes disoriented and moves only in the direction of the group that exerts the most force. This is a distressing situation for all economic actors, except, of course, those powerful agents who implement policies that increase their own profits or well-being.

Even more problematic is modern economic's seeming neglect of all ethical topics other than the distribution of income or wealth. For example, in the United States, crime is an issue that deeply concerns most citizens, and yet economics offers no solution, not even an idealistic one, to this difficulty. Indeed, crime even appears justified by the assumptions of mainstream economics, one of which is that people maximize their own self-interest, without regard for their neighbor. Is not someone who steals merely trying to maximize his own self-interest? Confronted with the social evil of robbery, society may strike back with intimidation. The threat of jail might be a deterrent, but only if the potential criminal is disturbed by the prospect. This is unlikely in a society in which even young criminals view a prison sentence as equivalent to having received a medal, or, alternatively, in situations where young people see prison as a safe place that harbors them from the chaos and savagery of street life. Similarly, drug use can be viewed as maximizing satisfaction in the short run and a means to block out vision of the long run. Though deeply injurious to human living, drugs and crime are too readily compatible with the assumptions of mainstream economics. Finally, although effective education is known to be important for the functioning of a modern economy, economists are unable to propose a strategy for improving education that is acceptable to a majority of the population. A voucher system, national testing, an expanded Head Start program—all these have been suggested, but the economic reasoning behind them is unconvincing to many.

Ethical arguments, in my opinion, offer more insight and can be more persuasive when such fundamental and troubling issues are under consideration. However, because mainstream economists have consciously separated ethical considerations from their economic analysis and believe that maximizing self-interest, along with other non-ethical assumptions, are necessary and sufficient explanations for human behavior, they view ethical reasons as superfluous.

Most people, including academics and researchers, do not lack ethical convictions to guide them in life. But economists do not distinguish between ethical convictions, on the one hand, and preferences, such as a predilection for a green sweater rather than a red one, on the other hand. Furthermore, even if convictions were acknowledged to be distinct from preferences, economists realize that people disagree about the validity of contending ethical principles. The plurality of moral codes among individuals is surely a salutary warning to economists and philosophers alike to discriminate carefully if they want to help people relate their ethical convictions to economic activity.

When faced with a diversity of plans and products, economists recommend competition. Strangely, however, they adhere to a single ethical tradition, namely utilitarianism, in their treatment of moral behavior, about which people have conflicting views. Utilitarianism prescribes that individuals should choose those actions that produce the greatest satisfaction or happiness, and that, similarly, society should be structured so as to maximize the general welfare. The latter prescription is inaccurately captured in the popular phrase "the greatest good for the greatest number of people." Despite the popularity of utilitarian explanations for human behavior, at least a superficial variety of ethical convictions about important personal and social issues exists. Given a diversity of opinions about practical, economic matters competition—provided it is feasible—is the process most likely to produce an optimal outcome, both because competition highlights qualities of goods that are attractive to consumers and because the price mechanism is a very effective means of conveying large amounts of important information to consumers. In this spirit, I recommend competition in morality, and I begin by examining a second ethical tradition that is the basis of many practices and institutions currently prevailing not only in the United States but in many other countries in the Western hemisphere. And just as utilitarianism is a broad tradition with many subtraditions, like a river with many eddies, so also the tradition I examine admits of many variants. Indeed, in order to appeal to a broad spectrum, I have intentionally formulated it in such a way that it encompasses or points to many different subtraditions.

This book attempts to demonstrate both the reasonableness of a distinguished ethical tradition and also the ability of this tradition to address a wide range of ethical issues—economic as well as personal and social. The particular tradition I have selected is the one that was commonly accepted by the framers of the U.S. constitution and by Catholic, Protestant, and Jewish churches until about the middle of this century. It is called the natural law tradition, so entitled because its adherents believe that just as there is one human nature that dictates the way a heart beats, a brain functions, or a lung breathes, so there is a common ethical law—admittedly quite general—to which all people are bound by conscience to adhere. But images of the human anatomy should not be pressed too closely since the natural law is not biologically or genetically determined. The primary criterion for human conduct in the natural law tradition is correct reason, a concept analyzed and developed at length in subsequent chapters.

This presentation of the natural law is a new articulation of a tradition extending back over two thousand years. Distinguished by its pedigree, the natural law also remains vital in modern times, as evidenced by natural law concepts used in ordinary moral language and precepts. The reader will find that the natural law as presented in this study strikes sympathetic chords as well as discordant notes. When either of these phenomena occurs, I recommend patience and critical reflection. To profit from this book, the reader must possess a willingness to contemplate an alternative to utilitarian thought and language, and some of the new concepts proposed here may initially appear alien. Indeed, an attractive quality of the natural law tradition is that it is markedly different, both in terminology and in its ethical principles, from utilitarianism—the ethical system that modern economics has relied upon and which many people employ to explain and justify their behavior.

My goal is to formulate the natural law in such a way that most readers will identify the contours of it in their own lives. I do this because an important claim of natural law is that it is embedded in human living and reason. The inquisitive person has only to look carefully to recognize it in her own life. Nonetheless, I realize that some people adhere to different traditions whose formulations contradict the tenets of the natural law and that those people will not easily change their allegiance. Realistically, therefore, the natural law tradition should be considered as one possible way to live one's economic life. The reader is challenged to consider whether the natural law tradition enables a person to live one's economic life better—an issue that cannot even be addressed within the narrow confines of the neoclassical tradition.

In order to help people understand better the patterns of the society in which they live, I apply natural law precepts to economic activities prevalent in the last quarter of the twentieth century. Two reasons especially motivate this endeavor. First, people should realize that, despite the many random components that contribute to the structure of various institutions in society, a unifying theme exists that justifies the basic structure of social institutions. Efficiency—the primary trait examined by mainstream economists—is an important principle of justice, since any society should not waste valuable resources. But, just as parents sometime tolerate waste because it is inextricably linked to the healthy development of their children, so efficiency must be balanced by application of additional principles of justice. Second, many people cannot work effectively unless they perceive that they make a contribution to the common good. An attractive feature of the natural law approach is that, in addition to placing the common good at the center of moral life, it specifies the contours of the common good so that people can identify the ways in which their activities promote the common good. If need be, people can modify their activities so that they more effectively contribute.

Once I have presented an expression and justification for the natural law tradition, I explore whether mainstream economics, as practiced in the United States and elsewhere, accommodates the natural law system. Although many people use a utilitarian framework to justify their ethical convictions, the natural law approach identifies values that, according to the natural law tradition, most people perceive to be integral to their lives. Because utilitarian explanations of human behavior are sometimes compatible and coincident with a natural law accounting of the same conduct, people often do not distinguish carefully between the two traditions. I show, however, that the natural law tradition has distinct ethical imperatives not found in the utilitarian tradition.

Ethics is critical reflection upon those activities that human beings feel constrained either to perform or to avoid. Because ethics considers elemental experiences of all human beings, any ethical system should be applicable to the broad range of activities in which human beings engage. In particular, an ethical system that touches the taproot of the human being should have some application to economic activities. Furthermore, the guiding principles in one's personal life should be seamlessly related to the principles that inform the way significant institutions in society function. Personal, economic, social, and institutional ethics should have a unified base.

Utilitarianism claims to be open to different ethical systems and emphasizes equal treatment of all people. But it respects ethical diversity by placing each person's ethical convictions in a black box. According to the neoclassical approach, people act only to pursue their own self-interest, and one person's ethical convictions are of no concern to another person. Because utilitarianism professes complete openness to all ethical systems, it pretends to an objectivity not available to rival ethical systems. Notwithstanding utilitarianism's claims and its favorable image in society, it has a narrow perspective that is incompatible with rival traditions such as natural law. I invite economists to explore this alternative ethical system and to examine whether it is indeed compatible with the neoclassical approach.

In addition to the assumption of narrow self-interest, neoclassical economics also assumes that each consumer maximizes his or her own self-interest and that each firm sets maximization of profits as its sole goal, assumptions that are not easily compatible with the pursuit of the common good and the avoidance of all actions that harm certain fundamental values. The strength of the neoclassical assumptions is that they yield an important result: a perfectly competitive economy is also an efficient one. The issue of efficiency is important to economists and philosophers alike, and I invite philosophers and ethicians to consider the questions of efficiency and motivation by examining the qualities of a free market system. If neoclassical economists did not so insistently claim and demonstrate that the free market system is efficient, ethicians would have to undertake such analyses themselves. As noted earlier, all other things being equal, society should prefer an economy which does not waste resources to one which does. In order to prevent dissipation of goods and resources, ethicians must understand how motives influence the efficient functioning of society. Neoclassical economists have many useful things to say about how institutions should be structured in situations in which it can reasonably be assumed that people act to maximize their self-interest. For example, when shopping in a supermarket or pondering which new car to purchase, a person legitimately pursues his or her own self-interest. Restricted to the right types of situations, maximization of self-interest yields efficiency within that segment of human activity. The important ethical-economic questions are: In what situations should self-interest be normative and what is in a person's self-interest?

As a Jesuit and a Catholic priest, I have lived many years in a community that professes to adhere to the natural law tradition. Some people might think that my experience introduces a bias. I agree. But there is no such person as the perfectly objective observer. Either one belongs to the utilitarian tradition or to the natural law tradition or to some other one. Long before people reflect on their moral tradition, they live it. The unbiased observer is a mythical figure that is a useful abstraction in certain disciplines, including economics and philosophy. However, no person is unbiased with respect to the moral tradition in which she or he has participated. What I have tried to do is what I ask readers to do. Standing firmly within their own tradition of moral living and inquiry, they should consider whether the natural law approach attends more carefully than their current tradition to the issues considered important by the reader.

If objectivity in the sense of not being affiliated with a tradition is a requirement for reaching the truth, I am as vulnerable as a neoclassical economist as I am as an adherent to the natural law tradition. My training has been thoroughly neoclassical, with an occasional dash of Keynesian economics. Living and thinking in the neoclassical tradition has helped me understand many facets of economic behavior in the United States. While it may also blind me to certain realities, it does not prevent me from noticing the ways in which the neoclassical system fails to fulfill my expectations as a moral agent.

Although the natural law tradition has been associated for many centuries with religious belief, I have chosen for tactical reasons to bypass this link. Even in our pluralist society, religion can be divisive, and I prefer that readers focus on the unifying aspects of the natural law tradition, not the particularities of individual subtraditions. Nonetheless, I do not deny that respect for the demands of one's conscience and belief in God are interwoven. If a person considers herself truly free but also sincerely believes that, according to her conscience, she must act in a certain way if she is to become more fully human, this person at least inchoately acknowledges the existence of a super-human, transcendent power to which (or to whom) she is free to respond yes or no. Therefore, a very close connection exists in the natural law tradition between belief in God and acknowledging that the fundamental values make preemptive demands that dictate the manner in which a person responds in certain situations not of her own choosing.

Because this book tries not to presume too much economics or philosophy, it can be used profitably as a text for students in undergraduate courses. Two types of students will especially benefit from the book. First, students majoring in economics or business who have taken an intermediate microeconomics course will understand better why utilitarianism is such a particular assumption of the neoclassical approach. Many examples have been chosen to stimulate students of economics to reflect more critically about the wisdom they expect to derive from economics. Second, philosophy students who have received a general introduction to different philosophical systems will find here a schematic presentation of one version of natural law. Also described and analyzed is the standard neoclassical model of consumer and producer behavior. Philosophy students will be familiar with a number of the ethical problems addressed by the natural law tradition, but the economic sections of the text will force them to examine seriously economic efficiency and how moral concerns should be integrated into economic models. As is true for economics or business majors, philosophy students can profitably use the book as an accompanying manual for an intermediate course. By exploring a particular moral tradition and one school of economics, they will understand better the differences among the traditions and be in a better position to select that mode of living and inquiry with which they wish to identify. Even if a reader is not attracted to natural law theorizing, responding to the challenges raised by the natural law tradition can sharpen the reader's appreciation of his preferred position. The charts and diagrams contained in the text are presented not merely as a welcoming gesture to economists but also as a visual summary of the arguments presented. They also relate new material to familiar economic models.

This book requests readers to explore different aspects of their personal and professional experience. It invites economists to consider their own moral convictions and to examine whether neoclassical economics has a broad enough base to support those convictions. Similarly, it summons philosophers and ethicians to review a modern version of natural law to determine whether it captures the salient components of that tradition. Finally, the book challenges philosophers and ethicians to treat realistically human motives for action, which are at times self-centered, envious, or altruistic.

How economists and non economists use the discipline of economics depends on personal aspirations. Many noneconomists approach economics groping for insight into the way they function and the way they ought to interact in the market place. Sometimes economists offer sound general policies, but if economics teachers are careful in applying neoclassical economics to reality, they must qualify most things they recommend with a host of conditional clauses. A second group of economists acknowledge the myriad restrictions that must be attached to their results and choose, therefore, to deemphasize policy recommendations A third group of economists turn the assumptions of neoclassical economics into moral imperatives. That is, in addition to assuming what the actual behavior of consumers is, e.g., that they maximize their own self-interest, this group of economists falsely raise the assumption to the level of a moral injunction. Thus, someone who maximizes her own self-interest becomes, by some arbitrary definition, a smart, rational person. Although such an approach is completely unjustified and is recognized by neoclassical economists to be unwarranted, many people nonetheless proclaim a moral principle where there is only a mathematical and economic assumption.

This text is unlikely to generate enthusiasm in people whose primary satisfaction comes from a fascination with the technical aspects of economics. Some economists enjoy the mathematical features of the science and delight in proving a theorem or deriving in rigorous fashion a significant result. Although not a kill-joy, I envision this book for people whose main concern is relating the human endeavor to economic issues. Some people are buoyed up by using economics to create a better society. Others come to economics looking for wisdom that will help them in their personal lives and in their understanding about society. This book is intended for them.

I sympathize with the desire of the student to discover something deeply human about herself or himself and others, even in economics. Many practices and features of institutions in U.S. society can be better explained by appealing to the natural law tradition, which circumscribes the human good by identifying important human goals. The first step that any economic agent must undertake is to set goals for herself or himself. But, economic goals should be related to general human goals and the means used to attain the goals should not conflict with the goals themselves. Such goals or fundamental values help define the meaning of a person. The natural law tradition provides the basis for addressing these issues in a rationally consistent manner. Furthermore, the wisdom contained in this tradition can generate excitement both for neoclassical economists as well as for those belonging to others schools of economic thought. Exploring the economic implications of a natural law ethics will revitalize economics, whether the economy is at the peak or trough of a business cycle.

CHAPTER 1

Introduction

Because economists consider themselves to be scientists while ethicians regard themselves as philosophers and humanists, both groups find it difficult to evaluate one another's work with an open mind. In their professional work, economists consciously avoid making ethical judgments, while philosophers think that mathematical rigor prevents economists from addressing weighty economic problems involving ethical issues. Instead, each group prefers to stake out proprietary areas of professional responsibility while remaining cordial to one another when they approach common borders. Mutual respect is offered, but not mutual appreciation. If, in the real world, the influence which ethics and economics have on one another was restricted to insignificant border territory, the inability of economists and ethicians to appreciate how their disciplines intersect would be of little importance. In fact, however, each discipline remains essentially incomplete without the other. Unless economics takes seriously the ethical convictions of individuals and groups in society, economic models cannot realistically be applied to a world in which behavior is guided not merely by preferences but by convictions as well. Similarly, ethics speaks only to saints if it does not take seriously people's ordinary desires to increase their income and improve their standing in society.

Communication between ethics and economics can occur only if thinkers in the two disciplines share some common ground. The purpose of this study is to identify the common territory shared by the two disciplines and to indicate ways in which each area requires the services of the other. In order to gain even reluctant acquiescence from economists that ethics has valid insights for them, one must explain to them how ethicists ply their trade, and to make the common perspective secure, one must allay their fears that by remaining open to ethical

1

arguments they are surrendering their most prized possession, namely, rigor. Then the same process must be reversed to assure ethicists that economic modeling captures important aspects of human behavior.

In the early chapters, considerable time is spent justifying an ethical framework which portrays the ways in which economic institutions have been shaped by or ought to be more influenced by the broad ethical principles derived here. In the final three chapters the neoclassical paradigm is subjected to a critique, the foundation of which is provided in the earlier chapters. The goal of this study is not simply to juxtapose ethics and economics but rather to integrate an established ethical framework into the neoclassical paradigm.

1.1 ETHICAL JUDGMENTS

In a pluralist society individuals make distinct, and sometimes conflicting, ethical judgments. One person may think it ethically wrong to take office supplies for personal use, to keep a wallet found on the street, regularly to spend weekends on the job and away from his or her spouse and family, or to use insider information for private advantage. Another person may find such activities undesirable or unsavory, but not condemn them as ethically wrong. Still another may have no qualms about performing such actions. The fact that three persons disagree concerning particular issues does not mean, however, that they lack consensus about more fundamental ethical issues. What constitutes greed for one person may be interpreted by another as merely the efficient operation of the market. Despite differences, substantial agreement is possible. For example, most people condemn lying and the dissemination of false information, whether in the marketplace or elsewhere. Although pluralism in modern society may be disconcerting to some, it tolerates many types of variety. However, pluralism is not a mandate to disagree on all issues, nor is it an injunction against seeking common ground.

Ethical judgments have consequences, and establishing a consensus about ethical judgments increases in difficulty as the number of people involved grows. Most people have diverse judgments about what constitutes a system of fair income taxes. Most also have strong and disparate ethical opinions concerning society's responsibilities to the sick, the mentally disturbed, and the homeless. For many particular social issues, solid reasons can be provided to justify sundry ethical judgments. But the diversity of opinions concerning social issues, which are inherently more complex than personal moral dilemmas, should not be taken as a paradigm for moral problems, which are more specifically personal, although even personal moral dilemmas invariably contain a social element. Personal moral issues—such as lying, loyalty, respect for one's parents, harming others, stealing—elicit a more uniform response. Most people, for example, condemn lying and praise loyalty or commitment even though they may disagree about what actions they judge acceptable in particular moral situations involving lying or loyalty.

The starting point for our ethical deliberations is a unity amid diversity, coherence in the face of variety, agreement about personal behavior but bitter discord concerning social issues. People appear to use some common approach in resolving personal ethical problems since many people condemn the same things and approve the same things about their personal actions. Social issues, on the other hand, provoke a baffling array of answers and approaches; they also produce great variety in the degree of certitude which people ascribe to the positions they hold. Some are stolid and unwavering in their support for one approach whereas others are tentative, even about matters which many other people address with clarity and conviction.

1.1.1 Faith and Human Reason

The general agreement that many share concerning some ethical judgments suggests a body of ethical imperatives or injunctions which are available to all people in a society. People should not steal; adultery is wrong; employers have to pay a fair wage—most people would support these judgments even if they are unable to provide reasons for their support. For some the weightiest reason may be that wise and religious people have always considered these judgments to be correct. Most people have not considered reflectively and critically the ethical prescriptions which they support and to which they try to adhere. Hence for them ethical prescriptions may simply be the distilled beliefs of previous generations that parents pass on to their children because parents continue to believe that traditional ethical prescriptions are valid. The belief of such people in their point of view is shored up by some evidence. They can point, for example, to their own experience in a community that confirms their ethical views. They can cite great thinkers, saints, or admirable people who espouse the same ethical views. They can depict the ways in which individuals or societies go astray if they do not adhere to the ethical principles or rules under discussion. In short, such people, given their own native endowments, may be acting reasonably by invoking their own experience and their own tradition, even if they never undertake a careful evaluation of their experience and tradition.

Because most people do not critically appraise their ethical principles and instead accept them as they are handed down, some thinkers equate ethical conviction with religious belief, although they acknowledge that the subject matter is different. But the striking phenomenon is that people share common moral beliefs. If the communality of ethical judgments is based on belief in a religious or secular sense, it is remarkable that significantly different traditions of religious beliefs converge in their ethical or moral prescriptions. Especially in the United States, which has been nourished by various ethnic groups over the years, the broad acceptance of the Judeo-Christian tradition requires an explanation. Some people are satisfied with the reason that "these are the traditions or beliefs of our forebears"; others legitimately demand a comprehensive and critical analysis of the foundation of ethical principles.

The explanation for widespread agreement about personal ethical judgments provided in this study is that a common rationality underlies all ethical reasoning. Economists have a particular concept of rationality. They say an economic agent is rational if he or she uses resources efficiently to achieve a desired goal. The ultimate goal of a consumer in the economist's model is human happiness or satisfaction. For most people to achieve happiness or satisfaction they need material goods and services: food and drink, a house, water, electricity, clothes, insurance, etc. Since goods and services are scarce and require time and effort to be produced, the consumer or producer does not waste resources, but, instead, uses them to the best advantage to attain happiness. From the economist's perspective such a person is rational.

In this work we adopt a broader view of rationality that includes the ethical dimension in the life of any economic agent. A person makes a rational ethical judgment when he or she uses those ethical principles that can be derived by human reason in the context of human community and applies the principles aptly to a particular case. "Lying is ethically wrong" is an example of an ethical judgment that, when experienced in a human community, can be derived from human reason by those living in the community, according to the approach taken in this study. Note that the word "ethically" is included in order to preclude the interpretation that lying is wrong because one may suffer ill consequences as a result of the lie.

The economist may agree that lying is ethically wrong and concur that each person has an obligation to adhere to this injunction in all situations, including economic ones. But the economist may justify her neglect of moral prescriptions because she thinks that ethical considerations have only minor implications for economic analysis and can therefore be relegated to ethicists for separate treatment and critical reflection. This study rejects that view and, relying on an ethical tradition which in various forms has existed in the United States since its inception and in Western society since Aristotle, analyzes the implications of ethical principles for economic behavior and analysis.

A complete ethical system should specify the meaning of different ethical concepts, including moral wrong, virtue, justice, and cruelty. The potential for moral misunderstanding is considerable because these concepts have indistinct boundaries. A moral concept is like a lake surrounded by a marsh area; it may be impossible to draw a line which everyone acknowledges separates the lake from the marsh. Nonetheless, notwithstanding the essential fuzziness of many concepts (not only ethical ones), I hope to show that, just as vast areas of a lake are clearly not marsh, moral concepts can be used unambiguously in a wide variety of situations. I intend to convince the reader that statements such as "Lying is ethically wrong" can be given an acceptably precise meaning and can be shown to be true according to the canons of human reason when they are exercised within a consistent human community. Having grounded personal ethical principles in human reason, I derive ethical principles that guide the manner in which at least some economic interactions ought to take place. Such principles have their marshy areas, and we cannot expect to solve every ethical, economic dilemma. Nonetheless, because a number of important ethical principles are near the center of the lake, people with open minds can acknowledge that such principles are properly used to resolve dilemmas because the principles are in clear water, away from the marshes.

From earliest times, reflection upon what is right and wrong took place in societies in which belief in God or gods was pervasive. Undoubtedly, a deep connection binds together religion, ethical theory, and ethical behavior. In this study I concentrate on ethical theory and practice. Without denigrating the impact of religion on moral theory and practice, I wish to emphasize the underlying rationality of ethical decisions, especially those concerning economic matters. In a later section I will use an example from sacred writings to show that purely secular ethical rationality can be consistent with ethical tenets stated or proclaimed in a religious context.

1.1.2 The Structure of Ethical Judgments

Ethical judgments conform to a certain grammatical syntax. The syntax requires three elements: a subject or agent of responsibility; an action to be performed or avoided; and a word, such as "ought" or "should" or "must" or a host of similar words, which indicates that the agent of responsibility is under moral pressure to perform or omit the action. The word that expresses moral pressure will be called the ethical imperative. Two examples, one positive and one negative, illustrate the matter.

Positive: An adult ought to help his or her parents in their old age.
Negative: As long as a person is married, he or she should not have sex with someone other than his or her spouse.

The agents of responsibility in these statements are, respectively, all adults and all married persons. In the positive statement the ethical imperative is "ought to"; in the negative example it takes the form of "should not." In the positive case the action to be performed is assistance to one's parents and in the negative case extramarital sex is proscribed.

For most people and in most circumstances, ethical judgments are personal ones that apply either to themselves or to people they know well. The agent of responsibility in these instances is the person making the judgment, in which case the subject or agent of responsibility is "I": "I have to get my parents into a home for the elderly." If the agent of responsibility is known to the person making the judgment, the form used is "you": "Your parents are old and you should help them" or "You are married and should not be playing around with other women."

The logic of all ethical norms is that, although the statement is presented as a "must" or "should" to a particular individual by a specific person, the particular person making the statement implies that other people in similar circumstances are under the same constraint to act in the explicit way indicated by the statement. Any moral prescription exerts pressure on a person to act in a certain way. Many people call the personal compelling force conscience, a faculty that appears to have some characteristics shared by all people as well as other features that are purely personal. However it manifests itself in a particular person, conscience is a force or "voice" that commands acquiescence. Although one may refuse to follow the "voice" of conscience, not only does one feel less a person for doing so but one makes similar judgments about others. Mr. Smith may experience conscience as the command: "You, an adult, ought to help your elderly parents." But if another person exists who is also an adult and is also in similar economic and social circumstances to Mr. Smith, Mr. Smith interprets the imperious command of his own conscience to extend to the other person as well.[1]

In our modern pluralist society many people deny the implication that a personal ethical prescription binds other people in similar circumstances. They may say to their friends: "I ought to help my parents. But that's my own personal judgment. That does not mean that you must help your parents." The first two statements contradict the third statement, unless some difference, other than point of view, is offered that explains why a person thinks his friends are under a different moral obligation than he himself. What the person means to say is: "Although I recognize my obligation to my parents, each individual must make his or her own judgments concerning their moral responsibilities in similar circumstances." This is certainly a correct statement. Every person does make his or her own ethical judgments. However, everyone is under moral pressure to "do the right thing." The nature of moral obligation is that the ethical principles and the circumstances determine what must be done, not the subjective opinion of the person making the judgment. A person making the judgment feels constrained by some higher authority to act in a certain way. When he or she decides what ought to be done in a particular set of circumstances, the emphasis is on the circumstances, not on the individual making the decision. Anybody else in the same circumstances would be morally constrained in the same manner.

Person A may assert "I ought to help my parents in their old age" while Person B states "I am under no obligation to help my parents in their old age." A and B are clearly of different opinions concerning their responsibility to their parents. They are entitled to their own opinions. But, if they consider their moral judgments to be correct, they judge that contrary moral judgments are incorrect. Once one makes a moral judgment, even if its formulation appears to apply only to the person making the statement, that person necessarily implies that all persons in similar circumstances fall under a similar ethical constraint. Since this is the case, the popular aphorism "I'm OK, you're OK" is not just trite; it is also wrong.

The attempt to restrict the application of ethical judgments to one's personal life is understandable, although misguided, in a society as pluralist as that of the United States. Because freedom of belief is a cornerstone of American society, no one should be inclined to impose their views on others. Nonetheless, people become mature only if they are willing to make personal, ethical judgments, and such judgments imply that other people in comparable circumstances should act in a similar manner. To be sure, just because one person thinks that people should act in a certain way does not mean that such a person necessarily wants to change the law so that everyone is legally bound to act in a certain way. Consider a particular case.

Ethical discourse in the United States in the latter part of the twentieth century is colored by the issue of abortion—whether it is morally responsible and whether it should have the protection of law. The case of abortion is singular because it involves a profound question about the inception of human and personal life as well as a question about the extent of human freedom. Understandably in this case, people want their private views, whatever they happen to be, transferred into public policy. On many issues, however, people can make different ethical judgments without seeking legal support for their views. Strong and opposing ethical views need not diminish the freedom of people to act in a democracy. On the other hand, refusing to acknowledge the implications of ethical judgments does not smooth interaction in a pluralist society, but only confuses people about the nature of an ethical imperative.

1.1.3 Casuistry

The previous section concentrated on the nature of the moral imperative, which is revealed by the language of constraint or pressure, in words such as "ought," "should," and "must." For simplicity, we assume that all ethical judgments can be expressed through the word "ought."[2]

Applying general ethical "oughts" or principles to particular situations is known as *casuistry*, a word which is derived from the Latin word *casus*, meaning "a specific case." Once general ethical principles have been enunciated, ethics consists of casuistry, applying the general principles to particular cases. Much current debate concerning disputed moral judgments can be labeled as casuistry. Abortion, euthanasia, insider trading, the plight of the homeless, Third World debt, ecological pollution, the fairness of income taxes, physical abuse—all these pose specific ethical questions, which are answered only by relating them to more general moral principles. When people try to determine which ethical principles are relevant and how the principles should be applied, they are engaging in casuistry. In this sense of the word, casuistry is an essential activity for those who strive to behave in a morally consistent way.

The art of casuistry, which enjoyed a distinguished tradition among moralists until the middle of the seventeenth century, also has a pejorative connotation, acquired mainly through the pen of Blaise Pascal, who in the mid-seventeenth century ridiculed casuists in general (and the Jesuits in particular) for what he considered to be the lax moral precepts that were tolerated by casuist thinkers.[3] Casuistry can refer to a specious type of reasoning that distinguishes so precisely among various factual situations that each situation is in effect completely different from all others. When a person uses the particulars of a situation to arrive at a specific ethical judgment that suits his or her own purposes, that person engages in casuistry in the bad sense of the word. The reasoning in these cases is sophistical because the person is using distinctions to reach a desired conclusion rather than a judgment warranted by the circumstances.[4] In the positive sense of the word, casuistry is required not only to act morally but also to make necessary qualifications to general moral principles.

1.2 ETHICS AND ECONOMICS

In the mind of the ordinary person economics and ethics are closely related since ethical questions often arise in business contexts and because fairness in business promotes good business. Economists admit the connection between ethics and economics, but they judge the effects of ethics on economic behavior to be either minor or unsystematic. They are also aware that no one ethical perspective enjoys broad support by ethicists. Hence, economists try to avoid using any ethical content in their analysis. One way to appreciate the strengths and limitations of the economist's point of view is to review some definitions of economics.

1.2.1 Definitions

Definitions about economics cannot be given apodictically because alternatives exist; therefore, choice justified by reason is required. In their popular textbook, *Economics*, Paul Samuelson and William Nordhaus offer a variety of definitions, all of which delineate common areas for exploration. A representative definition from the list is the following:

> Economics is the science of choice. It studies how people choose to use scarce or limited production resources (land, labor, equipment, technical knowledge), to produce various commodities (such as wheat, beef, overcoats, concerts, roads, and missiles), and to distribute these goods to various members of society for their consumption. (pp. 4–5)

This definition appears to be very broad inasmuch as it includes all material goods and services produced by and distributed to any conceivable group in the United States or in any other country. Nonetheless, the definition is considerably narrower than other possibilities. For this reason, it is referred to as the narrow economic definition while the following one, with an ethical component, is designated the broad definition:

> Economics is the study of choice. It studies how people choose *and ought to choose* to use scarce or limited production resources, to produce various commodities, and to distribute these goods to various members of society for their consumption.

The first definition concentrates on a factual description of an economy. By stating that economics is a science of choice, it seems to suggest that economics analyzes both the factual question, how people choose, and the ethical question, how people ought to choose. But the second sentence of the first definition limits the analysis to the factual aspect: how people choose. Nonetheless, inasmuch as it embraces everything that is used, produced, and distributed in the entire economy, it has indeed an expansive outlook, especially since the concept of goods and services is broadly construed. Within the concept "goods" are included the following categories: final goods, such as wheat, automobiles, food, clothing, and computers; intermediate goods, such as steel, chemicals, fibers, and raw materials; and public goods, such as roads, quiet, clean air and water, safety, and knowledge. Furthermore, the concept "goods" also includes the processes or activities by means of which the goods themselves are produced. Services is a particularly vibrant sector of modern economies and every year new types of services are generated. Banking, transportation, insurance, brokerage activities, telecommunications, and education are all examples of services offered in a modern economy.

In economics, the various inputs used to produce goods are referred to as "factors of production." Usually, three general categories are used: land, labor, and capital. Occasionally, entrepreneurial ability or managerial expertise is considered an additional factor of production, but more frequently is not treated at all, just assumed to exist in the background. Factors of production are examined from two points of view: how much of each is needed to produce a definite amount of a good or service, and how much each factor is paid in equilibrium for its services.

A pluralist society allows great diversity in actions and beliefs. One person may think it fine to be married and concurrently have an intimate relationship with another woman, as long as his wife does not discover the liaison. Another person may find such behavior reprehensible. A similar diversity exists concerning ethical economic judgments. For example, one person may consider the production of computers to be ethically justified, independent of the ultimate use to which they are put. Another may balk at the prospect of selling computers to a white government that is going to use the computers to trace the activities of black people in order to keep them separate from and/or subservient to the whites. When treating ethical issues in economics, one cannot appeal to the objective judgment of a disinterested observer or rely on the usual technical analysis of an economist. In ethical matters, each person is an observer with a set of standards, which are often unclear to the individual. We address this ambiguity when we look more specifically at ethics as a discipline.

The issue of ethical diversity is a thorny one and will be addressed at length in later chapters. For now, it suffices to argue that economics and ethics are not separable areas of study, although they are distinct disciplines. Individual economists may choose to focus their efforts on technical aspects of the economy, but ethical principles influence not only individual economic behavior but also the macroeconomic functioning of the economy as well. The purpose of this text is to highlight ethical problems, to derive ethical principles, to address specific ethical issues that occur in any modern economy, and to arrive at reasoned ethical judgments about these issues.[5]

The point of view presented here is that economics is not merely about which goods are produced, how much is produced, and why those goods and quantities are generated by the economy. Economics also has as an integral part of its subject matter an analysis of whether such goods should be produced at all, whether a lesser or greater amount of such goods should be produced, and why one should produce more, less, or none. Economics ought not to be concerned solely with the manner in which production is organized. Simultaneously with the factual and theoretical analysis of "what," "how much," and "why" of production processes and factors of production, the discipline of economics must also analyze whether the relations among factors of production are as they "ought" to be; whether salaries, wage rates, and profits are as they "should" be; whether certain goods "ought" to be produced at all; and whether the production of some goods "ought" to be increased in order to provide for the needs of people who are not adequately cared for through the normal functioning of the economy.

1.2.2 Private Ethical Norms and Rational Analysis

The justification for segmenting ethical economic analysis from positive and empirical economics is that positive and empirical economics can be treated in a "scientific" manner, although economic methods and scientific procedures in the hard sciences are analogous, at best. Ethical economic analysis examines ethical judgments about economic issues.

Because ethical convictions are essentially private in the sense that they are held by individuals who choose when and how to divulge them, they are not amenable to scientific analysis. They are, however, subject to a rational critique. We have already shown that the language of ethical statements implies that one's personal ethical conviction is also binding on other people in similar circumstances. To this extent, every ethical judgment implies a norm for public action, even if a person chooses not to reveal his or her ethical judgment to others. Despite disagreements, many people share an extensive range of ethical convictions, and the area of agreement is sufficiently broad to enable economists and ethicians confidently to pose the ethical question in economics.

When considering whether to include an ethical component in the definition of economics, one should note the many ways in which productive activities depend upon common standards of decency and behavior. Whether one adheres to a contract, respects the right of private property, carefully disposes of toxic wastes, speaks forthrightly about corruption in one's place of work, or does a "good deed" to a person beset by misfortune, one is abiding by standards that one expects are shared and appreciated at least to some extent by other people in society. Furthermore, many economic decisions are influenced by ethical standards. Whether one spends money on alcohol, clothing, or entertainment is in part an ethical decision. Similarly, a person can work so hard that she destroys her marriage. Most people spend time pondering how to make good economic decisions that are also ethical, and, in my opinion, all people ought to engage in such reflection.

To the extent that the macroeconomic functioning of an economy is driven by the microeconomic foundations, microeconomic analysis that omits ethical considerations may derive results that apply to a nonexisting world, that is, a world in which ethical principles do not have consequences on economic behavior. Of course, economists live in a free country and anyone who wishes can offer a truncated view of reality.[6] However, one should not expect that free citizens will espouse the conclusions of a discipline that neglects such an important component of personal experience. Indeed, I will be arguing that moral standards, because they are shared, are important elements not only in the personal lives of individual economic agents but also in the maintenance of efficiently functioning markets, as well as in the provision of goods for which markets are thin or nonexistent.

1.2.3 Schools of Economics

At present, one can distinguish four broad traditions in the discipline of economics:

> **Neoclassical Economics**: According to this approach, competitive markets exist for most goods, for both present and future

production and consumption. Individual consumers pursue their own self-interest by maximizing their welfare, without regard to the well-being of other individuals in the economy. Firms are assumed to be profit maximizing and, for the most part, to operate in competitive markets. Prices adjust in a timely fashion to reflect scarcity or surplus. Barring government intervention or interference, unemployment and inflation are temporary phenomena that disappear as prices adjust to equilibrate supply and demand. Neoclassical economics assumes that because people have rational expectations, intervention by government is not effective. (One should note that rational expectations is a strong assumption about the ability of individuals and markets as well as an arbitrary assumption about the meaning of rationality.) Monetarism, a small but vocal school within the neoclassical universe, advises a steady and predictable increase in the money supply to stabilize the economy and is opposed to all government intervention in markets.[7]

Keynesian Economics: This brand of economics is similar to neoclassical economics, especially at the level of microeconomics (the study of interactions among economic groups in individual markets). With neoclassical analysis it assumes that consumers are self-interested, well-being maximizers and that producers are profit maximizers. In macroeconomic analysis, i.e., the study of how all markets and government policies interact at the aggregate level, Keynesians differ from the neoclassicals in that they assume prices in some markets adjust slowly, with the result that markets can be in disequilibrium for long periods of time. In particular, they reject the neoclassical assumption that real wages adjust promptly to changes in aggregate demand and supply. As a result, an economy can reach a temporary equilibrium at a level of economic activity which does not employ all people who want to be employed or all machines, some of which are left idle. A latent demand cannot emerge because prices, especially the wage rate, give false signals. The Keynesian prescription is to have the government intervene to stimulate aggregate demand through appropriate fiscal and/or monetary policy.[8]

Institutional Economics: This branch focuses on the structure of economic institutions. It attempts, on the one hand, to explain why economic institutions, such as the modern firm in its different guises, assume the form they do, and, on the other hand, it tries to show how these same institutions influence the level of economic activity in the economy. Because its primary concern is with economic units such as the firm, the government, the family, unions, etc., its focus is primarily at the level of microeconomics. For macroeconomic analysis (the study of how all markets interact together at the aggregate level), most institutionalists follow analyses offered in the Keynesian and neoclassical schools. Though belonging to the institutionalist school, Marxist economics presents a trenchant critique of capitalist institutions and offers its own distinctive analysis of macroeconomic phenomena.

Institutionalists emphasize that important information is only acquired through the expenditure of economic resources (research and analysis) and that institutions (factories, corporations, and partnerships) are established in part because they provide efficient structures to process relevant information. Economic resources must also be expended to draw up contracts and make sure that the parties adhere to the terms of the contract. Some institutions create important structures used to facilitate economic agreements and to verify compliance with contracts. The institutionalist school views certain institutions as the means by which a society efficiently orders economic interactions. Included within this category are economists who emphasize time, i.e., how the sequence in which information is transmitted and decisions are made influences economic equilibrium. The Austrian School is known for the significance which it ascribes to the timing of events and the passage of time. Although the Austrian School has a heritage of distinguished economists, such as Menger and Hayek, it is not currently popular in economic circles.[9]

Humanistic Economics: This school incorporates an ethical perspective and considers the types and amounts of goods which ought to be produced and the types of relationships which ought to exist among different factors of production. It rejects the notion that goods should be produced according to the demands of consumers as expressed in the market, but claims instead that consumers have certain fundamental needs. Essential goods should be produced to alleviate these needs before other less important or even frivolous goods are produced. Similarly, workers and employers ought to work in an environment and under a system of rules which cultivate respect and dignity. There is no commonly accepted appellation for this group, which includes a number of schools. The Post-Keynesian School, the School of Social Economics, and the school of Marxist Economics share common themes and approaches, although each differs in some ways from the others.[10]

The most popular of the various schools listed above is the Neoclassical School. Without prejudice to the other schools, a fair generalization is that the neoclassical approach constitutes the mainstream of modern economic thought. Contrary points of view have to struggle to gain a hearing, and even those who differ with the neoclassicals in particular areas often agree with their analysis on a wide range of issues. The Keynesians, for example, who also appeal to a broad spectrum of the economic profession, generally concur with the neoclassicals (or vice versa) at the level of microeconomics. As indicated above, institutionalists also rely on neoclassicals for their analysis of macroeconomics. The school of humanistic economics conflicts most directly with the neoclassical approach, and the Humanistic School attracts the fewest followers. In short, neoclassical thought rules, despite disagreements about particular issues, and the neoclassical assumptions are the starting point for all rival systems.[11]

In order to relate economics to ethics, one must choose both an economic school and an ethical system. The choice of the ethical system is treated in Chapter 3, while the economic system to be used in this volume is neoclassical economics. We begin with neoclassical economics because, despite its shortcomings, it appears to offer the best explanation for many economic phenomena. Once we encounter economic phenomena that are at variance with standard neoclassical assumptions, we do what any economist would do: change the assumptions.

The Neoclassical School distances itself most clearly from the realm of ethical values since its avowed concern is with the maximizing firm or individual. For this reason, the neoclassical approach appears to be a curious starting point in a book that explores the relationship between ethics and economics. Icy self-interest, which is a bedrock assumption of the neoclassical approach, does not allow much room to consider the plight of the poor or the ethics of lying for the sake of increased profits. In fact, the Neoclassical School seems the least sympathetic to ethical questions, while the Humanistic School is the one most open to ethical considerations.

The Neoclassical School is generally antipathetic to ethical questions but protects itself by asserting that ethical questions, though valid in their own sphere, fall outside the realm of economics. As we have seen, this is true provided one defines economics in such a narrow fashion as to constrain its applicability. Some neoclassical economists (see Mishan [1975,1981]) show just how narrow the interpretations must be in order to avoid important ethical questions.[12]

The school of humanistic economics is, indeed, closest in spirit to the general approach taken in this volume. Two reasons, however, suggest why we should begin our discussion using the neoclassical framework. The first reason is that, were we to choose the school of humanistic economics, we would be speaking to a very limited audience. By choosing the Neoclassical School as a base for ethical thinking, we address a significant body of public opinion. By including Keynesian and institutionalist variants on neoclassical theory, the group of benevolent listeners among economists is enlarged even further. Since ethical reflection belongs, I argue, at the heart of many economic decisions, I use the most respected analysis of economic decisions as a starting point and then show how neoclassical analysis can be enriched as well as modified by incorporating ethical components. Since the Institutionalist School and the school of humanistic economics offer clear areas for ethical questions, if I can demonstrate where the ethical questions occur in the neoclassical system, a fortiori I will have demonstrated that they are, in principle, to be found in the other schools as well.

CHAPTER 2

Approximating the Real World

Academic disciplines are distinguished both by the objects of their attention as well as the manner in which they investigate the particular object or phenomenon. Chemistry and biology, for example, employ similar methods, but explore different objects; biology analyzes cells and other more complicated living organisms, while chemistry examines interactions between substances that are more simply structured than cells. On the other hand, in the fields of both English literature and psychology one examines the human psyche, but English literature explores the images used and tales told by different authors, whereas psychologists conduct experiments on persons. In this chapter I explore the distinctive approaches and subject matters of economics and ethics.

2.1 *STATUS QUAESTIONIS* OR WHAT IS AT ISSUE?

The appropriate degree of abstraction depends on the problem being addressed. What is the problem we are addressing in this volume? In medieval universities, before any professor would ever discuss his analysis of a problem, he would first present what he thought to be the state of the question. Since lectures in medieval universities were in Latin, the professor first reviewed the *status quaestionis*, the state of the question, or, expressed more simply: What questions are being asked and what answers have been offered to date?

The questions addressed in this book are the following: (1) Is the modern economy, which relies on the free-market system, ethically justifiable? (2) What actions are ethically unjustifiable for a moral agent participating in a modern, free-market economy? (3) What actions are ethically mandated for a moral agent participating in a modern, free-market economy?

The following example illustrates the type of analysis to be undertaken. Suppose empirical studies show that the largest ethnic group with members living below the poverty line is the Hispanic group and that current programs are unlikely to improve their situation during the next ten years. In this case, it would be morally wrong for the government to do nothing, and it would be equally wrong for citizens, motivated perhaps by their disinclination to pay more taxes, to urge the government to do nothing. It would be even worse for citizens to support actions or policies that impoverish U.S. Hispanics even further. Thus, one could condemn as ethically unjustifiable a decision to terminate health-care programs such as Medicaid without implementing a realistic alternative for providing health-care services to Hispanics and to others below the poverty line. This is an example of a negative moral prescription involving economics.

It is both more useful as well as more difficult to establish what positive actions will lead to the greatest improvement in the situation of Hispanics in the most efficient manner, i.e., with the least cost to taxpayers. Some people may feel that an affirmative action program with jobs for Hispanics is the best way to lead Hispanics out of poverty. Others may find affirmative action morally repugnant and may recommend increased expenditures on education and job training. Still others may despair of the government setting up programs and providing services that ought, in their opinion, to be supplied by the private sector, and they might recommend instead that Hispanics be given enough money to bring them above the poverty line. Because of the complexity of the situation, reasonable people have legitimate differences concerning the policies that will have the most beneficial effects. No single policy can be identified as the only reasonable one. The important point is to undertake some action that has a reasonable prospect of improving the situation of those who are judged to be in acute need.[1]

One can expect from the economic and ethical analysis conducted in this volume a list of actions, at a suitable level of abstraction, that are morally unjustifiable. One will also be in a position to outline various positive actions or policies that can be taken to remedy injustices. However, people will have differences concerning the effectiveness of such actions. A person need only select one action or policy and pursue it as best they can.

The second and third questions of the *status quaestionis* refer to a moral agent, who is a person, group of persons, or institution that is free to make choices. Because moral obligation begins with the individual, whom we assume to be capable of free choice, the primary moral agent alluded to is the individual consumer or producer in the economy. He or she has the moral obligation to act responsibly in a complex world. Every individual, however, associates with other groups of people in the economy. Some of these groups are moral agents by reason of the concerted actions they regularly undertake. Certainly, a corporation is a moral agent that incurs responsibilities in conducting its economic affairs, and multinational corporations have an important impact on the international economy. Whether a corporation is multinational or not, practically every major corporation either imports or exports significant quantities of goods, borrows money, buys and sells currencies, etc. Such corporations are active participants in and beneficiaries of the system of international trade and finance. Units of municipal, state, and federal government are also moral agents since they make important decisions influencing the development of the economy. Any group of economic agents acting in concert incurs moral obligations. If they engage in the purchase, sale, production or distribution of goods, they have an obligation to consider whether their activities can be justified ethically.

An important question is the subject of moral agency in a corporation. Is the chief executive officer (CEO) in a corporation, for example, responsible for the morality of all activities undertaken by the corporation in its role as an economic agent? As far as the corporate structure is concerned, he, along with the board of directors, is held ultimately responsible for the conduct and profits of the corporation. In theory, the CEO and the directors are responsible to the stockholders, who are the true owners of the corporation (although during most of the twentieth century stockholders of publicly held corporations have chosen not to assert their authority). In recent years, however, stockholders have made it clear that they do not wish to relinquish their moral responsibility for the activities of the corporation. Many corporations have received resolutions submitted by stockholders who oppose certain practices of the corporation. Since these practices have already been approved by the CEO, the CEO and the stockholders are pitted against one another when voting on such resolutions. Although this is an important area for ethical deliberation, I will not address it in this study. Rather, in my treatment I abstract from (disregard) all confusions of moral responsibility that stem from the complexity of individual organizations. Instead, each economic grouping is assumed to constitute a moral agent.

The area of government offers a bewildering array of various agencies with overlapping responsibilities. Elected politicians also have responsibilities—to their constituents, to their families, to the nation, to those in need, to other nations in the world. Individuals working for large governmental agencies also have a responsibility to assist in the elimination of unethical activity in their own agency. Sorting out the ethical priorities in this area would be a useful undertaking, but it will not be attempted in this work.

Due to the large number of identifiable groups that can be classified as moral agents active in a modern economy, we abstract from the many differences among them and consider only two types of groups: corporations and the federal government. For each unit we assume that when it acts, it does so in unison with its members, without internal division or dissension. In the United States, the Congress, the president's office, and the judiciary all constitute units of the federal government and each unit has a large number of agencies. Although often times these individual components act at cross purposes, such differences are neglected in what follows. The government is assumed to act as a single agent, and the same assumption applies to a corporation or business firm.

2.2 THE CORRECT LEVEL OF ABSTRACTION

All thinking involves some abstraction from reality. Therefore, the standard objection to a theoretical analysis that "it is unrealistic" is not telling unless the critic can show how the omission of details substantially changes the results of the analysis. Although thinking implies abstraction, different disciplines choose to neglect certain segments of reality. This section examines the manner in which economics and ethics abstract from reality and their grounds for doing so.

2.2.1 How Economics Abstracts from the Real World

The precise level of abstraction in economics depends on the particular question being asked. In the modern economy the subject matter might be unemployment, taxes, rates of interest, etc. Since concepts of neoclassical economics are being used to understand the functioning of a modern economy, the level of abstraction employed in neoclassical economics is the norm. Traditionally, in neoclassical economics one considers an abstract corporation and identifies it only with respect to its scale and technological characteristics. A firm is located in a market and is considered either small or large depending on its size in relation to other firms in the same market. The name, geographical dispersion, and historical characteristics are not normally of interest to the economist when he or she is trying to understand what the optimal level of output is for the firm or under what conditions the firm earns monopoly profits. In many instances one assumes that a firm has available to it the same technology available to other firms. The financial structure of the firm, the layers of management, the number of plants, the type of goods produced, the ethnic composition of the work force, the training that workers receive—all these are assumed to be unimportant. In other words, one abstracts from such contingencies in order to focus on more important issues, such as pricing, profits, wage rates, and the use of capital.

In the neoclassical world all goods produced in a market are assumed to be of identical quality. If automobiles are being produced there are no lemons, unless a particular economist chooses to examine this phenomenon (see Akerlof [1984]). Not only are goods homogeneous, but so too are factors of production. Occasionally, in order to analyze the effects of policy changes on different classes of labor, one may distinguish between skilled labor and unskilled labor. For the most part, however, labor is labor, without differentiation. Each laborer works with the same care and intensity: there are neither eager beavers nor slouches. Furthermore, all laborers have the same skills within a firm; if one worker has both electrical and carpentry skills, all other workers in the firm have the same skills. Capital usually refers to physical machines, and all capital is identical. Any machine that is useful in producing clothing can be used equally well in producing food. Each machine is assumed to be fungible, in the sense that it can be used in any industry whatever. In many analyses it is assumed that machines last forever, which is not particularly unrealistic since such models are only used to analyze economic activity for a short period of time—two or three years. In the usual neoclassical analysis, machines neither fail nor do they become obsolete. Land is of the same quality in New Mexico as in New York, and management is equally efficient in different industries. By assumption, entrepreneurs are neither more imaginative nor more competitive than managers in factories.

As is apparent from the above comments, there is a vast uniformity within every factor of production and every good and service. Economics abstracts from particular firms, particular goods and services, particular differences among goods and services, and differences in quality and functions for each factor of production.

To those unfamiliar with economics, these assumptions appear distressingly unrealistic and patently false. Neoclassical economists, however, do not claim that they are realistic assumptions in the sense that they are literally true in all cases or even in most cases. They merely claim that they are legitimate abstractions from details that are not important to the overall analysis. Economists admit that automobiles are made by Ford, Chevrolet, Toyota, Datsun, Volkswagen, BMW, Audi, etc., and that each of these corporations produces automobiles that are of widely differing quality. In understanding the general patterns of production, however, such differences are deemed to be relatively unimportant, given the current state of economic understanding. Similar unrealistic assumptions are made about the behavior of consumers, markets, prices, and many other economic variables. Despite their implausibility, the assumptions lead to results that many economists consider interesting and applicable, with some adjustments, to the real world.

2.2.2 How Ethics Abstracts from the Real World

Like economics, theoretical ethics conducts its theorizing at a lofty level of abstraction.[2] It takes no note, for example, of different individuals, and, to this extent, its level of abstraction is comparable to that taken by economists when studying the behavior of the firm or the behavior of the individual consumer. Each individual is assumed to live in a community, to have a conscience, a rational facility, a memory, and an emotional facility, all of which are used to arrive at concrete ethical decisions; but differences among individuals in emotional make-up, intellectual ability, and the ability to recall are neglected. Similarly, when in later chapters we examine how moral agents can act contrary to common understandings embedded in the social institutions of society, we abstract from the particular characteristics of the institution. As in the case of economics, abstraction in ethics is a necessary prior step in order to make sense out of the plethora of individual cases. At the point when theory is applied, it is important to note the significant individual characteristics of the case, i.e., to engage in casuistry, as we will do to demonstrate the practical implications of the theoretical structure. Thus, although ethics is mindful of the travails suffered by any person wrestling with what is right in a particular instance, the function of theoretical ethics is to determine what is right not for a particular instance but for a whole class of incidents that share similar characteristics.

The formal way in which the ethician abstracts from the individual is analogous to the manner in which the neoclassical economist abstracts from the individual. The neoclassical economist assumes that the individual has a well-ordered set of preferences about the types and quantities of goods that he or she likes to consume, and the economist encapsulates the consumer's preferences in a mathematical utility function. The function refers to the utility, satisfaction, well-being, or wholeness of the individual. Various terms have been suggested to interpret the mathematical function, but, for our purposes, wholeness or well-being comes closest to the mark. A person is always assumed to desire more wholeness, and a person's wholeness is solely dependent on the amount of goods or services that he or she consumes. The form of the mathematical function indicates that the individual pursues his or her own self-interest. If the person were altruistic, the function would have to take on a more complicated form and the economist's analysis would not be as straightforward.[3] In fact, the theorem stating that the free market is efficient requires an assumption that individuals are self-interested in their pursuit of wholeness. With few exceptions, neoclassical economists assume that individuals are self-interested whenever they are engaged in economic transactions.

The absence of concern for and interest in others in the neoclassical model and the dependence of satisfaction solely on the consumption of goods constitute very stringent assumptions; indeed, they are so strict that they preclude important ethical questions from arising. For this reason, the characterization of the individual consumer will be one area in which we are forced to modify the neoclassical paradigm. For our present discussion, however, it is sufficient to note that although the neoclassical economist recognizes that each agent has particular tastes and preferences, she does not try to specify what they are. Similarly, the ethician acknowledges the differing preferences, abilities, and experiences of individuals, but does not take particular note of specific, personal endowments because in most instances morally correct behavior does not depend on such preferences, or, if it does, the adjustments to the general rule are obvious.

For each individual the neoclassical utility function is assumed to fulfill certain conditions, known as regularity conditions. If one accepts, for the time being, the fact that wholeness (or satisfaction) depends only on the individual's own consumption of goods and services, the regularity conditions impose constraints on the types of preferences for goods and services that consumers are allowed to have. These constraints, three in number, are quite reasonable. The first condition is that consumers always prefer more goods and services to less, i.e., they never reach a point at which they become satiated. Although every person in the real world does have a point of satiation, it is a reasonable approximation to assume that a consumer never gets close to her satiation point, in part because she switches to a more sophisticated model of the same good as she approaches the satiation point. For example, if a woman knows that she would never use more than ten business suits and that she can easily afford ten off-the-rack suits, if her income is sufficient she might purchase instead eight custom-made suits. The point is that people increase the quality of the good they purchase as they approach their private satiation point.

A second regularity condition is that a person be consistent in her preferences: if good x is preferred to good y and if good y is preferred to good z, then x must be preferred to z. Provided the conditions under which the person makes her choices remain the same, this condition or assumption is also reasonable. The third condition is that a consumer has an opinion concerning every good and service offered in the economy and that the person has preferences about all possible baskets of goods. For example, the consumer is assumed to be able to judge whether she prefers three apples to one peach or vice versa. Consumers must be able to do this for all goods and services in the economy and for all different quantities of these goods. In short, they must have an accurate map of their preferences for all goods and services.

In ethics, similar regularity conditions must be fulfilled. In the approach taken in this book, certain ethical values are assumed to be fundamental, both in the sense that they are the necessary conditions for the realization of other human values, and also in the sense that they are so basic that it is inconceivable that any person in society would not pursue these values, at least to some extent, in his or her life. This is only a brief and lapidary treatment of something that will be examined in great detail in chapters 3 and 4. It is mentioned here because there is an analogy between the utility function of the economist and the fundamental values that are assumed to be sought by all individuals, even if the ethicist does not express this assumption with as much mathematical rigor as the economist.

Note that neither economists nor ethicians claim that every person in society has a utility function satisfying the regularity conditions or pursues the fundamental values. When there are exceptions in economics, the resulting theorems still can be applied to the economy, as long as the exceptions are not too numerous. The claim is that to abstract from such exceptions is a reasonable way to focus on establishing how the economy functions. In ethics, just because some people are not committed to the fundamental values does not mean that the ethical principles or rules derived from this assumption are not binding. As long as those who do not pursue the fundamental values are infrequent exceptions, the ethical principles derived in this volume *ought to be* binding, as this is understood in an ethical sense to be clarified in later chapters.[4]

Another similarity shared by economics and ethics is the inability to verify the axioms of each system, because the axioms address realities that cannot be observed. In economics, the preferences of individuals are observed only indirectly. Furthermore, any action that suggests altruistic behavior can be interpreted as a type of long-run selfishness. Even if one observes that some people have inconsistent preferences and thus violate the second regularity condition, it is possible to assert that they have modified their preferences or that the conditions under which they have to choose have changed. There is always some explanation that allows the neoclassical economist to justify his assumption.

An analogous indeterminacy in ethics applies to the presumption that all people are committed to the fundamental values. Any person's dedication to the fundamental values is observed only indirectly, through the actions that she posits, and these actions admit a variety of interpretations. Also, survey results cannot decide the issue because a person may say that she is not committed to the fundamental values but perform actions that in fact increase her participation in the fundamental values. In ethics as well as economics, an appeal is made to some foundational experience to justify the initial axioms of the system.

2.3 CONTRAST IN METHODOLOGIES

Although economics purports to be an empirical science, one could easily get the impression from paging through modern economics journals that its sole focus is either theory or highly theoretical empirical estimations. In fact, both theory and empirical estimation are essential to economics, although theory enjoys a certain priority.

2.3.1 Economics as a Quasi-Science

The reason why economics emphasizes theory is that in economics, unlike chemistry and physics, one cannot repeat experiments under identical conditions with the expectation that certain patterns will become apparent. Since the conditions are connected to the events, one observes economic events exactly once. Even though two recessions might occur in a decade, the historical nature of economics prevents the two events from being the same.

The first difference between the two recessions arises because between the first and second recession the economy has developed new goods and services, new firms, new consumers, and new factors of production. Although economists valiantly try to adjust for such changes by use of sophisticated econometric techniques, some insurmountable obstacles impede complete adjustment. But, in the physical sciences one can replicate events precisely. For example, in a chemical experiment the chemicals are the same each time the experiment is conducted and the scientist can calibrate the temperature and pressure to whatever level is desired. In an economic experiment the "chemicals" of the experiment are people and goods, and they change continuously.

Consider conducting an economic experiment in which economic conditions are maintained over a period of time by transporting people to a special, self-sufficient colony. One could then observe how people react and how this mini-economy functions. In effect, one would have performed an experiment under conditions similar to those encountered by the chemist. Even in this case, however, there is no reason to believe that economic behavior will be the same under the experimental conditions, which are known to last a finite amount of time, as it would be in the real economy.[5] People react differently under experimental conditions than they do when facing long-term economic realities. Economic behavior is influenced by the structure of the situation as well as by the economic events themselves.

Because economic events do not occur in the laboratory but in the real world, they are historical. People gain valuable information from events, which they put to use when similar events occur in the future. The second reason why the second recession is different from the first is that the actors in the second recession have acquired important information during the first recession.

To illustrate this reality, assume that a second recession occurs five years after the first recession, and, implausible as it may appear, assume that everyone who was alive and participating in the economy during the first recession is also participating during the second recession and that no new consumers have joined the economy. Also, assume that technology and capital have all remained at constant levels during the intervening five years. Even under such stringent circumstances, the new recession would be *essentially* different from the old recession because the economic agents all have more information. Consumers, producers, and the government all lived through the prior recession and made decisions based, in part, on what they thought the other economic agents would do. They have now observed how other agents actually acted in the previous recession, and many agents will take this information into consideration as they formulate their own economic plans for reacting to the new recession. Because individuals accumulate and use information, every economic agent is different and, therefore, every economic event is new and different from the ones which preceded it.

Even though economic events are not repeated exactly, some factors remain more or less fixed. Therefore, economists make assumptions about which variables change over time and which ones remain fairly constant. Depending on the circumstances it may be reasonable, for example, to assume that consumers have not changed their preferences for peaches or for other goods. Over the period of six months it is highly unlikely that preferences, whether for peaches or for any other staple, undergo any fundamental change. Even over a few years, preferences might remain fairly constant. Over a twenty-year period, however, it is likely that tastes will change, even dramatically. Science might discover that peaches, like many other foods people enjoy eating, cause cancer. Alternatively, economic research might indicate that peaches inhibit the formation of cholesterol. The longer the interval of time, the more likely it is that economic variables change, whether in a beneficial or detrimental way for the consumer. Economists strive to make the least innocuous assumptions, the most realistic ones, and those which enable them to estimate how the economy reacts to changes.

In economics there is an interaction between theory and estimation, but theory holds the dominant position since it is impossible to estimate any economic relationship unless one has some theory to suggest what variables can be considered constant. Furthermore, theory develops the nexus between one economic variable and another and indicates what type of empirical relationship one should search for. For example, both at the aggregate level and the personal level, economists expect disposable income to influence consumption. As national income increases, the level of consumption expenditures is also expected to increase, and one anticipates that this theoretical prediction will be verified by empirical data. In order to confirm it, however, one first needs a theory to explain whether income influences consumption or consumption influences income. If there is a mutual interdependence, an adequate theory must specify the form the interdependence takes because the empirical methods used in economics cannot by themselves distinguish between cause and effect when, as is most often the case, variable x influences y, and variable y simultaneously influences x.

Certainly, economists could not formulate good theories unless they were also careful empiricists, noting patterns in the massive amounts of data available in a modern economy. In this sense empirical observation is a *sine qua non* for theoretical reasoning. Any science, whether hard or social, tries to ascertain why events occur and how to influence the outcome of events. But in economics the mere examination of data and statistical relationships cannot determine causality. For this reason, theory is more crucial to the discipline of economics, even though economics is also inconceivable without empirical observation.[6]

2.3.2 Ethics and Experience

As in economics, theoretical reasoning in ethics is paramount, although, as in the case of economics, ethical reasoning presupposes extensive experience in making ethical decisions. In both economics and ethics one distinguishes between pre- and post-theory observations. In economics post-theory observation, i.e., usual empirical analysis, is considered more important than pre-theory observation. In ethics, however, the situation is reversed, because theory indicates what one ought to do, which is logically distinct from what people actually do. So pre-theory observation is crucial because it provides the basis for moral reflection. Each person becomes aware of moral reasoning in the act of reflecting on his or her moral experience.

Although each person may reflect on a different event or pattern in his or her life, moral experience always involves a response to some interior force, which demands action of a certain kind. For example, a child may steal something from a store, realize it was wrong, and at a subsequent stage in his life question why it was wrong. Or, a person may feel an interior demand to assist a friend who is unemployed, and sometime after he helps the friend or chooses not to offer assistance he might reflect whether he had a moral obligation to help a friend. Usually at a young age every person experiences a moral imperative to perform some act. Some reflection may take place at that time, but since the study of ethics comes only after the experience of good and evil, the thoughts and hesitations one has at this early stage of development are not ordered systematically. It is this primary experience of good and evil, or at least the temptation to good and evil, that provides the crucial basis for moral reasoning.

Long before a person conducts an ethical examination of an issue, he or she has made many ethical or moral decisions based on implicit moral reasoning. Pre-adolescents and adolescents use moral values or ethical principles taught to them or assimilated from their culture to make moral decisions. Until one undertakes a study of ethics, however, ethical values or principles remain unexamined, uncriticized, and, therefore, somewhat arbitrarily bound to significant persons, groups, or events in one's life. But the fact that principles and values have not been subjected to critical reflection does not make them any less valid. It merely means that a person has not formally asked himself whether the particular moral principles to which he adheres are consistent with each other and compatible with the actual decisions he makes.

For most people, there is a divergence between the principles or moral standards they proclaim and the actions that purportedly flow from those standards. A manager in a corporation, for example, may be adamantly opposed to lying, yet she might instruct her secretary that when her boss calls and asks about the person she was supposed to fire, he should be told that the employee was indeed dismissed, even though she has not yet done so. This may not be a big lie, because she intends to fire the person soon, but it is a lie. By a process of ethical reasoning the manager may uncover this discrepancy and rethink her position. If she feels that telling an untruth to her boss is justified, then she must find room in her moral standards for this untruth. She might, on the other hand, realize that her instruction to her secretary was wrong, because it deceived someone who relies on her and who has the reasonable expectation that he will be given a truthful answer.[7]

Since moral issues are complex and people often disagree, some people are inclined to resolve the disagreement by seeking an empirical consensus among individuals. However, consensus plays no role in determining what any individual person ought to do, and it would be completely inappropriate, for example, to use an opinion poll in order to determine correct ethical behavior. Consider again the woman who instructed her secretary to tell her boss that she had fired the employee. After her director calls, she may be afflicted with pangs of conscience and with fear that she will be found out. These reactions may cause her to wonder whether she has acted correctly. She could take an informal survey of her friends or she might even hire a professional polltaker to determine what other people would do in such circumstances. The results would undoubtedly be interesting, but the only bearing the results should have is to make her better informed of the expectations that people have in the situation. She has to justify her actions in the light of *her* moral values and ethical rules, not others'. The opinions of the masses constitute empirical evidence, but they do not resolve ethical dilemmas. In personal decisions concerning moral matters, the moral majority ought to be of no consequence.

Realistically, the opinions of others certainly make a difference. It is easier to tell a fib to your boss if others equivocate frequently. For individual A, it is easier to perform a certain action if it is supported by a group of people whom individual A admires and who admire individual A. Although this is a natural reaction, in this study I abstract from that influential aspect of human nature. However, I do stress the importance of performing one's moral reflections within a community of ethically concerned individuals that adheres to a particular tradition. Genuine novelty is not to be expected in ethical reflection;

instead, one hopes to show how a particular ethical tradition, such as utilitarianism or the natural law, illumines ethical experience in the modern world.

Granted that both economists and ethicians require empirical evidence, the sources of empirical evidence germane to the economist and the ethician are very different. The economist looks at objective, statistical data and analyzes it, while the ethician introspects, i.e., considers his or her personal experience, and uses this as a basis for further reflection. In complicated cases, the ethician also needs detailed information about the effects caused by actions, because the moral worth of an act is often influenced by the effects it has on others. Although the sources of evidence are different for economics and ethics, both types of evidence rely upon a tradition of inquiry. The economist who collects data on consumption patterns adheres to a tradition that considers consumption patterns significant in the explanation of economic phenomena. Another economist, in another tradition, may collect data on surplus value in production. Similarly, an ethician in the natural law tradition examines her experience of beauty or knowledge while another ethician in the utilitarian tradition examines the good effects caused by particular actions.

Ethics, as well as economics, is related to history. The questions asked today depend on previous discussions concerning problems addressed, and perhaps resolved, in earlier eras. Indeed, this study uses neoclassical economic theory, chosen because of its venerable history, to investigate proper moral behavior in the economic sphere. The tradition I have chosen to guide the study is the long tradition of natural law theory. To use a concept developed by Gadamer, natural law tradition constitutes the justifiable "prejudice," which provides direction to the undertaking. As Gadamer demonstrates, knowledge in the human sciences is unattainable without some "prejudices"; but such prejudices should not be viewed in the negative light cast by the Enlightenment.[8]

2.3.3 Dialectical Reasoning

Although economists and ethicians want to be rational in their investigations, they adhere to distinct, but not necessarily conflicting, canons of rationality.

The economist devises theoretical models that approximate the real world. As we saw earlier, some of the assumptions at the heart of economic models are admittedly unrealistic. In fact, economists, with few exceptions, make no attempt to test directly whether the underlying assumptions of the model are accurate.[9] Rather, economists proceed pragmatically. First they try to verify the predictions of the theoretical model and then, if the predictive ability of the model is good, the assumptions are considered reasonable approximations to reality.

Consider, for example, one popular model of international trade, called the Heckscher-Ohlin model.[10] It predicts that a country which is abundantly endowed with capital relative to labor will export goods that use a large amount of capital relative to labor in the production process. Since this prediction can be tested empirically, the applied international economist uses data, runs regressions, conducts statistical tests, etc., to determine whether the prediction is true for a variety of countries. Because aggregating the total amount of capital in a country is both a theoretical and empirical challenge, for several decades scant attention was given to verifying whether one country is more capital intensive than another, which is a crucial condition for the theorem to be true. In many empirical studies one country was simply *assumed* to be the capital-intensive country.[11]

Consumer theory offers another illustration of how impervious assumptions are to empirical data. In this instance a large literature exists suggesting that consumers are not rational in the manner described above, and in section 7.2.2 I examine those findings. Furthermore, consumers are not rational when they maximize expected utility.[12] But because these assumptions yield results that are considered reasonable and that are not patently false, economists continue to assume that consumer preferences are indeed rational.

The ethician makes no attempt to predict whether people will behave according to the ethical principles she derives.[13] Predicting the behavior of individuals is a task for the psychologist or for the psychiatrist, not for the ethician. The ethician wants to arrive at rules that can be justified in terms of the fundamental values, or of alternative ethical standards. There is no strictly empirical test to determine whether the rules are true, although one can compare the experience of societies that adhere to differing sets of rules. Like the economist, the ethician draws out the implications of ethical principles. That is, the ethicist shows what implications the rules have and then considers whether the implications can be reconciled with the ethician's moral intuition. The ethician checks the correspondence between the type of activity prescribed by the rule or principle and the actual behavior that the ethician thinks appropriate. The ethician's moral intuition or judgment plays the same role performed by empirical data for the economist. Moral intuition is the reality test for the ethician just as empirical data is the reality test for the economist.

There is a necessary tension between the ethical rule and particular actions. Suppose an ethician considers the fundamental values and formulates an initial principle stating that all lying is morally wrong. Having enunciated the rule, suppose the ethician feels that in certain cases a doctor may deceive a patient concerning the gravity of her illness. The justification may be that this information causes the patient to despair, thereby making recovery even less likely. Since a moral decision is a combination of reasoning, emotions, and experience, the ethician may judge that telling the patient an untruth in such circumstances is justified. In this case, the ethician has to modify the rule that was derived from first principles. The moral investigator must make a distinction that allows for an untruth in the case of a person who reacts to truth in a way prejudicial to his or her own life. Having made this adjustment, the ethician must then pursue its implications. He could ask, for example, whether a person whose life is being threatened may lie in order to save her life. In particular, could a person deny that she loves her husband in order to save her life, or could she deny that she is a Christian in order to avoid the lions? Every modification of the rule has implications for particular circumstances. The ethician must move back and forth among the principle, the consideration of particular cases, and moral intuition before he arrives at a principle in which he has confidence.

This type of reasoning is not as clean and straightforward as the model building undertaken by the economist.[14] The economist makes assumptions, links them together, shows how such a concatenation of assumptions leads to results, and then conducts an empirical analysis to determine whether the predictions of the theory are confirmed by the data. Although the economist does not question the assumptions and although the theoretical predictions are rarely verified completely, the process of moving from assumptions (step 1), to deduction (step 2), to empirical confirmation (step 3) is straightforward. The ethician, on the other hand, starts with a group of primary values or standards (step 1), derives a principle (step 2), and then checks to see whether the implications of the principle correspond in all particulars to his or her intuition and overall judgment (step 3). If not, the ethician returns to step 1 and step 2 to consider what general principle can be justified in terms of the primary values or standards. After he formulates a new principle, he checks it with his moral intuition, insight, or experience and continues this process until there is a congruence between the ethical principle and his moral intuition. The process of moving back and forth between general principle and particular cases is called dialectics and it is the preferred method of ethical reasoning.[15]

Moral intuition and dialectical reasoning are important moments in the process of ethical argumentation that require further explication. Consider first moral intuition. An ethician makes a judgment whether a rule in all particular applications corresponds to his moral intuition, which is formed by many factors, including his country, family, schooling, and friends, and which is honed through the study of past masters. Ceteris paribus, the better an ethician understands an ethical tradition the better will be his moral intuition.

The word "dialectical" evokes the names of two philosophers, Hegel and Marx. As used here, however, "dialectical" reasoning simply means undertaking an argument by making an assertion and then examining whether the statement is true in test cases. The individual case might show that the statement is too general, i.e., that it holds only for a more restricted set of circumstances. If this is so, the individual case itself often suggests how to restrict the class to make it true. Alternatively, the individual case may indicate a way to expand the ethical prescription to include another set of circumstances. Thus, dialectics refers to the movement back and forth between general statement and particular instance, with emphasis on the truth relationship between the particular instance and the general statement. It is the process of resolving contradictions between general statements and particular statements.[16]

The dialectical method can be frustrating, for ethicians as well as for students of ethics. The expectation is that the process will converge on a principle that has general validity in the area being studied, although it is conceivable that the process does not converge on a resolution.[17] Even though many people use this mode of reasoning to reach decisions in the ordinary affairs of human life, dialectics, when used in a formal argument, appears indecisive and confusing. The reader should be patient (one of the virtues necessary for implementing a reasonable life plan) and become familiar with the process of moving back and forth between principle and particular case. The student of ethics must also become adept at juggling principles, since ethics usually involves applying several different principles to a particular issue. Ethical principles are related to one another, and each principle deserves appropriate attention, where "appropriate" is determined by the particular issue. One ethician is inclined to give more weight to one principle, while another ethician offers reasons why the additional weight is excessive. Dialectical reasoning is a demanding exercise, but it is also "the" method by which one arrives at what is "reasonable."[18]

In economics, in ethics, in every academic discipline, even in ordinary conversation one encounters the word "reasonable" again and again. Sometimes "reasonable" is simply a synonym for "what I think." When "reasonable" is used properly, however, it means a statement that balances many points made in an ongoing discussion. "Reasonable views" most often do not follow strictly from explicit assumptions, formulated with mathematical precision. Rather, they are the outcome of a process of reconciling the demands of a plurality of true statements and states of affairs.

This text would become unbearably tedious if I adhered strictly to the dialectical method in considering the multifarious aspects of economic justice. As useful as this method is, careful application of it would yield few results by the end of the volume. The analytical, deductive method of the economist is the better choice as an expository device, with one significant exception. Justification for the primacy of the fundamental values can only be given dialectically. Accordingly, in the next two chapters I repeatedly analyze the experience of the pursuit of the fundamental values. In each repetition I highlight another aspect of the fundamental values and urge the reader to confirm that this aspect exists in his or her own experience. Because the fundamental values are grounded in a basic, universal human experience, their justification is not purely logical, but combines logic and experience.

A caveat concerning the dialectical method is in order. Because the dialectical method is being conducted in the background, the general principles that are deduced here apply ceteris paribus, as in economics. In economic theory, particular circumstances of the worker or consumer or the firm have no bearing on the analysis, but the circumstances affect the way in which the theory is applied, and this is true in ethics as well. For example, if the United States had been experiencing a depression for ten years, this condition would influence the way in which the economic principles are applied. Similarly, a lie to a boss who unscrupulously denies workers legitimate benefits would be evaluated differently from a lie to a boss who acts uprightly in all matters. I, therefore, rely on the reader to make reasonable adjustments to particular circumstances. The general principles still apply in unusual circumstances, but one must engage in careful casuistry.

2.4 ECONOMIC FACTS, ECONOMIC MODELS, AND ETHICAL PRINCIPLES

An ethical argument applies general ethical principles to particular situations and arrives at an ethical judgment that prescribes a certain type of action. Consider what particular judgments, prior to reaching the ethical judgment, are necessary in order to arrive at an economic prescription. As an example we select one important (and rather obvious) ethical principle that will be derived and justified in Chapter 5: resources, human or physical, should not be wasted without good reason. In order to apply this principle to some particular situation or circumstance, one must judge whether current resources are being wasted and, if there is unreasonable waste, whether a better method of production or distribution or consumption exists. In devising a policy to eliminate or reduce current waste, one should avoid policies which have been wasteful in the past and one should also avoid policies which are likely to be wasteful under conditions that are likely to prevail in the future.

Any ethical judgment about economics requires analysis of the past, present, and future. It is useful to list the individual components of an ethical decision concerning economic practice.

1. **Current Facts**: Current facts are the set of statements that accurately describe the present situation. At any point in time, one can distinguish three qualitative types of facts: economic, institutional, and cultural.

   Whether a fact is economic, institutional, or cultural is based on its subject matter. One can further distinguish facts on the basis of their structure: simple or complex. Simple facts present data or describe states of affairs at a given point in time. Complex facts join simple facts, from different points in time or referring to different aspects of a reality, into an array.

2. **Past Experience**: How the economy has functioned in the past, how effectively institutions have provided various goods and services, how much one relied successfully on nonmarket motivation to accomplish important social goals—all these may be important in determining what type of policy is likely to be successful in the future. The same threefold division of economic, institutional, and cultural facts is applicable in the past as well.

3. **Future Projections**: One makes reasonable projections about the likely effect of a particular economic policy. Institutions are assumed to change slowly over time. Occasionally, dramatic changes occur, but they do so with little warning and are almost impossible to predict. Cultural facts are even more impervious to short-run change.

Current facts, past experience, and future projections involve varying degrees of subjective opinion or feelings. Any ten people, not just ten economists, will give ten different descriptions of current facts, past experience, and future projections.

Based on the division given above, there are eleven "elemental" ways in which two persons can potentially disagree concerning ethical economic policies. For each time category of past, present, and future, people can dispute economic, institutional, or cultural "facts." Thus, theorists can disagree concerning any of nine time-facts. The tenth possible area of disagreement is the group of ethical principles that various people, including economists, may cite, while the eleventh area is the manner in which the ethical principles are applied to the factual situation. Aggregating the nine time-facts together into a category called "the true state of affairs" produces three areas of potential disagreement: the true state of affairs, the ethical principles, and the application of the ethical principles to the true state of affairs.

Economists use models to analyze complex facts. However, an economic model, usually formulated with daunting mathematical rigor, is never uniformly confirmed or uniformly rejected by economists, since some economists judge the model to offer a good explanation for some facet of past experience and others judge that the model is flawed and the facts are in need of a more thorough explanation.

In the past two decades economists themselves have become cynical about purported facts and empirical confirmations of models. After World War II, economists developed an empirical estimation technique called regression theory, which spawned a new area of economics called econometrics, the study of the measurement, forecasting, and testing of economic models. Although enthusiasm was high during the 1970s and 1980s that these techniques would enable economists to select those models that most closely conform to reality, most economists now admit that empirical studies, as important as they are, are not decisive for or against a particular theory or model.[19] Institutional and cultural facts are less precisely defined and generate even deeper disagreement.

This study focuses primarily on ethical economic principles, without denigrating the importance of the nine time-facts. Neoclassical analysis provides a crucial set of facts, and some time-facts of a general nature are used to show why a particular arrangement is just or unjust. However, a careful examination of all the time-facts pertinent to the complete justification of various economic policies is beyond the scope of this book. At times it may seem as if I handle time-facts in a cavalier manner. This occurs for lack of space, not because I underestimate their significance or the importance of stating the facts in a more nuanced way than is appropriate in a volume of this scope.[20]

2.5 POLITICS

Economics is a study of how the economy works, and ethics is a study of what one ought to do. Politics as practiced is the art of the possible; as a discipline, however, politics is the study of how governments and public institutions of governance are formed and interact. To the extent that politics uncovers the patterns according to which people interact, politics reveals institutional, and perhaps cultural, facts. Neither institutions nor the culturally conditioned views of individuals are easily changed. Politics teaches that there are constraints on the types of activity that a person or government can undertake to change society. These constraints are significant when a change in policy is being contemplated that is motivated by an ethical concern or derived from an ethical principle and that affects the institutions and culturally conditioned views of individuals. Even when an ethical principle demands that some action be undertaken to correct an injustice, it may be more effective not to introduce a change that directly achieves the intended goal but that brings it about indirectly.

Suppose, for example, that an outcome of a combined ethical and economic analysis were that rich nations had a moral obligation to provide greater assistance to poor nations. Also, assume that via some democratic means people indicate their readiness to assist poor nations, even poor nations with inefficient governments.[21] Assume also that all poor nations are run by inefficient tyrants and that all rich nations are run by efficient saints. Finally, suppose that aid provided by rich countries to inefficient tyrants goes directly into the coffers of the inefficient tyrants. Under such circumstances, are the rich nations still morally obligated to provide aid to the poor nations? The ethically correct answer, although no attempt is made to justify it here, is: No, but the rich countries still have a moral obligation to do *what they can* to assist the poor in poor countries. (The reader should not be distracted by the austere assumptions used in the example. The example can be made equally cogent if inefficient tyrants are running rich nations, but in that case the tyrants in the wealthy nations would not be disposed to grant aid to the poor nations. The obligation would then fall upon the individual citizens in the rich country to provide what aid they could.)

Moral imperatives must be feasible and realistic. Rich countries are under no moral obligation to make inefficient tyrants into wealthy or wealthier tyrants. If it becomes impossible to assist poor people in poor countries through the normal political channels, one has an obligation to undertake other, more realistic means. A rich country could send aid with the proviso that it be distributed to the poor. This type of restriction is definitely intruding in the internal affairs of a foreign sovereign nation. According to a principle that will be enunciated in a subsequent chapter, one should allow the smallest feasible unit to make decisions to provide for its own welfare. On this principle, once aid is granted, under normal conditions one should allow the authorities in the local country discretion over the disposition of the aid. However, interference is sometimes required by reason, and in the particular case described above, some interference is expedient. It would require another volume to describe the type of interference that can be justified, since the justification depends on the reaction of citizens within the country as well as on the reaction of other nation-states.

The point is that although political necessities do not remove moral obligation, they may mandate that the moral obligation be fulfilled in unusual ways. In the unrealistic example of the inefficient tyrant in the poor country, one possibility is that the rich country could try to work through the good offices of a neighboring country to have the inefficient tyrant removed. Less drastic measures, however, are usually more realistic and reasonable. For example, it may be that even though all the citizens in the rich country voted that aid should be given to the poor country, they cannot agree that some plan A is the best plan. The reason for their inability to agree is politics, in the best meaning of the word.

Assume that the wealthy country is the United States and that every U.S. citizen of voting age belongs to a political party. Also assume, realistically, that different parties have different views of human nature and what motivates people. Adherents of party A espouse plan A while party B people support plan B. No moral principle can reconcile these differences, because the differences stem from conflicting descriptions of cultural and institutional facts. We can assume that the success of the plan depends on the response of individuals to various incentives and that people have legitimate, nonethical differences about effective incentives.

For all these reasons, people of goodwill may differ about how to undertake morally good actions. This should be neither surprising nor discouraging, inasmuch as the motives for individual as well as collective action are not transparent but must be deduced from the experience of the way in which people act. Because ethical principles require institutional and cultural facts in order to be applied correctly and because people of different political allegiances perceive different institutional and cultural facts, the conclusions presented in this volume are either of a general nature, allowing further discussion and qualification according to political points of view, or, if the conclusions are particular, they assume that there is no disagreement about the institutional and cultural facts relevant to the case.

A plan is no less desirable simply because politics influences the selection of the plan. Politics is an essential ingredient in all situations involving collective action.

CHAPTER 3

Fundamental Values

In this chapter I begin the articulation of an ethical system that provides guidance both for decisions made by individuals and for policies pursued by economic and social institutions in society.

3.1 ECONOMIC LACUNAE

Since ethical concerns are foreign to most economic treatises, I begin the examination of ethical values by pointing out two areas in which economists, using their normal methods, have not been able either to analyze or to obtain results that people living in modern societies would plausibly expect. These economic lacunae suggest ways in which ethical analysis can both complement and modify economic analysis.

In recent years, writers have spoken about the imperialism of neoclassical methodology and how it has infiltrated demography, sociology, political science, and history.[1] Although "imperialism" suggests unwarranted force or intervention, a more benign interpretation is possible: the fact that the neoclassical model has been so readily exported to a variety of related disciplines is a sign both of its adaptability and its inherent appeal.

Despite the conquests of the neoclassical model, it remains essentially incomplete in a number of areas. I highlight two lacunae, i.e., two crucial areas of inadequacy, with a view toward appreciating the contribution that a well-developed ethical system can make to the neoclassical model by filling in these gaps. The first area of deficiency is in defining the goals of the consumer and the second is in identifying the goals of institutions in society. At this point, I wish merely to suggest the gravity of the problem; in later chapters I analyze the specific difficulties and the proposed solutions.

The neoclassical model assumes that each consumer has a set of preferences subject to a budget constraint, that is, the consumer has a limited amount of money at her disposal. The model assumes that the consumer purchases those goods that, given her budget, maximize what is variously called the utility, satisfaction, or well-being of the consumer. A strong assumption of the neoclassical model is that a person's well-being is determined solely by the amount of goods that she alone, not others, has available to herself. Even if it were the case that narrow self-interest is a good approximation to the behavior of individuals, assuming that a person's primary interests pertain to the consumption of goods does not capture the complete array of aspirations and goals that people have. People are indeed interested in consuming goods and services, and, to a certain extent, their well-being does increase as their ability to consume more goods and services increases. However, people also have personal goals, things that they want to do, to achieve. A person wants to get married, to create something beautiful, to become the head of a corporation, to help people in a community, to cure people of diseases, to invent something new, to educate people about the traditions of a community.

Amartya Sen, noting that personal goals and aspirations cannot be incorporated into the standard neoclassical model of consumer behavior, speaks of a duality in the treatment of an ethical subject. On the one hand, one can attempt to measure the extent to which a person achieves certain goals. Calculating the satisfaction or well-being of a person is a good, though not perfect, approximation of the extent to which a goal is reached. On the other hand, one can consider a person in terms of agency, i.e., her ability to formulate and set goals, to choose values, to make lasting commitments. This latter capability of the human person is not captured in the neoclassical approach.[2]

The second significant gap in the neoclassical model is the distance between the personal decision of an economic agent and the corporate decision of some group of economic agents. One would think that the best way for a group of economic agents to decide upon a course of action is to vote and let the majority rule. As sensible as that seems, Kenneth Arrow (1963) demonstrated many years ago that majority rule leads to inconsistencies. That is, more people in a group may prefer plan A to plan B and also prefer plan B to plan C, but, following a majority voting rule, the economic group may choose C.[3] In other words, there is a lacuna between personal economic rationality and group economic rationality. Research has shown that the anomaly of majority voting disappears only when one person is allowed to impose his decision on others or when the people in the economic group have similar preferences.

Ethical principles serve both a positive and negative role, although the latter is more pronounced in popular perception. The negative role is to single out actions that are incompatible with decent human behavior: promising someone a raise and then reneging, stealing, lying, destroying things of beauty, etc. But the positive contribution of ethics is equally if not more important. We noted earlier that the neoclassical paradigm does not allow a consumer to form "agency" goals. The main contribution of ethical principles is not merely to identify agency goals but also to show that some goals are valid for all consumers. That is, no matter what their individual preferences are about the goods they wish to consume and no matter how they choose to use goods, all consumers assign and should assign positive value to certain common human goals, which we call the fundamental values. These goals are admittedly quite general and allow a multitude of different strategies to pursue them. Nonetheless, they give a binding direction to individual lives. To the extent that a person conscientiously seeks these goals, she becomes a genuine person, one who ought to be admired by the community in which she lives.

The neoclassical model is unable to generate a consistent system of choice that remains compatible with the liberal democratic emphasis on majority rule. One way to resolve this difficulty is to impose not a personal dictator but moral imperatives, informal rules that need not be incorporated into the legal system but that guide everyone in society. By adhering to these rules, society can make decisions that respect the views of individuals but also acknowledge the claim that ethical values make on all people in the community.

In this chapter the focus is on rules that morally bind individuals, while chapters 5 and 6 show how a similar set of principles should guide major institutions in modern society. Any society has a responsibility to fulfill central functions that enable people to flourish. If these functions can be carried out by a system of competitive markets without intervention by public authorities, the private route is preferred. If, on the other hand, sound reasons exist why the private sector cannot provide goods in sufficient abundance or to the people in the population most in need of the goods, then the government or other quasi-public entities should develop a reasonable, alternative plan.

The ethical system developed in this chapter is a large structure, and examples of the way ethical principles are applied I often take from ordinary, noneconomic activities. This is done for two reasons. First, common applications often illustrate the principle better than economic ones, and, second, economic examples often require lengthy explanations and detailed qualifications. When I do consider an economic example, I distill the essence of it and omit irrelevant, but realistic, details.

3.2 ETHICAL SYSTEMS

Like economics, ethical systems also have foundational statements. One distinguishes different ethical systems by the fundamental assumptions that they make. There are two general classes of ethical systems:

Deontological Ethics: Deontology bases ethical standards on the intrinsic rightness of an action. Immanuel Kant is perhaps the best-known proponent of a deontological system, the cornerstone of which is that a person should never treat another person as a mere means to an end or goal. He tried to show that a person could not with rational consistency demand respect from others and act against this principle. Kant argues that the principle is self-evident, in the sense that adequate reflection reveals it to be true. According to Kant, a person acts ethically only if she performs an action because of duty; undertaking an action for the good consequences it achieves makes the action a practical one, not an ethical one. Rawls's theory of justice as fairness, though often described as a contract theory of justice, is also deontological since the demand to do justice to others comes before the demand to do good; by his own admission, the description of the self and of the original position relies heavily on the Kantian critique.[4]

Teleological Ethics: This system examines the end or goal of an action. If the intention motivating the action is good, then the action itself is considered good, as long as it leads directly to a justifiable goal. Aristotle took this approach and many other philosophers have followed in his footsteps. Aristotle was careful to argue against the proposition that the end or goal justifies any means whatsoever, a statement that might appear to some as a valid inference from the assumption that the goal of an action determines its moral worth. One must, he said, look at each individual action and justify it in terms of its own goal or end; only those means may be used that are compatible with the end for which the particular means exists.

Three types of teleological ethics continue to be analyzed and developed by philosophers and therefore warrant attention.

Natural Law Ethics: This system claims that human beings all share certain "natural" aspirations and that, therefore, all human beings esteem certain fundamental values. What is "natural" is discovered by human reason as it reflects on human beings, in particular, how they act and interact in community. "Natural" does not refer solely to biological facts or laws; rather, correct reason considers not only biological facts but also human aspirations in order to determine what actions are "natural" and, therefore, ethically acceptable. According to this approach, society should be structured in such a way as to foster the realization of human aspirations, which correspond to the *teloi*, the Greek word for ends or goals, of all human action. The individual human desires to acquire knowledge, to create beauty, and to sustain life are examples of human aspirations that are natural. An action is good if it is natural, that is, if it is consistent with the end or goal of a human being; otherwise it is ethically bad. Because in the natural law approach human beings are to act in a way consistent with the finality or the ends of human nature, natural law is a teleological ethical system.[5]

Consequentialism or Proportionalism: A consequentialist judges the rightness or wrongness of an action by the amount of good or bad long-term consequences it has, and whether the consequences are good or bad depends on the often unspecified goal of human activity. For example, lynching a person is wrong because if it became the accepted way of dealing with suspected criminals, innocent lives would be lost. Proportionalists differ from consequentialists by adding a requirement that limits actions with evil consequences. An action with evil consequences can be justified, according to the proportionalists, only if the good consequences of the action are greater than the evil ones *and* if the action is proportionate to the amount of good created. In other words, it is not sufficient that the total sum of good consequences outweigh the bad; unnecessary bad consequences cannot be tolerated. Both consequentialists and proportionalists stress that *all* consequences, direct as well as indirect, long-term as well as short-term, must be taken into consideration.

Utilitarian Ethics: In its most undifferentiated form, utilitarianism judges an action to be good or bad by its effect on the utility (or happiness or satisfaction) of all people in society. In this form of teleology, utility, happiness, or satisfaction is the single goal for all people. An action that increases utility is deemed good, and one that decreases it is bad. The modern version is referred to as rule utilitarianism. According to this variant, a rule for society is to be adopted if the rule results in the greatest good for the greatest number; otherwise the action is to be rejected. In summing individual utilities, society may wish to give greater weight to some classes, e.g., the poor or those especially gifted, such as artists or entrepreneurs. Even with greater weights given to certain classes, however, for utilitarians the maximization of utility remains the criterion for judging the moral rectitude of an action.

Contract theories, which are theories of justice rather than general theories concerning ethics, can be deontological, as Rawls's system is, or teleological, as is Locke's system, which is based on the natural law.[6]

Each of these ethical systems has a distinguished history and each program has theoretical advantages and disadvantages. In the latter part of the twentieth century, rule utilitarianism appears to be the most popular and "natural" approach, in the sense that it seems most plausible to both ordinary people and modern thinkers in a variety of disciplines. However, if one takes a longer perspective and considers traditions accessible to Americans, the natural law approach is the one that has been generally followed in America since Revolutionary times and, more generally, is part of the Judeo-Christian heritage.[7]

Utilitarianism has emerged as a popular ethic in the past half century because it seems to offer a reasonable way to decide how society ought to be structured. In particular, many people who have studied economics find utilitarianism congenial to their thinking, in part because it offers a way to avoid confronting the various ethical systems that people use to guide their lives. Utilitarianism uses a conception (utility) familiar to them, and it has a slogan that rings true: "The greatest good for the greatest number."[8]

Despite such appealing characteristics, utilitarianism has significant theoretical and practical problems. The first is that it is difficult, some would say impossible, to estimate either the relative or absolute utility of an individual. In fact, economists never try to estimate utility directly. Rather, they make assumptions about the nature of utility and attempt to show that human behavior does not contradict such assumptions. However, such tests do not have much power to reject alternative models since it is possible, of course, that people undertake actions based on motivations other than utilitarianism and that the alternative motivations also generate the type of economic behavior expected and predicted by the neoclassical model.

A second, more intractable problem with utilitarianism is that once utility is broadened to include moral values, it becomes impossible to combine several moral values into a single measure of happiness or satisfaction. How, for example, does one add together the satisfaction of having material goods with the satisfaction of having told the truth or with the satisfaction of having been faithful to a commitment made to some individual? Such additive comparisons are necessary if utilitarianism is to be a viable moral as well as economic theory. The fundamental difficulty with utilitarianism as a philosophical system, however, is that the sole justification for it is utilitarian. That is, utilitarianism is considered valuable for the pragmatic reason that it produces "better" results, where "better" is defined within a utilitarian matrix. As Hannah Arendt pointed out, utilitarianism as a system cannot distinguish between utility and meaningfulness.[9]

Many ethicians have found utilitarianism too imprecise to yield useful results, and they have turned instead to the traditional way in which Americans have conceived their moral obligations, i.e., the natural law. In a recent monograph, Alasdair MacIntyre (1990) argues that only three broad traditions of moral philosophy offer a plausible basis for making moral decisions. He refers to them as the encyclopedic (typified in the unitary approach to knowledge taken in encyclopedias, culminating in the Ninth Edition of the *Encyclopaedia Britannica*), the genealogical (according to which there is no truth-as-such but only truth-from-a-point-of-view, best represented in Nietzsche's *A Genealogy of Morals*), and the natural law (which, following Aristotle and

Aquinas, claims that a human being has an essence which each individual should strive to attain and which can be grasped in a community with a tradition of moral living) traditions.[10] In MacIntyre's view, the natural law tradition offers the most comprehensive and convincing analysis of moral phenomena, but the reader will be able to make her own judgment as the advantages and drawbacks of natural law in the version presented in this study become apparent. Weighty arguments and positive assessment offered by MacIntyre notwithstanding, I begin defensively by mentioning two drawbacks to the natural law system that must be answered to assuage the apprehension of the reader.

First, the natural law appears to put too much emphasis on human nature as a static, inert mass, neither changing nor developing, adjusting to new circumstances not by accepting the circumstances but by rejecting them. Moreover, in recent decades the "natural" in "natural law" has been misinterpreted to refer to biological rhythms and processes. At a time when biology was a new science and scientists were uncovering the wonders of the human body, the natural law approach was appealing. During the past fifty years, however, doctors have regularly intervened in the "natural" functions of the human body. Brain surgery, organ transplants, gene research—all these are performed regularly by morally responsible individuals. Although these activities are indeed consistent with the natural law, people unacquainted with the tradition erroneously perceive intervention in natural processes to be contrary to natural law.

An ethical approach is out of tune with the times if it cannot adjust to changes that most people consider to be morally legitimate. In fact, however, natural law neither makes biological rhythms and processes determinative of ethical principles, nor does it neglect these processes. Every process, biological, psychological, or artificial, must be interpreted and judged by human reason, which is the primary determining factor of ethical principles in natural law. A priori, an ethical system that concentrates on biological processes is likely to be confining, and it is rightly suspect. Undoubtedly, the natural law approach assumes that some core of what it means to be human is constant for all people, in all societies. Were this not the case, modern people could not make sense of earlier societies or communicate ideals and aspirations to people from radically different cultures in our own day. Because human beings judge that such communication takes place and is deeply satisfying, it must be the case that human nature creates similar ideals and aspirations in all people. Guided by a tradition, human reason decides and acknowledges what the essential core of human nature is. Identifying this core does not, to be sure, eliminate all disputes since the human core expresses itself in specific actions, which are legitimately subject to diverse judgments.

A second drawback to the natural law approach is that through the centuries it has been closely related to religious beliefs. In our own presentation, we will be careful to stress the role of reason, not religious faith, in the derivation of ethical principles.

3.3 VALUES

The starting point for the natural law approach is the human experience of significant moral or ethical values. My contention is that certain fundamental or basic values are significant and essential for all human beings, no matter what their religious conviction. After discussing the philosophical meaning of value, I list the values that are essential according to the natural law tradition.

For the philosopher, a value is an abstract good that individuals try to incorporate into their lives by performing some appropriate action.[11] The value of friendship, for example, is the abstract ideal of what it means to be a friend to another person. One participates in the value of friendship by being the recipient of a favor by one's friend or by performing an action for one's friend: by cooking a meal, by sympathizing with her, by spending time together, or by helping him paint his apartment.

Before trying to define the value of friendship, consider a more pragmatic approach to value, contained in the question "How much do you value your friendship?" This is a question neither about the monetary value of friendship nor about the value itself, but about the meaning and significance of friendship to the individual. A person determines the how-much-value of friendship by setting boundaries, by specifying what one is willing to surrender for the sake of friendship: "I am willing to give up this much, but no more." In fact, most people try to avoid delineating the borders of friendship or other values, because boundary setting is such a difficult and distasteful task. As a result, the borders of friendship and other values are usually not defined until events compel a person to stake out the importance of friends or other values. Events in a person's life may bring him right to the border and tempt the person either to move beyond the border or to redefine the border. Particularly in countries that value individual freedom, people are not normally forced by other people to surrender their values or trade them in for another value. For the most part, individuals spend their lives well within the boundaries of their values; they live and work undisturbed by questions about the location of the periphery and do not concern themselves with the value of friendship or any other value.

Having sought the location of boundaries for a value, i.e., the how-much-value question, I now ask what a value is, or—in terms of boundaries—what it means to be within the boundaries of a value. "Boundary" is a geographical image for an entity that is intangible, indivisible, and not located in any specific place, although it exercises a real effect on people. A value is an ideal, intangible good that is cherished and esteemed by someone; it exists independently of a person and exerts an attraction on him. The value, by its power of attraction, applies pressure on people to undertake some particular action so that the value is realized in the individual's life. Through the particular action the person shares or participates in the value. The result of performing the action is that the person makes a value a part of himself and, consequently, becomes more deeply human.[12]

Speaking as if the value were the agent in an economic transaction, one can say that the value offers a feeling of deep human satisfaction to the person in return for the person's action to implement it in her life. The individual would express it more strongly: "Not only do I feel more deeply human; I know that I am in fact more of a human being as a result of participating in this value." Through a specific action a person partially assimilates the value, makes it "her own." The process of assimilation is an unusual one because, although it transforms the individual and makes the individual more human, the value itself is undiminished in intensity by its "assimilation" by another human being. Even if an entire country participates in the value of friendship, friendship is not therefore less of a value. A value is not consumed by participation.[13]

The description of value may sound mystical to some people and appear too fuzzy to be helpful in analyzing a modern, worldwide economy. Nonetheless, participation in a value always involves something specific because a person can only share in a value through actions. For example, a person assimilates the value of knowledge by studying or by encouraging others to acquire knowledge. When a person acts in such a way as to acquire more knowledge (reading a book, having a conversation), the person "shares" in the value called knowledge.

Since values are ideals, they contain within themselves an intimation of perfection. Any particular action a person performs only enables a limited, finite realization of a value. The more actions a person undertakes to realize a value, the more fully the individual shares in the particular value. "Beauty" is a value, and the person who puts flowers in his home makes present in a specific way the value of beauty. He can also spend money to make his home more attractive, and by so doing he also participates in the value of beauty. When he goes out to the countryside on a beautiful day, he has yet another opportunity to realize the value of beauty in his life. One of the challenges of life is to discover more interesting, significant, and imaginative ways to realize values. Children participate in beauty by mimicking the actions of parents, but adolescents begin the process of establishing beauty as a value for themselves, independent of their parents, by finding new ways to realize old values. The mature person who continues the growth process searches not just for numerically more ways to instantiate values but for more significant and meaningful ways, which are interesting for the person's own life and perhaps, if she is fortunate, meaningful for a wider circle of friends or admirers. The economic significance of values is that people spend money to realize them. For example, in order to participate in the value of beauty, people spend money on homes, clothes, art, personal appearance, cars, vacations abroad, etc.[14]

A concrete action (or plan of action) reveals the person's commitment to the ideal. The action, however, is not merely a signal to himself and to others that he is committed to some particular value but also the means by which the person shares in the value. The phrase normally used to describe the sharing is "to participate in the value," although "realizing" and "assimilating" a value are also used. The significance of the word "participate" is that it indicates a sharing that preserves the integrity of the value itself. The person shares the value without diminishing (or increasing) it and without making it less available to others. Even if everyone in a particular town put fresh flowers in the living room every day, each one of them would participate, through this action, in the value of beauty. An individual's participation is no less intense because many others participate in the same value in the same way, although it is true that most people seek variety in the pursuit of values.

The relationship between values and the individual is illustrated in Figure 3.1. The acts compose one part of the rectangle, which represents the person. A person performs acts that enable participation in values, and by sharing in the values, a person fulfills herself and becomes a better person. The expansive effect of acts that enable participation in values is suggested by an expanded rectangle, bordered in part by dotted lines.

The philosopher's concept of value, which we call a human value, bears a striking similarity to the economist's concept of a public good. In the case of a human value, one additional person can share in the value without causing any diminution in the "amount" available for others. Described in this way, a human value is analogous to what economists call a public good, that is, a good or service that is not diminished when one additional person consumes it. The difference is that a public good is decreased if many additional people share in the good. For example, security is a public good, but there is no less security in a town if one more baby is born to a family living in the town. However, if one thousand more babies are born, security in the town may be diminished because existing police resources are spread too thin. In the case of a human value, it makes no difference how many

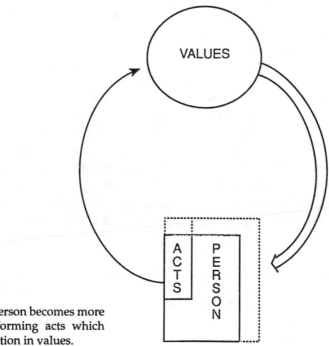

Figure 3–1. A person becomes more human by performing acts which lead to participation in values.

additional people decide to participate in the value. All people share to whatever extent or intensity they choose, and the value itself is never changed, either diminished or amplified, by increased participation. It may appear as if escalating popularity strengthens the value, but the vitality generated by popularity is not intrinsic to the value itself. In fact, the strength revealed in the enthusiasm of the populace is likely to diminish with time, without the value suffering any essential loss.

As uneconomical and unscientific as my description of value appears, it is nonetheless a straightforward, phenomenological portrayal of what every person experiences.[15] The individual deeds one performs are actions directed at different values. A particular deed, if oriented toward a value, changes the individual and grants him a fuller participation in the particular value he strives to attain. A person who helps a friend in need not only wins the appreciation and affection of his friend but also realizes or instantiates more fully the value of "friendship."

3.4 FUNDAMENTAL VALUES

People seek so many different human values in their lives that they appear to be infinite in number. The following values should be included in any comprehensive list of values: loyalty, friendship, optimism, realism, persistence, competitiveness, equanimity, creativity, resoluteness, devotion, charity, love, beauty, honesty, neatness, spontaneity, accuracy, understanding, wisdom, prudence, astuteness, cleanliness, rationality, simplicity, tenderness, solicitude, courage, generosity, temperance, resiliency, objectivity, maturity, vigor, refinement, resourcefulness, kindness, piety, compassion, justice, patience, punctuality, etc.[16] Some of the "values" in the list overlap with others, while others are antithetical to one another; some values are attractive to certain people but distasteful to others. Some are values for all seasons, others only appropriate when the circumstances dictate. Each value has a slightly different meaning, a particular attraction, and a distinct class of actions that enable a person to participate in the particular value.

The natural law approach to ethics claims that certain values are fundamental, in the sense that all other values that people legitimately strive to realize either fall within the category of one of the fundamental values or can be derived from some combination of the fundamental values.

3.4.1 Seven Fundamental Values

From the list of values given in the preceding section one could try to sort, distinguish, and compare, and in this way derive a set of fundamental or canonical values. Heuristically, however, it is better for the reader to ponder what he or she thinks are values to which every human being would subscribe.[17] In performing this exercise, the reader should be aware that whatever category or name is used, it should be quite broad, in order to include many of the particular values listed earlier. Likewise, it is important to remember that people differ in the words they use to describe fundamental values—a fact especially true for Americans, since, as researchers have pointed out, Americans lack a language about values that expresses more than just private, personal support for certain human values. This difficulty must be linguistic or cultural in origin since the same research shows that people are committed to human values.[18]

Ethicians working in the natural law tradition have identified seven essential values that produce wholeness and harmony in the individual. My list of these fundamentally human values relies on John Finnis (1980, pp. 59–99), as he presents them in his book *Natural Law and Natural Rights*. Grisez and Shaw (1980) offer a slightly different list, but the list in Grisez (1983, pp. 121–125) is identical to that given by Finnis.[19] The seven fundamental values are knowledge, beauty, life, friendship, playfulness, practical reasonableness, and religion. These are the values for which one works and is willing to endure hardship, and they are also the ones that are so central to the human project that one should never want to choose directly against them in any conceivable set of circumstances. In order to describe each of the fundamental values, we have to list the actions that lead to the realization of these values. Because the values themselves are ideals, any definition that did not refer to particular actions is necessarily dependent upon further abstractions, which require their own definition or clarification.

> **Knowledge:** Participation in knowledge is achieved by undertaking specific acts that produce greater information or comprehension for the individual. Among those acts are the study of the physical world, the human person, society, the cosmos, the liberal arts, all sciences, and the particular ways in which people react to one another. Knowledge includes fiction, because it unveils human life, and poetry, because it reveals the world to us and us

to ourselves. It also includes facts, because the real world is important, and comprehension, because facts without comprehension are only partial knowledge. Casual conversation, arguments, newspapers, magazines are all instruments for attaining knowledge. Self-knowledge, acquired through personal experience, reflection, and conversations with others, is also a form of knowledge.

Beauty: Beauty is a value in which people participate by creating beautiful things, by appreciating and admiring beauty, or by being beautiful. People create beauty by the clothes, jewelry, and adornments they wear, the home or office they decorate, the gardens they landscape or have landscaped, the pictures painted, operas sung, ballets danced, music played, sculptures sculpted, buildings built, etc. People also participate in beauty by seeing and experiencing beautiful things. Observing the beauty of nature; of attractive men, women, and children; and of buildings, paintings, artifacts, manuscripts, etc., is a way of participating in the value of beauty.

Life: Life refers first and foremost to physical life. One participates in life by being physically alive, by being active and maintaining one's health or the health of others, by supporting measures that extend the lives of human beings, by passing life on to others through procreation, by protecting people whose lives are threatened, by using the various functions of the human body and mind. Animals and plants also participate in life, and by nurturing and cultivating them people participate in life.

Friendship: Friendship includes all relationships in which people share their lives with others and make a commitment to others. It includes family relationships, marriage, ordinary friendships, business and professional relationships, and relationships that are created by joining various groups, such as local civic or church organizations, educational institutions, business groups, or national and international associations. Because friendship embraces all relationships, even citizenship, it also includes justice, which renders to each person what is due to him or her.

Playfulness: Recreation, relaxation, and a certain aimlessness compose this value. It is realized by playing games, participating in sports, traveling, and "kidding around" with one's friends. The games one plays can be very personal (involving sex, for example), or they may be impersonal, involving large numbers of people, as in marathons or lottery drawings. One can also recreate by being a spectator: by watching sporting events, cultural events, movies, television. Whimsical conversation and behavior are also forms of play.

Practical Reasonableness: This is the value of acting reasonably and can be described as "using common sense," provided this implies critical reflection and not simply a folksy regurgitation of values prevalent in the community. Practical reasonableness is the value of coordinating the many talents and desires of an individual to form a plan, method, or process by which one pursues the fundamental values. This value is an organizational one that is also self-reflective, inasmuch as it gives each fundamental value, including practical reasonableness, its due. Human reason and the human person are so interrelated that reason itself grasps when it is that the faculty of practical reasonableness functions in a reasonable manner. Practical reasonableness also means that one knows when one has spent enough time thinking about an issue.

Religion: Religion is the value of awe and wonder at the physical world, society, and one's individual person and personal life. In response to the awe and wonder, most people believe in a personal God and express their belief by joining a religion, praying alone, worshiping in common, and giving thanks to God. Awe and wonder exist not merely because human comprehension is incomplete but also because one has the conviction that any satisfactory explanation for the human situation is to be found on another, "higher" level, not accessible to human reason. By accepting those mysteries in life beyond comprehension, the human person acknowledges that God belongs to this "higher level" and is deserving of praise.[20]

Because the fundamental values are elemental goods that people strive to achieve through their actions, they can also be called basic goods, elemental values, or essential goals.

Although the seven fundamental values are self-evident to a person living in a community, this does not mean that no objections can be raised to their formulation or to the manner in which one seeks them. It means only that, upon reflection, no further evidence for the existence of the values can be offered other than the experience of the values themselves.[21] Different societies may use other concepts for the fundamental values than those listed here, have eight or five values instead of seven, and yet still capture the essence of the natural law approach. The seven values listed above are derived from a particular tradition. But much can be learned, knowledge advanced, and friendships formed by subjecting these values to review by alternative traditions that group essential human values in another way. Despite the possibility of eventual enhancements to the fundamental values approach, I contend that the taxonomy presented here captures the significant aspects of moral reflection in the Judeo-Christian tradition.

Let me justify the list of seven by examining a value that is not included, namely aggressiveness. Why is it not one of the fundamental values? In order to qualify as a fundamental value, the value itself must be fulfilling, even if it were the only value one pursued, and the value must also be so deeply human that a person should never act directly against the value. Aggressiveness is undoubtedly a human value for many people, especially business people, in the United States. But a person who acts aggressively in all situations is a fool and is recognized as such by everyone, except other fools. An aggressive person may choose to be aggressive, even with his mother, but in most instances his mother would not understand, nor would most other people. Likewise, one does not usually act aggressively toward one's spouse, children, or friend. Acting contrary to aggressiveness means being complaisant or appeasing someone. The previous comments suggest that appeasement is appropriate in many situations. Thus, by reflection on our own experience, every reasonable person can be led to the judgment that being aggressive is not fundamental, although there are some circumstances in which it is admirable.

Someone may object that the seven fundamental values are merely ways to express the preferences that many, if not all, people have, and that these preferences are adequately represented by neoclassical indifference curves and the utility function, since, ultimately, a person seeks human values because they yield satisfaction. According to this objection, anyone who espouses the seven basic goods is simply stating that she obtains satisfaction by pursuing these goods.

Admittedly, a person who seeks the basic goods does find satisfaction in the pursuit of them, but the desire to be fulfilled is not the reason why a person seeks the values. Neoclassical economists assume that satisfaction, fulfillment, happiness, or pleasure is the motivating force, but they offer no evidence for their assertion other than their own experience and their own introspection. The fundamental values approach also appeals to the evidence of experience, but unveils a different interpretation of that experience. Even if a person pursues the fundamental values for the sake of pleasure, there is no reason to believe that pleasure (or happiness and satisfaction) is homogeneous or commensurable. For example, the happiness one experiences from having spoken honestly about abuses occurring in the factory at which one works differs from the happiness attendant upon water-skiing, which also differs from the happiness that comes through one's children.[22] Uneasy with the assumption that satisfaction motivates consumers, some economists have theorized about the underlying causes of satisfaction. Scitovsky (1976), for example, claims that physiological psychology supports his claim that novelty is the primary determinant of comfort and stimulation. The fundamental values approach does not dismiss the relevance of novelty, but links it to the fundamental values. Unless a person is pursuing these essential human values, no amount of novelty can bring the type of satisfaction with which a consumer can be ethically content.

3.4.2 Private and Public Knowledge and Truth

A complete ethical system based on fundamental values should explore the distinctions among the values and determine whether each value fulfills the dual conditions mentioned earlier. Since the goal in this study is to apply the framework of the fundamental values to economic issues, we need only develop those aspects of the ethical theory that have implications for economic interactions. Because knowledge is not merely a personal goal but also a goal of society and because it plays a pivotal role in economic theory and practice, it is important to distinguish not only the ways in which knowledge is transmitted but also the types of knowledge that are sought and communicated.

A distinction can be made between publicly available knowledge and personal or private knowledge. Personal or private knowledge is known by a single individual or a small number of people, such as a family or circle of friends, or whatever group of people are privy to the information. Private or personal knowledge may become public knowledge, if one or more persons in the informed group choose to reveal it to members outside the group. When information concerns the purely private sphere, the perimeter of which is often difficult to define, the "public" should respect this private sphere and not seek to make private knowledge public. A person's sexual preferences, conversations with a friend, faults, aspirations, beliefs, promises made to friends, emotional responses in times of stress—all these belong to the realm of private knowledge.

Private knowledge is a legitimate value for the individual person or group of persons from whom the knowledge derives but not for others. It is important to note that this distinction is not merely a logical one, but one based on the experience and personal history of any individual living in community. Every person is at times acutely aware that he does not wish his interior thoughts or aspirations or even his private deeds to become publicly known. Furthermore, he would consider it extremely unfair if a person with whom he shared this information revealed it, without his permission, to others. This experience and conviction are, I claim, universal to any mature, reasonable adult.

Private knowledge is not accessible unless the person himself, or other persons who share in his private life, reveal it; but how does one distinguish private knowledge from public knowledge? One can distinguish three types of private knowledge: knowledge that is de facto private, essentially private, or morally private. Knowledge is de facto private if it is known only to one person or a small group of people, even though it could be known by a larger group. Knowledge is essentially private when it is only accessible to the person himself or herself. For example, whether one man truly loves another woman or is just feigning love for her, is known at best only to the man himself. Finally, knowledge is morally private if it pertains only to the person or a small group but has no general consequences for society. An example is the knowledge that a mother has of the fears and apprehensions of her child.

Public knowledge includes all knowledge that is not private. A person's height is not private since it can be observed by many people. A person's sexual preferences are initially private, both de facto and morally, but they become part of public knowledge once a person reveals them through public actions or statements. The possessor of private knowledge retains the option to keep the knowledge private. Once the knowledge becomes known in the public domain, however, it no longer enjoys the moral protection appropriate for private knowledge. In general, public knowledge encompasses all knowledge available to objective observers and thinkers. Science, history, theories, facts about nature, facts about individual persons and groups of persons, psychological analysis of public figures—all this belongs to the realm of public knowledge.

The distinction between the private sphere and the public domain becomes fuzzy when knowledge which was originally de facto private becomes known to a wider circle. As this happens, people in the wider circle may still have a responsibility, depending on circumstances, to protect the privacy of the individual about whom they have been given private knowledge in an unethical manner. Alternatively, some people, by reason of their position, may legitimately seek to make private knowledge more public, because it is related to their position, though not to their own person. In a family, for example, a parent can ask a young child about his or her conduct and legitimately expect that the child will speak truthfully. As the child matures most parents realize that the sphere of the child's private life increases and that parents must therefore not ask questions which pierce the veil of privacy. These are important moral issues, but they are beyond the scope of this study.

In society everyone should be interested in the pursuit of public knowledge and of his or her own private knowledge. Unfortunately, experience teaches that many individuals, both on the job and at home, also crave private knowledge of people other than themselves. Similarly, firms have "private" information that other firms seek to acquire. It may be regrettable that people and firms are so inquisitive about the private activities of others, but no harm is done unless a person or firm is pressured by someone to reveal private knowledge. No one should be forced to divulge morally private knowledge, i.e., knowledge about the private sphere of the individual or economic enterprise. For example, no man or woman should be asked by a reporter "Are you faithful to your spouse?" Since responding to the question forces the person to turn private knowledge into public knowledge, one can make a reasonable case that the reporter is acting unethically. For the person being pressured, the proper response is that it is none of the reporter's business. The difficulty is that such a reply can be interpreted as a concession that the person is indeed unfaithful to his or her spouse. Society should be protective of private knowledge and not require disclosure. Of course, some people freely choose to make private knowledge public because they seek money, power, or a variety of other goals. There is nothing wrong with this, provided the person doing the revealing is making known his or her own private knowledge and not someone else's.

Telling the truth differs from truth itself because the telling is supposed to lead the hearer to greater knowledge. One should always tell the truth if it leads people to knowledge that is legitimately public. But, as indicated earlier, by asking an improper question a person may wrongly seek private knowledge. The optimal answer to such a question should be truthful, but evasive. If evasion is not possible and if truth leads person B to morally private knowledge reserved to person A, then person A may tell an untruth and not act directly against the fundamental value of knowledge. Similarly, if truth does not communicate knowledge, as may occur when an elderly woman seeks information about her medical status, then telling an untruth which more clearly communicates that status is appropriate.

The situations referred to above are exceptional. In general, people should be disposed to tell the truth because knowledge is a basic good. A society in which individuals and institutions regularly communicate the truth not only participates more fully in the value of knowledge but also is, I believe, more efficient, because people base their actions on the true situation. Efficiency, however, is secondary to knowledge as a motivating factor for creating a society in which the truth is told.

3.4.3 Acting Against a Fundamental Value

According to the natural law tradition, each fundamental value makes a claim on every human being, a claim that is experienced by all persons as they grow to maturity in community. An examination of this experience reveals that a person understands that he is under a moral obligation to pursue these values in appropriate circumstances and that he should never perform an action that is directly opposed to them. The dual character of the claim, positive and negative, rests on the human experience of these values—an experience that is grasped and articulated by the intellect as it pursues the fundamental value of practical reasonableness.

An action is directly and objectively opposed to a fundamental value if it negates, reverses, or countermands another action that was previously taken to realize a basic good. An action is subjectively opposed to a fundamental value if the person intends by the action to induce other people to perform acts that do not lead to the realization of the essential goals, even though the persons positing the acts reasonably expect to realize the fundamental values.

A few examples of actions contrary to the fundamental values are useful. A person who willfully destroys a painting which he or she thinks is beautiful acts against the fundamental value of beauty, because he or she negates the previous action of the painter who created the beauty. A person who destroys an original manuscript of some literary or musical masterpiece acts against the fundamental value of knowledge because the act prevents people from acquiring a complete understanding of the work. A person who tells a lie to people who legitimately expect the truth misleads other people and may induce them to act in a way inconsistent with the pursuit of truth or knowledge. A mugger who stabs a person acts against the fundamental value of life, and a person who divorces his wife for no reason at all not only acts directly contrary to the fundamental value of friendship but also to the basic good of practical reasonableness. Finally, a person who ruins a game which adults are playing because she is envious of their enjoyment acts contrary to the value of playfulness, even if no physical damage is caused.

Since the fundamental values are all equally primary or central, they cannot be hierarchically ordered. One value is as valid or essential as the other, and, therefore, one ought not weigh one value against another, although a person may legitimately choose to pursue some basic goods more actively than others. Even though one essential goal, such as life, is not uniformly more important than knowledge or beauty, a hierarchy does exist within each fundamental value, an issue which is addressed later in this chapter. Thus, human life is higher than animal life which is higher than plant life, a fact that influences our understanding of what constitutes an action directly contrary to a fundamental value.

One should not think of the basic goods as stepping-stones on the way to some greatest value, called human happiness. The experience of fundamental values means that there is no overriding value or all-embracing criterion that allows judgments to be made about the particular fundamental values. Because the primacy of fundamental values is at variance with the modern emphasis on happiness as the overarching goal of all human activity, their sovereignty requires further explication and justification. Let us first consider a popular way in which "the modern person" pursues values.

The modern person avoids fanaticism; he wants to be reasonable, even objective, about values. An action that causes greater overall happiness is sanctioned by some, even if it is directly contrary to one of the fundamental values. If a lie makes more people happier, it is permissible, according to this mode of thinking. If a divorce makes both people happier, it is morally correct. This strain of modern thought sees human happiness as the final goal of all human activity, and any action that increases the amount of happiness is considered ethically responsible and correct. This type of thinking is either utilitarian, consequentialist, or eudaemonistic, because it assumes that the utility or happiness of people in society is the primary goal of all individual actions.

Modern utilitarianism and consequentialism perform a moral calculus. Consider an act x that has several consequences. The consequences can be divided into two mutually exclusive groups: G is the set of good consequences, and B is the set of bad consequences. The set G has individual elements that we label g, and the set B has individual elements that we label b. Suppose there are n good consequences and m bad consequences. The total good achieved by an action x can then be expressed as $T(x)$:

$$T(x) = \sum_{i=1}^{n} g_i - \sum_{j=1}^{m} b_j$$

According to the eudaemonistic view, an action x is ethically correct provided $T(x)$ is greater than or equal to zero; otherwise the action x is morally objectionable. I call the summing up of good and bad consequences the moral calculus of consequences.[23] The formula $T(x)$ applies equally to utilitarians as well as to consequentialists (but not to proportionalists), since both groups determine morality by weighing what effect consequences have on human happiness.

The fundamental values approach disagrees with the moral calculus of consequences for three reasons. First, fundamental values are not comparable among themselves. Second, even in the case of the single value of happiness, happiness for one individual is not commensurable with happiness for another individual. Third, consequences of many, though by no means all, actions are not merely uncertain but also unknowable.

Values are not comparable among themselves. The seven essential goals are not means toward an end but ends in themselves. They cannot be assigned weights and added together, even if one allows different weights for different individuals. Weights usually sum to the number one. A possible choice of weights would give .30 to life, .25 to friendship, and .10 to each of the other five fundamental values. Although these weights add up to one, they are essentially arbitrary. There is no reason, and can be no reason, for choosing one set of weights over another set. How does one rationally compare life with knowledge or friendship with life? People will want to give different weights in different circumstances. In order to have a consistent ethical system, one would then need a criterion for deciding which circumstance warranted which set of weights and would have to assign different weights to different categories of circumstances. How does one compare the importance of different circumstances if not by reference to the fundamental values? One therefore returns to the initial difficulty of choosing weights for fundamental values. It cannot be done in a rational manner; to choose in an arbitrary manner is inconsistent with the demands of practical reasonableness if the result of the choice is an action against one of the fundamental values.

Rejecting the moral calculus of consequences does not mean that distinctions cannot be made in order to resolve difficult moral problems. For example, consider lying in order to save someone's life. Is one permitted to tell a potential murderer that the police are outside in order to distract the murderer and run away? Under normal circumstances a person's actions should not be influenced by whether the police are outside or not. For a potential victim to say that the police are outside is to state something which is false, but which should be of no consequence to a law-abiding citizen. The whereabouts of the police is important only to someone breaking the law or to a potential victim of a crime. Furthermore, the situation is one in which neither the murderer nor the potential victim expects the truth to be told. One is bound to tell the truth only if the parties involved can reasonably expect the truth to be told. One aspect of determining what is ethically correct involves an evaluation of the situation. In the case mentioned, stating a falsehood is not directly against the value of knowledge because the intent of the lie is to lead the murderer to greater knowledge about himself. The lie is a lie, but it is intended to be an integral part of a more complex action that results in greater knowledge.[24]

The reason for examining the above example is not to suggest that the resolution offered is the only one consistent with the natural law approach but to illustrate that the fundamental values approach is sufficiently robust to apply to all situations, even morally difficult ones. One does not have to resort to a moral calculus of consequences just because distinct basic goods appear to come in conflict with each other.

Consequentialists might argue, however, that in many cases fundamental values do not conflict, in which cases the moral calculus of consequences is appropriate. But even in these instances, a simple summation of "goods" and "bads" is, I claim, incompatible with the moral judgment of the reader. Consider the value of life, and suppose an Iranian terrorist threatens to blow up a plane of four hundred tourists unless the U.S. government hands over a completely innocent American citizen, who was born in Iran, to the Iranians to be murdered. Killing the innocent Iranian-born American results in four hundred lives saved and one life lost. According to the moral calculus of consequences, the act is justified since $T(x)$ is greater than or equal to zero. Our moral intuition, however, rejects killing innocent people to save other innocent lives. The basis for the moral intuition is that one is never permitted to act directly against the fundamental value of life.[25] Thus, the happiness of the community or the overall welfare of the community is not a higher good than life itself. As we shall see, in every economy every moral agent has a responsibility to contribute to the common good, properly defined. One operates against the common good, however, by acting directly contrary to one of the fundamental values.

The third objection to the moral calculus of consequences is that in many cases the consequences of actions involving the fundamental values are not merely uncertain but also unknowable. Because actions cause reactions in other people, the effect of any particular action is frequently uncertain. Since every moral judgment is universalizable, if a particular moral judgment is eventually adopted by all other people, it induces a pattern of activity that is so vast in scope that the individual consequences, i.e., the good g_i's and the bad b_j's, are often innumerable.

The utilitarian would respond that it is exactly by enumerating all the consequences of an act that one arrives at moral decisions which agree with moral intuition, and she would respond to the example of the Iranian terrorist threatening four hundred lives in exchange for the death of one innocent person by saying that such a rule in the long run would lead to greater human misery since terrorists would know that their threats produce results. Consequently, terrorists would make more frequent and drastic threats. Therefore, according to the utilitarians, the rule of killing one innocent person to save the lives of many actually results in more deaths than never yielding to terrorism. Killing an innocent person to save a greater number of innocent lives is rejected, therefore, by the utilitarians and consequentialists as a viable principle because it does not lead to greater satisfaction or happiness for a greater number of people.

The problem with this neat calculus is that it assumes that terrorists will react only in one way, namely, with more frequent and violent threats. The terrorists themselves, however, can use the utilitarian calculus. They can reason that they should limit the deaths of innocent people to, say, ten per year. Adhering to this strategy, the nonterrorist utilitarians, when they perform their calculations, discover that yielding to ten terrorist actions a year really does result in greater good for a greater number. Any assertion by the utilitarians about how terrorists will respond in the future to present capitulation is an assumption, not a reasoned calculation. The only way to determine whether the assumption is correct or not is to observe a world based on the principle that it is morally correct to kill innocent people in order to save the lives of other innocent people. One must then contrast this world with a world in which the moral rule is that it is never acceptable to kill innocent people. Even if such an experiment were possible, it would be a false one because people would know beforehand that the experiment is merely an experiment. Once the results of the experiment become known, a decision must be made concerning the correct rule. The terrorists could reason that it is better not to kill too many people in terrorist actions during the experimental period when killing innocent people is tolerated. By adopting this strategy, the experimental results will show that it is better to allow the killing of innocent people. Once the rule is established that innocent people are to be killed when this action is expected to save the lives of other innocent people, the terrorists know they can exploit the rule to their own ends.

The utilitarian approach is not without some merit since there are many situations in which it is feasible and acceptable to weigh the probable consequences of different private and public actions. As will be seen, efficiency within reason is an ethical principle, and this means that, for the most part, one should not waste resources. When an action is not contrary to any of the basic goods, it is rational to calculate which policy achieves the stated goals with fewer expenditures, and in such instances the more efficient policy is also the ethical one. But just because utilitarian-type calculations are sometimes appropriate does not mean that they can be used to decide all moral issues.

An important distinction is that within the category of any single basic good a hierarchy of ways exist by which people and things participate in that value. For the fundamental value of life, nonhuman animal life is lower than human life, and, therefore, killing an animal can be justified if the animal threatens human life or if killing it enables participation in the value of life at a higher level.

More generally, within the category of any fundamental value, the ways in which we can participate in the value are ordered. For example, the surgeon who performs a mastectomy is acting against the basic goods of life and beauty. If she did not have a good reason for performing such an operation, the act of the surgeon would be unethical because it is directly contrary to a fundamental value. On the other hand, if the surgeon believes that the mastectomy prevents the spread of cancer in the patient, she has performed an action which, if she is correct, enables the patient to participate more fully in the essential goal of life. The operation, because it prolongs the patient's life, also allows the patient to participate more fully in the fundamental value of beauty, even though personally the patient may be less physically attractive.

Some ethicians refer to a mastectomy or any act that causes damage to an organism as a physical or ontic evil, but not a moral or ethical evil. This terminology acknowledges that the act may be directly against a fundamental value if one merely considers the direct consequences of the act. But human reason, which relies on personal experience in a community of individuals, decides whether something is ethically evil not on the basis of the physical evil caused by the act but on the basis of whether the act enables greater participation in the same basic good against which the physical evil offends. In a mastectomy, some harm is done to the patient, but only in order to achieve her better overall health. By acting in this way, the surgeon respects and fosters the fundamental values of life and beauty.

In section 4.4 I address the problem of establishing a hierarchy of actions leading to any single fundamental value. The task of determining when simple and complex actions are ethically permissible is an arduous one that has occupied ethical theorists for centuries; indeed, most ethical dilemmas and controversies concern the hierarchy of values within any fundamental value. For the most part, I am not concerned with identifying hierarchies in this study; I presume that ethicians have established such orderings and that they are available to any person committed to the essential goals. Nonetheless, at times I will presume the existence of a specific structure in order to cite illustrative examples for the ethical principles deduced.[26]

The fundamental values make an absolute claim on people. It is by examining the nature of this absolute claim that a person derives the injunction never to act directly against one of these values. We call this the noncontrary principle.

> **Noncontrary Principle:** Commitment by a person to the fundamental values implies that the person ought never freely to perform an act or approve an act directly contrary to one of the fundamental values.

An action is directly contrary to a fundamental value if the action itself diminishes rather than increases participation in the basic good. For this reason, consequences are important, as long as they are the direct result of the action undertaken. For example, the direct result of a successful operation may be that lethal cancer cells do not spread throughout the body. This is an intended consequence of the mastectomy, and it flows from the action of the surgeon performing the mastectomy; therefore, the mastectomy is justifiable. On the other hand, a doctor would act unethically if she amputated someone's arms because the person wanted to be a circus freak.

In some situations killing an innocent person may be unavoidable. To focus on the central moral issues, ethicians have traditionally pondered the situation of a trolley, hurtling out of control down the tracks. A switchman stands at a switch; he can switch the trolley to Track 1, where one innocent person will be killed, or to Track 5, where five people, all of the same age, background, and innocence as the person on Track 1, will be killed. To which track should he switch the trolley? Clearly, he should switch it to Track 1. It is true that the life of one individual is just as valuable as the life of another, but since the switchman must choose, he should pick that action which results in less harm or damage to the fundamental value of life, i.e., he should let one person be killed rather than five. Note that the situation is structured so that the consequence of the switchman's action is the death of one person or of five persons. In circumstances where one does not freely choose to kill a person but by dint of the circumstances must choose who is to be killed, the person deciding should choose in such a way that the least damage is done to the essential value of life. For correct ethical behavior in situations in which a fundamental value is threatened and a person is forced to react, I formulate the reaction principle in the following section.

One other characteristic should be considered in determining whether actions against fundamental values are ethically justifiable. Suppose that in the example considered earlier the surgeon performing the mastectomy knows that the mastectomy itself will not increase the chances of the woman living unless it is combined with chemotherapy, a separate action to be undertaken by another doctor. What makes the mastectomy ethically justifiable is its position in a more complex action, namely, the entire treatment given to the patient for carcinoma. The surgeon relies, therefore, on the desire and willingness of the patient to proceed to chemotherapy, as well as on the skill of the chemotherapist, for an ethical justification of the mastectomy she performs. More generally, some actions are complex and only the congeries of individual acts leading to the desired result justifies the actions. In such cases, it is legitimate for one person to assume that others act ethically in completing the entire action.

Since many human actions are complex, it is useful to introduce a distinction between an act and an action. An act is some deed or initiative taken by an individual, while an action is defined as a sequence of individual acts that is comprehensible as a coherent unity because it achieves a goal. Because most acts are positioned within a larger complex of an action, any single act can take on a different complexion as it is integrated into a different action or series of acts. For this reason it is impossible to state ethical principles applying to individual acts which never admit of any exception; the best that one can do is to state general principles that apply to most cases.[27]

People participate in the fundamental values by taking specific actions, many of which require goods or services, which are the means to the end of participating in an essential value. People have a responsibility to choose reasonable means to attain the end of participating in the basic values. In this sense the end justifies the means, or, expressed more precisely, the end justifies reasonable means taken to achieve that end. What else could possibly justify the means other than the end? But the end does not justify all means, and the noncontrary principle designates some means as unreasonable: any action directly contrary to a fundamental value can never be justified by claiming that it allows greater participation in some other essential value. In short, the end justifies reasonable means. The next section further articulates "reasonable means" by making the noncontrary principle more specific and by enunciating three other principles of personal justice that are derived by reflecting on the basic human experience of pursuing the fundamental values in a community.

Sometimes a dramatic cultural shift is required for people even to realize that they are acting directly against a fundamental value. For hundreds of years people have gone hunting for food, but, according to the fundamental values, hunting for the sake of playfulness is directly contrary to the value of life (of an animal). Although killing an animal for fun cannot be justified, it can be explained as a remnant from earlier times when hunting was primarily a food-gathering activity. Some people hunt animals to put the hands, head, antlers, or skin of the animal in their living room. Their intention is to increase beauty in their homes, but they attain this goal by violating the life of the animal. This behavior is inconsistent with the absolute demand of each basic good. Because moral sentiments derive from attitudes in society, certain people may feel no compunction for killing animals either for the beauty they create in a person's life or for the playfulness that the hunt provides. But, if people are committed to the fundamental values in the manner I have indicated, they should come to the realization that killing for beauty or fun is unethical.

3.4.4 Four Personal Principles of Justice

The preceding discussion showed that the words "action" and "directly contrary" have to be qualified in the noncontrary principle. "Action" may refer to a series of acts involving a number of people. The people may either cooperate with one another to achieve the desired goal of the action or a well-based understanding may exist that each person contributes his or her own act or action to the complex action. Considered separately, each act of each individual in the sequence may be a physical evil. The comprehensive action, however, legitimates each individual action. Also, an "action" is only directly contrary to an essential goal when the direct result of the comprehensive action is contrary to the essential value. Put positively, a person shows respect for a basic good even though parts of the complex action are contrary to lower order realizations of the fundamental value, provided the direct result of the action is participation at a higher level.

Although a doctor is ethically justified in removing a limb from a person to save that person's life, no action directly contrary to the highest level of a fundamental value can ever be justified.

We restate the noncontrary principle and provide the qualifications, which clarify the meaning of "action," "directly," and "contrary."

> **Noncontrary Principle:** Commitment by a person to the fundamental values implies that the person ought never freely choose to perform an action or approve an action directly contrary to one of the essential goods, where "action," "directly," and "contrary" are understood in the following way:

> **Action:** An action is either an individual act performed by one person or a series of acts performed by one person or many persons that constitutes a coherent process.[28]

> **Directly:** The action includes an act which itself offends against the fundamental value. If an act does not itself offend against the essential value but has uncertain consequences that may offend against the fundamental value, the action is indirectly against the basic good.

> **Contrary:** The action contains one or more acts that individually undermine a single fundamental value because they do not realize the same fundamental value at a higher level. Provided the acts against the lower level values are necessary to achieve a higher level result, such an action is not contrary to the basic good in question; such an action is said to be "against" the basic good, in recognition of the fact that some part of the action, when taken in isolation, moves away from, rather than toward, the essential goal.

> **Directly Contrary:** An action is directly contrary to a fundamental value if the action violates a fundamental value directly and is contrary to a fundamental value. An action that is either indirectly or simply against, in the sense defined above, an essential value is ethically responsible.

A freely chosen act which offends against a basic good at its highest level can never be justified, since one cannot claim that it enables the value to be realized at a higher level. No possible amount of "good" consequences at the highest level of the same basic good or of other basic goods can justify such an action.

The qualifications presented above accommodate the complexity of human actions and are motivated, on the one hand, by the commitment to pursue the fullest possible realization of the essential values, and, on the other hand, by the acknowledgment that the fundamental values are so fundamental that one may never act directly contrary to them. Thus, we have not introduced ethical principles based on a distinct experience of the pursuit of the fundamental values; these are rather an explication of the primary commitment and insight. The definition of "contrary" states that complex actions which promote a fundamental value should be undertaken, while the meaning of "directly" indicates that some actions can never be justified, as was evident in the examples discussed earlier.[29]

In order to decide whether an action is ethically justifiable, one must consider all the consequences of the action, personal as well as social, although one must be careful not to add together consequences of two distinct essential human values. Estimating the social consequences of an action requires prudent deliberation. For example, when an ethician terms an action morally permissible or mandated, she must reckon with the fact that, if her reasons are persuasive, many people will perform the act that she terms permissible or mandated. These are consequences not of the act itself but of approving the act in a social setting. Similarly, if a certain action is performed in an institutional setting, the ethician, always keeping categories separate, must evaluate the impact on the manner in which the institution functions. Because institutions are difficult to establish and maintain, ethical guidelines for actions which change the functioning of an institution are different from those which only affect personal activity.

The presumed commitment by all people in society to the fundamental values is mocked if many or all in society regularly act directly contrary to those values. Should a society accept such deviations from the prescribed pattern or should it intervene to prevent them from occurring?

First, the presumed pledge to the basic goods by all individuals presupposes that this commitment is a free one, at least on the part of adult members of society who do not hallucinate about reality. One can force or induce children to pursue the fundamental values in the hope and expectation that one day they will freely chose to pursue such values on their own. Although education may and should include some indoctrination when children are young, at some point children become adults and compulsion becomes inconsistent with the free pursuit of the essential values.

The presumption made in this volume is that all people are and ought to be committed to the basic goals of a human being; however, seeking essential values in one's life is not a biological instinct, coded in the double helix containing a person's genetic information. Rather, the fundamental values approach asserts that each person has a basic disposition to seek these values, and this disposition, although it requires support through neurological processes, is transmitted through experience in community, which expects adherence to some standards. Various groups in society help people to understand and appreciate which actions lead to deeper and more profound participation in the basic values. Thus, people have a nonbiological orientation as well as a moral calling to realize the fundamental values. But because the orientation in children is inchoate and requires nurturing by persons and institutions, society should be more prescriptive with children, especially in the family and schools.[30]

Is a person or society better off if society prevents an adult contemplating some action directly contrary to the basic goods from carrying out that action? According to the fundamental values approach, society prospers and flourishes to the extent that more people are enabled to pursue these values and actually do pursue them. Preventing someone from acting against the essential goals implies some prior knowledge about the intentions of the individual. In many instances, a person can act privately against a fundamental value and no one in society would even have the opportunity to intervene. However, many actions directly contrary to basic goods may be known beforehand.

Consider two examples involving private actions that people announce they intend to take. In the first example a person says that he is going to divorce his wife because he has a passing attraction for another woman. Suppose, furthermore, that he publicly admits that his reason for divorcing his wife is not cogent. In the second example, person A is about to tell a lie to person B, and the friend of person A realizes this. Both instances occur in the private sphere, that is, between people who have a voluntary or familial relationship with one another. Both actions also influence other people, but we can assume that their effects touch only friends and acquaintances. Although the person about to divorce his wife makes the information public, we assume that the effect of the action is only on individuals known to the couple.

Two interventions are possible: one to persuade and one to compel. Certainly, a friend should try to convince a person about to divorce his wife that he is acting rashly, without good reason, and directly contrary to the fundamental value of friendship. Similarly, the friend of A should try to convince her not to tell the lie, since a lie is directly contrary to the basic good of knowledge. If persuasion fails, is compulsion required by the presumed commitment of all people in society to the primary values? It depends whether compulsion produces greater participation in the basic values. If a man wants to divorce his wife but, if prevented from doing so, remains committed to his wife, society may make the reasonable judgment that laws or customs prohibiting divorce promote the pursuit of the fundamental values. Similarly, if social custom requires the friend of person A to tell person B the truth, person A will be less inclined to tell a lie.

In both cases, society must make a judgment whether, given the circumstances of a particular society, the use of social pressure promotes the pursuit of the fundamental values. Social coercion at least prevents person B from suffering the effects of a lie and, in the first example, the wife from suffering the effects of a divorce. The effects of the lie could be significant, and they can justify intervention by the friend of A. Similarly, society may have an interest in supporting the institution of marriage; if it does, it could prevent the husband from divorcing his wife for a frivolous reason.

The examples suggest that intervention is sometimes advisable and even required when the action of an individual influences other individuals or other institutions in society. In cases when the well-being of others is entailed, however, preventing a person from performing an action directly contrary to the fundamental values does not prevent the person from intending to do something directly against them. Where actions contrary to the essential values contemplated by individuals are purely personal and have no effects on others, no compulsion is warranted, although advice by friends is recommended.

The experience a person has of himself or herself pursuing the basic goods in community includes the realization that some actions are private in the sense that, although they occur in a community of individuals, they do not have a significant impact on others. It also includes the affirmation that such private actions should be respected by others. One way to express this is that a person is bound by conscience to respect the privacy of others, where "conscience" is shorthand for the demand experienced by people to adhere to the requirements of the fundamental values.

In dialectical fashion the preceding discussion used examples, appealed to experience, and suggested different formulations of general principles. The discussion is offered as a partial justification for this formulation of the principle of personal freedom.

> **Principle of Personal Freedom**: Individuals should follow their conscience in pursuing the fundamental values and should allow others to do likewise, to the extent feasible with the requirements given below. Society, for its part, flourishes through the free pursuit of the fundamental values by individuals. People should not be required by other people or society to pursue the essential values in particular ways which are contrary to their personal convictions. Individuals can, however, be prevented by appropriate agents from performing actions if:
>
> 1. the actions adversely affect other people in a direct way, or
> 2. the actions, when they are likely to be imitated by others, adversely affect significant institutions in society which enable people to pursue the fundamental values.

An action "adversely affects" other people if it prevents a person from pursuing a fundamental value or impairs his ability to participate in a fundamental value. The principle of personal freedom elucidates the consequences of seeking fundamental values in society rather than as an independent person functioning without any reference to other people in society.

The principle of personal freedom makes a distinction between positive and negative coercion. Positive coercion, which forces someone to perform an act which, in the estimation of society or others, leads to a participation in the fundamental values but which is contrary to what the person believes, i.e., against his conscience, is never permitted. This is the foundation in morality for freedom of religion and freedom of conscience.[31] Negative coercion prevents a person from carrying out an action that is directly contrary to the basic goods, although the person performing the action may not realize or admit that it is directly contrary. This type of intervention is possible or even mandated if others are adversely affected.

Suppose a person feels that he is bound by his conscience or religion to undertake an action that others deem to be directly contrary to the fundamental values. Is society bound to respect his freedom of conscience? Society has a dual responsibility in this instance: It must respect, although not necessarily grant, his freedom of conscience, and it must also protect the interests of others. By preventing a person from carrying out a plan that hurts others or impairs their ability to pursue the fundamental values, society shows no disrespect for the person's conscience. Basic respect is shown by an absolute prohibition against positive coercion. The person who is prevented by society from carrying out some action required by conscience, such as killing a person or destroying some object, can console himself with the thought that, according to his religion or conscience, his intention was pure and that he would have performed the action were he not blocked by society.

Related to the issue of intervention is the question concerning what the required response ought to be when, through no fault of one's own, one of the fundamental values is threatened. The threat may come from a person, a group of persons, nature, or some other force beyond the control of the person who perceives that the fundamental value is threatened. A person may be dying of cancer, a notorious killer may threaten a hostage, an elderly person may be about to be run over by a car, or a child may be trapped in a cave. Each of these examples involves the essential good of life, but examples involving other fundamental values can also be cited. A beautiful building may be threatened by industrial pollutants, or a rain forest—which is an abundant source of knowledge, life, and beauty—may be threatened with extinction by the functioning of the free-market system.

In the life-threatening instances listed above, a person who is aware of the threat has a responsibility to take reasonable steps to save the life of the individual. Perhaps nothing can be done in the case of the person dying of cancer. Force may be required against the known killer. A shout may be sufficient to warn the person in the street of the oncoming car. Heavy equipment or skilled workmen might be required to rescue the child in the cave. The person's moral responsibility to act is a consequence of his or her commitment to the fundamental values. Although people in society have their own plans to implement the fundamental values, in the examples cited they are confronted with a direct threat to the fundamental value at the highest level. They achieve a greater participation in the basic good by undertaking an action that may take but a minute but which saves the life of an individual. People in such situations do not freely choose the situation, although they freely determine the manner in which they react to the situation. In the noncontrary principle we stated that freely chosen acts directly contrary to a fundamental value are unethical. We now emphasize the qualification "freely chosen" and note the difference between the type of moral response permitted in a situation where one freely chooses a course of action and the type of response allowed when one is confronted with an imminent action that threatens a fundamental value. In the latter case, one can act directly contrary to the fundamental value as long as the response is proportional to the (physical or ontic) evil being threatened. Proportionality is the main guideline contained in the reaction principle.

How much effort does one have to expend to ward off the evil? For example, must the best doctors be called in to try all possible procedures to save the life of the person dying of cancer? No, the magnitude of the response depends on the extent to which the essential values can be sought in the situation and the extent to which the person desires to seek them. We enunciate the principle, which we call the reaction principle, and then justify it.

> **Reaction Principle**: An action, initiated by persons, by nature, or by some combination of both, may directly threaten a fundamental value. The obligation, ceteris paribus, of an onlooker or someone directly threatened by the action is to react by attempting to prevent the action or the effects of the action by means of the appropriate expenditure of resources. The following criterion specifies the meaning of "appropriate expenditure":
>
> 1. Resources should be expended to prevent the action in proportion to the anticipated ability of people to participate in the fundamental values once the danger is averted. An action directly contrary to a fundamental value should only be undertaken to prevent a threat to the same value.

In the case of the fundamental value of life it is useful to make more specific the meaning of "in proportion to," contained in criterion

1. Therefore, two implications of condition 1, as applied to the fundamental value of life, are noted:

2. If the process or event threatening the life of a person leads irreversibly to death and intervention does not enable any substantial participation in the fundamental values, the person responsible is only required to take ordinary means to prevent the threatened event from occurring.

3. If a person's life is threatened, the person who desires greater resources to be expended than would be allocated by society's adherence to 1 and 2 above, may expend them. However, one's moral obligation is satisfied by following 1 and 2. In case of a direct threat to a fundamental value other than life, intervention should respect the legitimate wishes of a person who has a reasonable claim to the goods being threatened.

Criterion 1 states that actions to ward off threats to a basic good should be in proportion to the "damage" threatened. (The use of "damage" is, of course, an image since the fundamental value itself experiences no harm. The true harm is done to persons or things. If a person could have prevented a directly contrary action but did not, the harm is that she is not as profoundly human as she could have become.) Since we earlier rejected the consequentialist moral calculus and also included proportionalists among consequentialists, some explanation is necessary. In the case where a basic good is threatened, proportionalism is correct as long as the measure of proportion is taken within the category of any single fundamental value.

The noncontrary principle asserts that any freely chosen action against a fundamental value at one level can only be justified if the action increases participation in the same essential value at a higher level. In the noncontrary principle the focus is on the individual, but in the case treated by the reaction principle a person is put in a situation in which he is forced to act in order to prevent some action contrary to the fundamental value. In such circumstances, the person has to make reasonable, not herculean, efforts to ward off the threat. "Reasonable" in this instance is to be judged by the ability and freedom of the person threatened by the event to participate in the basic goods subsequent to the event. Different circumstances must be distinguished, as is done in criterion 1. Nevertheless, the goal remains the same: participation in the fundamental values.

The criteria explicitly allow people to gauge the expenditure of resources on expected participation in the fundamental values subsequent to the event. The reason this is permitted in the reaction principle is precisely because one is reacting to and not instigating a situation. By reacting, one is expending resources that could be used in the positive pursuit of the fundamental values. Since the ultimate goal is to participate as fully as possible in the fundamental values, a decision has to be made about the most effective use of resources. Even when a fundamental value is threatened at its highest level, one should not spend resources unless intervention is likely to allow greater participation in that fundamental value than if no intervention had occurred. One is not required, for example, to expend significant economic resources (the expenditure of which prevents others from participating in life) in order to provide a few extra days or months of life to someone threatened by a debilitating disease.

Consider again the examples given earlier. Criteria 2 and 3 apply to the person dying of cancer. The person and those caring for the person are morally bound only to ask for and to take the ordinary means usually given to sick people to keep them alive. If the person desires extraordinary efforts to be made to save his life and has the necessary resources to pay for these efforts, he is free to do so. Society, however, is not required to provide those resources should the person not have disposal over them. The second example was of the person about to be hit by a car. The person observing what is about to take place has, according to criterion 1, a moral obligation to take proportionate action to prevent the accident from occurring. In this case a shout, hardly a great expenditure of time or resources, would suffice to warn the pedestrian. Criterion 1 also applies to the child trapped in the cave. Since the child can recover completely from the ordeal, proportionate efforts should be undertaken, without endangering the lives of others, to rescue the child.

When a society is forced to weigh lives against lives, it should choose to protect those lives that have the greater chance of participating in the fundamental values. Ceteris paribus, more resources should be expended to save the life of a child than the life of someone who is elderly. Similarly, society should devote more resources to preserve the life of someone who, because of his or her role in society, can contribute more to save the lives of others. For example, more resources should be committed to saving the life of a doctor or of a national leader known for his or her ability to maintain peace between nations than for a person of ordinary ability. One can justify the expenditure of more resources for an extraordinarily talented person who uses this talent to enable others to participate in the fundamental values.

An individual person may volunteer to offer his life in exchange for the lives of others, but the person should do this only if he judges that his action will be effective in saving the lives of others and that, as far as he can judge, those whose lives are saved will be able to participate more fully in the fundamental values. These reflections justify condition 1 of the reaction principle, which, although it applies primarily to individuals, also indicates the way in which society should coordinate its activities.

Condition 2 states that only ordinary means need be taken to preserve the life of a terminally ill person. While condition 1 demands some proportional effort, condition 2 sets the "absolute" level of effort, relative to the standards of society at that time. In this case "ordinary means" are the usual activities that would be undertaken for someone who is moderately ill. Doctors and ethicians differ about what constitutes "ordinary means," especially since the standards of society are in constant flux. Particularly in times of rapid technological change, it should not be surprising that the determination of the precise level of "ordinary means" is disputed.

Condition 3 acknowledges that some people desire to cling to life more than others. The presumption should be that such persons are willing to expend great resources to avoid death not because they fear death but because they desire to pursue yet other ways of participating in the fundamental values. On the basis of the principle of personal freedom, people should be permitted by society to spend their resources as they see fit. Nonetheless, it is possible that the person who expends large resources to prolong life for only a few additional days acts unethically. The reason is that the person is bound by condition 1. Although society, following the principle of personal freedom, assumes that the person is acting to promote his own welfare and the welfare of society, the person may be partially aware of the folly of spending large amounts of money in futile gestures to keep death at bay. Those who seek to avoid death at all costs are often gripped by a blinding fear that impairs their judgment and, consequently, diminishes their moral culpability. Theoretically, however, an individual acts immorally if he spends large amounts of money to prevent the inevitable. The money and the resources it represents could be better used by others to pursue the fundamental values.

Although the reaction principle is not always easy to apply in practice, its virtue is that it offers a theoretical guide for allocating resources in situations in which fundamental values are threatened.

The last personal principle of justice that flows from the presumed dedication of everyone to essential human values is a commitment on the part of everyone to the common good of society. Since the common good can erroneously be interpreted as some undifferentiated value such as happiness or satisfaction, I often make more precise what is meant in this study by the common good by using the term "the flourishing of all people in society."[32] Flourishing suggests growing luxuriantly, as in the blooming of a flower, and the way in which a person flourishes is in the pursuit of the fundamental values. In this study the common good is always to be understood as the multiple flourishing of all people in society through the diverse pursuit of the essential human goals.

How does one justify the responsibility of everyone in society to pursue the common good? The justification derives both from the experience of pursuing the fundamental values in community and from reflection upon that experience. The reflection itself is a participation in the fundamental values of knowledge and practical reasonableness.[33] Consider first the experience of the pursuit of the fundamental values in community.

People grow, mature, learn about right and wrong, accept the expectations of the community for their actions, perform good actions and bad actions, develop aspirations, and criticize other members of the community—all within a community. People are formed by the community and, long before they reflect on the fundamental values, they have pursued them alongside others in some community. Because this all happens naturally, the community is an integral expression of the social nature of men and women, and other animals as well. The community itself sets ethical and social boundaries within which members of the community operate, as MacIntyre (1984) has emphasized in his influential study *After Virtue*.[34] As a person matures and becomes more aware, experientially as well as vicariously, of different communities and their customs, she notes features common to the various communities she knows.

One experience everyone has in community is pressure to behave in a certain way. Although the pressure may come from the community, it is initially experienced as something internal. As a person becomes familiar with new communities, she may recognize that some pressures generated by her community do not exist or do not exist to the same extent in other communities. She also recognizes that some pressures to do certain things and avoid others are constant in the various communities which she experiences. If her experience is limited to only one or a few communities, she may, for example, conclude incorrectly that all communities bury their dead or that all communities eat with utensils. But if her experience is broad and if she is insightful, she can recognize that, no matter how various societies dispose of their dead, all societies show respect for the dead. By reflections of this sort, the inquisitive person can be brought to realize that all good communities pursue the fundamental values and that the community is structured to assist them in the pursuit of these values. A person is always a part of a community, and thus she cannot step outside it and judge whether it is good or bad based on some external criterion. The judgment about the good of community comes from someone committed to one community, though aware of other communities.

By experience a person may also realize that once the community perceives a better way to allow people to pursue the fundamental values, pressure develops in the community for an adjustment in the traditional way of doing things. She also realizes that, if in her own family or in the community she sees something which can function better (in the sense of achieving the fundamental values at a higher level) and she can explain it well to the community, she expects that the responsible people will make the proper adjustments. If she pointed out anomalies to the authorities which prevent people from pursuing knowledge or beauty or playfulness or any other essential human good, and if she gave reasons for a suggested change, and if the authorities agreed with her but then, for no reason, did not carry out the suggested reforms, she would judge that they have acted unreasonably. In effect, she makes the judgment that society should be structured in such a way as to enable all people to flourish in the pursuit of the fundamental values. Even though her view of flourishing may be quite constrained by her own experience, she still can perceive the fundamental values and, what is important for our purposes, she can perceive that society should be ordered so that it promotes the pursuit of these goods.

A second component of a person's experience in community is the realization that people are better able to strive for the fundamental values when they have goods and services at their disposal. Goods and services, however, require human labor to produce them and to make them available to people in the community. This realization is elemental and has two components. First, it is the experience of every person in community that he must make a contribution to the production of goods and services; second, as one reflects on this experience, he judges that everyone should make some effort to produce goods and services for the community. Different people have distinct abilities and roles in the community; nonetheless, each person is expected to contribute his or her "fair share" to the common enterprise of generating the goods and services necessary to pursue the common good. Ascertaining what constitutes one person's fair share is a laborious undertaking, since it cannot be determined without examining the detailed contours of society as well as the abilities of the person. Even though people may have differences about how much an individual ought to contribute, they agree that each ought to contribute in proportion to the person's abilities and to the position he enjoys or role he performs in society. Most people make this contribution through work, which is effort devoted primarily to the production of goods and services rather than time devoted to the consumption or use of goods and services.

The experience described above of a person living in society, pursuing the fundamental values, trying to improve society, and making a contribution to the common good, is the basis for the following principle.

Personal Principle of the Common Good: Through reflection on one's experience in community and society, each person is called to acknowledge the following moral obligations.

1. Everyone ought to desire to establish conditions in society so that all people can flourish in the pursuit of the fundamental values. The flourishing of all members of society in their pursuit of the essential human goals is called the common good.

2. Every person, in proportion to his or her abilities and position in society, should make a contribution to the common good by working, inside or outside the home, to produce goods and services for society.

In the fundamental values approach the claim is not merely that each person has the experience that grounds this principle, but also that each person in her own way reflects on this experience and realizes that it is an essential component of what it means to be a human being.

CHAPTER 4

Other Values and Traditions

The fundamental values approach is a modern expression of the natural law tradition, a prominent ethical school of thought, but the prominence of the school cannot guarantee the validity of the approach. Therefore, in this chapter I subject the fundamental values approach to criticism from opposing schools of thought. The responses to the objections demonstrate the extent to which the fundamental values approach incorporates a plurality of views.

4.1 OBSERVATIONS ABOUT CERTAIN FUNDAMENTAL VALUES

Freely acting directly contrary to a fundamental value is never permitted—this is the result of the investigations in the previous chapter. This prohibition applies equally to each basic good, and in this sense each essential value is due equal esteem, as measured by human actions. This "negative" equality notwithstanding, reasonable people are practically constrained to grant one value a priority over the others. Physical life, because it is a necessary condition for participating in the other values, is more elemental than other values. One should never choose to act against any of the fundamental values, but individuals and society ought to promote the value of life by positive actions. In singling out physical life for special attention, emphasis is given to the proactive responsibility of society to sustain life. It is important to remember, however, that the basic good of life includes much more than physical life: Health, procreation, and maturation are all included under the value of life. Life is a contextual value without which no other values can be sought.

Fundamental values are often sought in the context of previously existing relationships among people. Friendship and familial relationships have a place of importance in people's lives long before family members understand the significance of friendship as a value. People are naturally drawn together in families and friendships because there is wealth to be created by sharing one's experiences with other persons. Economists suggest that people form communities for less lofty goals and claim that people have needs for food and shelter that can be better met by a division of labor and specialization. According to the economists, modern people, like their prehistoric forebears, come together out of need, in order to survive in a hostile environment as well as to increase the material resources available for their use.

Although scarcity and relative need form an important aspect of the human experience, it is also true that people come together even after their needs have been taken care of. The economist might claim that even in this case they have a need because otherwise they would not come together. But, to argue this way the economist must assume what he wishes to show, namely, that people come together only to fulfill needs. According to the natural law approach and the Judeo-Christian tradition, people come together not primarily because of economic or physical need but because they can create more in common than they can alone. The economist motivates community by claiming that specialization creates material wealth more efficiently, but a plausible, alternative motive for community is that it creates spiritual wealth.

A balanced explanation for human community is that people come together to share the wealth they already have and create new riches, first, by interacting with one another and, second, by cooperating to produce goods and services. Even if people were unable to create increased material wealth by forming bonds with one another, they would form ties of friendship in order to experience the wealth provided through friendship and shared relationships. Living is essentially a social enterprise. Healthy people do not exist in isolation. The "solitary" scholar working to expand the horizons of knowledge communicates with other scholars, either of the current age or of past and future ages. The religious hermit bands together with other hermits and studies the writings of holy men and women who have preceded him or her. Forming bonds with other people is an essential component of life.

Some will claim that religion should not be included in the list of fundamental values because they note that many people do not believe in a supreme being or do not practice a religion. Although it is true that religious belief is not universal, all people seem to experience awe and wonder at someone or something which they acknowledge to be beyond them and superior to them, and this domain is designated "religion." The vast majority of people would consider their lives poorer if they did not act in pursuit of the value of religion by practicing the particular religion which is the bearer and sustainer of their beliefs. In fact, many people experience religion as so fundamental that they would risk their property and lives in order to practice their religion. Economists like to make plausible assumptions, and since skepticism about religion is confined to the relatively small group of better educated and wealthy people in industrialized societies, the assumption that religion is a fundamental value for all people is certainly more realistic than the assumption that religion is not important for most people.[1]

Since for the purposes of this study religion does not play a significant role in the derivation of the principles of economic justice, those who find its inclusion among the fundamental values problematic may omit it mentally from the list.[2] But if the reader decides not to include it as a fundamental value, it should at least be acknowledged as a value about which many people have strong convictions. Without good reasons, individuals should not prohibit people from practicing their religion or force them to perform acts contrary to their religion.

The seven values are fundamental in two senses. First, they are all (with the possible exception of religion) considered by all human beings to be values. This does not mean that everyone implements the values in the same way since every culture and subculture has different ways of realizing the fundamental values. Even within one particular culture or subculture people may have contesting views, for example, about how best to realize the value of life, beauty, or friendship. Disagreements multiply when distinct cultures are compared. For example, some primitive societies ritually killed certain members of the tribe once they reached a certain age, but one need not agree with their practice in order to assert that, even for them, life was a fundamental value and that taking another's life was restricted by certain norms, although the norms were drastically different from those commonly observed in modern society.

Because the essential human goals are intended to include all significant areas of human existence and striving, they are defined broadly. As in any definition, there can be uncertainty as to whether certain aspects of a value (is pornography knowledge or beauty?) are included in the definition or, if they are included, are considered directly contrary to that value. Initially, one can include debatable activities within the categories of the fundamental values. In fact, issues such as pornography (as part of knowledge or beauty), prostitution (as part of playfulness), drugs (as part of playfulness), etc., pose significant questions of fairness in a modern economy, but they need not concern us at this point.

4.2 OBJECTIONS

Objection 1: Is the list of fundamental values complete?

> **Response**: In the previous chapter a long list of values was presented in order to demonstrate how numerous and ubiquitous values are. One can legitimately ask whether the list of seven fundamental values captures all that is essential from the earlier list. The best way to answer that question is for the reader to reflect on his or her own experience. Are there other values, which are essential in the sense defined, but which cannot be included in the list of seven?

Objection 2: Why is "happiness" not included as one of the seven basic values? It would appear that everyone desires to be happy. Furthermore, people take concrete steps to ensure their happiness: A woman marries the man she loves, people work hard in order to enjoy their leisure and provide for their children. "Happiness" is also one of the many interpretations of the utility function used in neoclassical economics. Certainly, happiness is a fundamental drive of human nature.

> **Response**: I grant that all human beings desire to be happy and that they also undertake actions which they hope will result in happiness. However, most people perform some actions that they anticipate to be painful without any expectation of happiness. They perform the action because it is the ethically correct thing to do. Furthermore, an action which has happiness as its thematic, conscious goal cannot result in happiness, unless one forgets about the goal. Happiness is a side-benefit of activities intended to fulfill other ends. An adolescent may say: "I want to be happy today, so I am going to go to the beach," but an adult realizes that

happiness is more elusive. Going to the beach may make one happy, but only if one is playing, talking, observing nature, etc. The claim of the natural law approach is that one becomes happy only by undertaking activities which one thinks lead to participation in the fundamental goods.[3] Literature is filled with examples of people who think certain persons or things can bring them happiness. In sum, happiness cannot be achieved directly; it comes about as a side-effect of pursuing the fundamental values. Indeed, happiness has many different levels. As Nozick (1989, pp. 99–117) points out, "Happiness rides piggyback on other things that are positively evaluated correctly. Without these, the happiness does not get started" (p. 113).

Objection 3: If happiness is not a fundamental value, what about suffering? Everyone has to suffer in his or her life, and everyone admires people who refuse to abandon their beliefs even if they are tortured. Some people even die for their beliefs or loyalties (for country, religion, race) and they are widely admired. At the very least, it appears reasonable to claim that, at times, suffering is an essential value.

Response: Suffering, physical and psychological, is an important component of everyone's life. For those people in industrial countries who are not poor, physical suffering usually comes only with sickness and at the end of one's life, whereas psychological suffering occurs more regularly. Concern for loved ones, disappointment in relationships, and rejection by friends or colleagues at work all cause suffering. A mature person knows how to accept suffering, but it is not something a person seeks out. If there is no other way to remain faithful to friends or committed to one's principles, one accepts suffering that is imposed by persons or circumstances outside of oneself. But a person does not choose to participate in a "value" called suffering. A person who looks for suffering when it is not necessary is considered deranged and maladjusted, while a person who accepts suffering when there is no other way to remain true to one's principles is admired, perhaps revered.

When possible, people avoid suffering. The entire medical profession and the pharmaceutical industry are committed to relieving people's suffering. Some suffering is unavoidable, and some suffering is senseless. Much physical suffering can be alleviated by drugs, and future research should produce new drugs and procedures that will further reduce physical suffering. Psychological suffering, however, can never be removed, because even when a drug offers short-term relief a person can get depressed that she has to be treated with drugs.

Objection 4: Is not work a value? Although unpleasant at times, it enables one to participate in the fundamental values. Moreover, everyone works. The fact that it is a value is immediately apparent to anyone who cannot find work. Everyone has either had the experience of being out of work or can imagine being out of work and can anticipate the discomfort it would cause. Because these feelings are universal, work must be a fundamental value. Also, every person has the experience that one participates in the value of work more or less intensely depending on how hard and conscientiously one works. Work has the characteristics of a basic good.

Response: Work is a value in the sense that through work a person makes a contribution to the welfare of society by producing goods and services. If people did not work, there would be fewer goods to be used for participation in the fundamental values. Moreover, a person who does not work would not be making a contribution to society. Society flourishes when *everyone* works. By working, people demonstrate their solidarity in the human situation and create goods needed to participate more fully in the essential values.

Despite this positive evaluation of work, it is an instrumental value, not a fundamental one. It enables a person (by earning a wage) to purchase goods and services to be used for participating in the basic goods. It is also an expression that all humanity exists in a state of scarcity with respect to physical resources, goods, and services, and one makes a contribution to decreasing scarcity through the work which one performs. That work is an instrumental value, but not a fundamental value, is evident in that people do not work for the sake of work. It makes no sense to work as hard as one can if the work does not allow participation in other values. A workaholic is the popular expression for a person who works excessively—one who does not stop to enjoy the fruits of his labors. Not only does the workaholic deny himself the opportunity to pursue the fundamental values, but he also robs work of its ultimate meaning by raising it to the status of religious commitment. A workaholic may be physically robust, but he is not well balanced, because he gives work a value it does not warrant.[4]

Objection 5: What about sex? The seven fundamental values are boring. If that was all there was to life, people would commit suicide. Sex is one essential drive that everyone would acknowledge, and it does not even appear in the list of essential goods.

Response: Sexual contact is an important value for many people, and sexuality should be important for everyone. Sex, however, is not a fundamental value because not only can one not rationally desire to have sex in all situations where it is available, but one does not do anything drastically wrong by acting directly contrary to sex, whatever that may mean.

Free sex without commitments may be the fantasy of many an adolescent, but it is not rationally desired by a mature person. One characteristic of a fundamental value is that one is never permitted to act directly against the value. If sex were a fundamental value, by refusing to have sex one would be acting against the value. A better way to express the value and worth of sex is to say that sexual activity is important for many people at some times, and sexuality—the way a person uses his or her body in all interactions, even the most casual ones such as conversation—is always important for an individual and always plays a role, whether a person is aware of it or not. The significant difference between the two is that a person has much more control over his or her own sexual contacts than his or her own sexuality.[5]

Using this distinction between sexuality and sex, it should be apparent that sex is to be desired in certain situations, but not in all situations. If one is married, sex with one's spouse is good, when both are willing. If a married man had sex with his office secretary, his wife would not consider sex in that instance to be a value. In its literal sense, sex is not a value at all since it is a physical act rather than an ideal good. Using language carefully, I should say that sex is an act performed to express love or friendship. Some might find this redefinition tendentious since it omits sex performed purely for pleasure and not as an expression of friendship. However this issue is resolved, sex is at most a value in certain circumstances. More generally, it is a value to be included under playfulness, life, and friendship since it is fun, healthy, potentially procreative, and expressive of a special type of friendship.

The significance of sex as a subsidiary or conditional value can change over time in society. At present, the main way to be procreative is through sexual union. In some future society science may offer other possibilities that are judged to be ethically responsible; at that time, the significance of sex as a value may change. Whatever future developments may arise, sex will always be one way to conceive children and it will also be one way in which couples can be playful, have fun with each other, and express their friendship in a special way.

Objection 6: In his book *A Theory of Justice*, John Rawls designates liberty, power, opportunity, wealth, and self-respect as primary goods. Could they be considered fundamental values?

Response: Rawls calls them primary goods because he claims that no matter what other goods people may desire, everyone desires to have liberty, opportunity, wealth, power, and self-respect. Liberty, power, and opportunity are closely related to the freedom to choose a life plan which maps out how one plans to achieve the basic values. Wealth is only an instrument, albeit a necessary one, for the attainment of fundamental values. Self-respect is conveyed to a person by members of a community in acknowledgment of his or her contributions to the community. It is not a value that can be sought directly, nor is it one which can be allocated on the basis of any criterion other than merit. To distribute self-respect to minorities, for example, because they have low self-respect is either an impossibility or an act in which self-respect evanesces in the process of being distributed. Like happiness, self-respect comes as a by-product of actions aimed at realizing the fundamental values, and it certainly cannot be "awarded" unless the recipient deserves it.

Objection 7: If one is never permitted to act against a basic good, then an artist must always produce a beautiful painting. He or she is never permitted to paint something that is ugly or repulsive in the estimation of the artist. In fact, however, artists, especially modern artists, depict inner city squalor, personal psychological angst, and natural disasters. Does this mean that they are acting immorally?

Response: No. An artist may legitimately attempt to highlight reality, even the seamier parts of reality, in a painting. Painting an ugly or repulsive scene is not the same as destroying something which is beautiful. After all, when portraying the real world, the artist does not create the original scene that is given to him by nature, by history, or by society; he or she makes it more vivid or emphasizes certain aspects of it. The artist's intent may be to draw out the poignancy of the situation or merely to call attention to realities which are so repulsive that people would ordinarily suppress them. Beauty and knowledge are both fundamental values, and the artist can enhance knowledge without acting directly against beauty. To act directly against beauty one would have to destroy (or fail to take reasonable steps to protect) something beautiful.

Objection 8: The categories for the basic goods are so broad and the force of the noncontrary principle so strong that the combined effect is to restrict severely the type of activity permitted. Consider the fundamental good of beauty. Nature is beautiful, for the most part. If one is not allowed to act directly against nature, shopping malls in the countryside never should have been built, because in order to build the malls one had to do violence to the beauty of nature. In a similar way, a new building replaces an older building which most likely had some beautiful features. The stricture not to act against the broadly conceived fundamental values appears to incapacitate people and stultify society.

Response: I concede that it appears as if in many instances a commitment to the fundamental values paralyzes an individual, but this is only because insufficient attention is given to the hierarchy of values within any individual fundamental value. Let us consider different levels of natural beauty. It is wrong to destroy the most beautiful natural phenomena, acknowledged as such by society. Only a boor or an unethical person would build a hotel over Niagara Falls and thereby ruin the beauty of the falls. Cities regularly designate certain buildings as beautiful and grant them landmark status, which means that the owner cannot change the building without municipal approval. Individuals and governments acknowledge their responsibility to respect beauty, person-made as well as natural.

Beauty is a fundamental value and developers *ought to* acknowledge the demands it makes on them and on all people. There is nonetheless ample scope for new buildings and large projects. After all, some natural sites are not particularly beautiful and some buildings standing on potential construction sites are rather plain. In such situations a developer is on morally sound ground when she clears the land for a mall or demolishes a building to replace it with another building, perhaps larger and, at least in the eyes of the developer, more beautiful. Although buildings are not made to last forever, each builder or architect ought to spend reasonable amounts of money to make the building beautiful. The expected life of the building will influence the amount of money spent to enhance the beauty of the building.

Objection 9: Some values which in our modern society are not as highly valued as in earlier societies appear to be missing from the list of fundamental values. For example, generosity and courage are important values which practically everyone admires in individuals, women and men alike. Why are they not essential human goals?

Response: Courage and generosity are certainly important qualities for individuals as well as society. However, they are not primary goals of a person's activities but modalities to decision making. Fear does not influence the courageous person when she decides what to do, while love of money or goods does not influence the decision of a generous person. However, a person does not wake up in the morning and say to himself, "I am going to seek out ways to be courageous." Although a person might decide at daybreak to be generous, this would not be sufficient since he would also have to decide who should be the beneficiary of his generosity. He presumably does not want to give the money to just anybody, but to someone who will use the money "wisely," that is, to a person who will use the money to pursue the fundamental values.

Courage and generosity are modes of being, important qualities in executing a life plan and in making decisions in pursuit of the fundamental values. However, people do not live to be courageous and generous, although they do live to discover knowledge and truth, to create and appreciate beauty, to have friends, etc.

Objection 10: Love certainly is a value, even if one omits its sexual manifestations. The simple fact that everyone desires to love others and be loved by others is proof that love is a fundamental drive in the human spirit. It is undoubtedly included within the basic good of friendship, but should it not be singled out for greater attention?

Response: Yes, love is a very important value, even a fundamental value. It would be acceptable to give the name of "love" to the basic value that we have called "friendship." The reasons for choosing friendship rather than love touch upon the way in which love is understood in modern society as well as upon the implicit hierarchy which society appears to give to love. Consider first the feeling of being in love. Many people identify love with emotions that accompany commitment, care, and concern for another human being or group of human beings. But the emotions are incidental to love, not essential—although it would be surprising if a person's devotion to another person or group of persons did not occasionally arouse strong emotions within the individual. The second difficulty with the use of the word love is that the media in modern society suggest that the highest form of love is that which results in physical and sexual expression. But this cannot be true, since a mother loves her child intensely without any sexual expression between mother and child, and one can be a best friend to another person without ever expressing that love in a sexual manner. Friendship implies some intimacy, but the intimacy need not be sexual.

Friendship is, I believe, a better description of the fundamental value that is pursued by commitment to another person or group of persons. Although love could also be used to describe the types of relationships which people value, one would have to distinguish love from feelings and from sexual expression, so that love is conceived broadly enough to include all types of personal commitments which people value.

It would require an entire volume to justify completely why the seven values are fundamental and why one's conscience says that a person is not allowed to act directly against them. My task is not to provide a comprehensive justification for the natural law approach, but to describe it, partially justify it, make it plausible to economists, and then apply it to the U.S. economy. Further motivation for the natural law approach is gained by analyzing more carefully the relationship between the fundamental values and human nature, the task for the next section.

4.3 HUMAN NATURE

The claim has already been made that all people would acknowledge that the fundamental values are important values in their lives and that these essential human goods are binding—in the sense that one ought not act against them—in all situations. The first of the properties can be designated the quality of universality, and the second can be called the quality of negative comprehensiveness. The previous sections justified negative comprehensiveness in detail. The quality of universality, on the other hand, has been more frequently asserted in this study than argued. Since there are certainly some people in the world who would deny the significance of one or more of the fundamental values for themselves, it is imperative to state in what sense the quality of universality applies.

The quality of universality is neither an empirical claim nor simply a moral claim, but a normative statement. Universality obviously cannot be an empirical claim because I have already pointed out that the fundamental values could be categorized differently without changing the underlying objectives of human actions. Even if there were only one possible categorization, however, some people might reject, for example, the assertion that playfulness is a fundamental value.

The natural law theorist replies to this rejection by stressing the consistency required by practical reasonableness in assessing the actions one performs in life. Often times theorists think of consistency merely in terms of logical coherence among statements. However, actions have purposes, and at different times the same action may have different purposes. Practical reasonableness demands that similar actions performed for the sake of reaching the same goal should not undermine one another or the goal one is striving to achieve. Consistency in acts is a requirement of practical reasonableness.

Consider the person who rejects beauty as a fundamental value. First, one should ask the person to examine her life and note the different ways in which the person pursues the value of beauty: colors, shapes, clouds, flowers, faces, bodies, clothes, homes, cars. Then the person should be asked to reflect that any action directly against the value of beauty undermines the positive actions which the person takes to realize beauty in her life. People who are emotionally or mentally disturbed may continue to reject one or more of the essential human goals, but undertaking these reflections should convince most people of sound mind.

Nonetheless, it is possible that some well-balanced, intelligent, and articulate people may reject one or more of the fundamental values. According to the natural law approach, these people are making a mistake because they are not interpreting their experience correctly.[6] The natural law approach establishes an identity between the rational person and the person who pursues the basic goods.

Once one accepts the normative quality of the fundamental values, a person sees the connection between the quest for the basic goods and the ultimate questions in life. Not only are the fundamental values important, but the meaning and significance of one's life is measured by the extent to which one realizes the values in life. A person does not have to realize all the values in the same measure, although practical reasonableness requires that all essential goods receive some attention in each person's life. Artists concentrate on beauty; business people on friendships (family), knowledge, and play; teachers on knowledge; politicians on friendship (their constituencies and their families), etc. Once the essential human goals are acknowledged, the worth of people's lives is not measured by the financial wealth or social status they attain, since these are, at best, secondary values. The more fully a person participates in the fundamental values, the more fully human a person is.

Although a commitment to the basic values conflicts with the neoclassical formulation of consumer behavior, commitment to the fundamental values does not mean that we have to abandon the entire neoclassical paradigm. After all, economists do not think that the assumptions in their economic models are exact descriptions of the way people behave. The economic models of consumer behavior *assume* that people are only interested in their own satisfaction and not in the welfare of others, an assumption made not because economists think it is literally true, but because they can prove that it leads to useful results. Our portrayal of the fundamental values approach suggests that the neoclassical version of consumer behavior is at best a rough approximation of responsible behavior by consumers. On the other hand, even in a world in which people are committed to the pursuit of the fundamental values, the assumption of self-interest is in some instances a reasonable approximation for consumers as well as producers. One task of this study is to define more precisely the circumstances in which one can plausibly assume that economic agents act in a self-seeking manner.

Human nature involves interacting with other people—for fun, life, friendship, and beauty, not merely for profit. One of the constituent components of human nature is an orientation toward other people, and the responsibility of one person to another is best realized if one puts oneself in a position of need. Suppose, through no fault of your own, you are starving to death and a perfect stranger walks by. He happens to be carrying a basket of apples. He is healthy, as are all the other people he knows, and he is taking the apples home, where he and his family intend to consume them during the next month. He realizes that you are starving and he also knows that, unless you receive some food immediately, you will die. According to the natural law approach, the person with the apples has an absolute responsibility to help you. For the man with the apples not to help you would be an act directly contrary to the fundamental value of life. No other value beckons participation as strongly at this point as the value of life. If he does not give you some apples, you die; if he does, you live. Society would praise the person who gives you the apples to eat because he acted out of charity, out of the goodness of his heart. Indeed, society should praise the man, but he should be praised not because he acted out of charity, i.e., he did something which he did not have to do, but because he did something which he was morally constrained to do.

Should this individual give you an apple, the two of you would be friends for life. Should he fail to give you the apple, you would rightly consider him among the meanest of men. With only the slightest inconvenience to himself, he could have assisted you, could have sustained you in life, but refused to do so. Anyone would judge that person to have performed a despicable act had he declined to give you the apple.

One can construct similar examples involving other fundamental values. Suppose, for example, that you had just finished painting a landscape. A person whom you do not know comes along and tells you how much he admires the painting. He offers to purchase it for a reasonable price, perhaps even a generous price, and you sell it to him. He then, in your presence, destroys the painting, not because he did not admire it, but just on a whim. Failing other exculpatory information, you or anyone else would judge him to have acted in a low and mean fashion, because he acted directly contrary to the fundamental value of beauty, even though he did not act illegally, since he owned the painting.

The fact that any human being would make these judgments is the justification for calling life, beauty, or any one of the other essential values a fundamental value and for referring to the system of fundamental values as the "natural law." It is not important to understand completely why a person makes this judgment or what the mental or psychological process is by which the person leaps over boundaries of ethnic groups, religion, and culture. The significant point is that you make such judgments and any human being you consider to be of sound and balanced mind does the same.

Some might object that these judgments are not culturally transcendent since an Oriental or an Egyptian from the year 2000 B.C. not only had a different world view but also a distinct set of values and principles. Many modern thinkers contend that one should not acknowledge the dominance of the fundamental values until one has undertaken an exhaustive study of all different cultures.

The objection that other cultures may have different values and that therefore a comprehensive investigation of the values of other cultures would be necessary before one has a firm foundation for adopting the fundamental values approach dovetails neatly with the empirical orientation of Western civilization. Certainly, anthropological investigations and psychological studies are useful aids to confirm or qualify a person's introspective insight. However, by focusing on what other people and civilizations do and by assuming that an "objective" evaluation is possible, one misses the point. The conviction of the individual about the centrality of any fundamental value is so strong that, even if another culture were identified in which, for example, life or beauty did not appear to be a fundamental value, the only way in which a person could understand the culture would be to discover some unusual way in which the culture expressed its commitment to life and beauty. The empirical reference for natural law is the individual himself or herself. Because the individual judges in the way she does, and cannot judge otherwise, the fundamental values are essential. One can express this reality in metaphysical terms by saying that the fundamental values are a priori norms for human action which become known to the individual in an explicit way when a person, by the act of reflection performed in community, participates in the value of practical reasonableness. In the act of seeking justification for the actions a person performs, human reason participates in the fundamental value of practical reasonableness and also acknowledges the basic orientation of a human being to strive for the basic goods. When a person imagines herself to be starving and meets a person with apples, i.e., food for survival, she cannot justify any other possible judgment, in any culture, than "the person with the apples ought to help me." This judgment defines in a partial way what it means to be practically reasonable.

By appealing to the individual experience which every human being in every culture has of the fundamental values, one can get the erroneous impression that every individual seeks to realize these values primarily on his or her own. Undoubtedly, there is an important sense in which each individual is responsible for his or her own life. Past factors—toilet training, teachers, significant experiences in grade school, the particular high school attended, an aggressive mother—all these people and factors may have influenced the particular values toward which one is currently oriented. But once a person reaches maturity, all the other people and events which had an influence in one's life should not and cannot reasonably be blamed for the way in which a person orders his or her life. A person is individually responsible for the way in which he organizes his life.

Individual responsibility, however, does not imply that one pursues values in solitary confinement. Teenagers may feel comfortable in a solitary world, listening to the stereo in their room or walking along, attuned only to their Walkmans, but they realize that such activities are part of a larger constellation that includes friends, family, and team members. All people pursue their values in communities, with a range of sizes and levels of complexity, and of all shades and hues. Life is inconceivable without the support, challenges, and interactions of community. Most people belong to several different communities: family; neighborhood; parish, synagogue, or church; business; town, city, or state; nation; schools; local bars or health clubs; sports teams or social clubs; civic organizations; professional organizations; travel or vacation groups; and one can add many others. Some of the bondings in these communities are admittedly weak. For example, if one takes an airplane flight, one might hesitate to call the group a community, whereas if one takes a month's vacation in Europe with a group of fifty people, that is a community in which people get to know one another well.

Whether weak or strong, exhilarating or oppressive, lasting or transient, community is the primary structure in which people seek the fundamental values and exercise their individual responsibility. Indeed, the attempt to distance oneself too completely from the demands of community arouses legitimate concern. If a person is a "loner" who eschews the companionship of others, if one seeks solitude not as precious time to reflect on past activities with others but as brooding time to pore over the past or fret about the future, if a person is not connected to enough communities, at least in informal ways, there is a justified anxiety that such a person is not, or will not be, able to handle the normal pressures of life. Communities create pressures, but they also relieve pressures or make them less onerous.

Participating in a fundamental value makes a person more deeply human, while acting against a basic good diminishes one's stature as a person. Since the general thrust of a human being is to grow and become more human, one chooses the fundamental values to become more fully human. When a person affirms her own existence, in the same act she also affirms the validity of the fundamental values and in this sense they are "true" values; they are not optional.[7] Someone may rationally choose punctuality as a value, while another person rationally rejects it as having no significance for her. But one cannot simultaneously affirm one's humanity and reject the fundamental values as essential goals, although, in moments of weakness, one can commit actions which are contrary to the fundamental values. Fundamental values constitute one of the essential truths about human beings.

Before generalizing the principles of personal justice derived in the previous chapter to make them applicable to an entire economy, it is important to be clear about the process, and so I review the progress to this point and illustrate it in Figure 4.1. A person's individual experience of the pursuit of the fundamental values is the starting point. When a person first begins to wonder about why one action ought to be chosen rather than another, this very act of seeking understanding is a participation in the fundamental value of practical reasonableness. Participation in this value eventually grants a person the insight that there are seven, more or less, fundamental values which all people seek to realize in their lives. The second stage is the realization that people in society have diverse ways to pursue the fundamental values, ways that are, in fact, so different that guidelines are necessary to ensure that each person has a fair chance to pursue the basic goods. The goal of this stage of reflection is to discover principles of justice that help people to flourish as individuals within communities of their

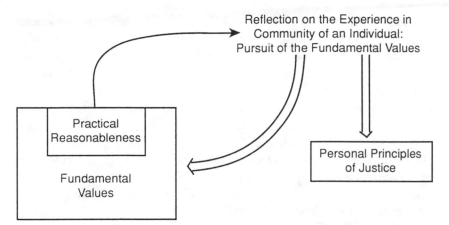

Figure 4–1. By trying to be reasonable, a person reflects on her actions and participates in the value of practical reasonableness. Participation in practical reasonableness generates the principles of justice.

making. We have already begun that process by deriving the principles of personal justice.

Since the starting point is reflection on the fundamental values, which are very broadly conceived, it is possible that in deriving principles of justice, too much emphasis is put on one fundamental value or one aspect of human experience. Therefore, every principle of justice must be tested by application to reality. If the application dictates a course of action which seems "unreasonable," as determined by one's experience in the community, one must study the way in which the essential values are pursued in communities and determine which important factor has been overlooked.

4.4 HIERARCHY WITHIN EACH FUNDAMENTAL VALUE

Although it is impossible to impose a lexicographic ordering on the fundamental values, within each category of a single basic value one can establish a hierarchy among the various ways to realize that value. Indeed, much of formal education can be construed as exploring hierarchies for each of the fundamental values. In order to act morally, a person or institution must establish some hierarchy, explicit or implicit, for each of the fundamental values.

Establishing a hierarchy for beauty is notoriously difficult and constitutes the somewhat neglected field of aesthetics. Even if beauty is partially in the eye of the beholder, the beholder must work with some implicit structuring of beauty in order to make daily decisions involving this value, i.e., whether to go to the museum, the hairdresser, the clothes boutique, the interior decorator's, the concert, the opera, the mountains. One's personal aesthetic hierarchy determines which of these activities yields a greater participation, at a given point in time, in the fundamental value of beauty.

If structuring a personal hierarchy for beauty is difficult, the choice of beautiful projects that a larger institution, such as a city, state, or nation, should support seems impossible. In fact, however, formal criteria do exist, and other social criteria can be introduced to guide the governmental unit in its selection.[8]

The practical necessity to distinguish higher and lower forms for the individual's fundamental values can best be seen by analyzing the value of life. The noncontrary principle states that no person should act directly contrary to life, which includes all life—human and nonhuman, animal and vegetable. For nourishment, every person eats vegetables and fruits; most people also eat meat and fish. Life must be taken away in order for people to be able to eat. Are these actions contrary to the principle that one not act directly contrary to the fundamental value of life? Or, suppose one kills a bothersome mosquito on a muggy summer night. Has this person acted against the fundamental value of life? Although the person who kills the plant to eat it and the person who kills the mosquito to feel more comfortable act against the value of life, presumably the motive for these actions is to enhance the life of the person. The action, therefore, simultaneously destroys life and supports it; it is not directly contrary to the fundamental value of life if the negative action against life at one level of life serves to promote life at a higher level. One must determine whether the action serves some higher form of life and thereby enables a deeper participation in the fundamental value of life.

Most ethical systems place human beings on a higher scale than animal life, which in turn is situated higher than plant life. Within such a hierarchy, a person can act directly against plants and animals when the action enables a greater participation in human life, which is a higher form. Since a comparison is being made of actions that lead to different realizations of the same fundamental value, one cannot object that one is comparing apples and oranges or, in this case, animals and vegetables, which are different entities and incomparable. The entities themselves are different; the judgment being made, however, is to what extent they participate in the fundamental value of life. Life is the common denominator that allows a hierarchy to be determined.

With respect to beauty, life, and the other fundamental values, disagreement about the true hierarchy will arise among people, religions, and ethical systems. Some people and religions are not convinced that meat is necessary to sustain human life and are therefore opposed to killing animals for food. Some religious adherents, such as the Jains in India, are very sensitive to the value of animal life and even prohibit the killing of insects. By appealing to a system of fundamental values I do not imply that all ethical questions can easily be resolved. The determination of the principles that establish a hierarchy within each fundamental value is a complex undertaking which, happily, is outside the scope of this work. Nonetheless, the examples I use will often rely upon some implicit hierarchy of fundamental values, which, I hope, is shared by the reader. Finally, any hierarchy within one fundamental value involves an assumption or assertion about the nature of human beings and about how the world is ordered. Generating even a limited hierarchy requires some philosophy of nature, as Hittinger notes (1987, pp. 65–92), about which considerable differences exist.

4.5 VALUES IN A PLURALIST SOCIETY

When a person states that she has a different value system from another person, she intends, in terms of the discussion in the previous section, to affirm one or more of the following six statements:

1. With reference to a particular class of actions which leads to participation in a fundamental value, I put more emphasis on certain particular actions than some other people do. Example: A particular woman has decided to use clothes more than cosmetics to participate in personal beauty. She expresses this commitment by saying that clothes are a value for her.
2. Within the category of one basic good, I put more emphasis on one or more forms of the good than another. Example: The artist seeks to create art (beauty formed by men and women) and is not concerned about his personal appearance (personal beauty).

3. I emphasize the pursuit of one or more fundamental values more than others. Example: The artist devotes more resources to the pursuit of beauty than to the pursuit of friendship.

4. I have different principles for structuring the hierarchy within any fundamental value. Example: One person may assert that personal beauty is always more important than beauty created by men and women.

5. I have different principles to coordinate the pursuit of the fundamental values. Example: A person states that no moral wrong is committed when a person acts directly against a fundamental value.

6. I reject one or more of the fundamental values as important goals in my life. Example: A person states that playfulness is equivalent to frivolity and certainly is not a value for him.

Only meanings 5 and 6 are inconsistent with the fundamental values approach, while meanings 1 to 4 are valid ways in which people in any society differ in their pursuit of the fundamental values.[9]

Because of the wide variety of disagreement possible within the framework of the fundamental values, a pluralist society committed to the fundamental values is not a theoretical contradiction, nor need it lead to inconsistencies in practice. There is ample room for disagreement among values even if everyone, or a large majority, enjoys consensus about the general pursuit of the fundamental values. Because values can be attained in a variety of ways and because knowledge, technology, and institutions in society constantly undergo change, every age offers new ways to realize the fundamental values, and certain "leader groups" demonstrate by example how to realize them. Artists, musicians, dancers, architects, and sculptors teach us important things about beauty. What one group of people thinks is beautiful another group may think is pornographic. What a hunting club considers playfulness another group may consider directly contrary to the value of life. In earlier societies it was considered natural and fair that for some particular job a married man be paid more than an unmarried man, who in turn would be paid more than a woman, but the same practice would be considered unfair by most people in society today. Opposition and tensions exist in every society, and there is no reason to believe that tensions should be greater in a society committed to the fundamental values. Even if they were greater, it may be that a commitment to the fundamental values offers a more realistic way to resolve the tensions.

A pluralist society with a commitment to the fundamental values does not merely tolerate differences among individuals; it cultivates the differences as a means to ferret out the truth and to discover better ways to participate in the fundamental values. Although the fundamental values approach allows great diversity of opinion, it is not consistent with all points of view. In particular, it clashes with the neoclassical view, which is essentially the modern liberal view so severely criticized by MacIntyre (1984) and Bloom (1987), according to which all opinions have equal value without any of them reaching "truth."

Although the liberal view is rejected by a society committed to the fundamental values, a natural law society still tolerates an enormous range of views. In fact, creating a society, as opposed to bringing together an indiscriminate group of individuals, always involves the selection of norms according to which all are expected to act. The norms of the modern pluralist and liberal society are essentially procedural norms, that is, norms which dictate how disagreements are to be resolved.[10] The natural law tradition claims that a society based on mere procedure neglects that which gives the human person his or her inherent dignity and that which provides the foundation for society, namely, a commitment to the fundamental values.

In *A Theory of Justice*, John Rawls argues that a theory of justice appropriate for a liberal democracy requires a "thin" theory of the good, i.e., one that does not specify the content of the good prior to establishing the norms for justice. It may appear as if I have proposed a "fat" theory of the good, inasmuch as I have enumerated seven values which I assert are fundamental and ought to be fundamental for all people. I would prefer to say that I have proposed a "slim" theory of the good. The reason is that, although I have indicated the general content of each fundamental value, I have not suggested a hierarchy. That is intentional. My position is that what makes a society radically pluralistic is the lack of agreement about the hierarchies within a fundamental value, as well as lack of agreement about a philosophy of nature and of the human being, which makes such a hierarchy possible. Even in a pluralistic society, however, people can agree that the seven basic goods are fundamental in the sense provided by the four personal principles of justice.

4.6 ORDINARY ECONOMIC DECISIONS AND THE FUNDAMENTAL VALUES

If ethics and neoclassical economics are to be joined in a fruitful union, it should be the case that the ordinary economic decisions made by agents can be analyzed in neoclassical fashion after incorporating a commitment to the fundamental values. For example, under general conditions consumer demand for a good should decrease if the price of the good rises and increase if the price of a substitute good rises. One should be able to determine whether a project is worth undertaking by calculating whether the benefits exceed the costs. Such predictions and calculations, however, appear at first glance to be precluded by the structure of the fundamental values. Because each of the fundamental values has an absolute quality to it, I have emphasized that an action contrary to one essential human value cannot be justified by calculating the good achieved by participation in another fundamental value.

As we shall see in the following chapters, a commitment to the fundamental values requires the economist to make an adjustment in the model which she usually adopts; in addition to preferences, consumers have goals, and they avoid, at all costs, actions directly contrary to a fundamental value. Despite such changes, the rule that the quantity of a good, such as clothing, increases when the price of a substitute, such as entertainment, increases is still valid. In other words, each consumer makes a decision concerning the relative importance of a good in pursuing a particular fundamental value. Similarly, one can calculate costs and benefits to determine which projects ought to be undertaken.

Such calculations are possible because every consumer imposes some positive hierarchy of the fundamental values, which determines how he responds to a price change. The hierarchy may be explicit, but most often is only implicit and is revealed through the behavior of the individual. The personal hierarchy, which is important for consumers and producers alike, is a preference ordering of the fundamental values, not an ontological hierarchy, which is impossible because each value deserves equal respect.

Setting a life plan means selecting certain fundamental values to receive greater emphasis than others. The doctor emphasizes life and knowledge, the juggler chooses playfulness to be his special human goal, and the musician stresses beauty. In a certain sense, determining a life plan is arbitrary, since a person usually has alternatives. A person may realize that she has great musical talent and foresee that if she chooses to emphasize music in her life she can become a famous musician. However, the basic call of human life is not to be famous or wealthy. The musically gifted person could just as easily choose to be a teacher because she thinks that teachers are needed in society or that she would make a good teacher. Even if a person selects a life plan that puts heavy emphasis on one of the fundamental values, the other values also make demands on the person. As an artist, one has an obligation to tell the truth, to respect life, and, if one is married, to spend sufficient time with one's family. Due to the complexity of life, everyone is called upon to implement all the fundamental values in a variety of ways.

Consider two economic examples, and recall that a person is free to pick one essential human goal for special emphasis, but she is not allowed to act directly contrary to a fundamental human value, except when the reaction principle applies.

Suppose a person has saved money and is inclined to use it in one of two ways: Either he builds a large house for his family or he continues to rent an apartment and puts the money in a mutual fund, from which he draws a specified amount each year to pay for elegant vacations for himself and his family. Both alternatives involve a commitment to his family and the value of friendship. Going on a lavish or extended vacation suggests a greater emphasis on playfulness. In the fundamental values approach, he is free to pursue either alternative. Suppose, in fact, he decides to have a house built. In bringing the construction to completion, he is not permitted to act directly contrary to any fundamental value. He cannot lie or cheat in order to pay a lower price for the house. He cannot jeopardize his marriage by working such long hours to finance the house that he has practically no time to spend with his wife and children. If he has to ruin some natural beauty in order to make a clearing for the house, he should be convinced that the house that he builds is at a higher level of beauty than that which he destroys; otherwise, he must choose another site. He should not needlessly tear down trees, which combine both beauty and life. On the other hand, if it is necessary to fell some trees to make room for the house, he can justify the action by saying that he needs shelter and that human life is on a higher level than vegetative life.

The second example examines a decision by the federal government to allocate resources. Each year the U.S. government, i.e., Congress and the president, has to set a budget. For simplicity, suppose the government has a fixed amount of money that can be spent in one of three ways: for basic research, for public transportation, or for the homeless. How much to spend on the first two areas depends on the priorities or preferences of the government. Like an individual consumer, the government can set priorities among the fundamental values. Basic research involves a commitment to knowledge while public transportation is an efficient means of helping a large number of people get to and from work and other activities each day. It enables people to contribute to the common good and also to interact better as a community. With respect to both basic research and public transportation, legislators must answer two questions: how important are these activities in themselves and how much money, if any, should the federal government be providing for these activities? It may be that legislators are hesitant to decide these issues and that they commission, instead, some economists to conduct a cost-benefit analysis. In carrying out an analysis of the benefits, the economists estimate the economic benefits. However, they should also place a value on knowledge in itself and on the contribution that transportation makes to community living. In both cases, they examine the behavior of people in the private sector to calculate how much they value basic research and public transportation. In effect, they take the decisions of many individuals, mediated by the free market in the private sector, and use this information as a guide in calculating benefits from public sector support. For a variety of reasons, the private market may not be a reliable guide for governmental priorities, but it usually offers a helpful benchmark. Despite the numerous problems encountered in cost-benefit analysis, in many economic situations it can be used fruitfully without paying explicit attention to the fundamental values.

The third area that requires a decision from the government is the amount of money which should be provided for the homeless. In this instance, a cost-benefit analysis which took views as expressed in the private sector as normative guidelines would not be appropriate. There are a number of reasons why the United States has so many homeless people, and it is important to know the reasons in order to be able to provide effective help for them. For the sake of our illustration, however, it is sufficient to know that people are homeless and that if they remain homeless their health will be impaired. Since health is related to the fundamental value of life, the existence of homeless people is related to the reaction principle. According to this principle, when a fundamental value is threatened, resources should be allocated to ward off the threat in proportion to the evil threatened. In a society committed to the fundamental values, society should commit sufficient resources to the care of the homeless so that their short-term and long-term health is not impaired. Because there are many ways to achieve this goal involving both public and private sector participation, prudential judgment must be used in deciding which approach is the best and how much funding should be allocated. Nonetheless, each legislator is bound by conscience to vote for a plan, backed with sufficient funding, that protects the homeless from short-term and long-term harm. Because a fundamental value is being threatened when the homeless exist, funding a program to care for the homeless takes precedence over funds for basic research and public transportation.[11]

The preceding examples show that incorporating fundamental values into the economic framework preserves ordinary economic analysis in many instances, but not all. Whenever an individual is tempted to act contrary to a fundamental value or when some other person or force of nature or society threatens a fundamental value, the usual calculation of personal or social costs and benefits is appropriate only to the extent that they are used to calculate the resources needed to keep the threatened evil at bay.

Empirically, it is interesting to know whether most people are committed to the fundamental values. This should be revealed in their economic behavior. A reasonable test of this commitment would be to determine whether behavior in circumstances in which fundamental values are threatened is statistically different from behavior in circumstances where there is no apparent threat.

4.7 FUNDAMENTAL VALUES BY TRADITION OR ASSUMPTION

The previous sections of this chapter and Chapter 3, taken as a whole, constitute a justification for a particular ethical system, i.e., the system of fundamental values or, using more traditional language, the system of natural law. Justifying an ethical system requires more detailed treatment than can be afforded in a work such as this, the primary focus of which is the relationship between ethics and economics. It may be that the reader has serious reservations about the suitability of the fundamental values approach to the modern economy. Granted sufficient time and space, I think I could explore those reservations and make the fundamental values approach more plausible to the skeptical reader.[12]

Rather than respond further to the many objections that can be raised, however, I adopt a popular stratagem of economists, that is, I resolve difficulties by assumption. If at this point the reader is wary and unconvinced, he or she is asked simply to *assume* either that the fundamental values approach is true or that it can be validated and justified. But, is it not important to verify whether the assumption is true? What are the individual assumptions that we make about what ought or ought not to be done by human beings? They are the following:

1. There are seven fundamental values: life, friendship (including justice), knowledge (private and public), beauty, playfulness, practical reasonableness, and religion. All other human values can be expressed in terms of these values.

2. Every human being has an ethical obligation to realize the fundamental values by undertaking actions which enable the person to participate in the fundamental values.

3. For each fundamental value a hierarchy can be established that suggests which actions lead to a deeper and more intense participation in the fundamental value. In other words, human existence is ordered and the human mind, through practical reasonableness, is capable of discovering this order.

4. One ought not freely to undertake an action directly contrary to a fundamental value, although actions against lower instances of the value are permitted in order to realize higher instances of the same value, and directly contrary actions are permitted in order to ward off a greater evil as measured within a single fundamental value.

I contend that the above assumptions are an accurate reflection of the ethical constraints which people experience in their lives, although they may use different words and concepts to express those constraints. The reader may judge that these assumptions correspond less to reality than I judge them to. Such a reader is asked to accept that the assumptions represent a reasonable, if less than perfect, approximation to reality. Even if the assumptions are wrong in some minor ways, they appear to capture significant aspects of the moral thinking not only of the United States but of many other countries as well.[13]

Another justification, perhaps more appealing to philosophers than to economists, is to state that the fundamental values approach stands solidly within a prominent tradition, that of natural law. In *Three Rival Versions of Moral Enquiry: Encyclopaedia, Genealogy, and Tradition* and earlier in *Whose Justice? Which Rationality?*, MacIntyre stresses the importance of exercising critical reflection within a tradition and examines at length three important philosophical traditions, which I noted at the beginning of Chapter 3. The encyclopedic tradition is empirical, scientific, and objective; it asserts that multiple motives, goals, and purposes are not needed to explain human behavior. Utilitarianism, which explains all human behavior by the single, simple motive of happiness or satisfaction, is located comfortably within the encyclopedic tradition. Nietzsche epitomizes a second tradition, a radically subjective one that sees power, desire, or arbitrary will as the basis of human activity. The third tradition is natural law, which asserts that human reason discovers, through reflection on life in community, goals that are common to all people and that determine morally acceptable behavior.[14] Although many more traditions exist in both Western and Eastern cultures, MacIntyre notes that the three he examines have had the greatest impact on Western society.

MacIntyre (1988, chs. 17–20) identifies the components of any philosophical, moral tradition and shows that any person can exercise critical reason only within such a tradition, which includes not merely a system of concepts related to one another but also a pattern of living which, when combined with coherent explanations, generates intelligibility.[15] A tradition can never be completely separated from the community that sustains the tradition, although people within a tradition have an ability to criticize it and respond to challenges emanating from other traditions.

MacIntyre argues that at this point in time, and perhaps for centuries to come, it is impossible to designate one of the traditions listed above as the "true tradition." Because the "true tradition" cannot be identified at this point and because liberalism is not concerned with ultimate truth, liberalism tries to embrace all traditions, but insists on doing so on its own terms. Liberalism thinks that it provides a rational foundation for utilitarianism, and it respects the right of each person to choose his or her own tradition because such a choice is, according to liberals, fundamental. By being so encompassing, it seems to occupy a superior position of rationality, and, as far as one can judge superficially, appears to be the tradition within which modern intellectuals most frequently operate. In fact, however, liberalism is as confined and arbitrary, at least as currently formulated and practiced, as any of the other traditions. The reason is that liberalism believes that it can comprehend any statement made by a tradition, without living or having lived in that tradition. However, liberalism's belief is just that: a belief, an assertion, an act of faith, for which there can be no convincing evidence. In MacIntyre's view, complete traditions are neither perspectival (which means that truth depends on one's perspective) nor relativist (which means that, in principle, one cannot decide which tradition is correct). Traditions prove themselves by being able to understand new challenges and problems, which are generated intermittently by new worldviews, such as the different paradigm arising out of the Copernican system. As critical reflection continues within communities of thinkers, one tradition may prove itself to be the true tradition because it gives more satisfactory answers to questions raised in different traditions.

Liberalism, according to Macintyre, does not possess all the features of a true tradition. It is committed to perspectivism, since it has rejected all but the barest, minimal notion of truth (MacIntyre [1988] p. 368). Therefore, liberalism is only a partial tradition, since it does not claim to discover truth. At best it offers procedures, which it claims are rational, without, however, relating the procedures to some ultimate goal. Happiness or utility may indeed be the goal of many people, but liberalism chooses not to ask whether it is a legitimate goal or what is the best way to reach this goal. Rather, it accepts the plans of individuals in society as given and simply tries to reconcile them. In other words, it offers procedures that partially satisfy canons of rationality.

The analysis in this book is an attempt to advance the natural law tradition. Because Americans use value language to express their moral commitments and because language, as MacIntyre (1988) notes in chapter 19, is an important component in any tradition, I have chosen to develop a moral system advanced by Finnis (1980), which recasts the natural law tradition in terms of fundamental values. It is my hope that the principles of personal justice as well as the applications of these principles in subsequent chapters to the economic realm represent a development and appealing interpretation of the natural law tradition.

To the person committed to liberalism and skeptical of the natural law tradition, I defend my approach by an assumption: Let the skeptic simply assume that everyone in society is committed to the fundamental values. To a person living in and committed to the natural law tradition, my defense is that the fundamental values are an accurate or at least reasonable statement of the ethical tenets of the natural law approach. To those persons living in and committed to the other two traditions listed above, I defend myself by my results. My claim is that, by use of the structure of fundamental values and by assuming that people in society are, by and large, committed to the pursuit of the these values, I can better explain the way in which people undertake economic activities and the way in which they conduct their economic affairs than can someone in another tradition. Note that a better explanation is one that more aptly reconciles the actions of people with their experience and with the language they use to describe their experience.[16]

As useful as MacIntyre's comments on traditions are, it is important to register one way in which the fundamental values approach is more than the type of philosophical tradition he describes. The natural law tradition claims that every person, no matter what the society or tradition in which he or she is raised, can and ought to acknowledge the binding power of the fundamental values and of the principles of justice that flow from the acknowledgment of these values.

The demands made by the basic goods transcend particularities of time and place, even though every offer to participate in these goods is a call to perform a particular action. The transcendent appeal and accessibility of the fundamental values are similar to an imaginary public garden, located in an ideal climate where flowers bloom all year round. Suppose that visitors from different countries, ages, and ways of life visit the garden throughout the year. Any person of any tradition can appreciate the beauty of the flowers, although the flowers will mean more to people who are familiar with the important flowers of their own tradition. Furthermore, even if people who lived five hundred years ago were brought into the garden, they also could appreciate the beauty of the flowers—flowers which may have different hues and shapes than the ones to which they were accustomed five hundred years ago. The fundamental values are similar to this perennial garden, visited and admired by people of all traditions and ages. Just as one appreciates flowers by walking in a garden, by looking, smelling, and perhaps even touching them, so one learns to appreciate the fundamental values by undertaking specific actions in one's life to realize them.

CHAPTER 5

Principles of Justice I: Efficiency, Subsidiarity, and Freedom

People do not usually think of fundamental values when they are asked about ethical matters. Instead, they cite rules, commandments, mottoes, or principles. I have begun this process by formulating the four rules of personal justice. My intent in this chapter is to reformulate the principles of personal justice proposed in Chapter 3 so that they can be applied to the various institutions that comprise an economic system.

Since goods are created and exchanged in society, society must agree upon the normal pattern of possession and use in order to determine what is acceptable and unacceptable. Therefore, in order to justify rules describing allowable use of goods, one must combine the following ingredients:

1. the fundamental values, with particular emphasis on the value of practical reasonableness, i.e., common sense, which among other things coordinates a person's pursuit of the fundamental values as well as society's pursuit of the fundamental values;
2. general knowledge of how institutions of exchange and ownership function;
3. the connectedness of individuals.

Although in this chapter I derive from the personal principles of justice several social principles of justice that should guide the economic structure of society, these are not the only possible principles that can be supported by the fundamental values, since business ethics, medical ethics, legal ethics, and other types of ethics also derive principles based on the fundamental values that are applicable in their own fields. Rather, they are the ones that a priori appear to be useful in determining whether the structures and policies concerning production and exchange in an economy are just.

At the outset, I restrict the range of issues under consideration to the domestic economy. That is, I assume that we are dealing with a well-defined society which, for the most part, is self-sufficient. Although international trade and finance are significant features of modern economies, except for incorporating international trade in an occasional example and a brief discussion of nation-states, no formal treatment of trade between nations is undertaken. International justice is a complicated issue and requires separate treatment.

5.1 IMPLICATIONS OF PRACTICAL REASONABLENESS

Any person who reflects on her experience realizes that she cannot pursue the essential values all at once; participation in the fundamental values requires individual actions, each of which takes time to perform. Furthermore, each person realizes that she or he matures and progresses in the ability to participate in the basic goods. Before a ballerina can dance the beautiful dance, she must spend many years learning and practicing the rudiments of rhythm and coordination. Before a scholar can acquire the knowledge conveyed in ancient Greek texts, he must spend many hours learning Greek. Once the foundation is laid, a person is in a position to realize the fundamental values in a deeper, more significant, and, often, more satisfying way. In many instances, each new experience of a fundamental value builds upon or adds to the foundation. Provided the person uses her memory and imagination to integrate past experiences into the present, she can use each new experience to make more profound her sharing in the fundamental values.

A person with common sense forms a plan for realizing the fundamental values, gradually and over time. Because these values are infinite, because one desires to participate as much as possible in the values through different actions, and because only a finite amount of time is allotted to a person in this life, one is under an ethical constraint to be parsimonious in the use of time. One should waste neither time nor resources; actions should be geared to achieve results. Wasted time means that one has less time to realize a fundamental value, less time to become more fully human.

Practical reasonableness requires that a person order her life so as to acquire primary capabilities before attempting more complicated things, and that she formulate contingency plans in case unexpected events occur that impede the acquisition of certain skills. Practical reasonableness, however, does not require that a person draw up a plan that binds one for the remainder of one's life. Rather, people are merely required to formulate a segment of a life plan, which guides the person for a few months or years at a time. As the person gains more experience in realizing the fundamental values and understands better his or her own talents and aspirations, the contours of the plan change. Life plans, in fact, are continually revised as new events modify either the goals one seeks or the means one chooses to arrive at those goals. Despite the plasticity, and sometimes even the obscurity, of any life plan, it is useful for our deliberations to be able to refer to it as a completed whole, and I subsequently assume that each person has formulated a comprehensive life plan.

Since the function of principles of social justice is to protect and foster each individual's pursuit of the fundamental values and since there are an infinite number of ways to pursue the basic goods, it is not to be expected that the principles of social justice which are derived from the application of practical reasonableness to society will be precise. In his treatise on ethics, Aristotle warns his readers not to expect too much precision in ethical matters because of the variety of ways to attain the essential values.[1] Despite this caveat, one can derive a number of principles that help either to structure the just society or to remedy injustices.

5.1.1 The Principle of Efficiency

Resources are required in order to realize essential human values. To sustain one's life, one needs food; to remain healthy, one needs a dwelling for protection and medicine to recover from sickness; to acquire knowledge, one needs books; and to create beauty, one needs materials or a musical instrument or a stage. Depending on the type of recreation one prefers, one needs transportation, a ballpark, a tennis court, etc. In addition to physical resources, all realizations of the fundamental values require the expenditure of time.

Not all activities, however, require the use of economic goods and services. For example, one can acquire knowledge by speaking to an intelligent person, since most intelligent people who are not lawyers or consultants do not charge money for conversing with someone. In conversations one spends time, but not resources. One can walk through a forest or climb to the top of a mountain and appreciate the beauty of nature. Despite the expenditure of time and energy, no physical resources are consumed. Although one can list many actions not requiring resources, it is difficult, although not impossible, to think of significant actions that do not require some expenditure of time. For instance, a married man may be presented with a situation in which he may be disloyal to his wife. The situation may be an offer of intimacy from some female acquaintance. The man participates in the fundamental value of friendship by refusing the offer, which may take but a second. Thus, although it is possible to think of actions that lead to participation in essential values but which do not require time or resources, most actions require at least one and, more frequently, both. In a modern economy particularly, most people expend both time and resources to realize fundamental values. People live in homes, eat food, travel to the mountains, become educated at schools, recreate at country clubs and ski resorts, worship in churches and synagogues, perform calculations on computers, and fly to Europe. In what follows, we assume that both time and resources produced in the economy are required for participation in the fundamental values. Therefore, any person who wants to realize the essential human goals in his life, and wants other people to realize them as well, must be interested in the production and use of resources.

The supply of natural resources in the world is limited, and readily available natural resources are even more scarce. The amounts of oil, iron, copper, uranium, coal, oil, etc., are finite, even though the total quantities available in the earth are not known with certainty. As best as can be determined at this point in time, minerals and energy sources will always be needed to produce physical goods. But each generation of people on earth needs physical goods to participate more deeply in the fundamental values. For this reason, efficiency in the use of minerals and energy is mandated by the commitment to the fundamental values.

All goods and services in a society are produced by work, which may be physical labor or labor embodied in a piece of capital equipment. Whether a machine or a person is doing the work, time has been expended by people in order to fashion the goods, or more accurately, to make the goods and services available to be used by people or institutions in society. If the main goal of people is to participate in the fundamental values and if time and personal energy are required to create goods and services, no individual should waste resources in striving for the essential human goals. He should marshal his time carefully and make effective use of the goods and services available to him; he should also be concerned that other people in society do not waste resources, which either he or future generations may wish to use. We formalize this principle of social justice by naming it the principle of efficiency.

The Principle of Efficiency: Natural resources, personal effort, and goods and services should not be wasted without reason.[2]

The justification for adding the qualification "without reason" is that some waste might be necessary in order to enable people to participate more fully in the fundamental values. Even a very efficient distribution system of milk, for example, involves some spoilage. Not every student who spends time and resources to attend a college acquires even a rudimentary education. Perhaps neither the student nor the system is at fault; in a large educational system it may be unavoidable that some students with special needs or backgrounds do not become educated. A municipal bus on a particular late night run may not pick up passengers, and as a consequence, the time, gasoline, and wear of the vehicle is wasted. But running the bus may reassure urban dwellers that they can always get home at night. Efficiency is but one consideration among many; even when inefficiency can be prevented, it may be justified.

Inefficiency can be tolerated in two types of cases. In the first category the efficiency exists and any attempt to remove it introduces another inefficiency. Suppose that although a firm is known by some members of society to produce shoddy, inefficient goods over a period of years, some ill-informed people continue to purchase goods from the firm until they learn from experience that the goods are indeed inferior. If the alternatives are government intervention or a campaign against this firm and other similar firms and if such intervention can be shown to cause even greater inefficiency, the current inefficiency should be tolerated. In the second type of case, the inefficiency can be removed, but other factors justify its tolerance. At a wedding party, for example, an abundance of food and drink may be offered to guests with the intent that some food and drink will be left over and cannot be collected and consumed at another time. The joy of the families in the new wealth created by the joining of bride and groom is expressed in many ways, and the violation of the ethical injunction not to waste goods can be a valid expression of the joy and personal wealth created by this new relationship. A more weighty example is the system of sales taxes and income taxes used in every modern economy. It is known that taxes introduce distortions yielding wasted goods and effort. A talented person may not work as hard to earn an additional $100,000 if she knows that 30 percent of the amount must be paid to the government in taxes. Despite such a disincentive, a just society may make the judgment that such inefficiencies are warranted by the greater good achieved by the redistribution of money from the well-to-do or middle class to the poor. In sum, everyone in society should be disposed to avoid waste; for a good reason, however, waste can be tolerated.

Efficiency is, of course, the primary, and sometimes the only, criterion of performance for neoclassical economists. Economists of most schools merely assume its importance and justify their assumption by appealing to the individual experience and behavior of consumers. In our approach we derive the principle of efficiency from a basic orientation of consumers to fundamental values. Scarcity of resources combined with a commitment to the fundamental values is sufficient to derive efficiency as a principle of justice.

5.1.2 The Principle of Subsidiarity

The mere fact that everyone seeks to realize the basic goods in his or her life does not warrant establishing structures in society. If the individual pursuit of the fundamental values constitutes a human being as human, then the best policy for government and other individuals to follow is to stay out of the way, to grant other individuals as much space as possible, and only to interfere when necessary. Interference, however, is often required, either because one individual's pursuit of fundamental values conflicts with another person's or because people sometimes act directly contrary to the fundamental values. Criterion 1 of the personal principle of the common good indicates that whatever structures are installed ought to enhance the ability of people to pursue the basic human goals. If a person lies, destroys, threatens, or kills in order to gain an economic advantage, some intervention by society is appropriate.

In the pursuit of practical reasonableness, human reason selects various aspects of reality as significant in determining just arrangements in society. It is useful to list together those moral prescriptions, i.e., *shoulds* and *oughts*, as well as those *facts* of human existence that cannot be neglected in the functioning of any society.

Oughts and Facts Common to All Societies:

1. All people *should* pursue the fundamental values.
2. People have different ideas and methods for pursuing the basic values.
3. People pursue the essential human goals both individually and in communities and *ought* to do so.
4. Some communities can be freely formed by individuals and do not interfere in the actions of other people or communities.
5. Some individuals and communities conflict in their interests and activities, and, therefore, some rule is needed to regulate their interaction.
6. Every community *should* foster the pursuit of fundamental values by all individuals within the community.
7. Goods and services are needed in order to pursue the fundamental values.
8. Some communities are essential.
9. In communities that are essential, a common understanding *should* prevail about which people assume responsibilities for other people and projects.

The items listed above are a combination of fact and moral prescription, as evidenced by *should* or *ought*. The individual *shoulds* are related to the most general *should*, namely, that people should pursue the fundamental values. The facts are derived from each person's reflection on the way in which people behave individually and in groups. As is apparent from the use of the word "community," we are assuming that people can belong to several communities simultaneously, although we assume that a person belongs to only one society.

Could the facts given above change? Are they true for all societies or only for some societies, or perhaps only for those societies that we have experienced up until this time? Our claim is that the insight about these oughts and facts proceeds from the drive of human reason to participate in the fundamental values, and this drive is invariant over time. In other words, these facts and oughts are essentially linked to what it means to be a human being.[3] The facts frame the human context in which a man or woman understands his or her responsibility to pursue the basic human goods. They are not independent of the realization of the significance of the fundamental values, because a person has the experience of seeking the fundamental values in a community, which, even if it contains only a few members, has sufficient complexity that the person seeking values experiences tension and conflict between community members in the pursuit of the essential values.

Some economists and philosophers may find this assertion unsettling because it appears too tightly bound to characteristics of traditional societies. Could not societies be different, they ask. If the question is how society ought to be structured or what particular rules a person ought to adhere to, is it legitimate, they object, to assert as facts and oughts things which should be proven and which appear in fact to be historically and culturally conditioned? Such critics prefer to see a statement of some first principles or axioms which are self-evident or true in all conceivable and feasible societies. For example, the assertion that some communities are essential and that, therefore, some common understanding is required to determine how responsibilities are allocated, is a mixture of fact and ought; once "ought" is introduced, many modern critics would claim that the statement is neither true nor false.

Their claims are wrong, although not foolish. In *After Virtue: A Study in Moral Theory*, Alasdair MacIntyre explains how it is that ethical prescriptions became dislodged from the situation in which they were formulated, how all oughts were severed from facts. Due to a series of philosophical developments that occurred prior to and during the period of the Enlightenment, people, and in particular philosophers, lost the image of what the ideal person should be. The ideal person, according to a long tradition beginning with Plato and Aristotle, was never much in question, until the critique generated during the time of the Enlightenment became convincing to thinkers. In the Aristotelian tradition, the ideal person is born in community and comes to maturity by being in community and reacting to the demands and encouragement of community. This fact cannot be separated from the ethical responsibilities the individual incurs within the community.

Let us examine more carefully observations 8 and 9 in the list above, which have important implications for just structures in society. The fact that some communities, such as those that rear children and those that produce goods and services, are essential is based on the universal experience of dependence and need. The complete dependence of a child—who requires some form of a rearing community—is especially obvious and compelling. Even if the community called "family" did not occupy the privileged position it enjoys in societies today, it would still be the case that some community would be necessary to care for an infant from the time she is born until she reaches maturity. In this sense the family community is essential, although it is not required that the parents be assigned responsibility for the child. We argue below on practical, not a priori, grounds that the arrangement involving parents as the primary providers of care and training is the one that *ought* to prevail.

Item 9 acknowledges the fact of conflict between individuals and communities and asserts that at least in some communities, which can be called essential communities, members of the community should know who bears responsibility for providing which particular goods and services. A person can only comprehend his or her position in the community by knowing what his or her responsibilities are in relation to other people.

The fact that people differ in abilities and aspirations and that there are many legitimate ways to pursue the fundamental values require that the individual, to the extent feasible, should be allowed to pursue the basic goods in the manner she chooses. A person is a better judge of her own abilities and aspirations than anyone else. But the facts also suggest that a person cannot be granted complete freedom, since in order to help all people attain the essential human goals some coordination of activities is required. The guiding motif for coordination should be to structure groups so that, to the extent feasible, the individual determines how best to pursue the fundamental values. When the group must make a collective decision and cannot defer to the individual, the group should be as small as possible, since this allows the group to weigh the needs, abilities, and aspirations of members of that group. By keeping the group small, whatever binding decisions it may take constrains as few people as possible. Furthermore, if the group functions efficiently, the group decisions reflect the views of most people in the group.

The result that groups in society should be as small as possible is stated formally as the principle of subsidiarity.

The Principle of Subsidiarity: The coordination and organization of humans and their activities should be designed so that the smallest feasible group regulates its own affairs. "Smallest feasible" is determined both by economic efficiency, i.e., the parsimonious use of materials, effort, time, and information, and by the effect that decisions by one group has on other groups, i.e., the degree of interconnectedness.

Changes in the facts of the situation may modify the way in which the principle of subsidiarity is applied. However, because it rests on basic insights about human nature, the principle of subsidiarity applies to all societies.

The principle of subsidiarity is the primary justification for a liberal democratic system of representation and of voting in modern societies. Although the facts of the situation in previous centuries were not always such that a liberal democratic system was possible, by definition a modern society has an educated populace and efficient means of communication, and an informed electorate is one precondition for justifying a liberal democratic system via the principle of subsidiarity. The political structure is a significant institution that contributes to the structure of justice in society. Although I will not examine the political system (or the legal system) in this volume, it must be analyzed in order to arrive at a decision concerning structural justice in the economy.

5.1.3 The Family

What is the justification for the privileges accorded to the family in all societies? Are these privileges which, perhaps, have outgrown their usefulness in modern societies? Since I do not have the space to give a comprehensive answer to these questions, I offer a brief justification for the position of the family in modern society and provide a few suggestions concerning how the role of family changes as the "facts" of a society change over time.[4]

As we noted earlier, some community is required to care for the young. A large unit, such as the tribe in earlier societies or an agency of state government in modern societies, could conceivably care for the young. One could also think of a private sector solution: a firm of professional nannies who care for the child until a certain age. If one is predisposed to think that the free market system provides an optimal solution for most problems, it is not unreasonable to look favorably upon a firm of nannies or a more sophisticated, private sector solution to the problem of rearing children. Obviously, some people make better mothers and fathers than others. Just as a profession of lawyers evolved in the early part of the twentieth century to meet the needs of corporate America, why not let a group of professional mothers and fathers, properly certified, take care of raising the children in a society? Why is the family the automatically preferred solution?

The family is not automatically preferred. Reasons must be given to support its position of preeminence among institutions that promote and sustain relationships of friendship. Reasons may be practical, but they should also rely upon the principles of justice and the presumed commitment of all people in society to the fundamental values.

As a first justification for the primacy of the family, consider its size. The family is the smallest feasible unit to nurture and educate a child. Because a child is the product of the love of a woman and man, in the practical order one expects that the parents of the child will be most solicitous in caring for and raising the child. Conceiving, carrying, bearing, caring for, and raising a child is a complete process in which one participates in the essential goods of life and friendship. Furthermore, personally caring for a child is a way to pursue a fundamental value not only for the individual but also for society. Provided that society is not "overcrowded," bearing and raising children prolongs society. If the privileges granted to a family were not sufficient to induce a large enough group of people to bear and raise children, society would have to devise other means to foster its own procreation. Community is itself a good, and communities, most fundamentally the human community of all women and men, seek to continue in existence through the generation of new members.

Second, although I claim that the pursuit of essential human goods is an ethical imperative for each individual by virtue of his or her status as a human being, the way in which values are pursued must be learned. One of the privileges and responsibilities of parents is to teach their children the best way to pursue the fundamental values. When children are young, they are prone to imitate what they see done by others, particularly those who care for them. Parents are their role models and children tend to imitate the actions of parents. To the extent that the actions of parents are rational ways of pursuing the fundamental values, the children become practiced in the pursuit of these values long before they can acknowledge the fundamental human goals as essential. Training and educating the child are the solemn responsibilities of the parents in a family. Although they may call upon other people to assist them, such as teachers in a school or coaches in a Little League, the parents retain ultimate responsibility.

In any alternative system of training and education, such as in a comprehensive school responsible for all facets of the child's life, one would have to rely on common methods that apply to a large number of students. Parents, on the other hand, can be as particular as they choose. Parents with many children know that treating their children "equally" by giving them the same amount of attention may be unfair, because children have different dispositions, needs, and talents. No one is in a better position to judge which mixture of affection and discipline is best than parents.[5]

Alternative arrangements which do not entail some small management group being responsible for large numbers of children are theoretically possible. One could conceive of a modern version of the practice in fifth-century Sparta, according to which children were cared for by parents until the age of seven and then sent off to a children's village, where they were educated and trained. Would this be against the pursuit of the fundamental values? It would be, unless one could demonstrate that the family structure is less effective than the children's village in training and educating the child to pursue the essential human goods. The advantage of the family structure, aside from the motivation of the parents to care for the product of their love, is that the parents follow the development of their child from infancy through adolescence and thereafter. They know the disposition, moods, inclinations, faults, strengths, fears, and aspirations of the child. They certainly do not know these things completely, but they know them better than any professional nanny in Sparta or elsewhere could know them for the twenty children in her charge. Because the child is optimally a product of the parent's love, the parents also have an incentive to communicate to their children the highest level of the essential values attainable for the child at the various stages of his growth.

Such ruminations notwithstanding and without undertaking a full analysis of alternatives, the family—in its many and constantly changing forms—at this time in the United States does not seem to have viable competitors. Therefore, because the family encourages the pursuit of the fundamental values and because it is the smallest feasible unit in which people can pursue the basic goods, it deserves not only protection within society but also a privileged ranking. Society should promote its operation and not lightly interfere with its workings. Some parents will, on occasion, not fulfill their responsibilities to their children. In such instances, it may be necessary for some other body to intervene to promote the pursuit of the fundamental goods by the children.

Family itself is not a fundamental value. As times change, the weight given to the family in society grows or diminishes, and the usual contours of interactions within families change. Historically, the word "family" has referred to entities of different size and extent. In some regions of the world today, "family" refers only to mother, father, children, and grandparents while in other areas it embraces aunts, uncles, and cousins of varying degrees. Although the composition of the family unit and the way in which the family interacts with other organizations undergoes intermittent change, this does not imply a change in the fundamental values; only the context in which the values are being realized is modified. For example, if family practices and social formation were to become so impoverished in the United States that young men and women did not receive training about the pursuit of essential human goals from their parents, in the schools they attend, or from the media, then entrusting the training of children to such parents would not conform to the principle of efficiency. Some alternative community would have to be devised. Changes in facts alter the set of opportunities which enable participation in the fundamental values.

In addition to providing a foundation for the institution of the family, the principle of subsidiarity can also be used to justify the existence of guilds, unions, clubs, corporations, civic organizations, governments of all kinds, political parties, and nation-states. Each of these communities has different responsibilities, but, since the web in which these communities interact changes over time, their responsibilities are not immutable, although the goals and activities of such organizations must always remain consistent with the pursuit of the fundamental values.

As in the case of the family, it is conceivable that what was feasible in a former society is no longer feasible. For example, in one hundred years the nation-state may no longer be the smallest feasible group to organize its own activities. The water, air, ground, and airwaves pollution caused by one country may so injure another country's ability to pursue the fundamental values that the nation-state is no longer a viable unit; a considerably larger conglomeration of nation-states may be required instead. Movements to larger affiliations of administrative units is already under way. In Europe the European Common Market, which in future years will likely encompass most of the countries of both Western and Eastern Europe, will assume some of the responsibilities of individual nation-states. As similar groupings of nation-states develop in the rest of the world, the nation-state may become an obsolete form of political organization or one restricted to a few countries that for historical reasons do not join larger communities of nations. Economic and social change can affect feasibility, and observant leaders have the responsibility to introduce changes in accord with the principle of subsidiarity.

5.1.4 Choosing a Life Plan

Because basic values can be realized at various times in a diversity of ways, each person should develop a plan to pursue these values over a lifetime. Becoming more mature implies, among other things, an increase in one's ability to participate in the fundamental values. To become more human with limited time and resources, fundamental reasonableness demands that the maturing person draw up a consistent plan for making progress in realizing the fundamental values more deeply. The tentative schema of one's life we refer to as a life plan because it covers all the stages of a person's life.[6]

As I indicated earlier, a person develops a life plan in fits and starts. Childhood visions of becoming a doctor or a firefighter acquire more realism as one moves through high school and college. Young as well as old frequently revise their plans for their occupation, profession, marriage, and life-style. Despite the chaos and sudden changes endemic to all such life plans, it is useful to think of the plan as consisting of three parts.

> **Activities and Values**: A person places priorities on activities that are most conducive to the realization of those fundamental values of particular interest to him or her.

> **Occupation**: A person selects an occupation and the number of hours worked per month to provide a level of income suitable for attaining the basic human goods. In selecting the occupation, a person considers more than the wage or salary. Since two-thirds of nonsleeping hours will be spent working, a person wants an occupation that is challenging and that fulfills her interests. Selecting a job implies that one must determine how much education and training, i.e., human capital, she plans to acquire.

Selection of Goods and Services: One chooses the most cost-efficient bundle of goods and services, designated as a vector x, for accomplishing activities (denoted by the vector q) which can be realized in a number of ways. Given one's limited income, one chooses that bundle of goods and services which enables the selection of the optimal q to achieve participation at the highest possible level of the fundamental values.

Some of the decisions in a life plan are not made by the person herself but by parents or guardians; in addition, people and institutions in society influence many decisions that a person makes. How much training or human capital is acquired depends in part on how much other human capital others in society have accumulated or plan to accumulate. This is true even if the attitudes and plans of others are not fully reflected in the anticipated benefits of increased training.[7] Practically speaking, a person makes a decision on these matters by moving dialectically, back and forth, among the three components: activities, occupation, and purchases of goods and services. Logically, one would choose the activities first, then the occupation, then the goods and services. Some people, however, follow the reverse order. They observe other people's consumption of goods and services, determine what income is necessary to support that life-style, and then determine which activities they will undertake in pursuit of the fundamental values. As we will see in Chapter 7, neoclassical economics constructs a model that compacts the three decisions into a single utility–maximizing decision that omits any reference to a plurality of fundamental goods.

Practical reasonableness also demands that one does not concentrate on one fundamental value to the exclusion of others, although every person selects certain values to be put at the center of his or her life plan. The scholar focuses on the value of knowledge, the athlete on the value of play, the musician on the value of beauty, but the scholar, athlete, and musician should all have friends, maintain their health, and seek some beauty in their lives. Even without a profession directly related to one of the values, a businessperson, tradesperson, or houseperson puts greater emphasis on some values than others. Such a personal emphasis on some values more than others does not violate the noncontrary principle, which requires that a person always respect all the fundamental values; a person can choose to emphasize certain values in his life and still show respect for all the fundamental values.

A life plan is not a technical blueprint of how one is to spend the next fifty years of one's life, nor is it a list of stages through which one hopes to pass. It is rather a vision, frequently changing and initially very idealistic, partly because the realities of one's own capabilities as well as the constraints of the real world are unknown to the person drawing up the life plan. Even after these realities become clearer to the individual, a good life plan remains idealistic, in the sense that it identifies the desired goals under the best of circumstances. In fact, most people realize that while compromises are sometimes required in life, at other times compromises are concessions motivated by fear, laziness, or a momentary lack of intensity in pursuing a goal one truly desires to achieve. In the process of acquiring greater realism, the planner also anticipates that she may drift away from the ideals she set for herself. The human spirit is aware that compromise is easier than striving high and hard; to combat this common human weakness every life plan should be idealistic.

A final characteristic of every good life plan should be an emphasis on acquiring virtues, that is, habits of acting in a certain way. Because the future is uncertain, one cannot anticipate the various situations in which one will be placed. And yet even when a person is surprised by various situations, she should act ethically. A person with a particular virtue is someone who characteristically responds in ways that promote the pursuit of the basic goods. Life is complex. Both by choice and happenstance, one is put in situations where one requires strength either not to act directly contrary to a fundamental value or to seize the opportunity to pursue a value. Acquiring virtue prepares a person to be strong in situations of temptation and alert to opportunities to pursue fundamental values. Therefore, the desire to attain virtues should be a component of every realistic life plan.

5.1.5 Emphasizing Certain Fundamental Values

Why does a person emphasize one value more than another? There are basically three reasons: personal history, personal abilities, and personal interest.

Personal history means the individual's familiarity with the manner in which an essential value has been realized in someone's life. If individual A's mother is a doctor, individual A may want to dedicate her life to keeping people healthy (life) and to understanding how the body functions (knowledge), because she has a greater appreciation of these values and a greater understanding of what actions to take to participate in the values. One's local community may have a long association with the performing arts. If at a young age one becomes familiar with the performing arts through the local community or through some significant individual in one's life, this can be a powerful incentive to make theater, music, or dance a central part of one's life plan.

One's personal abilities also play an important role in selecting favorite fundamental values. A person with a nimble mind becomes acknowledged as an intelligent person and, aided by the esteem of others, she realizes that she has a comparative advantage in knowledge. Although she is not thereby constrained to become an academic or writer, she may realize that she can make great strides by pursuing the value of knowledge in her life. Economists usually think of personal abilities and comparative advantage in terms of one's productive abilities in the marketplace, and productivity is indeed a viable consideration when selecting basic goods for special emphasis. Time and effort are required to achieve the essential values. A person with more ability in a certain area can achieve more in a limited space of time than a person with more modest ability, and this can be an important factor in selecting a primary value on which to concentrate.

Personal preference is also a legitimate reason for the choice of a primary value or values. Each person is created differently, and every person is endowed not merely with different abilities but also with different interests. One need not be reductionist to explain personal interests by personal history or individual ability; interests can be an independent ingredient in making a decision. For example, practical reasonableness does not prohibit a person with musical ability from becoming a lawyer or a basketball player. A highly intelligent person may enjoy working with children and decide, therefore, to eschew the life of academe and concentrate his efforts on raising children in the best possible way. These are personal preferences, which are acceptable reasons for determining the outlines of one's life plan.

In all the cases presented above, the person chooses. The choice is always an individual one, even though there may be different reasons why the person chooses one way of life over another. In some societies the choice may be severely constrained by tradition because certain jobs are essential, and training for such jobs is best achieved within the family or the community. Despite such constraints, common sense, i.e., the activity of participating in practical reasonableness, reveals that free choice is an important component in pursuing the basic values.

Because there is no hierarchy among the values and because one fundamental value is as important as the other, it is usually the individual who can best gauge how effective he or she will be in pursuing the fundamental human goals.

Two additional aspects of personal preferences affect the selection of an occupation: remuneration and the thrill of the job.

For most people, the wage one expects to earn influences the selection of a job, and there is nothing crass about a person wanting to know the figure on a paycheck she will receive. Wages indirectly make goods and services available to the person, which can then be used in the pursuit of basic values. For some people, the wage they receive for a particular job is a secondary or even negligible consideration. An artist, for example, is often depicted as indifferent to the amount of money she receives for her painting, musical performance, or book. Such indifference is warranted and admirable if the job itself is the activity that enables a person best to realize the essential values. Someone might accept a very low salary in return for the opportunity to fly to Mars or to work with an exciting actor or actress. In such instances, the job itself is thrilling. Some jobs, however, involve what many consider to be extremely unpleasant work: collecting garbage, laying asphalt, working on top of a skyscraper, caring for the terminally ill. If one thinks of "thrill" as a variable with different intensities, unpleasant jobs have either very low thrill or negative thrill, depending on what measure one selects.

From introspection and one's knowledge of how people react to situations, one can assert with confidence that the following factors are significant in the choice of a job: personal history, personal abilities, and personal preference, which includes remuneration and thrill.[8] If all jobs were equally thrilling, an economically efficient society should offer an array of jobs, from low paying to high paying, and it should use some mechanism to assign high wages to those jobs which are the most difficult to fill, i.e., those for which demand relative to supply is highest. If, contrary to fact, society needed the same number of people in each job, the highest-paying job should be the one with the most personal disincentives: high level of ability required and low level of thrill offered. The high wage would induce the person to take a job that she would otherwise decline. In a just society, a high wage is justified because the services of the highly paid person enable society to produce many more goods and services, which can then be used by people in the pursuit of the fundamental values.

5.1.6 Free Choice

Freedom of choice is not an absolute value. In fact, it is not a value which can be desired in itself, without any qualification. When faced with a decision, one wants to be free from irrelevant constraints, but one cannot rationally expect to be free from all constraints; some constraints are relevant because they are the consequences of previous decisions made by the person or by society. For example, faced with the opportunity to move to another state to start a new business, a person does not want the government or some other group to make the decision for him or her. However, the person may not want to transfer to another city because the move would disrupt the education of his children. This is a relevant constraint based on previous choices, and there is no reason why one should wish to be free from that constraint.

Although a person prefers to decide matters for herself, making decisions can be burdensome, and there is no value in making judgments all day long. In fact, because most people are happy not to have to make many decisions, social mechanisms exist whereby very important judgments affecting an individual's welfare are made without consulting the individual. A pilot does not confer with his passengers concerning the proper angle and altitude of his landing approach to the airport, nor does an engineer question future users of a bridge about how sturdy the bridge should be or what type of steel should be used.

Despite constraints, allowing people to choose freely allows people the best pursuit of the fundamental values, ceteris paribus. Adults usually have the most complete knowledge of their personal history and preferences, and often they also have the best knowledge of their abilities. Thus in a society which promotes these factors as determinants of choice, allowing the greatest amount of personal freedom is likely to result in the most effective pursuit of the fundamental values. However, even in a society structured to promote individuals rather than groups, there is nothing admirable about postponing a choice so that one is always free to decide whichever way one wants. "Keeping one's options open" is a slogan, not a value or an ethical principle. If one always tried to keep one's options open, one would never make a serious decision in life.

Even though free choice is not a value in all situations, some freedom and personal autonomy is required to pursue the essential human goals. The precise amount of freedom depends on the society in which one lives. Toward the end of the twentieth century, a young person in

Western society would be appalled if his spouse were chosen for him by his parents, or if his job had to be the same as the one which his father holds. This would be considered an unreasonable constraint on personal freedom. On the Indian subcontinent or in Southeast Asia, on the other hand, a young person might find it very "natural" that his or her parents play a large role in the formation of his or her life plan. In many Asian and African countries, as was the case for centuries in the Western countries, knowledge concerning one's abilities and interests is still deemed to reside more fully in the family and the community than in the individual. In such societies, individual freedom is constrained by the desire to make a good decision and follow the directions of people whom society considers to have greater information and perhaps better judgment as well.

Free choice is an important component of every person's life plan because it provides an important motivation to take the necessary steps to pursue the fundamental goods. But granting preeminence to free choice is not the only possible way to structure a society. History indicates that some societies, using autocratic or communal methods of distribution, have functioned well. That is, such societies, when compared with other societies existing at the same time, appear to have been successful in pursuing the essential human goals. It is at least conceivable that a person will be more motivated to pursue a basic value if the community designates him or her for a particular role since she then has the stamp of approval of the whole community.

The areas of free choice in society continue to change. At one point in the not-too-distant past, a parent automatically chose the college which a son or daughter was to attend. Now, the child plays a more significant role and the freedom of the parent is more constrained. As recently as twenty years ago, if one wanted to move up the corporate ladder, one had to be willing to move family and home to the new city or country where one was assigned. New methods of transportation and communication have made such displacements less frequent. Despite such increases in freedom, a totally free choice is unimaginable because a person is bound by past decisions and because a tension will always exist between the individual and any social group with which he or she is closely bonded.

5.1.7 Required Goods and the Noncontrary Principle

Earlier we listed certain ethical oughts and facts, common to all societies, which established the context in which an individual pursues the essential human goals. In addition to those ethical facts, there are facts about the goods and services necessary to pursue the fundamental values. Just as within the category of a basic value there is a hierarchy of values or goods that can be used to attain higher and higher levels of that value, so an ordering exists among goods. Some goods are more essential for society than others because they make possible the production of other goods and services. We distinguish four types of required goods: energy, raw materials, materials of personal sustenance, and security. Let us consider each in turn.

Goods cannot be produced without some source of energy. For many millennia, human energy was sufficient to provide society with a modest amount of goods. With the invention of fire, humankind found a new way to stay warm, to prepare food, and, eventually, to mold minerals for use as tools and ornamentation. Each discovery of a new energy source enabled humankind to increase its potential for participating in the fundamental values. Without abundant sources of energy the modern world would be inconceivable. Even though, according to the Second Law of Thermodynamics, the amount of energy in the universe is decreasing, the amount of energy contained in the earth and available to people is enormous. One can distinguish between renewable sources of energy and nonrenewable sources. Renewable sources include the sun, rivers, forests, and individual chemicals, such as hydrogen and oxygen, or compounds formed with them. Nonrenewable sources are coal, oil, natural gas, geothermal energy, nuclear power, and others.

The second required good is raw materials, which I define as elements (other than energy sources) used in the production of goods and services. These elements include minerals and other substances that are transformed in the production process. All such elements are derivative from the elements of the periodic table. However, although minerals and other raw materials can be refined and processed by people, they cannot be created out of more primitive elements, either now or in the foreseeable future. Minerals and other substances were formed in the cataclysmic process that led to the formation of the solar system and in particular the earth. Since we do not anticipate that humankind on earth will be able to survive another cataclysmic event of this order, we must reckon with the fact that we have a finite amount of raw materials available to us on earth. Future excursions to other celestial bodies may increase the available supply of raw materials, but any significant use of other planetary minerals is not likely to occur in the next fifty years.

The third required good is materials of personal sustenance, in which category I include food, beverages, health services, clothing, rest, and the home.[9] Food materials refer to agricultural goods as well as animals and animal products. People eat cultivated products such as grains, vegetables, fruits, and nuts, or animal products such as milk, cheese, and eggs, or animals themselves, including fish, fowl, and other types of meat. Although the meat of animals is a traditional form of nourishment, it may be that killing animals for food cannot be ethically justified at this point in the development of the United States. We set that question aside and note merely that people require some food to survive, and that the more nutritious the food, the more likely it is that people will live longer and, consequently, will be better able to participate in the fundamental values. In addition to food, people also need drink and housing. Since the category of materials of sustenance is meant to include those goods essential to maintain people who work, either at home or elsewhere, in a state in which they can pursue the fundamental values, it implicitly includes whichever goods are necessary to keep people healthy.

The fourth required good is security. Although security is not a physical good, it is as essential for human existence as the production of goods and services. Security is necessary because it enables a group of people to pursue the essential values, even when they are threatened by another community. Among the ethical oughts and facts listed in section 5.1.2, the fifth ethical fact was that some communities conflict in their interests and activities; therefore, some rule is needed to regulate their interaction. Indeed, some communities have serious disagreements and resort to violence. Whether the inclination to violence is an instinct in human nature or merely an attitude embedded in most cultures, it is sufficiently prevalent that most, if not all, communities require measures to protect themselves so that the members of the community are not hindered in their pursuit of the fundamental values. Under ordinary circumstances people will only formulate a life plan if the expectation prevails that they can fulfill it. Security enables people to formulate a fuller and more realistic life plan. Furthermore, because security is a public good, it has a certain democratic quality since, at least in a given neighborhood, the fact that one person enjoys security does not diminish the amount of security available to other people in the locality or society.

Security can be achieved in a variety of ways. Force, threats, and mutual agreements are the three most popular methods. Force, the most costly way to purchase security, is most effective in warding off an immediate danger, but also corrosive of long-term security. Threats are cheap, but ineffective unless they are backed up by force or mutual agreements. Mutual agreements are cheap in terms of goods, but costly in terms of time; least effective in the short term, since an agreement can easily be broken, they build secure relationships in the long term.

The means one society or community chooses to implement security has an effect on the welfare of other societies or communities because, in economic terms, security generates an externality. In the international sphere, force, as well as threats of force, are intended to adversely affect the security of a second, threatening nation, but force and threats of force may also either strengthen or weaken the security of a peaceful nation not directly involved in the conflict. Similarly, if a nation were simply to make a unilateral promise that it would not interfere in the affairs of other countries, this would constitute, provided it is credible, a positive externality for other countries. Which type of instrument of security ought to be chosen depends on the effectiveness of the instrument as well as on the externalities generated by the instrument.

There is a fifth good which is required in the production of goods and services but is not included in the list of primary required goods. The fifth good consists of human services, i.e., labor and management. Although this good is as essential as the others, it is not produced; no one makes a decision to produce labor or management. Workers and managers are trained, but this does not mean that one produces them. The only way to get an employee to work is if the worker chooses to work, and similarly for managers.[10] Remote training of workers takes place in the home and in schools, and society has a responsibility to make sure that the activities undertaken on behalf of the young prepare them to participate fully and effectively in adult society.

The common element in the four required goods of energy, raw materials, food (broadly conceived), and security is that they are absolutely essential. Energy and raw materials are required for the production of goods and services while food is needed for good health. Security is an umbrella good that protects all people in their pursuit of the fundamental values. As society advances, additional goods become essential for the pursuit of fundamental values. To the extent that it can reasonably be expected that they are necessary or very helpful in the pursuit of the basic values, they also are required goods. Education, transportation goods and services, communication goods and services—all these are required goods in modern twentieth-century society. Since even these, however, cannot be produced without energy, raw materials, food, and security, we distinguish between two levels of required goods: level 1 required goods (energy, raw materials, food, and security) are necessary to produce level 2 goods. Level 1 required goods are always necessary, i.e., they always indirectly serve the pursuit by individuals of the fundamental values. A level 2 good should also promote the pursuit of the fundamental value or at least contribute indirectly to the pursuit of a fundamental value.

When is the production of level 1 goods or level 2 goods ethically permissible? Goods and activities should be used, but not squandered, in the pursuit of the fundamental values. Therefore, as long as the activities are not directly contrary to the pursuit of the essential values and provided resources are not being wasted, the activities can be justified. This means that the planned production of level 1 and level 2 goods should reasonably be expected to lead to a general increase in the ability of people to pursue the essential human goals. Provided many specific conditions are fulfilled, the prices prevailing in a free market economy reflect the true costs of producing goods and services. Under such a system, energy, raw materials, and food will be generated only if producers expect to cover their costs by selling the goods and services at prices that consumers find acceptable.

The market system does not work, however, for the good I call security. One cannot presume that benefits accruing to society by producing more security exceed costs of production. The reason is that security is a public good, shared by everyone and purchased by no one in particular. Security is provided by the police, the fire department, the courts, and many law enforcement agencies at different levels of community. In a special way, the armed forces and the equipment they use, such as nuclear weapons and conventional weapons, provide security for the entire nation. Aside from the empirical question whether any particular strategy, such as deploying more nuclear missiles, truly produces greater security, the moral question is whether additional security enhances the ability of people to pursue the fundamental values and whether a particular strategy is consonant with the principles of justice. This is an important moral decision to be made by each community.

A requirement of the noncontrary principle is that no action can be justified that includes an act that itself directly violates a basic value at the highest level. In the production of goods and services, no possible good consequences for consumers can provide a basis for a productive activity that violates the highest level of a fundamental value. For example, if a general consensus in the United States existed that Niagara Falls is a natural landmark of overwhelming beauty, it would be ethically wrong for a firm to destroy the landmark, even for the sake of providing energy to producers and consumers at an extremely low price.

In order for the noncontrary principle to be applied to production activities, individuals and society as a whole must establish a hierarchy for each basic good. Individuals are free to determine the hierarchy they consider binding, but one of the responsibilities of society and one of the ways in which it forms itself as a culture is that it generates at least partial agreement concerning the hierarchy of each fundamental value.

5.2 CRITERIA FOR ETHICALLY RESPONSIBLE PRODUCTION

Drawing upon reflections in the previous section and applying the noncontrary principle to the process of production yields the following criteria for ethically responsible production:

> **Criteria for Ethically Responsible Production**: Business firms should produce goods and services which are to be used by consumers in the pursuit of the fundamental values. A particular production process is justifiable if and only if the following criteria are fulfilled:
>
> 1. the contemplated action or activity is reasonably expected to lead to a general increase in the ability of people to pursue the fundamental values;
> 2. the contemplated action or activity achieves the desired increase in resources with least direct offense at each level of each fundamental value;
> 3. the contemplated action or activity produces a net effect, including its effect on consumers, that respects and fosters the pursuit of each fundamental value; expressed negatively, the activity should not be directly contrary to any fundamental value. The exception is an activity, such as production of armaments or any level 1 good, that wards off a threat to a fundamental value; in this instance, the evil caused by the

production activity should be proportional to the gravity of
the threat.

The foundation for criterion 1 is that goods should not be wasted.
If, for example, a power plant is not needed in a particular area
because energy is abundant, it should not be constructed. Criteria 2
and 3 apply to each basic good individually. When an action directly
contrary to a fundamental value is contemplated, no attempt to compare effects on one fundamental value with effects on another is warranted since, as I have said before and will repeat many times in the
future, such comparisons implicitly reject the insight that each basic
value is essential. The exception mentioned in criterion 3 is justified by
the reaction principle.

These criteria are binding on individual producers as well as on
society at large. Although the criteria for ethically responsible production are developed with production activities in mind, they apply more
generally to any situation or act that causes damage to a fundamental
value at some level. For example, one way for society to set parameters
for firms is to designate certain land as unsuitable for commercial
development or for certain types of productive activities. A society
also sets safety standards by determining parameters that delimit production activities. When the guidelines set by society are themselves
not immoral, a firm has a moral responsibility to function within these
guidelines.

Ceteris paribus, in a just free market system, if a firm can make
profits by producing some good, this potential provides an initial justification that criteria 1 and 3 for ethically responsible production are
fulfilled. As long as consumers act in accordance with the dictates of
the fundamental values, they purchase only those goods enabling
them to pursue the essential values more effectively or at a higher
level, and as long as all the costs of production are born by the producer and the benefits of consumption accrue to the consumer, prices
in competitive markets reflect true costs and benefits. When markets
are not competitive, however, or when prices do not fully reflect costs
and benefits, prices are not reliable guides for the production of goods.
In such instances, because the market does not function properly, some
intervention into the market mechanism by the government or some
other institution in society is appropriate.

Criterion 2 addresses the issue of squandering resources. When
the firm does not produce the good as efficiently as it could, it thereby

violates criterion 2. Of course, one of the attractions of the free-market system is that it exerts pressure on the firm to abandon wasteful practices and become more efficient.

In the absence of a free-market system that fulfills the conditions for economic efficiency or in the absence of some other system of evaluating the costs and benefits of certain economic activities, any single producer of a level 1 good cannot determine whether criteria 1 and 3 are fulfilled. This is especially true for energy and raw materials, since an individual producer cannot gauge how these goods will be used in society. For this reason, especially in the case of level 1 goods, society has an ethical responsibility to make sure that these conditions are fulfilled.

Even in a well functioning free-market system, there are many situations in which prices do not reflect true costs and benefits to consumers of producing certain goods or services. For example, because beauty is a public good whose worth is not accurately reflected in the price system, what is widely acknowledged to be beautiful farmland may be purchased by developers who build unattractive housing on the sites. Because the price of the farmland does not incorporate the desire of consumers for beautiful land as they tour the countryside, and, perhaps, because the individuals who own the farm cannot make judgments about beauty, both society in general and the potential purchaser of the farmland in particular have to make a judgment about levels of natural beauty desired in their community. Is the natural beauty of the land at a lower level than the person-made beauty which is contained in the home designed for the site? When society has a justified conviction about the relative levels of such beauty, i.e., when it can specify a subsection of the hierarchy of beauty, society should act to protect higher levels of beauty.

In dialectical fashion in what follows I apply the criteria for ethically responsible production to several particular cases. Because the production of goods often comes in conflict with the three fundamental values of beauty, friendship, and life, the cases examined will focus on these values.

Consider first an example involving the mining of coal. Suppose coal is needed for the production of goods and services, and let us also suppose that in this unrealistic society no other source of energy exists. I also assume that any coal mine is a blemish on the beauty of the landscape. Despite the fact that a decision to open a mine involves an act directly against the fundamental value of beauty at one level, the decision may be a moral one if the criteria for ethically responsible production are fulfilled. Does this principle justify all types of damage to the beauty of the environment for the sake of increasing the productive power of the nation? No, because criteria 2 and 3 must be met. The first criterion, that the activity lead to a general increase in the ability of people to pursue the basic goods, is assumed to be true. The producer would not undertake the activity unless she thought that it would be profitable. In a market society this means that the coal will be used by other producers to generate goods and services to be used by individual consumers.[11]

Criterion 3 requires a measure of proportionality. Suppose the coal producer is faced with the possibility of opening mine A or mine B, both of which contain equal amounts of ore. If mine B involved greater damage to the natural beauty of the surroundings, it would be ethically wrong for the producer to choose mine B for her site, and it would be wrong for society to allow the selection of mine B. Criterion 3 also requires that the net effect not impair the pursuit of the fundamental value against which the activity of production offends. Since in this case we are not considering the safety of the mines (which affects the value of life), the only essential value under consideration is beauty. Although criterion 3 does not apply directly since mines do not produce final goods, the assumption is that the coal produced from mines generates energy which allows factories to produce goods, some of which are either themselves beautiful or make beautiful things more available to people, such as automobiles. If mine A or mine B did not indirectly generate beauty at a sufficiently high level to compensate for the beauty that it destroyed, society could not justify production at mine A or mine B.

Let us add a further complication by amending the example slightly. As above, suppose that mine A and mine B are equally productive and that mine A does less damage to the natural beauty of the environment. But, in addition, suppose that, in order to set up activities for mine A, one hundred families would have to be moved. We can assume that the producer already owns title to the land where the families are located and she is willing to pay moving expenses for the affected families. Although the families experience no monetary loss, they personally experience great disruption. Assuming that they will not all move to a new community together, friendships are broken up. But frequency of contact with friends typically varies during a lifetime; furthermore, friendships can sustain separation, provided occasional contact takes place. Choosing mine A may be against friendship, but it is not directly contrary to it.

Is mine A, which is less damaging to the environment, still superior to mine B? Yes. Some economists would be inclined to resolve the dilemma by using cost-benefit analysis, including all costs, social as well as private. However, cost-benefit analysis in this case is unwarranted (and unethical) because an action directly contrary to a fundamental value is being contemplated. Using cost-benefit analysis would be justified only if opening either mine did not involve an action directly contrary to a fundamental value but each mine involved an activity *against* different fundamental values.

Let us switch the example involving mine A and mine B to compare automobile plant A and automobile plant B. These plants cause some damage to the environment, which may be justified if the criteria are satisfied. By making people more mobile and reducing the time needed to get to various places, cars enable people to participate more fully in the fundamental values; cars (and roads) also allow people to see beautiful things which they otherwise would not be able to reach. Criterion 1 is therefore satisfied. To fulfill criterion 2, it must be the case that the plant cannot operate with less damage to the environment; we suppose this to be the case. Criterion 3 requires that beauty be "created" at a higher level. Automobiles save time and allow people to dedicate more time to creating beauty in their lives. This beauty may be of the garden variety, or it may be the care of the home or the beauty of public pageantries. As long as one of these is at a higher level in the hierarchy of values, criterion 3 is satisfied. Of course, it is possible that a society has so many automobiles that the environment is being polluted or that many of the automobiles remain unused, although not unpurchased. In this case, society would be justified in intervening to prevent an additional plant from being built because criteria 1 and 3 would not be satisfied.

Consider another example which involves individual acts against the basic value of life. Although killing animals, such as chickens, is at one level directly against life, the killing can be justified if the three criteria for ethically responsible production are fulfilled. In the case of food, the first condition means that the animal food is truly required to keep people healthy, that is, there are no other substitutes which are just as effective in preserving people in good health. Criterion 3 requires that the killing of animals has a net positive effect. In this case it means that people must be so much healthier as a result of eating meat that one can justify killing a lower form of life for the sake of a higher form. In order to make a definite decision whether criteria 1 and 3 are fulfilled, one has to establish a hierarchy within the value of life. Suppose, for example, that reasonable evidence exists which supports the contention that chickens are higher on the scale of life than fish. Thus, killing a chicken is worse than killing a fish. Were this the case, one would need a stronger reason for killing a chicken than a fish. For example, it may be that eating chicken makes one healthier than eating only fish, or that some variety in eating fish and chicken is beneficial.

Since knowledge about the way life evolved influences judgments people make about the hierarchy of life, what people consider morally acceptable with respect to food may change over time as their understanding of the hierarchy of life changes. But the transformation occurs not only because society has a better appreciation of the significance of chicken on the scale of life, but also because, as a result of research in human nutrition, people realize that they can get sufficient nourishment without killing animals higher on the scale of life than fish. If and when that change occurs, eating chicken will be considered immoral because it is against the fundamental value of life and does not qualify for an exception.[12]

Yet another illustration of how the criteria for ethically responsible production can be applied involves the possibility of war between societies. Since security is one of the required goods, society has to decide the best way to achieve true security. War is the ultimate defense of security, and the pertinent criterion for justifying war, if it can be justified in a modern society, is the reaction principle, which is contained in the last part of criterion 3. In the case of war, the important task is to determine the meaning of "proportional."

First, consider the traditional conditions for waging a just war. They are (a) that all efforts at peaceful resolution have failed; (b) that the war is to right some previous wrong or in defense against foreign aggression; (c) that the means are proportional to the end; and (d) that the country can reasonably expect to prevail and so succeed in either defending itself or in righting the wrong. Condition a is similar to criterion 2, which requires that, within the set of feasible actions, the contemplated action have the least direct offense to the fundamental values. Since peaceful resolution is usually much less damaging to the pursuit of the basic human goods, war should be a last resort. Conditions b and d for a just war can be taken together; they correspond to criterion 1, which requires that the contemplated action is reasonably expected to lead to a general increase in the ability of people to pursue the essential human goals. Condition *c* for a just war, that the means are proportional to the end, corresponds to criterion 3 for responsible production, which, applied to this case, requires that one should not use more force, cause more injuries and loss of life, destroy more buildings and territory, etc., than is necessary to achieve the required objective of self-defense or righting a previous wrong, such as expropriation of territory, inflicted on the country. Since war always involves actions with terrible consequences for participants and nonparticipants alike, decision makers have a weighty responsibility to verify that all the conditions for ethically responsible production are strictly fulfilled, and because great potential harm is involved, in cases of doubt decision makers should err on the side of peaceful resolution.

For a final illustration of the applicability of the criteria for ethically responsible production, consider an economic action that is partially against the fundamental value of life. In the United States both in this century and in the previous century, various cities have undertaken significant building projects. One such project was the building of the Brooklyn Bridge in New York City. In order to build the foundations for the two towers which, via the cables, support the central span of the suspension bridge, men had to work about 100 feet underwater in pressurized chambers. At the time, workers as well as managers knew that working in this environment produced various ailments. Furthermore, occasional blowouts occurred causing the pressurized chambers to lose pressure, and hurling workers in the chambers into the deep waters. Some men were rescued, but others drowned. Such blowouts were not intended and, as best as can be judged from our present vantage point, could not have been prevented. The supervisors of the operation took reasonable precautions, but there were enough contingencies which could not be anticipated that a priori it was likely that there would be several blowouts in the course of the construction project. In fact, approximately twenty workers died due to accidents while constructing the Brooklyn Bridge.[13] If supervisors and workers knew that some people would be killed in the course of the construction project, was there an ethical justification for building the bridge?

In terms of the fundamental values approach, the objection to a dangerous construction project is that the supervisors and workers act indirectly against, and perhaps contrary to, the essential value of life, since they know that some workers will be killed on the project. Neither the supervisors nor the workers directly violate the basic value of life because the supervisors do not commit an act whose direct effect is the death of one of the workers, and neither do the workers, since the act of entering into a pressure chamber to mix and pour cement is not itself against the fundamental value of life. It is true that engaging in such an activity is riskier than working in a factory, at home, on a farm, or in an office, and a complete development of the fundamental values approach requires a careful analysis of the acceptable levels of risk and uncertainty. For the present, however, we can assume that the personal risk assumed by a worker is minimal. Thus, if one views the activity narrowly as pouring cement in a pressure chamber, we assume that no individual worker commits an act directly contrary to a basic good.

When one takes a broader perspective, however, and views the entire length of the construction project as an action composed of individual acts, both management and workers realize that a number of people will be killed in the course of carrying out their jobs. In particular, the person with overall responsibility for the project can anticipate with virtual certainty that some workers will be killed. In this sense, a decision to undertake the construction project involves a choice that is directly against, and possibly contrary to, the fundamental value of life, although no individual worker or lower-level supervisor acts directly contrary to the fundamental value of life.

The supervisors with oversight responsibility for the project must make sure the criteria for ethically responsible production are fulfilled in order to proceed with the project. Criterion 1 requires that the activity should be expected to increase the ability of people to pursue the fundamental values. In the case of the Brooklyn Bridge, this was a reasonable surmise since it made family and business contacts between Brooklyn and Lower Manhattan easier and safer. Criterion 2 requires that building a bridge at this location be safer than building, for example, a tunnel or a bridge at a different location. If the bridge were safer at another location and just as effective, those responsible would be morally obliged to try to build the bridge at that location.[14] Criterion 3 requires that the services offered by the bridge generally promote the value of life at the highest level.

If the building of the bridge necessitated the direct killing of a person, it would be immoral to build the bridge, because a direct killing is an act contrary to the value of life. Even if the action of constructing the bridge involves activities which one can anticipate are against the value of life in the passive sense that it would be most unlikely that some workers would not be killed in the process, then undertaking the activity is directly contrary to the fundamental value of life. It is *directly* contrary because the person who has overall responsibility for the project can foresee with virtual certainty that some workers will be killed. That is, the action of building the bridge entails many individual acts; the effect of the totality of acts is directly contrary to the value of life at its highest level.

Criterion 3 allows an exception to the prohibition against acts directly contrary to a fundamental value when the value is threatened by someone or something. In this case, the value of life is threatened by the best alternative activities that have to be undertaken if the bridge is not built. Not to build the bridge also involves a conscious act, and this act may result in more deaths than the act of constructing the bridge. Building the bridge can be justified if it is thought that the bridge enables more people to live longer, reduces drownings which would otherwise occur in the ferries which used to go back and forth between Brooklyn and Manhattan, allows doctors to provide more effective assistance to patients in grave danger, provides greater security for the populace, etc. Furthermore, the loss of life in the first building project of this type is undoubtedly much higher than in subsequent ones because supervisors and workers are learning a new technology. Thus some "costs" are incurred immediately, while "benefits" materialize later. In evaluating the ethical quality of the project, one calculates the consequences and compares them with the effects of not building the bridge. Like the switchman at the juncture of Tracks 1 and 5, the supervisor of the bridge counts lives gained and lost to justify the building of the bridge. This is a type of cost-benefit analysis that is clearly a moral calculus of consequences. However, as we indicated earlier, the moral calculus of consequences is appropriate as long as the consequences all belong to a single category at the same hierarchical level, which in this case is the value of human life.

The building of the Brooklyn Bridge appears to satisfy the criteria for ethically responsible production. About twenty men lost their lives in the construction project, and, using an arbitrary number, we can assume that during the lifetime of the bridge an additional one hundred people were expected to die in a variety of accidents occurring on the bridge. To justify the loss of 120 lives, the project managers would have to anticipate, as a result of the presence of the Brooklyn Bridge, fewer fatalities in ferry disasters and more lives saved by doctors reaching patients earlier, totaling 120 or more people. Since ferry disasters occurred every few years, this was a reasonable assumption.

The basic insight used to derive the criteria for ethically responsible production is that goods and services enable people to participate more fully in the fundamental values. Without them, people would be not only financially and physically poor; they would also be unable to pursue the basic human goods in novel, interesting ways and at deeper levels. The production of goods and services exposes people to risk, changes the environment, and even modifies the manner in which people interact with one another. Under some circumstances, production activities are directly contrary to the fundamental values of life, beauty, and friendship at various levels in their hierarchies. But, it is contrary to reason to eschew activity that is against an essential value at one level if it leads to greater participation for many people in the same fundamental value at a higher level.

In applying the criteria for ethically responsible production the significance of level 1 and level 2 goods becomes apparent. The important distinction between level 1 and level 2 goods is that level 1 goods have beneficial effects which are so pervasive that only the vaguest calculation about the net benefits even within the category of one fundamental value is possible whereas level 2 goods require careful calculations of benefits if their production is to be allowed. In order to protect and promote the fundamental values, society has to make a general decision about the appropriate level of economic activities which are contrary to essential human values. In order to limit damage to natural beauty, for example, society has to set boundaries for the amount of damage firms and individuals can do to the environment. Similar boundaries must be set to protect friendship and life. As society changes the boundaries also change. However, society must set parameters within which economic agents in a free market society or any other form of economic organization must operate. The boundaries should be set conservatively so that there is no question but that production of level 1 goods within these boundaries will have a net beneficial effect on any single fundamental value against which it offends, directly or indirectly.[15] Society's decision is meant to ensure that the net effect on the fundamental values is positive. By specifying such parameters, society demonstrates its responsibility for making sure that criterion 1 is fulfilled. The individual economic unit, subject to review by appropriate groups in society, has the responsibility to ascertain that criteria 2 and 3 are fulfilled.

Level 2 goods differ from level 1 goods in that the firm cannot presume that criteria listed above are satisfied. Each producer must make the ethical judgment that the level 2 product which he or she produces is expected to lead to a greater participation in the fundamental values and does not offend against the fundamental values. Although he or she may be assisted by the price mechanism in making this decision, in many instances the price mechanism needs to be supplemented by a direct consideration of the issues involved. The fact that a producer makes profits producing a good is no guarantee that the criteria for ethically responsible production are fulfilled.

Consider an economic activity that does not fulfill the criteria for ethically responsible production. Back scratchers may enable some minor participation in the fundamental value of life, but one can legitimately question whether electric back scratchers can be justified, except perhaps for medical ailments. The producer who proposes building a factory to produce electric back scratchers, which, according to his own admission, do not make a significant contribution to the pursuit of the basic human goods, would be doing something unethical, even if he knew that he could make a profit.

The criteria for ethically responsible production are binding on all production units in society as well as on society at large. Organizational structures should incorporate reasonable procedures to make adherence to the criteria highly probable. That is, whatever decision-making machinery is used by a group in society, some safeguards are necessary to prevent uninformed or unethical actions, in violation of the criteria for ethically responsible production. For example, any economic group, such as the board of directors of a firm that relies on democratic voting to determine actions taken by the group, ought to allow, in extreme cases, for intervention by some responsible person when the outcome of the vote is in violation of the criteria for ethically responsible production.

5.3 CONNECTEDNESS

People are connected or related to each other by virtue of the common human nature which they share, and this bond draws a person outside the confines of his own interests. The basic insight that a commitment to the fundamental values is an integral part of being human and that the fundamental values are not merely "my personal preference" or "my own options" implies that each individual in the world ought to have a general concern for every other individual in the world. No person is or ought to be an island, and everyone is and ought to be his brother and sister's keeper. A common nature and a general concern for the welfare of all does not mean, however, that everyone is Big Brother or Big Sister to everyone else. Every person should be "concerned" with the opportunity of every other person to participate in the basic values, but the exact manner in which any individual chooses to participate in the fundamental values may not be of great concern to others because it depends not only on the degree of bonding but also on the types of actions other people are contemplating. If individual A is thinking of robbing, killing, or demeaning individual B, this should be of concern to everyone, not just A and B. If, on the other hand, individual A wants to participate in the value of playfulness by going to a movie or attending a baseball game, that should be of no interest to person C, unless C is a friend of A.

The actual degree to which people are connected or bonded depends on their past history, their current situation, and their common projects for the future. Although the strengths of bonds differ among individuals, some bondings are predictable because they are the result of people interacting through institutions. Institutions create bondings which are then amplified or attenuated by individuals.[16]

5.3.1 Common Understandings and Individual Conscience

Institutions exist in every society, and they are identified either by the people who belong to them or by the practices which they espouse. If they are identified by their members, they are groups of people who share some common expectations. Banks, firms, sports teams, neighborhood groups, religious bodies, civic groups—all these are institutions defined by their members. Other institutions are defined by the expectations of the people who use them. When one walks into a retail store, one expects to purchase something and pay money for it. When one goes out on a date, unless other arrangements are made the woman expects that the man will call for her at her house or place of work. When one meets an old friend, one shakes his hand or gives her a kiss. These are conventions established by a community or an institution.[17]

Since both types of institutions establish and reinforce expectations, individuals are never completely free as long as they are members of or participate in institutions. Despite the imposition of expectations, institutions both constrain and encourage individuals to be free. People must conform to the expectations of an institution, but the institution allows people to express themselves in novel ways that are unavailable if one is not a member of or does not participate in the institution. Even if three persons—A, B, and C—had identical dispositions and talents, but differed in their aspirations, the institutional structure which exists in society would constrain their free acts in different ways. Figure 5.1 uses a spatial metaphor to propose that institutions are the supporting frameworks in which people perform free acts, even though they are constrained to operate within the frameworks of their institutions. Therefore, every institutional structure both enables and inhibits free acts.

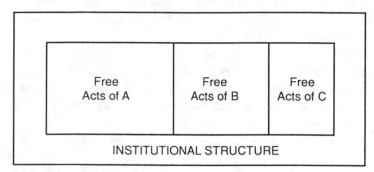
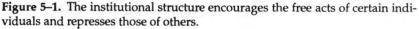

Figure 5–1. The institutional structure encourages the free acts of certain individuals and represses those of others.

Institutions generate common understandings, which may be local, shared only by a few, or may be affirmed by a large majority of the population. If a common understanding is sufficiently broad based, it is identified as part of the culture of the society.[18]

In a free society the particular desires of a person may conflict with a common understanding of society. What does one do when one's particular preference is at variance with the common understanding or convention, even one which appears trivial? In his book *Choosing the Right Pond: Human Behavior and the Quest for Status*, Robert Frank presents an interesting illustration of the way in which common understandings clash with particular understandings:

> Consider, for example a recent episode involving a member of the immigrant community of Tongans living in Salt Lake City, Utah. The Tongan went one afternoon to purchase a pony for his son's birthday. After agreeing with the pony rancher on a price for a particular pony, the Tongan backed his pickup truck up to the

barn and emerged with a stout section of lumber. With it, he then delivered a powerful blow to the pony's head, killing the animal instantly. The horrified rancher quickly summoned the police, who tracked the Tongan to his home, where they found him roasting the pony on a barbecue spit. Their interrogation revealed that it is a common practice in Tonga to honor a loved one by killing and roasting a pony. (Frank, 1985, p. 15)

There are laws in the United States against killing pets but not against killing ponies, presumably because most people are not inclined to kill ponies. Ponies present a particularly poignant case of a common understanding, but more routine examples of common understandings concerning prohibited activities abound. In certain states gambling, except with a state license, is prohibited. Sexual acts in exchange for money are also outlawed, although the sex industry is not intimidated by such laws. Spitting, smoking, and undressing in certain public areas are not permitted. Ought there to be such laws? What is the moral justification for such laws?

In the laid-back and uninhibited land of California, everyone purports to "do their own thing." In fact, practically no one, in California or elsewhere, does solely her own thing. All of us rely on common understandings, both to discover meaning in our lives and to express ourselves. Handshakes, driving on the right side of the street, funeral services, a dozen roses, Thanksgiving, the Fourth of July, marching bands—all these are examples of common understandings. Doing one's own thing, except for the unusually gifted person, means taking a few common understandings and introducing an interesting variation in a particular case. Because people must express themselves in ways that are intelligible to others, there is an unavoidable conflict among common understandings, individual understanding, and action.

Let us return to the example of the Tongan and his pony. In the United States, the pony is not only an animal but also a figure that embodies innocence, playfulness, freedom, and tenderness. These emotions are not necessarily, i.e., by instinct or human nature, connected with ponies. Ponies, however, have some characteristics which allow society to see in them qualities that, strictly speaking, are only applicable to humans. It is a quirk, perhaps, of the U.S. historical experience with the Wild West in the nineteenth century and the current tendency to romanticize the Wild West that at the current time the pony receives much attention and affection. Whatever the reason, parents encourage these feelings in their children, and the feelings are widely disseminated in the media. A common understanding concerning ponies, therefore, exists in American society.

If the extension of a common understanding is broad but not complete, e.g., 90 percent of the group subscribe to the understanding, group members may be inclined to prohibit contrary behavior. Is such a constraint consistent with the free pursuit of the fundamental values? We have previously distinguished two types of behavioral constraints: negative and positive. A negative constraint is one that prohibits someone from performing an action because it offends a common understanding or a fundamental value (about which there should be common understandings). Prohibitions against having sexual intercourse in public, killing pets, and desecrating graves even though one owns the property on which the graves are located are examples of negative constraints.

A positive constraint, imposed by some dominant group, enjoins a person to perform a certain action. The controlling group can command people to wear seat belts in cars, to be respectful during the playing of the national anthem, or to practice the religion of the group. Imposing positive constraints is ethically justifiable *only if* the action is not contrary to the conscience of individuals in the state. Forcing a person to violate her conscience diminishes the person as a human being because it means that one is compelling an individual to perform an act which is, in her estimation, contrary to a fundamental value. For example, it is hard to imagine anyone objecting to a seat belt on grounds that it violates the person's conscience. But, even in a state in which almost all the members were of one religion, it would be ethically wrong to compel the few who do not believe in the state's religion to practice that religion. Christians ought not compel Jews to attend Christian worship. This is an ethical stricture binding in most conceivable situations and it is the basis for freedom of religion.[19]

A society can impose negative constraints for the common good, even if the person whose actions are restrained by law feels compelled by conscience to act in a certain way. A person's religion may dictate, for example, that a leader of a tribe be killed once he has attained a certain age. The state is morally justified in preventing the tribe from killing the leader, because by so doing the state prevents a group from acting contrary to a fundamental value.[20] Even if a basic good is not involved, society can prohibit certain actions if the actions violate shared understandings that are deemed valuable to society. Because a society cannot function without certain shared understandings, an individual's freedom is not absolute. Common outlooks bind a society together and enable both the society and individuals in the society to express themselves and communicate with others. Although a community cannot force a person to share a common understanding, society may prevent the individual from jeopardizing the common understanding.

Some common understandings that currently prevail or have existed in society are unreasonable; it is and was unethical to impose them on others. Indeed, the danger of appealing to common understandings is that they can be used to justify institutionalizing the prejudices of a society. For example, it would be wrong to prohibit an interracial couple from holding hands in public because it offends the general sensitivities of people in society. In this instance, society is being inconsistent, since there is no reason to allow people of similar race to hold hands but deny the same freedom to people of different races.[21] Copulating in public, however, could be prohibited because it is considered both offensive and a threat to family values, and a law against public copulation is directed neither at the racial characteristics of those committing the act nor the act itself, but rather at the performance of the act in public.

A society committed to the fundamental values is allowed greater freedom to impose negative constraints than positive constraints. In the negative case a person cannot reproach himself or herself for not carrying out an action that he or she is not permitted to carry out. Had the Tongan not been permitted (by law) to kill the pony, he may have regretted the fact that in the United States he could not celebrate his son's birthday in typical Tongan fashion. However, he could not accuse himself of not wanting or not trying. Even if killing a pony were part of a Tongan religious ritual, he could assuage his disappointment with the reflection that he did not do anything wrong, since he was prevented by the power of the state from doing something he considered to be right and necessary. In the positive case, however, a person is required to perform some act which—the person is convinced—diminishes his stature as a person. For this reason, society should be very sure that the common good is served by requiring positive constraints.

Freedom of conscience is not a right independent of the pursuit of fundamental values. In the case of prohibiting an action, society potentially blocks someone from realizing a fundamental value in a particular way. However, since there are many ways to realize a basic value, preventing a person from acting in a certain way does not mean that the person cannot participate in the value. On the other hand, when a person is forced to perform a particular act that he judges to be a violation of an essential value, his conscience is violated; accordingly, the person judges himself to be less of a person. Since the goal of individuals and society is to participate in the basic values, society should avoid forcing someone who is psychologically competent to perform an act which the person considers to be a violation of a fundamental value.

In some cases the state imposes common understandings because they are required for good order, although the particular common understanding sanctioned by the state may be of little significance. For example, whether people drive on the left or right side of the road is unimportant, but it is crucial that all people in a country drive either on the right or on the left. Colors and designs have to be chosen for a country's flag. Words and notes must be selected for a national anthem. Once they are chosen and accepted by society, they gain an aura which inhibits change because they form one way in which a nation links the present with past experiences.

Common understandings not only constrain the free acts of people in society but also modify the set of possible free acts. Consider a society whose common understanding concerning the importance of music is reflected in an elementary school requirement that every child learn how to play a musical instrument. If all adults in society are capable of playing a musical instrument, society has qualitatively different ways of expressing itself. It may also have numerically more ways, since a person cannot play a violin or piano at the age of fifty unless she had learned how to play at some earlier time.

In Figure 5.2 the three panels refer to three societies, each with the same population size and at the same stage of development, but each of which has a different pattern of common understandings. Let us suppose that areas in the three diagrams represent the quality and quantity of free acts or common understandings, i.e., the greater the area the higher the quality and quantity of free acts or common understandings in a society. Panel 1 has fewer or less pervasive common understandings than panel 2. The society structured according to the common understandings in panel 1 grants more freedom to its members than that of panel 2, since the area designating free acts in panel 1

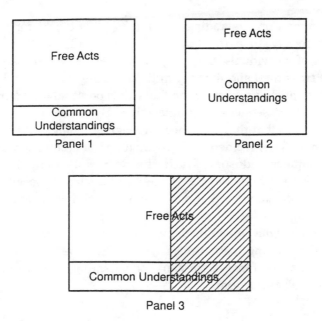

Panel 1

Panel 2

Panel 3

Figure 5–2. Common understandings constrain free acts as well as make free acts possible.

is larger. Because panel 3 illustrates a society that has more common understandings than the society generating panel 1, one might be inclined to think that the society behind panel 3 is more restrictive, inhibiting, and conservative than the one depicted in panel 1. However, the society in panel 3 uses its common understandings productively to enhance the free acts of its members. Compared with panel 1, panel 3 has either numerically more or qualitatively more pervasive common understandings, as measured by the area, but also more or qualitatively higher free acts as well.

The diagrams illustrate what was argued earlier, namely, that common understandings can promote communication and free acts among people, or, put more strongly, common understandings create the potentiality for personal freedom. The goal of society should not be to minimize common understandings or to decrease their binding effect on members of society, nor should society maximize them or seek to constrain all members of society to think or act in a prescribed way. After all, compared with panels 1 and 3, panel 2 is unattractive, because the common understandings in that society do not enhance personal freedom. The goal should be, rather, to promote common understandings to the extent that they foster free acts.[22]

Common understandings are the building blocks for all institutions in society. In particular, because they influence the economic behavior of individuals, they play an important role in the way markets are structured and the way individuals are expected to behave in firms. A common understanding that extols personal freedom, no matter what the consequences on others, is likely to result in more claims by individuals that they have been wronged by others in society. This results in a higher incidence of litigation and, therefore, a more developed insurance industry, which shields people from the harmful effects of large liability payments. On the other hand, a society with the common understanding that one's actions should never cause another economic agent to suffer a direct loss will probably have fewer lawsuits and a less developed insurance industry. In a corporation, a common understanding that shirkers will be dismissed produces a more productive work force. Common understandings can promote efficiency as well as freedom.

5.3.2 The Principle of Freedom

The desire by all people to pursue the fundamental values imposes constraints on the way individuals act toward one another, on the extent to which common understandings are imposed on others, and on the distribution of resources in the economy. The standards discussed in the preceding section are summarized in the following principle:

> **The Principle of Freedom**: A society should be structured in accord with the following criteria:
>
> a. All people should be encouraged to pursue the fundamental values.
> b. Common understandings should encourage people not to act directly contrary to any of the fundamental values, especially the fundamental value of life.
> c. Common understandings should encourage respect for personal decisions of others. If people are doing no harm to others and if they are not violating any common understandings in society which are necessary to promote the pursuit of the fundamental values, people in society should not interfere to prevent activities contrary to the fundamental values.

d. Actions contrary to widely shared common understandings can be prohibited. However, widely shared common understandings should avoid requiring a person to perform some positive act that is contrary to a person's conscience.

As formulated above, the principle of freedom is an admonition to individuals not to interfere needlessly in the lives of others. The principle, however, applies not merely to individuals, but also to society itself and all institutions in society. The positive requirements in the criteria of the principle of freedom make specific demands on the way in which any particular society operates. People in society should have a de facto liberty of choice and not merely a de jure liberty of individual opportunity.[23] We examine two essential areas of freedom: governance and employment.

In any society, people disagree about the shape particular institutions should assume and about which policies should be pursued. Differences of opinion are in large part due to diverse backgrounds and interests, and, even though one opinion may in fact be more correct than another, it is difficult or impossible to find an impartial arbitrator upon whom society can consistently rely to choose the objectively right opinion. In these circumstances reasonable processes can be instituted to arrive at a decision, although none of them will enjoy unanimous consent. One sensible approach is for society to have a thorough discussion of the issues, followed by a vote, and then let the majority opinion rule. As long as people are well informed, the outcome over the long run is probably the best that can be expected. Individual decisions may be wrong, the electorate may be misinformed on several issues, and people may choose to vote on the basis of narrow self-interest instead of on the merits of the issue. All these possibilities can and will occur. However, these potential errors speak against a liberal democratic form of government only if they are expected to occur with great frequency. If they remain isolated instances, liberal democracy appears to be a reasonable way to order society, although more analysis is required to determine whether a liberal democracy can be described as just.[24]

Note, however, that liberal democracy is not the only way to order society. In some societies, in fact, it may be unrealistic to assume that people are informed, or that they are capable of voting on the merits of the case and not according to self-interest. In those circumstances, some other form of government might conform better to the principle of freedom. If the United States discovered that self-interest voting was becoming the norm, the entire society would exercise practical reasonableness if it amended the Constitution to make a change which effectively thwarted the advance of narrow self-interest.[25]

No particular form of government is mandated by the fundamental values, by the principle of freedom, or by other principles of justice enunciated here. The particular form depends on the circumstances within the country. In earlier centuries, for example, monarchy was the preferred form of government in many parts of the world, and different groups in society had distinct privileges and responsibilities under the monarch. In descending order, the king, his family, nobles, landowners, town dwellers, freeholders, and serfs had various advantages and duties. Because such societies had limited means to share information, it is possible that a society headed by a monarch was one that afforded the most freedom, consistent with a commitment to the essential human goals and given the limited education of the populace, and that it was a reasonable structure through which society could pursue the fundamental values.[26]

The goal of any society, monarchical or liberally democratic, should be to provide as many opportunities for people to pursue the fundamental values as possible. Since some coordination is required in order to pursue the fundamental values at a national, regional, and local level, as long as voters are informed about the issues, the rule of "one person, one vote" is a reasonable rule, but not a necessary one.

Because work is an important way to actively pursue the fundamental values, an economy should not be structured in such a way that makes the pursuit of basic values very difficult. Ceteris paribus, the greater the variety of jobs available, the more freedom a person has to choose the job which corresponds best to his or her individual talents and interests.

In recent years in the United States, people appear to value permanency and stability in their job more than variety and upward mobility. This may be because modern society, which places a heavy premium on personal freedom, also makes it more difficult to form new friendships after one has passed into middle age or old age. If the maintenance of old friendships and the establishment of new friendships is difficult in a society, ceteris paribus a person should not be required to sever old friendships and search for new ones in a society that can reasonably afford to function in this manner. For example, suppose that a firm that has operated in New York for fifty years con-

siders transferring its operations to Chicago, even though the economic benefits from the move are small. It would be wrong for the firm
to transfer to Chicago if the move would cause much hardship for its
workers in New York. It would be even more reprehensible to move if,
for example, the motive was that management wanted to teach the
employees' union a lesson for some policy which the union had pursued in the past. Because the closing of a plant or an office causes
human suffering and impairs people's ability to pursue the fundamental values, a firm needs substantial reasons, consistent with the pursuit
of the fundamental values, to close a plant.[27] And even if a particular
firm has a good economic reason to close a plant, the economy should
function in such a way that people who have long been employed in
one region should not be forced, without good reason, to move to other
parts of the country in order to find employment.[28]

Society must be careful lest it speak frequently and glowingly
about freedom of choice but subtly restrict it by imposing conditions
that inhibit freedom. For example, prima facie it appears reasonable to
insist, in the name of freedom of access, that no group can be selective
in its membership. While this constitutes one aspect of freedom, true
freedom of choice for workers means that they have a great variety of
potential employers from which to choose. Some firms may have traditions that many people consider confining, even outmoded. However,
if no one is forced to join the firm, society should not interfere to abol-
ish the tradition. Suppose a corporation happens to have a strong religious tradition. People would join the organization knowing that, for
example, it followed the Jewish religious calendar with respect to cele-
brating holidays and adhered to Jewish dietary laws. Prior knowledge
means that the employees enter into an informal contract to abide by
the code of the corporation. Although this arrangement may appear
constraining, it actually allows greater freedom. Two types of people
will work at the firm: the person who wants to have his or her religious
beliefs integrated with the work environment and the person who for
nonreligous reasons likes the firm and does not mind adhering to the
schedule of religious practices and the dietary laws.

The same logic might appear to approve of a firm that hires only
women or refuses to employ people belonging to a certain group
looked down upon by the owners of the firm. But this is not the case.
Any restriction on access to a group must be justified by a reason
related to the pursuit of the fundamental values. Arbitrary preference
is not sufficient for a corporation since it is an institution recognized by

society for the purpose of contributing productive goods and services to society. In the latter part of the twentieth century, a firm that does not hire women has to show why the presence of women would impair productivity and other goals of the corporation. Even if the firm can demonstrate diminished efficiency if a certain group is hired, society, to emphasize broad access to a variety of ways to pursue the fundamental values, may stipulate that firms are not permitted to discriminate on the basis of a variety of factors. Efficiency, as we know, is only one principle of justice, and, as we will see in the next chapter, so is impartiality.

CHAPTER 6

Principles of Justice II: Distribution, Responsibility, and Impartiality

In the previous chapter we demonstrated how the principles of efficiency, subsidiarity, and freedom are applications to institutions, i.e., groups of people, of a society-wide commitment to the fundamental values. Each of these principles has an effect on the distribution of goods in society, although distribution is not their primary concern. In this chapter we derive principles directly relating to distribution that foster the pursuit of the fundamental values. The principles of distribution and relatedness are mainly concerned with the allocation of goods and services, whereas the principle of impartiality covers positions of prestige in society as well as physical goods and services.

6.1 THE PRINCIPLE OF DISTRIBUTION

During the French Revolution the cry from the people was for equality, fraternity, and liberty. In our day the primary call is for liberty, especially from government intrusions or from the bureaucracy of large social institutions. The call of freedom is particularly strong in the U.S. public media. It is a reasonable assumption that the poor still cry for equality and fraternity, not just for liberty, but that their weak voices are not heard in the marketplace.

There are many different types of equality. U.S. law, for example, mandates equality of opportunity in hiring: People with similar skills should have roughly equal chances of being hired for a position. The judiciary strives to provide equality of treatment before the law: All members of society should have fair access to due process and, if convicted of a crime, receive punishments which do not differ because of irrelevant considerations, such as personal wealth, social position, the color of one's skin, or the shade of one's beliefs. Equality before the law is not of much value, however, if one does not have the minimum resources necessary to participate in society. The late nineteenth-century novelist Anatole France caustically remarked: "The law in all its majesty forbids the rich and poor alike to sleep under the bridges of the Seine." Equality before the law is a necessary but not a sufficient condition for a just society.[1]

There are two important reasons why a society committed to the fundamental values may desire a more equal distribution of benefits than that generated by a free-market system. First, a more equal distribution may better provide for the basic needs of the poor and enable the poor to pursue the fundamental values at a level considered appropriate by society. Second, a more equal distribution has been shown to foster fraternal spirit and decrease divisiveness. An elevated spirit or a decrease in abrasive conflicts is directly beneficial to the individuals involved, but it often has the added effect of enhancing the productivity of society. One of the most effective ways to make the distribution of income more equal is through a progressive income tax. For this reason, most modern societies have income taxes that are levied at a higher rate for higher-income people than for lower-income people. Are systems of taxation which take from the rich and middle class to give to the poor justifiable? We seek the answer in terms of people's abilities to pursue basic values.

As we have seen, to recognize the fundamental values as elemental is to admit that they are essential to the well-being of all people in the world. In situations where a group's ability to pursue the values are jeopardized, every person outside the group should be ready to help, although, as we argue in a subsequent section, the obligation to help falls more heavily on those who are more closely bonded with those in jeopardy.

In order to pursue the fundamental values, goods and services are necessary, and the normal way to ensure that all individuals can pursue the essential values is to devise a system that allocates goods and resources in sufficient quantities. This formulation of the relationship between fundamental values and material goods suggests that justice is limited to the concern that every person should have the minimal amount of goods and services to sustain him in life and to pursue the fundamental values. Such a formulation of justice, however, is inadequate because it does not come to terms with the dynamic aspect of "minimum." What a society considers the minimum amount increases over time as the standard of living increases. As technology advances and new goods become available, a society forms new standards that determine a new minimum amount of goods and services needed to live with dignity.[2]

Neoclassical economists examine the effects that various policies have on the distribution of income. However, because the utility functions of individuals remain private, neoclassical economists cannot add the functions together, either in weighted or unweighted fashion, to form a social welfare function that renders some income distributions more desirable than others. Economists can only offer their personal opinion about what the distribution of income ought to look like, but they cannot conduct a scientific analysis. Since many neoclassical economists have an aversion to distorting markets by intervening in them, they rely on the free-market system to provide for the needs of the poor through the trickle-down effect, i.e., the activity of the industrious and energetic in society (the wealthy) indirectly benefits the poor by generating jobs for them.[3] Neoclassical economics offers little substance to the discussion of income distribution, although it has developed some formidable mathematical techniques.

6.1.1 The Rawlsian Approach

Although stress on the minimum amount required to pursue the fundamental values is not adequate to the task of structuring a just society, it is an important starting point. In his influential study *A Theory of Justice*, John Rawls argues that impartial people would opt to structure society in such a way as to benefit those who are at the lowest economic rung of society. In the Rawlsian system, impartial people agree to two principles of justice: equal opportunity for all and the difference principle. Equal opportunity for all means that individuals have equal access to different goods and positions in society, i.e., positions should be distributed on the basis of merit, while the difference principle states that any method for allocating goods and services is just only if inequalities in income or wealth benefit those at the lowest end of the income distribution. In particular, the difference principle implies that the competitive market system in the United States, as amended by income taxes, is just only if the system helps the poorest classes in society. The difference principle is referred to by economists as a maxi-min principle, because the rule maximizes the flow of resources to those least well off (those at the minimum) in society.[4] Rawls claims that this is a principle to which all objective people would agree.

Rawls is meticulous in describing exactly what he means by "objective." People can be purely impartial, says Rawls, if they have some general information about human society and the way human beings function, but are ignorant of their own position in society. He asks us to picture a group of people sitting around a table: They are clear-thinking individuals, but a veil of ignorance about their own talents and their own future incomes forces them to consider sympathetically the situation of all people in society, rich and poor alike. Rawls calls this the original position, in which people are asked to decide upon the contours of a just society.[5]

Rawls wants us to imagine people deciding on ethically just structures before a society is actually established. The people in the original position know a fair amount about human nature, but they know nothing about their own endowments. They do not even know what they consider to be the ultimate goods or goals in their own lives.[6] More practically, they do not know how successful they will be in the business world or in society in general. Given this type of ignorance, Rawls argues that the people setting the rules would unanimously agree to structure society so that any inequalities in society would serve to benefit those who are least well-off in that society, since each of the decision makers may himself or herself wind up as least well-off. That is, society would maximize the amount of resources going to those at the minimum level of income in society. Note that Rawls does not say that resources to the poor "should" be maximized, merely that they "would" be maximized in this original position. Indeed, no "should" can appear in the Rawlsian original position because people in this position are assumed to be concerned not about what ought to be done but about what people will actually decide.[7]

One attractive feature of the difference principle is that it includes a dynamic concept of the minimum, because as general standards increase over time the minimum standard rises as well. As it increases, the people who are at the new minimum should benefit most by the difference principle. Note that no emphasis is put on the means by which people acquire goods and services but only on the amount of goods and services accumulated by different distinguishable groups in society.

One of the most frequent criticisms proffered by economists of the Rawlsian approach is that it assumes that people are absolutely averse to taking a risk when the risk involves their very lives.[8] Rawls assumes that people in the original position, deliberating behind the veil of ignorance, are so frightened or disturbed by the specter that they might wind up at the minimum level of income or wealth in a society that they protect themselves by agreeing to the maxi-min principle. Economists point out, however, that Rawls has canonized only one possible reaction to uncertainty about one's life. Other reactions appear plausible. Suppose, for example, a person has two alternative positions in life. According to the first alternative, the individual lives a moderate, middle-class life; he or she has no great wealth, but the person knows that there will always be a home and adequate food. The second alternative is a lottery ticket. If one accepts the ticket, one's fate in life is decided by choosing from a deck of ten cards. The reverse side of one card, hidden to the chooser, is painted red; the reverse sides of the other nine cards are white. If one chooses the red card, one is poor for life, a life which may be cut short due to the ravages of poverty. A white card means that one lives in great wealth one's entire life. The lottery offers either a life of poverty, with probability 0.1, or a life of opulence, with probability 0.9. Given a choice between a middle-class life and the lottery ticket, many people would choose the safe life of a middle-class citizen. There would be at least some people, however, who would prefer the lottery ticket, which offers a chance of great wealth and presumably excitement. Economists, political scientists, and philosophers dispute Rawls' contention that *everyone* would choose the safe route.

Consider the practical effects of the difference principle. In a Rawlsian world, an entrepreneur who already makes $10 million per year would be allowed to make an additional $1 million per year, provided the $1 million incentive prompts the entrepreneur to undertake activities which help, directly or indirectly, those people who are least well-off in society. The entrepreneur might build a new factory that puts more people to work in society, and even if the factory produces no net increase in jobs, it may pay those who are working more than they had been paid in their previous jobs. Their higher income results in higher tax receipts for the government, and the government can use the tax receipts for programs that benefit the most disadvantaged. The point is that the entrepreneur need not have any personal interest in helping the poor. Indeed, she might be quite greedy and only wish to accumulate as many assets as possible. Provided the entrepreneur's greed increases the well-being of those least well-off in society, society should tolerate such greed, according to the difference principle.

Rawls's concern for the least well-off in society is certainly admirable. However, justice must be concerned with treating all people fairly, not just the poor. Even a middle-class person may feel disadvantaged when contemplating the resources of the wealthy or the care lavished on the poor. A person who earns an average income may think that he is being treated unfairly, compared either with the best or the least well-off in society if, for example, he must work much harder than the highest-paid person in society or if he has to work harder than the person to whom benefits, such as food stamps and housing, are granted by the government. A person's concerns extend beyond the minimum amount of goods and services necessary for survival. Since an unavoidable reference for one's own well-being is the well-being of others, each economic agent is also concerned about one's relative position, even if everyone in the economy has sufficient goods and services to live in dignity.[9]

At first, the desire to compare one's own situation with that of others in society may appear mean-spirited, especially if everyone has been given sufficient goods and services to pursue the fundamental values. Put another way, even if it is true that most people are concerned with the distribution of goods and services in the economy, is this a justified concern or, rather, one born of selfishness and envy?[10] Since our approach has been to focus on the meaning of essential values, a concern, if it can be legitimated, for the distribution of goods and services must be related to these values.

Rawls departs from the neoclassical assumption that one cannot compare the utility of one person with that of another,[11] and argues that in the special case of political and social justice, interpersonal comparisons in the possession of primary goods, among which are respect, honor, and position, are possible.[12] The principal focus of the fundamental values approach, however, is not on the primary goods of society but on the fundamental values themselves and on having sufficient goods and services to pursue them. We agree with Rawls that interpersonal comparisons are possible, but disagree that the relevant consideration is the primary goods themselves. Depending on the amount of goods and services used, the fundamental values can be realized with greater or lesser intensity. Suppose the system which distributes goods and services (think of the competitive-market system) were one which also guaranteed that the people who received the most goods and services were more adept at using these goods to realize fundamental values than others. Then one could, reluctantly perhaps, admit that the distribution was fair. But are the wealthy more adept or assiduous pursuers of the fundamental values?

If one only considers a summary measure of the goods and services available to a person, i.e., her income or wealth, there is no reason to believe that people of greater wealth are more capable of realizing the fundamental values than the poor or those in the middle-income range. Indeed, except for narrowly defined classes, it is almost impossible to make an objective judgment about who is inherently more capable of realizing the basic values if they had a wide range of goods available to them. Musicians are one example of a specific group that are clearly more capable of realizing one fundamental value (beauty) in a particular way. Both the ability and the desire to create beautiful music may be revealed in an objective way; in music competitions, for example, people reveal their ability and their accomplishments. People who score high on examinations seem more suited to pursue the value of knowledge than those with ordinary intellectual talent. Society can make judgments such as these, and society may wish to reward gifted people with resources that promote their pursuit of music or knowledge. With the exception of cases of this kind, however, there are no external means by which one can judge whether one person is better at realizing fundamental values than another. Therefore, other things being equal, one person should not be given more resources to pursue fundamental values than another. Of course, other things are never equal. Nonetheless, if they were equal, society should tend to distribute goods in an egalitarian manner, and this is the justification for the initial inclination of many people to espouse an egalitarian society. Egalitarianism's appeal springs from the realization that all people have the same responsibility and the same basic abilities to pursue the fundamental values in the ordinary ways.

If all things except ability were equal, society ought to have a strong egalitarian bias, although more resources should be designated for artists, musicians, intellectuals, or others with above-average capacity and capability for realizing the fundamental values. In fact, however, people differ not only in ability but also in their effort, interests, responsibility, willingness to assume risk, etc. Although none of these characteristics is directly related to the attainment of the essential human goals, these particular qualities are either helpful for the production of goods and services in society, or they reveal a person's determination to acquire goods and services in order to pursue the fundamental values. Precisely because other things are not equal and because a basic tenet of fairness is that a person should merit or deserve the goods or services which she obtains through the market system or some other system of distribution, an equal distribution of income is not ethically defensible. Morally sensitive people have a legitimate interest in making sure that allocations are not too large or too small, i.e., the distribution of income and wealth should correspond to contributions that people make to society. Therefore, it is to be anticipated that, in certain circumstances, society will redistribute income and/or wealth because the distribution produced by the economic system prior to redistribution is judged to be unfair.[13]

Note that the expectation that a person should merit or deserve the goods or services which she receives is not an arbitrary assumption but rather an expression of the lived experience of every person in society. From the time a child receives less candy than her brother to the point at which a woman receives less pay for performing the same job as her male colleague, people have not merely an emotional reaction but also a moral reaction to any arbitrary distribution of goods. Of course, by pointing out that merit and deserts are significant conditions for any distribution of goods, we do not solve the difficulty of what it means to merit or deserve a good. For instance, some will claim that one merits a good by adhering to the free-market rules of the game. If, for example, a person invests in the stock market and a firm in which he holds stock happens to discover a new source of energy, the person, because he holds shares in the company and because a rule of the game is that shareholders allot the profits of the company, deserves to receive a share in the millions of dollars earned by the company. Arguing in this way, however, leaves unanswered the question about what constitutes a justifiable source of merit or desert. By appealing to the rules of the game, one simply repositions the question about merit or just deserts. The question about deserts becomes one about whether the rules of the game reward people according to merit, a topic we will take up after we address arguments for and against redistribution.

6.1.2 Arguments Against Redistribution

Despite the justification offered above, redistribution of income and wealth can be criticized on a number of counts. First, as has already been discussed, the redistribution may not be in accord with contributions individuals make to the production of goods and services. A response to this objection is that a person's productivity is only one consideration in determining a fair distribution of income. After all, the mentally disturbed and the severely handicapped still deserve to receive resources from society even though some of them cannot make productive contributions.

Second, any redistribution which is based on how much one currently earns neglects the ability of people to realize the fundamental values. Consider first a meaningful redistribution of income. Suppose a person has assets worth several billion dollars, all of which was earned by adhering scrupulously to the rules of the game. It is reasonable to assume that the person is incapable of using all these resources personally in pursuit of the basic goods. For the sake of argument, assume that when some of this billionaire's resources are transferred by fiat to the people with the least resources in society, the productive output of the economy is not affected.

Also suppose that a billion dollars of the billionaire's money is redistributed to the poorest members of society, and each family receives $500. Provided one can presume that the poor will have better ways of spending the money than the billionaire and provided that future, potential billionaires do not become dejected by the redistribution and decrease their efforts, the transfer should be made, because the goal of society should be the realization of fundamental values. On the other hand, if it is expected that the poor will not use their money wisely, the state (or the person herself) should not redistribute the resources. Suppose there were sound reasons to believe that the poor recipients would use their checks from the government (or from the billionaire herself) to purchase alcohol or to divorce their spouses. A just society should not redistribute in this case. (See Finnis [1980, pp. 173–77].) These two different hypothetical cases show that redistribution, even when the billionaire earned her billions by adhering to the rules of the game, can be justified in terms of the fundamental values in some cases but not in others.

The third basis for criticizing income redistribution is that it decreases the incentive for talented people to use their proficiencies for the benefit of society. Oftentimes this objection takes the specific form that increased wealth for the wealthy trickles down eventually to other people in society and that taxing the wealthy is therefore counterproductive. But the ill effects of a diminished incentive may be operative not only on the rich, but on the poor and the middle class. A poor person, for example, may have to work very hard to earn a paltry income. If enough poor people feel that their recompense is not commensurate with their effort, they may diminish their efforts and may decide to rely instead on the meager benefits provided by the state. Which income class the person belongs to is not significant. More important is the contribution a person or group can make to society. If a revision of the income-tax rates elicits greater efforts on the part of a large body of middle-class people, and if this increased effort redounds to the benefit of the poor, middle class, and wealthy alike, then a revision of the income-tax schedule should be undertaken. The distribution of income (and wealth) should encourage productivity on the part of all individuals in society. Admittedly, redistributive mechanisms which can be implemented empirically usually generate disincentives to some groups as well as losses in well-being. But even in these cases, the redistribution can be justified if the legitimate expectation exists that more people will pursue fundamental values more intensely.

A fourth objection to redistributive mechanisms is that they do not address the real concern of ordinary people. According to this view, whether a redistribution improves the productivity of society and whether it enables poor people to pursue the fundamental values more intensely are irrelevant since people do not conceive of justice in terms of the ideally correct distribution of income. Rather, people judge whether a society is just or not in terms of the status quo and one's ranking with respect to other groups. As the economy grows over time, a just society is one which advances all classes and groups at approximately the same rate. What counts is not the absolute level of one's wealth or income, but one's ranking relative to others. As long as one's relative ranking remains approximately stable over time, the society is just, in the view of the relativist.

It is undoubtedly true that many people *think* that a just society is one which maintains relative rankings as the economy grows. This view, however, is erroneous. If it were true, it would condemn blacks and Hispanics to the lowest level in the United States for ages to come. It would also mean that people in less-developed countries would always have an income per capita lower than that of people in developed countries.

The maintenance of fixed relative rankings as the economy grows is a sufficient condition for a just society if two stringent conditions are fulfilled. First, the initial starting point must be just. Second, there must be no substantial changes over time in the needs of individuals, the contributions made by individuals, or the opportunities offered by the economy. Since the first condition is as unlikely to be fulfilled as the second, maintaining fixed relative rankings is not a justified goal for a society committed to the basic goods.

From an empirical point of view, when an economy is growing at a healthy rate and relative rankings of groups in society are maintained, people are often satisfied, but this does not mean that society is doing justice to all. Any person is pleased to receive regular increases in income because he likes to purchase, use, and enjoy the additional goods made possible by the increased income. As long as one's relative position has not deteriorated, the person is not inclined to agitate to demand an even larger income, nor is he inclined to listen to people who claim they should get more. Although the abundance of the moment silences critical questions in many people, one cannot conclude from the fact that people do not object that society treats them fairly.

People are concerned about how resources are allocated both because they want to receive their fair share and because they do not want goods and services to be wasted in society. Goods and services are squandered when the economy (through the competitive-market system or some other system of allocation) apportions goods and services to people who cannot use them as effectively as other people, i.e., goods and services are misallocated. In a free-market economy, a maldistribution of resources can be prevented by adhering to two rules. First, the process by which goods are acquired should be basically fair or just. Second, the resulting distribution of wealth or income should be fair or just, and, if it is not, income should be redistributed.

6.1.3 The Economy as a Fair Game

In *Anarchy, State and Utopia*, Nozick argues that redistributing income is not necessary to achieve a fair allocation of goods and services and may even work counter to the intent of making the ultimate distribution fairer. Instead, Nozick claims, in order to achieve a just distribution it is sufficient that the rules of the game be fair, provided people start the game from an initially fair allocation of goods. In his view, if the initial allocation is fair and if people acquire goods according to rules which are judged to be equitable by all involved, then the resulting distribution must be fair. This position is also taken by Buchanan, who justifies it by analyzing the characteristics of a fair game. He asserts that a game or rule is fair if it is "agreed to by the players in advance of the play itself, before the particularized positions of the players becomes identified."[14] By insisting on the game analogy, Buchanan disallows any external criteria to judge whether the end-state, i.e., the outcome of the game, is fair. He refers to the willingness to enter the game as a contractarian logic. Not surprisingly, both he and Nozick dismiss those who do not accept the contractarian logic. The emphasis on the fairness of the game and the refusal to examine end-states or outcomes are diametrically opposed to the spirit of the fundamental values and the principles of justice.[15]

Nozick's and Buchanan's positions are persuasive as long as one's primary concern is with goods and not with the ability of people to pursue the essential human goals. If the economy is only a mechanism for producing and distributing goods, these functions are carried out most efficiently if one establishes rules that everyone agrees to and that are strictly enforced. In such a world there is no need to examine the resulting distribution of goods since it is fair by definition. Only its efficiency requires detailed analysis.[16]

Let us examine whether a modern free-market economy is a reasonable approximation to a fair game. Based on people's experience with different games, especially games of sport, we note five significant characteristics of a fair game:

1. Everyone agrees to the rules and understands the ways in which one performs effectively in the game.
2. No one begins the game at a disadvantage compared to other participants.
3. All participants abide by the rules of the game or are justly penalized if they violate the rules.
4. The game is one pursuit among many in a person's life. People do not play games, least of all a single game, for their entire lives.
5. The activity has the characteristics of a game, i.e., an activity: (a) which depends partially on skill and partially on luck; (b) the outcome of which is not known with certainty before the game is played; and (c) which does not cause incapacitating injury to many of the players.

In most games, such as sports or cards, the rules are rather straightforward and in playing them one can easily develop a strategy.

Chance certainly influences the outcome, as is specified in the third characteristic, but, provided one understands the rules, a person should be able to make the judgment that the rules do not favor one group of participants over any other group. In most games making such a judgment is usually not difficult because the game is repeated many times over, in different contexts, with a variety of players who possess an assortment of skills. Let us consider each of the rules and examine whether a modern economy operates in accordance with the rule.

The first characteristic requires sufficient understanding by all participants. Are the rules of any free-market economy sufficiently straightforward so that they can be implemented by most or all participants? Certainly not in the United States, where, for example, the tax code alone numbers thousands of pages, and regulations concerning the transportation and sale of goods are voluminous. Even if, as Nozick and Buchanan would recommend, no such tax code existed and government legislation were simple and straightforward, the rules for interacting in the economy—such as futures contracts and bankruptcy agreements—would still be complicated and under constant revision. Would a person of modest intelligence agree to a game if he knew that clever people who understand the rules more thoroughly than he have a better chance of succeeding in the game? Hardly. In fact, in a dynamic economy the rules are constantly changing as new markets appear and old markets vanish.

Since the economy is under constant revision, is the game repeated frequently enough so that a person can ascertain that it is fair? In one sense, the economic game is only played once for each person, since each person has but one life. On the other hand, it is true that one can measure who is ahead in the game at many discrete intervals. Every year, for example, each person in the economy earns some particular income. If this information is made available to people, one could consider such an annual sampling to be one play of the game and determine who won and lost during that year. The more frequently one samples the outcome, however, the more variable the outcome becomes, because chance has a larger impact in the short run than in the long run. In the long run the law of large numbers applies approximately equal doses of good and bad shocks to individual fortunes. The greater the variability of outcomes, the less inclined many people, though not all, will be to play the game. In a dynamic economy, one cannot plausibly argue that the game is played sufficiently frequently that most participants have confidence that they understand the game and, therefore, that it is fair.

The second characteristic is that no player should begin at a disadvantage. Many writers have commented on this feature and have made proposals which would make the assumption less discordant than it currently is.[17] For example, one way to equalize the starting position of each participant is to levy a 100 percent inheritance tax. Although steep inheritance taxes are unpopular, they were a device envisioned by some of the early framers of the U.S. Constitution as preventing the accumulation of power and advantage.[18] Even with steep inheritance and gift taxes which prevent parents from transferring wealth to children, current wealth can permanently effect offspring, and some people would still have more human capital than others. Wealthy parents can hire the most qualified people to train and instruct their children and can introduce those children to influential people. In addition to increased human capital, children of the wealthy would also enjoy substantial material advantages, since the parents would be able to share their wealth with their children during the parents' own lifetime. Theoretically and practically, a program to prevent the transfer of wealth during the lifetime of the wealthy person would be problematic at best and probably not feasible. Even a young country such as the United States has an entrenched wealthy class that is unlikely to surrender its privileges. Despite this skeptical attitude about the possibility of challenging the structures that support the accumulation of wealth, a steep inheritance and gift tax may make sense, not because it makes the game fair but because it conforms to the principles of justice.

The third characteristic is that everyone should abide by the rules of the game, that the system of penalties is fair, and that the judges or referees who assess the penalties are informed and impartial. In other words, a fair economy requires some system of penalties that are fairly assessed. In some instances it may be difficult for the person or agency maintaining surveillance over the economy to ascertain whether an infraction of the rules has occurred. For the most part, however, it is reasonable to assume that this condition can be fulfilled in a market economy.[19] Although egregious examples of favored treatment abound, one can plausibly argue that such aberrations will occur under any rules.

According to the fourth characteristic the game should be one pursuit among many. People should have some options other than participating in this particular game. In a modern economy, however, one cannot realistically opt not to participate in whatever economic system prevails. For example, to produce all one's goods on a farm in Vermont means that one must accept a much reduced standard of living. Although the state does not prevent a person from acting in this way, if a person has goals that require certain types of goods or even the minimum goods needed to live decently, the person must participate in the economy that produces those goods.

We have already discussed (a) and (b) of the fifth characteristic of a fair game, its randomness. While some randomness is acceptable, the allocation of goods and services should also incorporate merit and desert. Furthermore, randomness is not a positive value, as it is in an ordinary game. Ceteris paribus, if economy A were as efficient as economy B but economy A experienced less randomness in the allocation of goods and services, economy A would conform more to the requirements of justice.

The last requirement of a fair game is that the probability of an incapacitating injury is low. According to this criterion, Russian roulette is not a moral game, because, according to the natural law approach, one is not allowed to act directly against the fundamental value of life. Similarly, when considering whether one wants to play the economic game of unhindered free markets, one possible outcome—absenting charity or state intervention—is the death through extreme poverty of many players of the game. One should not choose to play the austere free-market game if one can participate instead in a variant of the unhindered free market that prevents people from dying due to extreme poverty or other causes associated with the functioning of the system.[20]

Because so many of the conditions are not fulfilled, a balanced judgment about the free-market game is that it is not fair. Despite such a conclusion, would people nonetheless choose to play the free-market game? When confronted with a particular economic activity, a person ought to ask the question: What is the opportunity cost of playing the game? That is, an individual or society must ask the question: Which game is better, which game is fairer? Even a neoclassical economist, therefore, cannot avoid posing the question of justice, since it is embedded in the question concerning the opportunity cost. Although the concept of a fair game was introduced to elicit a straightforward acceptance of the basic fairness of the free-market economy, the previous discussion demonstrates that no such simple, unqualified response is possible. All the questions that engage us in the chapters to come need also to be addressed if one is to answer the question whether the economy is a fair game. It is a telling criticism of Nozick, Buchanan, and the neoclassicals that they have no basis on which to make a judgment about competing economic systems. Like all modern liberals, they can only appeal to consistent procedures.[21]

In a stable and just economy the rules of the game should change in a way that promotes fairness. As the economy experiences different shocks, people are concerned about the well-being of others, and the rules should be changed in a direction that supports justice.[22] Maintaining justice does not emerge as a concern in the neoclassical paradigm because the neoclassicals, in the tradition of Adam Smith, assume that the goals of various individuals can be joined harmoniously through the functioning of the price mechanism. An alternative view is that unrestrained competition leads to conflict and, therefore, that competition must be constrained. In fact, unconstrained competition is not viable. Etzioni (1988, pp. 199–216) argues that the germane economic question is not whether the private sector or the government should be involved in the production or allocation of a particular service but rather what level of competition is appropriate for each type of good produced in the economy.

6.1.4 Arguments for Redistribution

According to the natural law approach, a society is interested not primarily in the production and allocation of goods and services but in participation in the fundamental values. Goods and services are important to the degree that they enable participation in the essential values. Although the pursuit of the basic values is undertaken by individuals, the ability as well as the desire to pursue the fundamental values is of concern to all people in society. If a person acquires moderate wealth, purchases goods and services and *never uses them at all*—surely an unrealistic assumption—society ought to intervene. It may be that when a person hoards particular goods society would not want to intervene for a variety of reasons, practical as well as theoretical. However, if such a pattern were repeated on a widespread basis, society would be justified in redistributing unutilized goods and services to people who would use them to pursue the fundamental values.

Although the example of a person who makes no use whatsoever of most goods and services which he possesses is unrealistic, the principle concerning the use of goods is clear. Society has to make a judgment not merely about fair rules for acquiring goods and services but also whether those who acquire the goods and services can use them as well as other members of society. Since society does not have accurate information on how goods and services are used by particular families or groups in society, it makes its judgment concerning the general way in which people use the goods and services. In the United States as well as in other nations, a common judgment of society is that if money is redistributed from the middle and upper classes to the lower classes the lower classes will purchase goods and services which they can use more effectively for the attainment of the essential human goals. This judgment relies in part on an agreement that certain goods, depending on the general standard of living which a society has achieved, are essential in a modern society.[23]

In the Rawlsian original position, people do not know what values they will be pursuing in life. According to Rawls, the rules, to which people agree unanimously in the original situation, must allow people to have conflicting values. Rawls assumes that no values are universal in any modern, liberal society because in the original position no values are raised higher than others. He therefore adopts the liberal position that a person can use the goods and services in a society to pursue whatever values he or she desires. Once this degree of openness is granted, it is difficult for Rawls to avoid Nozick's libertarian criticism: The difference principle is inconsistent with the fair acquisition of property in a well-ordered society.[24] Even though Nozick rejects any intervention in the economy based on an evaluation of end-states or final outcomes, the position which I take is not susceptible to Nozick's criticism that only fair rules should count, and not the resulting distribution itself. Although Nozick would repudiate the designation of any values as fundamental and binding on all, once the binding character of certain basic values is granted, a concern that the resulting distribution of income favors the pursuit of the fundamental values can be validated.

There is a second reason why Nozick's emphasis on fair rules should be supplemented by an examination of the distribution of wealth and income. It is impossible for a society to specify entirely just rules of acquisition in an ex ante manner. For competitive markets, monopolistically competitive markets, oligopolistic markets, and quasi-markets in public goods—for each of these market structures one would need not only different rules of fairness to regulate the current state of those markets but also rules that correctly anticipate the manner in which markets change. But this implies knowledge not merely of expectations about future prices but also knowledge about the future structure of the economy, surely a type of information that no institution in the economy has. In reality, the best one can do is designate rules or principles that cover markets as they exist now and make adjustments as patterns of interaction change.[25]

It is instructive to consider some objections to the position I have outlined:

Objection 1: Whatever else a free market may be, it is voluntary. No one is constrained to buy things they do not want to buy, nor is anyone compelled to sell things they do not wish to dispose of. This is true whether the market is competitive or not; no one is forcing anyone to do anything against his or her will. What possible objection can there be to such a system? By definition, all trades in free markets are fair because if they were not fair, people would not enter into the market. Why is any corrective mechanism necessary if all people voluntarily participate in market exchanges?

> **Response**: First, admittedly, the principle of personal freedom developed in Chapter 3 and the principle of freedom developed in the previous chapter highlight the importance of free will, and freedom is also a strong motivating factor for the principles of subsidiarity and impartiality. Nonetheless, free will is not a fundamental value; it is neither the only value nor the highest value in society. It is fundamental only in the sense that people ought to be given as much freedom as possible to pursue the basic goods. The principles of freedom, subsidiarity, and impartiality must be joined with the other principles of justice and applied to institutions in society to determine the scope of freedom.
>
> Second, even if freedom were the highest personal value, which it is not, freedom is always exercised within a structure, and the structure determines the options available. Restraints on freedom can increase the range and quality of options for all. For example, no free-market system can exist without important public goods. Because a public good is by definition a good that is not diminished by an additional consumer of the good, free markets for such goods do not exist. Examples of public goods are a stable currency; a system of roads, airports, and telecommunications; and clean air and water. Without such goods efficient exchange

would not be possible. In order to conserve and develop such public goods some constraint on the free will of economic agents is necessary. Thus, in a free-market system there is an unavoidable conflict between freedom and efficiency, and it is not surprising that other principles of justice also clash at times with the principle of freedom.

Objection 2: The principle of distribution encourages people to be lazy; therefore, it is an unrealistic and inefficient principle. Because people at the lower end of the distribution of income know that they will receive resources from the upper- and middle-income regions of the distribution, they realize that they do not have to work. People near the low end of the distribution can just wait until they are poor enough to receive a transfer of resources. The principle of distribution is diametrically opposed to the principle of efficiency. It cannot, therefore, be a principle of justice.

    Response: Granted that the principle of distribution stands in opposition to the principle of efficiency, it is not diametrically opposed to that principle, just opposed. People at the lowest end of the spectrum can indeed expect a transfer of resources to their benefit in most modern societies. The transfer of resources, however, is not sufficient to move them to the next higher income class; the transfer is designed to be modest and allows them to pursue the fundamental values in a most basic way. In addition to providing the poor with means to pursue the essential values, an aim of a system of transfers is to make the distribution of income thinner. That is, the poor are moved up to a higher average income, but they still remain poor relative to others in society. Competition with the Joneses, even the poor Joneses, continues to be an effective motivation in a society with income redistribution. People at the low end of the distribution can still improve their relative standing by working hard, something they cannot do if they are content to receive handouts from the state.

Objection 3: The principle of distribution leads to self-seeking legislation that takes income and goods from the rich to make the poor and middle class better off. All talk about deciding who can use society's goods to best advantage in the pursuit of the fundamental values means nothing in the face of greed—not greed by the wealthy, but greed by the poor and middle class. The middle and lower classes just want to get their hands on wealth earned through the hard work of others, or through superior talent, or through the willingness to take chances.

Response: Realistically, greed by the poor and middle classes is a factor society uses to determine the proper amount of redistribution. It *ought not* be a factor, but it sometimes is. Poor people may vote for a politician who will push for programs that help the poor, even though the poor may already be receiving sufficient help from the state. Theoretically, one should make a decision concerning the proper distribution of wealth and income independently of what one personally earns and owns because impartiality, as we shall see, is a principle of justice. In order to guarantee objectivity, Rawls has the people in the original position make their decision behind a veil of ignorance about their own location in the distribution of income.[26] In theory, the argument for any particular type of redistribution should be as persuasive to upper-income people as it is to lower- and middle-income groups. In reality, selfish and unjust redistribution is a definite possibility, although it becomes less likely in an economy in which the poor have little political power.

Objection 4: Representatives of different religious denominations have stated in recent years that the proper criterion for a just ordering of society is how an institution or policy affects the poor. It calls upon people of goodwill to make a "fundamental option for the poor."[27] But the poor, although not neglected in the principles of justice enunciated so far, are not the focal point of any redistributive scheme. Should not everyone exercise a "fundamental option for the poor"?

Response: Yes, if one interprets "fundamental option for the poor" as a commitment to provide the poor with materials of sustenance, i.e., goods sufficient to maintain their health and to enhance their ability to pursue the fundamental values. Almost without exception, the poor throughout the modern world do not have the bare minimum to keep them in good health and allow them the modest pursuit of essential human goals. A bare "minimum" means goods and services required to pursue the fundamental values at a level that society judges to be barely adequate, relative to the overall income in society. By setting a minimum standard, society affirms that the poor with a standard of living below this level can use goods more effectively in pursuit of the fundamental values than other people in society.

The real world of the poor is one of disease, poor health, uncertainty, hunger, danger, simple clothes, and usually inadequate housing. To alleviate these needs, society usually transfers resources to the poor in the form of food, clothing, medical services, housing, and other basic goods.[28] However, a realistic concern for the poor may mean that, instead of direct assistance in the form of food, clothing, medical services, and housing, they be given education and training, which create the opportunity to compete effectively in the economy.[29] Such an approach may be a more effective way to provide them with the ability to attain the essential human goals at higher levels. Truly effective education requires an array of well-developed social institutions, including schooling, family life, and civil discourse. In recent decades in the United States, these institutions have undergone dramatic changes and, as a result of the ensuing disruption, education of those who are young and poor has not been sufficiently intense to enable poor youngsters to break the cycle of poverty.

The distribution of income reveals the percentage of the population that earns an income greater than any stated amount. Indirectly, the distribution of income is a measure of how goods and resources of a society are allocated. A society must judge whether resources, if redirected to the poor, would be better used in the pursuit of fundamental values. Society may observe that large groups with approximately the same amount of talent, drive, willingness to assume risks, etc., wind up with dissimilar allocations of resources. Society should take action to redress the resulting injustice because fair rules of acquisition have not been specified, implemented, or adhered to. The *principle of distribution* has two components: the first part states what constitutes a fair distribution, while the second part lists conditions that are to be fulfilled if income is to be redistributed.

The Principle of Distribution of Wealth and Income: The distribution of wealth and income in a modern economy should be based on contributions that people make to generate goods and services and on the ability of people to pursue fundamental values. Society ought to make objective judgments about the abilities of different income groups to pursue the fundamental values. Redistribution is appropriate when at least one of the following conditions is fulfilled:

1. Individuals or a class of people have earned their income or wealth unjustly.
2. Society has a reasonable expectation that the redistribution from one group, called the donor group, to another group, called the target group, fulfills both of the following conditions:
   a. The target group will use the funds to pursue the fundamental values better than the donor group.
   b. Redistributing does not so decrease the incentives of the donor group that their decreased efforts make the target group less able to pursue the essential human goals. (This is the Rawlsian difference principle in the context of fundamental values.)

As a special instance of condition 2, transfers to people of outstanding talent or who make exemplary contributions to society can be justified if society judges that such talented people are not appropriately rewarded in the market or in whatever system is initially chosen to allocate goods and services.

The criteria listed above are helpful; they are not, however, sufficient to select some optimal distribution from a set of many different possible distributions of income. Consider, for example, the two distributions given in Figure 6.1. The tighter and taller distribution reveals that incomes are more equal because the distribution has less dispersion. The fatter distribution, however, has a mean of $40,000, compared with a mean of $20,000 for the tighter distribution. The fatter distribution does not decrease the standing of the lower echelons of society in any absolute sense. In fact, many poor and middle-class people are better off in an absolute sense in the fatter distribution. But, relative to the richest members of society, the poor are worse off in the fatter distribution. In a latter section we argue that, under a broad range of circumstances, concern with relative standing is a legitimate moral and economic concern. Only if relative position does not count could one argue correctly that the fatter distribution is the ethically mandated one.

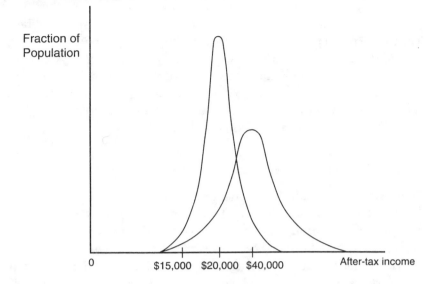

Figure 6–1. Ethical principles do not designate one of the distributions more just than the other in a static economy.

The principle of distribution is a corrective principle because it implies that however fair the social institutions are thought to be, an essential test of their justice is the end result, that is, the way in which resources are actually distributed in the economy. Using general knowledge about people's motivations and their willingness to work hard, one can state that fair rules are not fair if 5 percent of the population is awarded ownership of 90 percent of the goods produced by society. The principle is a safeguard and corrective for a basic indeterminacy in establishing what constitutes a fair price and a fair reward to a factor of production.

6.2 OBJECTIVITY AND SUBJECTIVITY

A just society acknowledges the role played by individual and group bondings in society. Because people and groups connect with one another, people form relationships which entail commitments to another person or group. Since a commitment either arises out of or leads to a positive evaluation of another person or group and because a person may be blinded by her desire to indulge the people to whom she is committed, she may not make objective judgments about people.

In a society committed to the pursuit of the fundamental values, personal or group relationships imply two types of responsibilities. The first is that a person or group has primary responsibility for taking care of those people or groups with whom he is most closely bonded; this is the principle of relatedness. The second responsibility is that in the distribution of goods, offices, and honors, society, institutions in society, and individuals should not show partiality to certain people or groups; this is the principle of impartiality.

6.2.1 The Principle of Relatedness

Discussion of practical reasonableness revealed that subsidiarity, which requires that society should be organized in such a way that the smallest feasible groups are given responsibility for their own well-being, is a principle of justice. This principle, along with other social forces, influences the size and function of various institutions found in nation-states: the family; local, state, and national government; business partnerships; corporations; unions; private property; private clubs, etc. We have already examined the special role reserved for the family, but other groups also warrant protection and cultivation. Many institutions in society were developed because they allow the smallest feasible group to make those decisions that influence its own welfare, i.e., its ability to pursue the fundamental values.

If a group is directly responsible for the people within its own organization, it will take care of those individuals in those areas over which the organization has control. A family, for example, is responsible for the welfare of its own children. Even after a child reaches majority, however, mutual obligations of family members remain binding. Since the family relationship forms lifelong bonds, the family arguably has the broadest area of direct responsibility, but other groups also have important obligations, which are limited by the narrower functions they perform in society. A corporation is responsible for assigning individuals to productive activities within the firm and for making sure that both explicit and implicit labor contracts are fulfilled.

What happens when a person is in need and no organization is directly responsible for the particular need encountered by that individual? Let us consider an example in which familial bondings are excluded. Suppose that Charles is an unmarried person who once worked at AT&T but is now unemployed, although he is able-bodied and physically capable of holding a job. For a variety of reasons,

Charles has not maintained contact with his family, and, although he is not psychologically disturbed, he has not searched for a job in over a year. Finally, suppose that Charles, who is currently in dire and obvious need of food, shelter, and medicine, is sitting calmly on a bench in the center of town. A person who encounters Charles on the street cannot, without spending some time with him, determine whether he is lazy or disoriented. Eventually it will be important to ascertain which of these is the case because it will determine the type of help he is given; but suppose that initially the information is unavailable. What is not in doubt for someone committed to the common good is that Charles needs help.

The question we pose is: Who ought to help? Because every person is a human being, every individual human being is and ought to be potentially concerned about every other individual in the world. In fact, however, most people legitimately restrict their concerns to a much smaller subset of individuals within the whole world. Should a Japanese student visiting some friends in the United States be concerned about this man whom she sees sitting on a park bench in the center of town? In a general way, yes. But unless there is some other connection, the responsibility to care for him is not hers. One could change some aspects of the situation, and then the Japanese student would incur some responsibility. If, for example, Charles had been beaten up by gang members and left to die when the Japanese student happened upon him, she would have a responsibility to do something because only she can prevent him from dying. That is the message contained in the parable of the Good Samaritan (Luke 10:30-37). The person who is our neighbor depends on the circumstances in which we happen to find ourselves. Without specifying some special circumstances, however, the Japanese student has less responsibility to act than an American living in the same town. If Charles's family were aware of his situation, the family would have a greater responsibility to act than any American passerby who happened to talk with the young man.

What principle establishes the degree of responsibility? Moreover, who has the responsibility to act when the person with the heaviest responsibility refuses to do what is necessary? These are important questions both for an individual as well as for society at large. When contemplating ethical burdens on an entire society, we should be interested in the responsibility that institutions or groups bear toward their members, because only institutions nurture common understandings that assign responsibility to individuals or groups. The principle of subsidiarity prescribes that an institution bears direct moral responsibility for its members only in those areas in which it is constituted to make decisions. But when a person's needs are not encompassed within the pertinent area, is there a principle that indicates which group bears primary responsibility?

In the example involving Charles, the goal is to help him satisfy his need for food and shelter. By assumption, the family is not involved. The only connection he has is with people in the town who observe him and with his friends at AT&T, who, by assumption, are aware of his plight. Of these two groups we assume that the people who know him best are his former co-workers at AT&T. If this is truly an individual case and not part of a larger pattern that requires a systematic approach by the town, country, state, or nation, Charles's former co-workers are in the best position to help this individual. Maybe they can provide only temporary help and eventually must turn to the municipality for help. The point is that, because, by assumption, they had a close, prior relationship with him at work, they ought to be assigned the responsibility by society, even though they may not consider him to be a close friend.

Ceteris paribus, effective, personal help is provided by people with tighter bondings to the individual in need, and, therefore, the general principle is that the degree of responsibility is determined by the degree of relatedness. People who have more binding connections with a person in need have a greater responsibility to help. In the case of an institution which is directly responsible for a certain need, this principle overlaps with subsidiarity. In many cases, however, there is no institution or community that is directly in charge of the welfare of the individual. In those circumstances, the degree of bonding through friendships, cooperative projects, institutions, or geographical proximity becomes the determinative factor, and it is incumbent upon society to make this responsibility known to people in society.

Depending on the situation, physical closeness may be one of the most important bonds. In a small town, two neighbors who live a thousand feet away share much in common and have close bondings whereas in a major city two people who live a thousand feet away may share the same apartment building but be located thirty stories apart and not even have a nodding acquaintance with one another. Neither physical propinquity nor family birth nor any other single relationship is a sufficient guide, although each one suggests an obligation. The goal is that assistance be provided by someone in a position to lend assistance and who both understands and appreciates the needs of the individual. This requirement of justice is called the *principle of relatedness*.

> **The Principle of Relatedness**: Those people or institutions who by reason of history, consanguinity, geography, business, or any other bond considered significant by society are related to persons in need have a stronger responsibility to respond to people in need than those not so related. The stronger the bonding with the person in need, the greater is the responsibility to act.

Like the *principle of distribution*, the principle of relatedness is a corrective principle. It does not state what must be rectified or how it is to be remedied, but rather who ought to do the correcting. Relatedness has no content in the sense that it does not help determine whether the underlying situation is unjust. Its importance is that it assigns responsibility in those cases when the person in need is not being attended to by some group that ordinarily bears responsibility for the individual. In effect, the principle states that every society should have a safety mechanism by designating a residual bearer of responsibility, namely, the group or person with the closest bonding. In this way some group or person always exists in society to care for someone in need.

A parallel justification as to why the principle of relatedness is included among the *principles of justice* is that a realistic society expects some injustice or inefficiency to exist in society. Human wills are weak and people do things they know they ought not to do. In particular, they fail to fulfill their responsibilities to those in need. A just society takes these failings into consideration by affirming and reinforcing a principle that creates a safety net to catch those uncared for because others—either individually or in groups—neglect their duties.

6.2.2 The Principle of Impartiality

Society enacts laws which embody common understandings about acceptable actions, stipulate punishments for infractions of rules, and outline processes to be followed in determining whether a law or a contract has been broken and whether people are entitled to compensation. The political system also establishes procedures for determining how laws are passed, how they can be changed, and who is responsible for implementing them.

In a just society the common good requires that all individuals and groups flourish. Unless there are particular circumstances that warrant treating one group or individual differently from others, it is to be presumed that all people are equally interested in pursuing the fundamental values in their lives. Therefore, people should be treated impartially as they undertake to pursue the fundamental values or accumulate the goods required. The color of a person's skin, the gender of one's co-workers, what a person does or does not do on Sundays, the language one speaks, the way a person dresses, what clubs one belongs to, what community one lives in, the weapon one carries, the gender of the people one chooses for sexual intimacies, the amount of physical strength one possesses, the access one has to the media, the honors one has received, how much wealth one has, who one's father is, one's views on communism, politics, or politicians—all of these facts or opinions *ought to be* incidental to the manner in which the law is administered and in which individuals and groups interact. It is a requirement of justice not only that laws be impartial and that they be administered impartially but also that they appear to be impartial and impartially carried out, because in the absence of the appearance of impartiality citizens would either waste time trying to have the laws changed or wrongly criticize lawmakers for passing biased laws.

Laws do not regulate all types of activities in society since many transactions are private in the sense that they are made verbally between individuals or groups. Even when the only parties present are those with an interest in the negotiation (i.e., there are no objective observers), the individuals making an agreement have a responsibility to act impartially toward one another as well as toward others. At a later time the agreement may be contested by one of the parties, and at that time each party to the compact has a responsibility to depict accurately what transpired. The fact that one person is physically stronger, more experienced, or politically more influential should have no bearing in the resolution of the disagreement.[30] Although, in the United States, contracts that are contested are often resolved in a court of law, many of these disputes could be settled amicably if parties to the contract were personally more committed to the principle of impartiality, which has at its foundation a commitment to the fundamental values of knowledge and friendship.

The Principle of Impartiality: In all transactions, meetings, exchanges, disputes, and resolution of disputes, people should be treated impartially in the sense that the pattern of treatment is the same for all people in similar circumstances.

For example, if society punishes a black man and a white woman for walking hand-in-hand but does not penalize similar behavior by white couples, the society acts with bias. The color of one's skin in this context is an irrelevant characteristic, though this may be denied by many because they lack insight or fortitude. Because the meaning of "similar circumstances" requires some concept of relevant characteristics, wise and brave people make an important contribution to justice in any society.

Impartiality does not imply that, when judging an action, the impartial person must be open to all ethical traditions. According to MacIntyre (1988, pp. 370–88), one tradition is not easily translatable or transparent to another tradition, and certainly a person who stands in one tradition cannot appropriate the point of view of another tradition without years of effort. Therefore, since every person is raised in some tradition and since objectivity is possible within a tradition but not across all traditions, impartiality implies objectivity primarily within one's own tradition. Rawls (1951) describes the characteristics of a person who is objective and capable of making fair ethical decisions. Many of these characteristics are relevant for implementing the principle of impartiality. Rawls, however, thinks that his list of qualities enables him to arrive at ethical prescriptions that are independent of any ethical tradition and, therefore, superior to all other ethical systems. In fact, however, some of his requirements for unbiasedness reflect his commitment to the liberal tradition.[31]

6.3 THE SIX SOCIAL PRINCIPLES OF JUSTICE

In Chapter 3 we derived four principles of justice applied primarily to individuals: the noncontrary principle, the principle of personal freedom, the reaction principle, and the personal principle of the common good. I refer to them as "personal" principles because each is rooted in a human being's experience of the pursuit of the fundamental values, and one arrives at them, in dialectical fashion, by pursuing the fundamental value of practical reasonableness. Although that experience always occurs in community, I did not refer explicitly to institutions in society when justifying such principles.

In this chapter and the previous one we have undertaken a parallel search for rules to orient the way in which society and the institutions in society function. We used three primary ingredients to produce these additional principles: (1) a commitment to the fundamental values, with a special emphasis on practical reasonableness; (2) some knowledge of institutions and how they function; and (3) the connectedness of individuals. The results are the six fundamental principles of justice, which we list below.

1. *The Principle of Subsidiarity*: The coordination and organization of humans and their activities should be designed so that the smallest feasible group regulates its own affairs. "Smallest feasible" is determined both by economic efficiency, i.e., the parsimonious use of materials, effort, time, and information, and by the effect that decisions by one group has on other groups, i.e., the degree of interconnectedness.

2. *The Principle of Freedom*: A society should be structured in accord with the following criteria:
   a. All people should be encouraged to pursue the fundamental values.
   b. Common understandings should encourage people not to act directly contrary to any of the fundamental values, especially the fundamental value of life.
   c. Common understandings should encourage respect for personal decisions of others. If people are doing no harm to others and if they are not violating any common understandings in society which are necessary to promote the pursuit of the fundamental values, people in society should not interfere to prevent activities contrary to the fundamental values.
   d. Actions contrary to widely shared common understandings can be prohibited. However, widely shared common understandings should avoid requiring a person to perform some positive act that is contrary to a person's conscience.

3. *The Principle of the Distribution of Wealth and Income*: The distribution of wealth and income in a modern economy

should be based on contributions that people make to generate goods and services and on the ability of people to pursue fundamental values. Society ought to make objective judgments about the abilities of different income groups to pursue the fundamental values. Redistribution is appropriate when at least one of the following conditions is fulfilled:

a. Individuals or a class of people have earned their income or wealth unjustly.

b. Society has a reasonable expectation that the redistribution from one group, called the donor group, to another group, called the target group, fulfills both of the following conditions:

   i.   The target group will use the funds to pursue the fundamental values better than the donor group.

   ii. Redistributing does not so decrease the incentives of the donor group that their decreased efforts make the target group less able to pursue the essential human goals. (This is the Rawlsian difference principle in the context of fundamental values.)

4. *The Principle of Efficiency*: Natural resources, personal effort, and goods and services should not be wasted without reason.

5. *The Principle of Relatedness*: Those people or institutions who by reason of history, consanguinity, geography, business, or any other bond considered significant by society are related to persons in need have a stronger responsibility to respond to people in need than those not so related. The stronger the bonding with the person in need, the greater is the responsibility to act.

6. *The Principle of Impartiality*: In all transactions, meetings, exchanges, disputes, and resolution of disputes, people should be treated impartially in the sense that the pattern of treatment is the same for all people in similar circumstances.

These are social principles of justice, not merely principles for individual human behavior, because they prescribe the manner in which society and its institutions should be structured. Since we are concerned primarily with the social principles of justice in subsequent chapters, we drop the qualifying adjective "social" whenever the meaning is clear.

Objection: The natural law tradition frequently speaks of the principle of the common good or the principle of solidarity. Concepts similar to the common good and solidarity appear in the above list of principles, but there is no explicit principle of solidarity or principle of the common good. Why not?

Response: The principle of the common good is a principle of justice, but since the commitment to the common good is a responsibility incumbent upon every individual in society, we include it among the personal principles of justice. According to the personal principle of the common good, everyone ought to desire to establish conditions in society so that all people can flourish in the pursuit of the fundamental values, and every person should, in proportion to his or her abilities and position in society, make a contribution to the common good by working, inside or outside the home, to produce goods and services for society. In short, the personal principle of the common good is the same as the principle of solidarity.

The principle of the common good could be the general heading under which all particular principles of justice fall. The terms "solidarity" and "the common good" are useful because they refer to a grave responsibility frequently neglected in a modern society, which stresses individual freedom and the individual pursuit of happiness without any reference to the higher ideals of the community. The usefulness of the principle of the common good is diminished if people understand it to require only a vague commitment not to harm others. Because the common good is better at motivating and directing individuals than at establishing guidelines for the functioning of institutions, we listed it as a personal principle of justice rather than a principle of social justice.

The principles of justice articulate the consequences for institutions of a commitment on the part of all or most people in society to the pursuit of the fundamental values. Figure 6.2 illustrates this connection between the basic goods and the principles of justice. The starting point is the experience that each person has of pursuing the fundamental values in her community. The reflection on the experience, which usually occurs many years after the person has actively been pursuing the fundamental values, involves an affirmation of the experience and

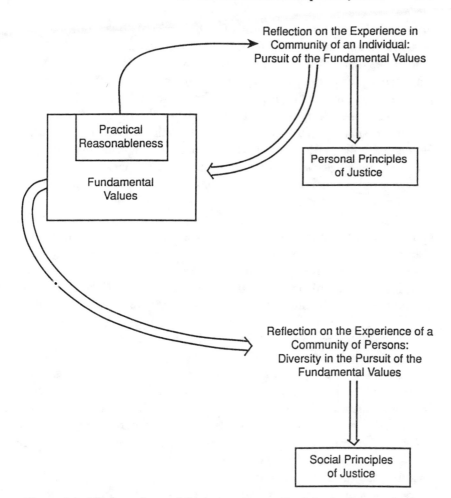

Figure 6–2. The experience of the common pursuit of the fundamental values enables a formulation of the principles of justice.

also the realization, through the pursuit of the basic good of practical reasonableness, that the world should be structured in such a way as to make it possible for all individuals to flourish by striving for the essential human goals. The six principles of justice express the requirements of fundamental reasonableness in light of the variety of ways in which people legitimately pursue the fundamental values by creating institutions and by enunciating rules.

In the principles of justice words like "reasonable," "plausible," and "feasible" occur a number of times. What is reasonable, plausible, or feasible in any single principle of justice can only be determined by referring to the other principles of justice, since an implicit requirement of justice is that it be coherent and rely on wise people. The principle of subsidiarity, for example, prescribes that the smallest *feasible* group be given control over its own affairs. What is feasible depends on the other principles. Suppose group 1 is smaller than group 2, both of which are smaller than group 3. Group 2 might have the size that allows individuals the most freedom in determining their own affairs, provided one neglects the effects of its actions on other groups in society. Once those effects are taken into consideration, it may be the larger size of group 3 becomes more efficient (principle of efficiency) and also provides more freedom (principle of freedom). As a specific example, consider the five boroughs of New York City or the subdivisions of any major city. The particular borough of Queens would have more freedom were it not forced by the city charter to coordinate its activities with Brooklyn, Manhattan, The Bronx, and Staten Island. However, to cite one vital disadvantage, transportation services would be woefully inefficient if instead of a single transportation authority five authorities, corresponding to the five boroughs, functioned quasi-independently of one another.

Reasonable people will disagree concerning which group size is "most just," both because they vary in their estimation of the factual state of affairs and also because they emphasize different principles of justice. We are not at a point in our deliberations where we can make a balanced judgment concerning the justice of institutions of any size, because justice cannot be determined until the structures of other significant institutions in society are specified. It may well be that one cannot select an optimal size and that groups 1, 2, and 3 are all consistent with the principles of justice, depending on the general structure of society. The only occurrence that would rob the principles of justice of their usefulness is a demonstration that *all* groups of *all* sizes in society are consistent with the principles of justice and that institutional structure is, therefore, irrelevant. But counterexamples exist to demonstrate that subsidiarity and the other principles of justice are not vacuous. Many different possible social structures are compatible with the principles of justice. Which structure becomes reality for a particular nation-state depends on several factors, one of them being the historical experience of the nation-state and the history of neighboring states. History and chance both play a role in the evolution of social structures.

A good test of the validity of the principles as well as of the reader's comprehension of the principles is to conduct a "negativity test." For each one of the principles one should be able to think of a situation which would violate the principle. As a first example of the negativity test, consider the principle of distribution. The task is to describe a situation that according to objective observers violates the principle. Two examples suffice to illustrate the two distinct components of the principle of distribution.

First, suppose Vincent, who is wealthy, operates a chain of private hospitals and health clinics that are located primarily in poor neighborhoods across the United States. He operates the hospitals in poverty-stricken areas because cities and municipalities decided that private health-care operators are more efficient at providing health care to the poor. The public authorities use a voucher system to pay what they deem to be a reasonable amount of money directly to the poor, who use their vouchers to pay for medical services when they go to private hospitals and clinics. Finally, assume that the primary reason for Vincent's wealth is that his hospitals and clinics, aware that the poor have no alternatives, have charged exorbitant prices for the health care provided. As portrayed here, Vincent has gained his wealth unjustly. Even if it is impossible to determine exactly how much of his profits were unjust profits, the principle of distribution is violated. Furthermore, the principle of distribution can be used to gauge how much of his wealth should be redistributed.

The second case involves a woman who has earned her money in a perfectly just fashion, as far as she or anyone else can tell. She was not born to wealth, but she took advantage of new opportunities in the economy as they presented themselves. On occasion she earned excess profits, but not because she acted deviously or unjustly. In fact, it is impossible to decide whether the excess profits she earned were reasonable incentives for entrepreneurs to be imaginative and take risks, or whether they were profits flowing from unjust prices in the marketplace. At the current time she earns $10 million per year, and there is no reason to believe that she will work less hard if income tax rates are changed and her after-tax earnings become $9 million per year. Although she may decrease her charitable giving if she is taxed $1 million, she will not decrease her giving by the full amount of the tax. If the government increases its tax revenues by taxing her an additional $1 million, it will distribute the money to the poor, who, we assume, will use it effectively to pursue the fundamental values.

In this case, the woman has done nothing wrong; indeed, she might even have been generous to various charities. Nonetheless, redistribution is appropriate both because she will not slacken her efforts, even though her after-tax income is $1 million less per year, and because society judges that the target group will be better able to use the funds to pursue the fundamental values.[32]

Devising negativity tests is also a useful way to apply the dialectical method and explore the robustness of the principles of justice. But the task before us is vastly more complicated than simply constructing examples of unjust circumstances. The principles of justice must be applied to the entire array of circumstances involving the production and exchange of goods and services; thus they must apply to situations of individual exchange as well as to institutions. Whether various institutions are just and under what circumstances they behave justly is an important question because the answer determines not merely our evaluation of overall justice in society but also our evaluation of particular economic activities. Because such activities take place in a larger framework of institutions, an activity can be just in one institutional framework but unjust in another.

A complete analysis requires that the principles of justice be related to the way in which various countries interact economically; but consideration of the international economy is deferred to a subsequent study. By far the most important economic institution is the free-market system of exchange since it sets parameters for many other institutions, such as corporations, unions, cooperatives, governments, and government organizations.

6.4 TOO MANY PRINCIPLES OF JUSTICE?

There are six social principles of justice, though they easily could be increased to fifteen if we chose to list every qualification as a separate principle. Furthermore, in Chapter 3 we listed four personal principles of justice. Although the demands of justice can be stated in different ways, the important point is that the formulation reflect a commitment to the fundamental values by individuals, by institutions in society, and by society as a whole.

The principles of justice are implications of the commitment to the fundamental values in a world in which people necessarily interact. If each person or group were able to pursue the basic goods without impacting on other groups in society, there would be no need for social principles of justice. In societies of earlier eras, when geographical regions were not as densely populated as they are today, when the means of communication between different parts of a continent or the globe were primitive, when most people earned their livelihood on farms or by raising livestock, the need to think carefully about social principles of justice was not as great because a person's actions impacted on only a small group of people. Modern society is characterized by complex interactions among many people and institutions.

Although the ethical imperative to pursue the fundamental values does not change over time, the institutional framework in which the basic human goods are sought is modified in every age. As society advances (or regresses), certain novel circumstances arise, and these circumstances are the context in which economic agents conduct their activities. Society may seek to regulate economic activity by establishing a new institution—such as the United States did in 1914 when, responding to a series of financial crises, it created the Federal Reserve System of banks to regulate the money supply and monitor lending activities by banks—with the mandate to oversee certain types of transactions. Alternatively, the costs of establishing an effective institution may be so high that society prefers to rely on the goodwill of the parties involved. In the latter case, ethicians may be prompted to make more explicit one or two principles of justice. In doing this they do not add a new fundamental value. Rather, through their commitment to practical reasonableness and by remaining alert to changed circumstances, they perceive new ways in which people *ought* to interact.

As an illustration of a potential future addition to the social principles of justice, consider the issue of labor mobility. It may be that in the twenty-first century it becomes apparent to wise people, reflecting within a particular tradition, that people should not be forced, without good reason, to emigrate or relocate. In the nineteenth century, many Europeans chose to emigrate in the hope of a better life. The travails on their journey to the United States were greater than the disruption caused to a modern family by being forced to move from one section of the country to another. Was the system which put pressure on them to leave their homeland unjust? Not necessarily. At that time not much was understood about the functioning of economic systems. In a nineteenth-century European country, private corporations and the government may have been concerned that economic conditions were forcing many people to emigrate. But, in all likelihood and given the state of economic theory at that time, they were unaware of any policies they could follow which would improve conditions in their land. Governments in modern, developed countries, on the other hand, have many instruments that can stimulate economic activity, either regionally or nationally. A change in understanding as well as a change in the ability of the government to influence the functioning of the economy has occurred. Furthermore, transportation and communication costs have been reduced so that the most significant change is the ease with which forced dislocations can be prevented. Modern corporations still have to move employees to different plants, but they can rely on incentives to induce people to move from one region to another. In view of such changes, it may be that future economies would be unjust if people were forced to move their residence merely to stay above the poverty level.[33]

A possible objection to the social principles of justice is that their very plurality inhibits their application. Someone can plausibly contend that, if there were only two principles of justice, such as the principles of subsidiarity and efficiency, they could be applied in a straightforward manner. But having four personal principles and six social principles of justice, with several qualifications, makes the application of the principles arbitrary, according to some people. Many ethical theorists would prefer an ordered hierarchy of principles, because, from the vantage point of ease of application, a lexicographic ordering is more straightforward. A lexicographic ordering specifies the sequence in which each principle is to be applied; if the first principle is insufficient to determine what is just, the second principle is employed, and so on until a principle on the list is reached which determines whether the situation is just.

Although a lexicographic ordering of the principles of justice would make application of the principles easier and less contentious, it is unfortunately not possible. The reason is that the foundation for the principles of justice is a commitment to the essential human good. No fundamental value receives absolute priority over the other values, nor does any group of people in society have an absolute priority over other groups in the pursuit of the fundamental values. Knowledge, for example, makes claims on people, as does the basic good of life. In some circumstances life has a priority and in others knowledge.

The basic requirement of justice is that society be ordered so that individuals flourish in their pursuit of the fundamental values. Individuals have different talents, interests, and drives, and a just society acknowledges those differences and tries to structure the economic system accordingly. Balancing the pursuit of separate values, on the one hand, and diverse talents, interests, and drives, on the other hand, means that we have to rely on experience and critical reflection for the application of the principles of justice to particular situations. The plurality of principles is a reflection of the many ways in which individuals acting alone and in concert pursue the essential goals of human existence. Provided we have interpreted the pursuit of the fundamental values in individual and institutional settings correctly, the principles of justice are equitable rules for coordinating the pursuit of the fundamental values. Indeed, it is possible to derive many more principles, maxims, and criteria for justice. The new rules or criteria, however, are not new ethical demands in addition to the requirement to seek the fundamental values; rather, they reflect the achievement of practical reasonableness in a particular set of circumstances.[34]

A society is just if the primary institutions of that society support the social principles of justice. The free-market system is the most important economic institution in modern society and, therefore, we explore whether its basic contours accord with the social principles of justice. In the next two chapters we evaluate the neoclassical paradigm of consumption and production.

CHAPTER 7

The Ethics of Maximizing Behavior

The free market is a system of exchange in which individuals interested in buying and selling various commodities agree to a price that is determined by supply and demand in an unconstrained manner. In some markets a manufacturer may initially set a price for the good he sells. This opening price, however, changes as the number of other suppliers in the marketplace and the strength of their demand are revealed. The difference between a market system and a free-market system is that in the market system prices or quantities may be controlled by economic agents, such as the government, whereas in the free-market system participants are unconstrained. A perfectly competitive market is a particular type of free market in which the participants are so numerous relative to the size of the market that no individual participant has power to determine the market price. In most modern economies, some components of a free-market system are joined with the institution of private property, which specifies that people are at liberty to acquire property to use, develop, and sell, with minimal interference by other institutions, including the government. One definition of capitalism is a system of free markets in which participants have the right to purchase, use, develop, and sell property.[1] When we speak of the free-market system we assume that, for the most part, people not only exchange goods without interference by dominant agents who have power to set the rules for interaction but also that people accumulate money and goods for their private use.

The free market is not an invention of the twentieth century, although free markets have become more developed and widespread in this century than in any previous century, including the nineteenth century, which experienced a burgeoning of the international free-market system. Furthermore, available evidence does not demonstrate that free markets evolve in the Darwinian sense: that once a free market in a particular commodity appears, it becomes the dominant form of organization as it asserts its superiority over other types of markets. Important markets that were once free markets have subsequently been controlled by different groups. The oil market, for example, was a free market prior to 1973, and then from 1973 until the present was controlled by OPEC, a cartel, in which a limited group of producers regulates the price by restricting the supply of a good. Also, markets for agricultural goods are rarely completely free since governments, both in the United States and abroad, traditionally play a role in setting the prices of farm goods. For certain commodities, free markets are prohibited by law. Drugs, nuclear weapons, and sophisticated military hardware cannot be bought and sold without government approval in many countries. In all modern countries, no person is allowed to sell his or her labor for a lifetime, i.e., there is no free market in slaves, although there was at one time.[2] In many instances, a free market is the norm until domestic producers are threatened by foreign producers. Whenever foreign producers start exporting commodities to the United States, for example, and drive domestic producers out of business, one can expect domestic producers to put pressure on lawmakers to enact protective tariffs, which transform what was formerly a "competitive free market" into simply a "market," since a dominant agent, namely the government, enters the market with power to determine the equilibrium price.

Free markets are not guaranteed by human nature since they do not "naturally" appear if the government does nothing. Rather, a free market is an institution, and like any institution, it requires cultivation if it is to thrive. As a structure for conducting business, the free market has rules, both explicit and implicit, to which participants and nonparticipants are expected to adhere. In order for it to function smoothly, certain political rights, such as the freedom of assembly and speech, are necessary. And like any other institution, it need not last forever. A society may decide that there are better ways to conduct business and downplay the significance of free markets, or a society may simply become careless and not realize what support is necessary to sustain them.

An attraction of the free-market system is that it appears to be more efficient than other systems. But efficiency is a difficult principle of justice to apply to an economy. On the one hand, economic theorists have focused much attention on this topic and provide useful theorems for our consideration. Applying these theoretical results to realistic situations, however, is all but impossible.

As we analyze the concept of efficiency let us set aside aspects of efficiency that are distinct from, though intimately related to, efficiency. In particular, let us only consider efficient production and consumption, without regard for the effect which efficient modes of production and consumption have on the distribution of income and wealth. With this focus, we can accept the economist's definition of efficiency, called *Pareto efficiency*, which looks only at production and exchange, not at the initial or final distribution of factors and goods. The Fundamental Theorem of Welfare Economics states that if certain conditions are fulfilled, the economy is efficient in the Pareto sense. Naturally, a careful study is required to determine whether conditions prevail so that the assumptions of the theorem are satisfied. Respecting this caveat, it is nonetheless reassuring to know that, if the conditions for the theorem can be verified, the free-market system is an efficient structure for the production and exchange of goods and services. The drawback to this result is that the framework for the analysis of efficiency is a static one, since the economic models assume that the economy does not evolve or develop over time. In addition, the Fundamental Theorem of Welfare Economics does not indicate how to measure the degree of efficiency in the economy when the economy does not adhere strictly to the assumptions of the theorem. Since the social principle of efficiency prescribes efficiency within reason, the theorem does not indicate how much intervention in the economy is required. In short, the question of efficiency is intricate and requires careful analysis in subsequent sections.

7.1 THE FUNDAMENTAL THEOREM OF WELFARE ECONOMICS

An attractive quality of an entire system of free markets is that it produces an efficient society. Economists have spent two centuries making more precise the claim of Adam Smith that, if people are given free rein to produce, buy, and sell what they wish, their actions, taken together as a whole, will produce an outcome beneficial to every individual in the economy. This result follows even if individuals undertake their activities without any concern for other members of the economy, i.e., they act out of narrow self-interest. "As if by an invisible hand" the activities of selfish individuals will redound to the benefit of all. In *The Wealth of Nations* Adam Smith gave cogent arguments for his claim, although he did not offer a mathematical proof. In the two succeeding centuries, economists have made more precise what structure or qualities an economy must have in order for the invisible hand to operate effectively. The results of this research, which in the past fifty years has been conducted with sophisticated mathematical techniques that are daunting even for people trained in economics, have been compressed into various theorems. Students of economics encounter one such theorem in a second-level course in microeconomic theory, and it is known as The Fundamental Theorem of Welfare Economics.

Singling out the Fundamental Theorem of Welfare Economics for special scrutiny may appear unwarranted, since neoclassical economics has produced many other theorems as well. While it is true that economists are often more interested in the results of the existence and stability of competitive equilibrium under a variety of types of competition, the theorems concerning these issues make use of the same assumptions that are necessary and sufficient to prove the Fundamental Theorem of Welfare Economics. Therefore, any critique of the assumptions required for the Fundamental Theorem is also an implicit appraisal of the neoclassical approach. In fact, the assumptions listed below are only those required to prove most neoclassical theorems concerning general equilibrium. In order to prove the Fundamental Theorem, it is also necessary to assume the existence of a social welfare function, a topic covered in section 7.2.2.[3]

The Fundamental Theorem states that an efficient economy is the outcome of a process of exchange if the economy possesses the following characteristics:

1. *Complete Set of Markets*: A complete system of competitive, unimpeded markets exists in which prices are set by supply and demand. The "completeness" of the markets also refers to the time at which goods are available. A complete set of markets, therefore, includes markets for goods produced in the future as well as in the past. That is, there must be markets for computers available today, computers available three years from today, and computers produced three years ago.[4]

2. *No Dominant Agents*: No economic agents operate in the economy who are large enough to influence or control prices. The economy must comprise perfectly competitive economic

agents, and there can be no government intervention, control of markets via cartels, or other dominant economic agents, such as monopolists.

3. *No Public Goods*: All goods are privately produced and consumed. There are no public "goods," like clean air and safety, or public "bads," like pollution or crime.

4. *No Externalities*: There are no externalities in production or consumption. That is, there are no effects (good or ill) that one agent has on another agent and that are not reflected in the prices of goods produced or consumed. If, for example, factory A produces computers, this assumption requires, among other things, that the activity at the factory does not produce more educated workers, who can then migrate to neighboring factory B, where they are hired at a higher wage because the training they received at factory A made them more productive. Similarly in consumption, the assumption requires that individual A's Mercedes causes no pollution, ill will, envy, or esteem in individual B.

5. *Utility and Profit Maximization*: All consumers act to maximize satisfaction and all firms maximize profits.

6. *Symmetric Knowledge*: Consumers have symmetric knowledge about goods available and their qualities, and producers have as much knowledge of their factors of production as the factors themselves. A factor of production is a good, such as land, labor, or physical capital (i.e., machines and factories), that is used to produce goods and services. If one agent, such as a potential patient, has more information than another, such as someone selling medical insurance, the price of the good exchanged (medical insurance) will not be an efficient one.[5]

7. *Homogeneity*: All goods and factors of production are homogeneous, which means that there are no lemons or defects in goods or factors of production. Labor is also homogeneous, and although there can be different levels of labor, such as skilled workers and unskilled laborers, all laborers in a given class are of the same quality. Similarly, capital machines are homogeneous.[6]

8. *All Contracts Are Fulfilled*: All economic agents fulfill their contracts, implied or explicit, to deliver goods, services, and

payments in a timely fashion. There are no bankruptcies, nor is there a need to fire workers for not doing an honest day's labor. Takeovers, unfriendly or friendly, are assumed away if they are motivated by a desire to install a more efficient management team than the existing one, because current management is assumed to act in the most efficient manner to maximize profits.[7]

9. *Independent Economic Activity*: No collusion among economic agents. Producers make their production decisions independently of each other. Similarly, consumers decide to purchase or sell goods based on their own preferences, not on group desires ascertained after collective consultation. Cartels, such as oil, coffee, and tin, are not permitted. A community that agrees not to sell homes to some ethnic group violates this condition as do employers who agree not to hire certain classes of individuals.[8]

10. *No DUPs*: No resources are expended on directly unproductive processes (DUPs). This means that there is no lobbying by economic groups for governmental policies that, though inefficient, produce benefits for particular groups.

11. *Normality Conditions*: Preferences and production sets must fulfill certain conditions. As we stated earlier, consumers must have consistent preferences. That is, if a consumer prefers bundle of goods A to bundle B, and also prefers bundle B to bundle C, then she must prefer bundle A to bundle C. Goods and services must also be perfectly divisible; for example, a consumer must be able to purchase 4.75 suits or 2.38 cars. For producers, the normality condition is constant returns to scale, which means that as a firm doubles its inputs (land, capital, and labor) output also doubles.[9]

Although the above assumptions are clearly not true for some economic situations, the question addressed in the following two chapters is whether they are a sufficiently close approximation to the reality of a modern economy to assert that the free-market system, as embedded in such economies, is efficient in the Pareto sense. Since we assume that part of the reality of a modern economy dedicated to justice is a commitment to the fundamental values, we also analyze whether the assumption is compatible with the pursuit of the basic goods.[10]

7.1.1 Efficiency as Defined by Economists

In common parlance efficiency refers to a person or economic agent who does not waste time and resources in getting things done. By extension, a system, such as a factory or a method of delivering goods to a market, is efficient if it does not waste resources. An economy is Pareto efficient if no rearrangement of production, exchange, or consumption patterns can make at least one person (or group) better off without making any person (or group) in the economy worse off.

The pedestrian concept of efficiency is occasionally at variance with the technical economic sense of Pareto efficiency. First, Pareto efficiency requires that consumers make an accurate evaluation of the usefulness of the good and not merely judge the quality or usefulness of the good by the price, as some consumers are inclined to do. Second, Pareto efficiency pays no attention to who actually receives the goods and services produced by an economy. Whether income is distributed equally or to a few fortunate individuals does not affect the Pareto efficiency of a society. A society with ten billionaires and millions of poor people may be judged efficient when the Pareto criterion is employed. We highlight the differences by using an example which focuses on a consumer's penchant to judge efficiency by price.

Consider the case of an airline that offers outstanding service but charges a high price for the service. Suppose ABC Airlines has a failsafe system which guarantees that all of its flights arrive on time (if not, the price of the ticket will be refunded) and hands people their luggage (not someone else's) as soon as they arrive at the exit of the terminal. Without further information about the airline, most people would be impressed with ABC's operation and would say that ABC Airlines is an efficient operation. But most people would also assume that ABC Airlines is charging the same price as other airlines. If ABC is charging $200 for a flight that costs $100 on another airline, people would be less likely to compliment ABC on its efficient operation.

Suppose ABC is aware that people think it is squandering its resources, and, in order to counter this erroneous impression, ABC decides to advertise in newspapers to convince people that it has the most efficient system. The advertisements present statistical evidence demonstrating that ABC pays its employees the same as all other airlines, has the same safety features, is not connected with organized crime, etc. Because it organizes its operations well and offers a service that people desire and are willing to pay for, ABC feels it is more efficient and, therefore, justified to the profits it makes. Note that ABC does not hire more employees, nor does it pay its employees more. Rather it simply has a better system of organizing its workers, and because the system is better, its profits are higher than those of other airlines.

An economist would say that ABC is indeed more efficient and legitimately earns higher profits.[11] Some consumers, on the other hand, would be reluctant to say the airline is efficient, because the issue for these consumers is whether the airline offers better service at the same price. These consumers are not interested in paying management or the stockholders or even the workers an extra $100 for their brilliant system or for the improved service. An economist, however, notes that ABC Airlines is using the same resources as the other airlines and is getting more done. She concludes that the other airlines must be wasting resources, and, therefore, ABC is efficient. ABC relies, of course, on consumer interest in their service; it can only continue to charge $200 if a sufficient number of consumers are willing to pay the higher price for premium service. Economists view the excess profits of ABC as deserved because of their greater efficiency; for an economist, excess profits never indicate greed, either of management or of stockholders. Even if the stockholders of ABC are becoming wealthy at the expense of consumers, ABC is acting efficiently in the eyes of economists. For economists, wealth is a separate issue from efficiency: efficiency is concerned solely with the use of resources, not with the ultimate ownership of goods produced.

The Fundamental Theorem of Welfare Economics uses the economist's notion of efficiency, not the pedestrian concept used by most people. The narrow, economic concept of efficiency, which concentrates on the waste of resources and not the income or wealth of various people in the economy, is known as Pareto efficiency. There is nothing unethical about the concept, since it is just a tool for analysis. One must simply be aware that it excludes consideration of the distribution of goods. Were the economist to use the man-in-the-street's concept of efficiency, one could not prove the Fundamental Theorem of Welfare Economics, since a requirement is that one set aside the issue of the distribution of resources. Because economists do not feel competent to discuss just or fair allocations of resources, and they admit that at the current time their mathematical models cannot capture many of the issues involved in the analysis of just institutions, they excise an aspect of justice, namely, what constitutes a just distribution of resources, in order to answer the question of efficiency. Economists think that philosophers, ethicians, and politicians should decide which distributions of income and wealth are fair.

Even when the concept of efficiency excludes questions of fairness and is narrowed to a consideration of waste, Pareto efficiency has a shortcoming: it assumes that whatever is purchased by consumers will be used effectively. At the turn of the last century, Veblen (1899) pointed out that people frequently purchase certain types of goods, not to use them but to waste them. In many societies, conspicuous waste, according to Veblen, is a sign of both good taste and high class. The fundamental values approach, in contrast, argues that conspicuous waste is unethical, no matter what the personal preferences of the person inclined to purchase the goods, because goods are made from scarce resources and they are to be used to achieve fundamental human goals, not to impress other people.

Given all its shortcomings, Pareto efficiency is nonetheless a useful tool, since it enables a judgment as to whether the allocative mechanism of distributing resources to various industries and firms within an industry is efficient. A Pareto efficient economy does not, for example, produce too few pairs of jeans or too many tons of steel, given the demands of consumers in the economy. Conceptually, Pareto efficiency applies to all areas and units of the economy, even within the individual firm. In a free-market economy, however, one need not analyze the operations of each firm, because inefficiency within the firm is weeded out by competition among firms and incompetent firms are driven out of business. In reality, most businesses do not operate at a peak level of efficiency; at least some workers and some managers do not work up to their potential or even at the intensity expected of an ordinary worker or manager. Some workers are lazy, some are sloppy, and some would work more purposefully if management created a more conducive working environment. This individual type of organizational slack or inefficiency influences overall Pareto efficiency within an economy.[12]

7.1.2 The Fundamental Theorem in a Graph

Economists give diagrammatical presentations of theorems not just because diagrams highlight the essential elements of the theorem but also because a picture suggests ways to modify the assumptions and produce different results. We introduce a figure here which is fre-

quently used by economists to illustrate the concept of Pareto efficiency.

The Fundamental Theorem assumes that the number of goods
produced in the economy is large, but in order to illustrate the theorem
in a two-dimensional graph, only two goods can be chosen; we select
the generic goods of food and clothing. The curved line bulging outward in Figure 7.1 is called the production possibilities frontier and
represents the maximum amount of food and clothing that can be produced by the economy. Note that point A is a Pareto inefficient equilibrium point, which means that it is possible at this point to make some
people better off without making anyone else worse off. If one moves
the economy from point A in a northeasterly direction, the economy
produces more of both food and clothing. At point B, for example, one
can provide more food and clothing to every person in the economy
than was possible at point A. Any point along the bowed-out curve—
the production possibilities frontier—is efficient with respect to production, because the only way to increase production of one good is to

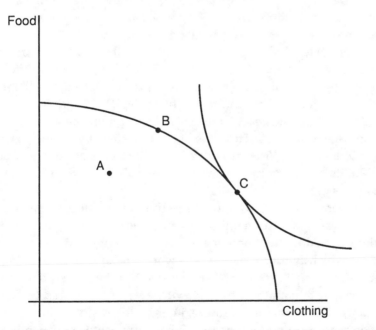

Figure 7–1. Provided all the assumptions of the Fundamental Theorem of Welfare Economics are fulfilled, the price mechanism brings the economy to an
equilibrium at point C, the only completely efficient point, in the Pareto sense,
on the diagram.

decrease production of the other good. That is, one moves along the frontier.

Although B is efficient with respect to production, it is inefficient with respect to consumption because consumers would prefer to have (and can afford) more clothing and less food. That is, they would prefer to move to point C. In an economy that fulfills the conditions of the Fundamental Theorem neither A nor B can be equilibrium points. At point B, for example, the price of clothing relative to food is too low. As a result, there is an excess demand for clothing and an excess supply of food. The excess demand for clothing pushes up the price of clothing, while the excess supply of food depresses the price of food. Factory owners then have an incentive to switch from food production to clothing production because initially they earn excess profits from producing more food. However, once supply adjusts completely to demand, factory owners earn only normal profits.

C, through which two curves pass, is the only completely Pareto efficient point on the diagram. The production possibilities frontier (the lower curve) identifies all points that are Pareto efficient with respect to production. The upper curve, bending away from the production possibilities frontier, is called a community indifference curve. For a certain level of satisfaction it depicts all the points that are Pareto efficient with respect to consumption. In fact, there are an infinite number of community indifference curves, most of which are to the northeast of the indifference curve we have depicted. Society would be better off if it could reach an even higher indifference curve than the one passing through C. However, it is constrained by technology, capital, and labor—all three of which combine to produce the production possibilities frontier. In Appendix A we analyze in greater detail why point C is the optimum point that can be achieved.

Before leaving the diagram, it is useful to point out how it can be used to visualize a dynamic economy, one that expands over time. Strictly speaking, the Fundamental Theorem applies only to an economy in which all future states of the world are known. Even if one cannot assign probabilities to all future states of the world, one must at least be able to name and describe whatever undiscovered technology might be discovered in the future, in order to extend the Fundamental Theorem to a growing economy. This requirement is sufficiently stringent to render impossible any reformulation of the Fundamental Theorem for an economy experiencing technological change over time. Nonetheless, evidence suggests that monopolistically competitive markets, i.e., markets in which firms have some freedom to set prices, work well in a dynamic framework. If a new and more efficient process of production is developed, producers in a free-market economy apply it quickly to their firms, because it enables them to make higher profits.

In terms of Figure 7.1, the production possibilities frontier shifts outward, to the upper right, in response to any of the following: an increase in the number of machines, an increase in the number of workers, or an improvement in technology. An approximate way of stating a dynamic version of the Fundamental Theorem in terms of the diagram is that an economy with competitive markets reaches a higher community indifference curve faster than an economy without competitive markets. In a constantly changing economy, competitive markets cause the production possibilities frontier to shift out faster than noncompetitive markets or markets controlled by the government. For technical reasons it is not possible to prove mathematically a Fundamental Theorem of Welfare Economics for a dynamic economy in which new products and new productive techniques are introduced over time. Nonetheless, there is good reason to believe that profit maximization and utility maximization work effectively in a dynamic setting and result in an efficient economy.[13]

7.2 ETHICAL IMPLICATIONS OF MAXIMIZING BEHAVIOR

Firms may or may not maximize profits, and consumers may or may not maximize their utility or satisfaction. Both these issues are factual. Alternatively, one can also ask whether firms ought to maximize profits and whether individuals ought to maximize utility. We look for the correct answer to the latter set of questions by applying the social principles of justice.

7.2.1 Profit Maximization

In a free-market economy a necessary condition for economic efficiency is that the firms in the economy be intent on maximizing profits. Although other plausible goals—such as total quality management or maximizing market share—exist for firms and although they may be pursued jointly with profit maximization, a reasonable approximation is that firms seek to maximize their profits, at least over the long run. Technically speaking, however, one cannot verify whether firms attempt to maximize profits in the neoclassical sense. First, even if via a questionnaire one ascertained that most firms state that they maximize profits, one would not know whether their assertion is true or whether they only intend to maximize profits. Second, the economist cannot determine a theoretical maximizing level of profits. The economist knows that if a firm is maximizing profits, marginal cost at that firm must be equal to marginal revenue. Thus if marginal cost is not equal to marginal revenue, the economist can be theoretically sure that the firm is not maximizing profits. But since an economist rarely has complete information about the marginal cost of a firm, in practice all the economist can do is observe whether a particular firm earns more profits than a competitor. Even when a firm earns more or less profits than its competitor, because there are many distinct explanations consistent with the neoclassical paradigm, one cannot conclude that the firm is not maximizing profits.[14]

Is profit maximization immoral? No, provided the firm adheres to the criteria for ethically responsible production. Because efficiency is a principle of justice, society should have a structure that promotes efficient production of goods and services. If a society relies on a competitive-market system to allocate its resources efficiently, if the firm fulfills the criteria for ethically responsible production, and if the fundamental institutions in society can be shown to be just, then members of society have the responsibility to abide by those rules that promote the efficiency of the system. Since one of the efficiency-enhancing rules is that firms seek to maximize profits, those firms, with workers and management in cooperation, have a moral responsibility to maximize profits.[15]

Moral approval of profit maximization can certainly be misunderstood. It is not a carte blanche to pursue profits without regard for other people, the environment, institutions in society, etc. The people within a firm are always constrained by the obligation to pursue the basic values, to abide by the personal principles of justice, and to comply with the criteria for ethically responsible production. For example, in many instances people working at major corporations become aware more quickly than government officials of damage done to the environment through harmful production processes or through the disposal of goods that are no longer serviceable to society. Such people have a serious obligation to warn society about present and future harm to the environment even if current legal statutes permit the economic activity threatening the environment.

Despite this and similar caveats concerning actions directly contrary to the fundamental values, each firm rightly focuses on profit maximization. In a complex society, each institution makes its own contribution to justice. The primary contributions of a firm to justice are to provide productive employment for people and to produce goods and services that can be used by individuals in their pursuit of the essential human goals. If goods are to be provided without wasting valuable resources, maximizing profits is one path to attain this goal.

Although this does not mean that firms have no other responsibilities other than to maximize profits, it does imply that in a competitive-market system profit maximization should be a central focus of every firm engaged in production for profit. One consequence of this result is that even though most large firms can afford to give money to charities or to the support of the arts, donations to charitable groups should never become a major focus of such firms.

Some people may make a much stronger assertion: that a firm should never give money to charitable causes. Instead, they claim, in order to have an efficient economy, the firm should maximize profits, distribute profits to shareholders, and let individual shareholders decide for themselves which charities should receive their donations. The correct response to this objection is to note that the corporation is not an impersonal entity that exists solely to maximize profits. As must be apparent, the assumptions of the Fundamental Theorem never hold exactly. For a variety of reasons, no economy is able via the free-market system to produce and allocate goods and services in such a way that even the essential needs of all economic agents are fulfilled. Some economic agents perceive more quickly than others those who are in need, and sometimes particular groups are in a better position than others to fulfill certain needs. A corporation may recognize these needs more quickly because of the type of business it is in, the clients it serves, or because of the people who work for the firm. For example, a firm that produces computers may be in close touch with changes in the world of education. It may perceive that if support were given to particular projects not currently being funded by the government or by other private donations, they would promote the common good. The firm should make contributions of this sort, provided it is not distracted from its essential function of producing and selling computers, and similarly, it should speak up if it notes that government funds are being wasted through the inefficient use of computers. Although a firm is not a person, because it functions as a unit in society, it has moral responsibilities.

Expenditures on lobbying are consistent with profit maximization for the individual firm, but lobbying is not productive for the entire economy if its main purpose is to persuade rather than inform. To the extent that lobbying conveys significant information to government officials, it is a useful service and should be encouraged. In many cases, however, firms or industries lobby against other firms or industries to gain an advantage for themselves. Ceteris paribus, lobbying cannot be justified when firms pressure government officials to introduce changes—whether efficient or inefficient—in the economy that are already known to the government but that bring greater benefits to particular firms.

Consider the usual situation, in which officials either are well informed or can become so without the assistance of lobbyists. In this scenario lobbying is a directly unproductive process (DUP), since the sole function performed by lobbyists is persuasion. The wastefulness of lobbying activities for the entire economy is apparent when one realizes that firm A spends money to convince a legislator to perform some action which firm B, or some other economic group, condemns. In response firm B naturally hires a lobbyist to attempt to sway the vote of the legislator. Even if both firms expend their funds in a legal manner, they use them wastefully from society's point of view. Directly unproductive processes require time and effort but provide no useful benefits to society. A legislator is elected to make good decisions, while firms are incorporated to produce goods and services. Far better for society if legislators attend to their affairs and firms attend to their own business. The analysis is much more complex if many different groups other than firms importune legislators as a matter of course or if the lobbyists have information not available to legislators. The ideal is that all firms and groups refrain from directly unproductive pursuits.

Because profit maximization is an important building block for an efficient and just society, all economic agents within society should respect the rules by which the corporation functions. In particular, they should not prevent a firm from maximizing profits.

Unions control pension funds for their members, and because many pension funds have substantial investments in individual corporations, unions can use their position to influence the policies of firms. A union might wish a particular corporation to make decision A, which will directly or indirectly benefit union members. Corporate management, however, may be inclined to make decision B, which is more profitable than decision A. The union can threaten to sell the firm's stock unless the firm makes a decision favorable to the union. This would be unethical on the part of the union if decision B is the profit-maximizing decision as well as a morally acceptable one. If in order to be efficient a society relies on the institution of free markets and profit maximization, different agents and groups in the economy should support the institution. In particular, they should not use their economic power to seek their own ends without regard to the overall functioning of the system.

The ethical evaluation is different if decision B is considered by union members to be immoral. For example, rightly or wrongly, the union may be convinced that corporations should not be selling computers to South Africa or to some other country. Because, in the union's estimation, the action is considered immoral and because corporations can make profits elsewhere, the union commits no injustice by using the threat of selling off stock in offending corporations to influence the decisions of the corporations. This analysis assumes, of course, that the union's actions conform to the principle of impartiality, i.e., it is not selecting one issue or one corporation to the neglect of others.

7.2.2 Utility Maximization

Do consumers also have a moral mandate to maximize utility? The argument used above is that, since society relies on the free market to achieve an efficient allocation of resources and since profit maximization is an essential condition for a Pareto efficient economy, people in society have a responsibility to support profit maximization.[16] Utility maximization is also a necessary assumption to obtain the result that free markets produce a Pareto efficient economy. Do ethically sensitive people have an obligation to maximize utility in the self-interested way assumed in the Fundamental Theorem of Welfare Economics? Are they, perhaps, forbidden to concern themselves with the welfare of others? The general answer is no to both questions, primarily because the Fundamental Theorem makes assumptions about consumer preferences that are inconsistent with the pursuit of the fundamental values.[17]

First of all, some economists doubt whether consumer preferences are sufficiently ordered so that it is possible for consumers to maximize utility in the manner understood by economists. According to neoclassical theory, consumer preferences are assumed to fulfill certain regularity conditions, the most important of which is transitivity.[18]

As was noted earlier, if a person prefers bundle A of goods to bundle B of goods and also prefers bundle B to bundle C, then it should follow, ceteris paribus, that the person prefers bundle A to bundle C. The difficulty is that people in the real world are not usually in the same situation when they face a choice between bundles A and B, a second choice between B and C, and a third choice between A and C. Therefore, it is not surprising that empirical work shows that consumers often violate the condition of transitivity, an essential building block for the maximization of preferences.[19]

Consider the questions posed previously. Must ethically sensitive people maximize utility in the selfish way assumed in the Fundamental Theorem of Welfare Economics? Are they forbidden to concern themselves with the welfare of others? To both questions the proper response is no, for a number of reasons. First, efficiency in production can be achieved without efficiency in consumption. If consumers do not maximize utility in a selfish way but producers do maximize profits, the only waste from the neoclassical perspective is that consumers could have reached a higher state of community satisfaction. Failure to achieve the highest possible community satisfaction may entail some waste, and, especially in a society at or near subsistence level, a waste of this kind could be unreasonable. In a wealthy society like the United States, however, the waste involved is not significant, provided people have some flexibility in the types of goods they use to pursue the fundamental values.

Second, even in the case of a subsistence society, the "loss" is unreasonable only if the "loss" as measured by economists corresponds to an actual "loss" in society. If consumers maximize their utility in a selfish way, without regard for the well-being of others, it is true that self-interest–maximizing individuals reach a higher level of individual utility. If consumers, however, are concerned about the welfare of other individuals and these concerns are reflected in their utility functions, then it makes no sense for individual consumers to maximize their own utility without respect to the welfare of others. Economists assume that individuals are concerned only with their own self-interest both because the assumption is convenient mathematically and because it leads to the desired result that an economy consisting of such individuals is Pareto efficient. In a wide variety of situations, however, the assumption is not verified in the real world.[20]

Third, I noted earlier that, provided people adhere to the Criteria for Ethically Responsible Production, profit maximization does not violate the assumption that people are committed to the flourishing of all people in society. Fulfilling the Criteria for Ethically Responsible Production still yields many opportunities for conscientious firms to maximize profits. Assuming self-interested utility maximization, however, requires that consumers violate the principle of the common good on a regular basis. As long as economic agents are altruistic in the sense that they care about other people whose welfare they do not directly control, no simple tampering with the assumptions of the Fundamental Theorem can produce the result that the economy populated by altruists is Pareto efficient. In particular, one cannot preserve the results of the Fundamental Theorem by assuming that people only act as if they were self-interested but in fact are genuinely concerned about the welfare of others. Concern for others is revealed in the actions of individuals, which are modeled in the utility function. The utility function is supposed to contain all the ethical convictions of individual consumers. In particular, the personal principles of justice, including the strictures to pursue the common good and never to act directly contrary to a fundamental value, must be embedded in the utility function. However, as I show in Appendix B, any realistic attempt to include the personal principles of justice in the utility function means that the normality conditions for the utility function are not fulfilled. Thus, utility as conceived by neoclassical economists is incompatible with the natural law approach.[21]

Another objection to the neoclassical concept of utility (or preferences) is that, according to the neoclassical outlook, preferences between individuals can neither be compared nor criticized. Strictly speaking, a neoclassical economist cannot say, for example, that some poor person has bad dietary habits, because the neoclassical economist professes not to know anything about "good preferences" or "bad preferences." Despite such a squeamish attitude by the neoclassical economist, most societies exhibit maternal and paternal tendencies when they provide help to the poor. Such societies are simply unwilling to grant normative status to utility functions of the poor, the homeless, the handicapped, the elderly, the sick, the providers of public goods, and many others. Such groups of people would have to live in conditions judged to be unacceptable by society if provision were not made for them according to norms set by society.[22]

From a technical point of view, what is required in the neoclassical system to express this concern for the unfortunate is a social welfare function that adds together the individual welfare functions by giving greater weight to certain people, such as the poor, the disadvantaged, etc. A social welfare function of this type respects the preferences of all individuals but gives greater weight to the preferences of some individuals. (A social welfare function is the mathematical function that produces the community indifference curve depicted in Figure 7.1.) The difficulty is that the only way to create a social welfare function is by fiat. Economists have shown that it is impossible, except under very restrictive conditions, to create a one-to-one relationship between individual utility and the utility of the entire society. As incredible as this seems, neoclassical economists do not have any consistent way to sum up individual utilities and obtain community utility.

In a democratic society, it makes sense to rely upon the expressed opinions of the electorate to determine the social welfare function. But a well-known result in welfare economics is the Arrow Impossibility Theorem, which states that a social welfare function cannot be derived by democratic voting.[23] The only ways around this obstacle are to make the draconian assumptions either that every individual in society has the same utility function and is allotted the same amount of income, or that a dictator determines the preference structure for society. The first assumption is as patently unrealistic as the second is absurd and contrary to the principles of justice. Thus, the only consistent way out of the dilemma is to grant equal weight to each individual, though this solution is also arbitrary. This suggests that an important reason why economists make assumptions about consumers is expediency: The assumptions allow economists to derive mathematically plausible results.

Most people are concerned with the welfare of other people and are affected by the sight of the sick and homeless. But once people's utilities or satisfactions are influenced by other people's welfare, there is no guarantee that the price mechanism of a free-market economy will achieve a Pareto optimum. Consider again Figure 7.1. When people maximize with respect to their own consumption and without consideration of the welfare of others, the optimal point for society is point C, and the price mechanism moves the economy to this optimal point. Suppose now we consider the same economy with the same productive capacity, i.e., the same production possibilities frontier, but we *allow* people to be concerned with the welfare of other people. Two changes are thereby introduced. First, a new curve bending outward from the production possibilities frontier is generated.[24] If people are disturbed when poor people do not have enough to eat, it is plausible that for the new set of community indifference curves the tangency between the production possibilities frontier and the community indifference curve will occur closer to the point B, which we assume to be the Pareto optimal point for the new set of preferences. At this point more food and less clothing are produced and consumed than at point C. Second, there is no guarantee that market prices in the economy will be such as to move the economy to point B. Nonetheless, if the government is sensitive to the wishes of the populace, more food will be produced than at point C since the government will increase demand for food by either purchasing food itself and distributing it to the poor or by giving food stamps to the poor. In other words, production will move to the northwest along the production possibilities frontier. However, the actual point reached by the economy may be to the right or left of point B, the optimal point. In this case there could be some waste in consumption.

Economic models cannot estimate how much loss results from following the price mechanism when people are interested not only in optimizing utility from their own consumption but also in making sure that others are adequately cared for. In view of our ignorance concerning the effects of nonselfish or benevolent consumer behavior and in light of our ethical concerns to provide for the welfare of all, consumers are under no obligation to restrict their maximizing to the satisfaction which they achieve by consuming or purchasing goods for themselves.[25]

Although narrowly conceived utility maximization is not supported by the ethical principles, consumers are not supposed to waste resources. In this restricted sense they are still expected to maximize their utility. If a consumer purchases an item, she should anticipate that the item will be used, and the more expensive the item, the greater the use that should be expected from the good. Note that "use" means more than mere possession. If a person buys a fur coat that hangs in a closet for years without being worn, the person made a bad decision, but not necessarily an immoral one. The decision was morally bad if the person could have foreseen that she was not going to use the coat frequently. Similarly, a wealthy person who buys a yacht which is used only one day a year violates the ethical principle of efficiency within reason. If the person anticipated that use would be restricted to one or two days a year, the ethically correct action would have been either to rent a yacht from someone else for the one or two days it would be needed or purchase one's own yacht and rent it out to others when it is not being used by its owner. An unused yacht represents a waste of resources.

For most people, the daily affairs of life involve ordinary clothes, food, television, and housing, not minks and yachts. Even in these circumstances, however, people are expected to make reasonable calculations about how often they will be able to use the goods they purchase. According to a long Puritan tradition at variance with an emphasis on personal gratification but which antedates the founding of the American republic, people are expected to act virtuously in the sense that they restrain their desires and focus on central realities: family, friends, honesty, beauty, knowledge, etc. If people are encouraged to moderate their desire for tangible goods in order to focus on the acquisition of more important intangibles, although such exercises are theoretically compatible with utility maximization, their emphasis is on restraint rather than on maximization. Utility maximization assumes that desires are insatiable; virtuous restraint, on the other hand, urges people to delimit their desires, precisely because, if unchecked, they cannot be sated.[26]

Even neoclassical economists acknowledge that some economic phenomena are incompatible with narrow self-interest. When people on a business trip leave tips in restaurants even though they never expect to return to the restaurant again, they are acting generously but not in their own self-interest. People vote in elections even though each person realizes that his single vote makes no appreciable difference on the outcome. At the beginning of his book *Passions Within Reason*, Robert H. Frank lists many other actions performed by individuals which do not fit the neoclassical assumption of self-interest:

> [Many people] give anonymously to public television stations and private charities. They donate bone marrow to strangers with leukemia. They endure great trouble and expense to see justice done, even when it will not undo the original injury. At great risk to themselves, they pull people from burning buildings and jump into icy rivers to rescue people who are about to drown. Soldiers throw their bodies atop live grenades to save their comrades. Seen through the lens of modern self-interest theory, such behavior is the human equivalent of planets traveling in square orbits. (Frank, 1988, p. ix)

Some economists dismiss these phenomena as being insignificant, relative to the vast number of situations in which people act out of a motive of self-interest, while other economists try to show that many of the economic actions serve to promote the interest of the person performing the action.

Frank considers the neoclassical paradigm inadequate to handle such phenomena and develops instead an alternative model, called the commitment model, in which people signal their commitment to perform an action without regard to its consequences. Frank shows that the ability to commit oneself and to communicate that commitment improves the long-run welfare not only of society but of the individual as well. He considers two general types of signals used to communicate commitment: physiological ones, which reveal emotional states, and moral signals, in which people indicate a commitment to a system of ethical principles or values. Since the fundamental values approach emphasizes the importance of commitment to basic human goods and the ethical principles, Frank's arguments suggest that such a commitment provides more material benefits to people committed to the fundamental values.

Frank's arguments neither support nor reject the claim that a commitment to the fundamental values is *more* beneficial to the individual or to society than a commitment to some other set of values. I contend that all people are called to pursue the fundamental values, whether or not they produce a society that is optimal according to some economic measure. Frank's result is nonetheless reassuring because it suggests that a commitment to fundamental values does not harm people in a material sense.

7.2.3 Cutthroat Competition

Business people, pundits, and people in the media often use bellicose, martial terms to describe the attitudes that rivals in the business world bear toward one another. One firm sets out to conquer another, a second firm is ready to devour a competitor, while a third is eager to wipe out the competition. Clichés abound: "a dog-eat-dog world," "cutthroat competition," "price wars," "white-collar jungle," etc. Are such images compatible with the pursuit of the fundamental values and with basic civility? The images, yes; the realities, no. Life would be dull indeed if language were not used to magnify and glorify ordinary events. A humdrum existence is often bearable as long as there are moments of glory, or at least moments of imagined glory.

Much of the language used to refer to competitive rivalry is generated by an understandable human desire for recognition and appreciation. Competitive language lets other people know that person A or firm A is exerting as much care and effort to produce goods as a person would expend if her very life were at stake. A person or firm may wish to communicate this to others because she is convinced that this effort has a beneficial effect on society. A second motivation is that a person may wish to set himself above others by asserting his personal willingness to undertake risk and to work hard. Other explanations are possible, but those that stress a desire to extol an agent's efforts or achievements correspond best to anecdotal evidence about exaggerated claims.

If the function of colorful, competitive language is indeed to assuage and promote rather than to describe with precision, one need not be apprehensive that people act exactly as they speak. The only danger with such imagery is that people may deceive themselves into thinking that the colorful language is an accurate description of the actual state of affairs. Deception is a common human problem, and it is no less likely in a free-market system than in some other system. Although self-deception hurts primarily the individual engaging in the deceit, it also impairs the efficiency of a firm or a municipal body when the false claims of the deceiver irritate fellow workers or cause other economic agents to react in a defensive manner.

Colorful language aside, does the reality of competition create an atmosphere in which people are more likely to act either contrary to the basic values or in a way that does not promote the flourishing of all people in their pursuit of the fundamental values? No, provided institutions in society (other than the firms and individuals who use the vivid language) remind people about their commitment to the essential human goods. In an alert society mindful of its commitment to the fundamental values, the firm's focus on profits helps to create a just society because the level of profits, in the absence of market imperfections, indicates how efficient the firm is. The dynamic force behind perfect competition is that each economic agent contrasts herself with a comparable economic agent and measures how productive she is relative to the other agent. Perfect competition allows the most direct comparisons among firms. But, even when competition is less than perfect, the market might be sufficiently contestable that producers may behave efficiently, because they face the threat that a competitor will enter the market, quote a lower price, and steal customers from the incumbents in the market.[27] In a contestable market each firm is cautious, apprehensive, and on edge because another firm may decide to enter. Whether the competition is actual or potential, competition does not violate the fundamental values. On the contrary, it increases the efficiency of the system because both competitive markets and contestable markets send signals to less-than-competitive firms to change their ways if they wish to remain in business.

In response to competitive pressure, economic agents may choose unfair methods to increase the productivity of the firm since acting unjustly may be an "easier" response than eliminating inefficiency in a just manner. For example, competition may induce a manager to squeeze more effort out of her workers, who are already doing their jobs, without granting them a corresponding increment in wages. The response that might have made more economic sense would be for the manager to make some hard decisions about quality control, lines of responsibility, inventory control, etc. The manager possibly shunned taking effective action in one of those areas because, all things considered, she found it easier in the short run to extract more work from the workers without granting them a corresponding wage increase. Although the manager acted unfairly (she violated implicit labor contracts), she was not forced or coerced into acting that way by the competitive system.

The danger in a free-market system is that agents become conditioned to behave in a consistently competitive, adversarial manner, without ever learning how and when to collaborate. For example, competition among economic agents at similar levels in the same firm is appropriate in certain areas, but managers should not be in competition with their own workers or with the stockholders. Unfortunately, people in the same firm often compete more fiercely with one another than with outside competitors. Plainly, the manager who takes short-term advantage of his workers will discover that the workers take long-term advantage of the firm by not working as hard and efficiently as they would if they thought they were being treated fairly. Firms have many avenues to attenuate the bitterness of competition both within the firm and between firms, and they can foster both competition and respect for the different groups in the firm as well as for other competitive units in society.

In a noncontestable market, the dominant producers have broad discretion to exercise their market power for their own advantage. In such situations, the pressure to maximize profits may induce people to take economic advantage of their superior position and deal unfairly with weaker members of the system. Thus, to a certain extent, competitive markets prevent exploitation.

A society that emphasizes the pursuit of profits and private satisfaction may find it difficult to give primacy to the pursuit of the fundamental values. Lest profit and utility maximization crowd out the pursuit of fundamental values, a just society needs institutions that either directly or indirectly support the fundamental values and the aspirations of weaker members of society to participate in these values.

Every nation must make a judgment concerning the ability of the populace to reconcile two goals which are in tension with one another. Promoting the free-market system, which entails competition and profit maximization, is at least partially opposed to the pursuit of the fundamental values, and there is no optimal method to resolve this tension.[28] One reasonable approach is to make sure that institutions such as schools, churches, the government, and other private bodies stress the importance of pursuing the fundamental values. Another approach is to promote the observations of wise women and men with insight into human behavior. Whatever the methods available, certain nations may find it impossible to sustain the tension between competition and a commitment to the fundamental values and opt, instead, for an alternative economic system that does not rely primarily on competition.

Some Third World nations do not have well-developed markets in many commodities, and for various reasons the governments in these nations are reluctant to introduce free markets. The explanation may be venality, i.e., that the leading classes would suffer comparatively if free markets were introduced. But other reasons are possible. The country may have an inadequate infrastructure, which makes the transmission of information difficult. Unless information about the volume of production and demand, the quality of goods, and the prices of goods is easily accessible, a market cannot function well. Alternatively, people may be so widely dispersed and transportation so slow that effective markets are impossible for many commodities, or the size of potential markets may be small. Finally, cultural and social factors may militate against establishing free markets. By allowing the profit motive free rein the authorities might dissolve centuries-old tribal or regional bondings.

In short, the country may not have the economic and social infrastructure that enables the self-interested profit motive to function without undercutting a general social commitment to the fundamental values. Given the situation in their country, leaders may therefore choose some form of socialist economy with managed markets. The fundamental values do not require a free-market system. The principles of justice only require that different agents work together to establish efficiently operating markets; for some countries, managed markets in a noncapitalist structure may conform better to the principles of justice.

A healthy society has ancillary institutions, in addition to the free-market system and the institution of private property, that promote the essential values and institutions of justice, especially in situations where the free-market system only weakly supports the pursuit of the basic goods. Among the variety of purposes which these ancillary institutions serve, offering incentives and generating attitudes that promote the common good are two services they ought to provide. In this way, ancillary institutions draw the person out of narrow self-interest and promote broader societal goals.

Chapter 8

Greed, Envy, and the Desire for Status

The desire to pursue fundamental values should be cultivated in society because it enhances the stature of a human being. But every person also experiences other desires, superficially less pure and ennobling, but nonetheless pervasive. At times, people act greedily; they envy the success of others; and they desire to occupy positions superior in prestige to those enjoyed by others. Evaluating these actions and desires in terms of the fundamental values concludes my analysis of how a natural law approach can be made partially consistent with the neoclassical paradigm.

8.1 GREED AND ENVY

In the eighteenth century, when the free-market system was first analyzed, some thinkers thought that trade would pit the passion for money against the passion for glory and honor. Since love of money was deemed to be less passionate and more well ordered than other passions prevailing at that time, people envisioned trade leading to a taming of the human spirit and to international peace, because countries would have to rely on one another. Similarly, it was expected that markets would break down feudal structures and replace them with "rational" structures conducive to the efficient functioning of markets. The pursuit of self-interest rather than fulfillment of one's duties was expected to produce shopkeepers who would be more solicitous of customers, since by pleasant service a shopkeeper could increase his own welfare.[1]

Despite such optimistic expectations at the outset, experience teaches that in addition to providing friendly service, a free-market system can also generate abrasive and abusive behavior, both in the marketplace and in the home. At a theoretical level, even if the neoclassical paradigm is only approximately correct, it appears to imply that economic agents are motivated by what many people consider to be base motives of greed and selfishness, which often produce misery when they appear in familiar settings. Producers and others who share in profits strive to maximize profits, while consumers, who by assumption never have sufficient goods for their desires, allocate their income in the way that achieves the highest utility for themselves. Part of the paradigm is that a consumer never has to look outside himself to know his preferences: What others desire and consume does not affect him. If the desires of others influenced him, they would constitute an externality (a good or bad effect of one agent on another for which the agent producing the effect neither receives nor pays compensation), which cannot be handled efficiently in the free-market system.

The Fundamental Theorem appears to condone a narrow concentration on profit maximization and self-interest, since, along with a host of other assumptions, they constitute sufficient conditions for an efficient economy. Envy is discouraged because envy means that the consumption patterns or honors of others become normative for an individual. Thus, the neoclassical approach appears to recommend greed because it is efficient, and discourage envy because is inefficient. But this is an instance of drawing ethical implications from a theory which by design eliminates all but one consideration of ethical issues. Recall that the Fundamental Theorem relies on the concept of Pareto efficiency, which avowedly lacks all ethical content other than efficiency itself.

In the popular press, capitalists are often accused of being greedy, and their greed is justified by the pragmatic reason that it generates benefits for others. Is it possible that "greed is good," as Ivan Boesky claimed prior to being caught trading illegally? Greed is the excessive desire for goods or for the accumulation of goods, where "goods" includes services as well as financial goods, such as money and stocks, and intangible goods, such as glory and power. What is excessive is to be avoided and cannot be good. As was apparent in the discussion of the fundamental values, physical goods are instruments; they are not ends in themselves. There can be no justification for the mere accumulation of goods without reference to their ultimate use. Since greed by definition focuses exclusively on goods and not on their use, greed is never good.

In our study of the Fundamental Theorem we pointed out that, if producers and entrepreneurs maximize profits and consumers maximize utility, their activities result in an efficient economy. Is it not good to maximize profits, and is not maximization a form of greed? Furthermore, if one adjusts the neoclassical paradigm to state that one should maximize participation in the fundamental values, maximization of this sort would appear to be harmless.

Greed is a personal disposition toward the accumulation of goods; the definition above states that it is the *excessive desire* for goods or the accumulation of goods. The mere desire to accumulate goods or the desire for goods is not greed; whether the desire is excessive depends on what one intends to do with the goods. A person who wants to accumulate a million dollars with the intent of leaving it to charity or funding some public work is not greedy, since there is no personal desire for goods or to accumulate the goods for one's own use; the desire is to make goods available to others. In the neoclassical paradigm each firm maximizes profits.[2] A person who maximizes the profits of his or her firm is making the most efficient use of resources by not wasting resources. She is adhering to one important ethical principle, the principle of efficiency. The desire to generate profits is not necessarily a manifestation of greed, although owners of the firm can reveal their greed by the manner in which they dispose of the profits or the conditions under which their employees work.

How does one determine the meaning of an "excessive desire" for goods or the accumulation of goods? A desire is rational or justified as long as the person seeking the goods or the accumulation of goods can put them to reasonable use, where what is reasonable is determined generally by the pursuit of the fundamental values and more particularly by standards within the community. At this point we do not attempt to derive standards of rationality in consumption but point to the possibility of two different communities, each with its own norm for consumption, reaching agreement about a common standard.

Consider an example involving two hypothetical societies. Suppose that in society 1, according to a prevalent common understanding, a person who wears an ordinary suit or dress only three or four times before discarding it does not make "reasonable use" of the item. Society 2, with a different structure and set of common understandings, considers the wearing of a suit or dress three or four times fully sufficient to qualify for reasonable use of the item. Since the meaning of clothing may be different in the two societies, it is possible that society 1 and society 2 both have meanings for "reasonable use" that are consistent with the pursuit of the fundamental values. However, it is also possible that society 2, perhaps unwittingly, fosters greed by promoting a common understanding that approves of infrequent use of clothing. One way in which civilization makes progress is through a meeting or clash of cultures. If society 2 feels challenged by the practices of society 1, society 2 may examine its own practices and reasons for those practices in comparison with the different practices and reasons offered by society 1. As MacIntyre points out (1988, pp. 389–403), one society or tradition can be more rational than another, and, given time and effort, one society or tradition can come to the realization that another society offers a better explanation for its practices. If this realization occurs, it is achieved through a dialectical process that includes action as well as reason. If society 2 feels strongly challenged by the practice of society 1, it must not only reflect on the reasons offered by society 1 for its practice or custom, but also, if society 2 finds the reasons intriguing or partially persuasive, it should *act* in the same way society 1 does. In practice, this means that a subgroup in society 2 starts imitating some of the practices of society 1. Only by acting in that way can society 2 have the experience of participating in the fundamental values of beauty and friendship that clothing makes possible.

Although greed is most directly related to the accumulation of goods by consumers, the pure desire to accumulate money, not goods, has been singled out for particular criticism by various religious traditions. But even the desire for greater profits or more money is not necessarily nor normally an indication of greed. As we have seen, maximizing profits does not imply that the profit maximizer deals with labor or management in a less than courteous and humane fashion. Civility, friendliness, and concern are compatible with efficiency and profit maximization, and even if systematic concern and respect for other people in a corporation or organization do not produce an organization which is more efficient in the Pareto sense, a commitment to the fundamental values mandates that a profit maximizer treat each person with respect and with a view to their own pursuit of the basic values.

Envy is a more mild form of greed that is often directed at a person rather than at goods. One may envy a person because of the qualities that she has, or one may envy a person because of the goods or other material advantages that she possesses. Envy of another person's qualities may imply admiration for the person herself as well as for her qualities, but one might just as well resent the other person precisely because she has desirable qualities. The alternative attitudes of admiration and resentfulness are also possible when envy is focused on the goods that another person possesses. Depending on whether the focus is on the fundamental values or mere possession, two definitions of envy are possible:

> **Type 1.** Envy is the desire to possess goods that other people have because the goods enable a person to realize the fundamental values in an attractive or novel manner.
>
> **Type 2.** Envy is the desire to possess what other people have solely because other people possess the goods, not because of the ways in which the goods can be used to pursue the fundamental values.

Type 1 envy is a natural means by which a person learns to pursue the fundamental values; he sees other people striving for the values through the use of goods, and the goods themselves become attractive because of what they can achieve. There is nothing reprehensible in type 1 envy because it is oriented toward the pursuit of the basic human goods. A person with type 2 envy, on the other hand, resents the ability of other people to pursue the fundamental values, but the resentment does not stimulate a similar desire in the envious person to pursue the same values. Type 2 envy, which we call selfish envy, is "bad" both because the envious person is annoyed at another person's ability to realize fundamental values and because the envious person focuses on the possession of goods, not on their use. It is the type that Veblen (1899) ridiculed so effectively at the turn of the century. Both type 1 and type 2 are pure forms of envy; in the real world one frequently encounters envy as a mixture of types 1 and 2. In general, society should try to discourage type 2 envy but encourage type 1 envy.[3]

Society has an interest in controlling the incidence of greed and selfish envy since these qualities distort the goals of a just society. Although greed and envy are personal attitudes and desires, their prominence in society and their frequency of occurrence are influenced by public acknowledgment by societal institutions of a commitment to the fundamental values.

Greed is an attitude antithetical to the pursuit of the basic goods because greedy and avaricious people seek to accumulate goods or the means to purchase goods without the intention of using the goods to realize fundamental values. Although greed itself is bad, it may have indirect benefits. As was pointed out above, it may promote a more productive society, for example, by providing a motive, albeit an inappropriate one, for a talented entrepreneur to use his abilities to improve production techniques or to launch a new firm. In this way the greedy entrepreneur puts to work people who otherwise would have been idle. But the indirect benefit of efficiency could also be generated by the motive to serve the common good, i.e., to promote the general welfare by enabling all people to pursue the fundamental values. Ceteris paribus, both the desire to serve the common good and greed are equally capable of motivating talented people to use their talents for the benefit of all in society.[4]

Greed and selfish envy are internal attitudes or desires of individuals. Theoretically, these desires can remain mere volitions, in which instance they would be of little concern to society. If enough people have greedy thoughts, however, the thoughts will eventually generate greedy actions which do have an impact on society. A society populated to a significant extent by greedy people acting on their thoughts and feelings would be inconsistent with the pursuit of the fundamental values. It would also be one in which the least well-off are neglected since, by definition, the greedy people, who may include some of the poor, are seeking only their own welfare. Since it would be difficult either for society or for an objective observer to specify greed or selfish envy as the motive for any particular action by an individual, there is no feasible way, consistent with the principle of freedom, for society to prevent people from acting out of motives of greed or selfish envy. Society, however, has instruments available that modulate the acceptability of personal greed and selfish envy.

Consider three societies with differing attitudes toward greed. Society A promotes the flourishing of all individuals as the goal of society and brands greed as a base motive, but one that is frequently encountered in society, while society B fosters the common understanding that greed is good and the flourishing of all individuals is of secondary importance. As long as the common understanding is sufficiently strong and effective, society A is more consistent with the principles of justice. Even though society A restricts the freedom of people by having a common understanding, which may be more or less binding, it is the correct common understanding, since it imposes a gentle restraint on individuals. A third society, society C, may have no common understandings with respect to greed or selfish envy and impose no indirect restraints on the actions or motives of individuals. Even if it could be demonstrated that society C were more efficient in a Pareto sense, society A would still be preferable because greed and selfish envy are incompatible with the flourishing of all individuals in society.

As indicated above, not all envy is bad. Since type 1 envy is a form of admiration and emulation—one person admires the ability of another person to pursue the fundamental values—let us refer to it as admiring envy. Although envy usually occurs in individuals in mixed form, i.e., admiring envy commingled with selfish envy, it is at least conceivable that an individual may have envious desires that esteem and revere the person to whom they are directed. Because admiring envy encourages people to find better ways to pursue the fundamental values, society should not repress such desires. However, for two practical reasons society may find it difficult to foster admiring envy without promoting selfish envy as well. First, because admiring envy and selfish envy usually come bundled together, it is difficult for society to use common understandings or institutions to foster admiring envy but discourage selfish envy. Second, every individual is called to realize the fundamental values in his own way. Other people may provide suggestions by their example, but no adult should become the slave of others' fashions or practices, even in the pursuit of the essential human goals.

Some imitation is necessary and desirable. Children mimic adults and learn how to pursue the fundamental values by observing and emulating role models. For their part, adults often rely on a religious or cultural tradition that suggests how goods are to be used in the pursuit of the fundamental values. But admiring envy should be mixed with imagination to discover a way to pursue the fundamental values that fits a person's abilities, experience, and aspirations. Heavily promoting admiring envy may diminish people's resolve to pursue the fundamental values in a way consistent with their own background and horizon. A society has to use great ingenuity to instill common understandings fostering admiring envy.

If one person has admiring envy, some other person is the recipient of this envy, and the recipient of admiring envy who is publicly acknowledged enjoys status. Status can be an influential factor in the way people make economic choices—for jobs or consumer goods—and it requires analysis, especially in a work that is willing to classify certain motives or emotions as more worthy of social approbation than others.

8.2 STATUS

Of most concern to economic agents in an economy is their local status, i.e., how they compare with people with whom they interact regularly. Concern about one's job position relative to one's co-workers, about one's consumption pattern relative to those of one's neighbors, about one's productivity relative to the productivity of co-workers—all these are issues of local status or what I call microstatus. Concern about one's position vis-à-vis most other people in the economy can also exert a significant influence on individual as well as corporate economic decisions. When concerns about status refer more generally either to one's position in the national economy or the global position of one nation compared with another nation, I denote this as macrostatus. Information at both the micro and macro level is necessarily garnered through statistics, sometimes mediated by anecdotes: Statistics as well as anecdotes can have a powerful effect on people's perception of status.

8.2.1 Macrostatus and Microstatus

Let us first analyze status at the microeconomic level. In the previous section on greed and envy I noted that admiring envy is good. In fact, admiring envy can be thought of as a type of good, similar to a real good but less tangible, that can be transferred from one person, the admirer, to another person, the one being admired. Since it is a good, admiring envy has a price, although not one directly observed in the marketplace and not one that is the same for all individuals. Some people are willing to pay more for admiring envy than others. The person who is the recipient of the good, the admired person, pays a price for the good while the person who hands over the good receives a payment in return.

This analysis may seem unrealistic because it appears in reverse, but there is abundant empirical evidence that the status people enjoy plays an important, quantifiable role in many different economic decisions and that they are willing to pay for it.[5] Consider Figure 8.1. Earnings are calibrated on the vertical axis, and the value of a worker's marginal product is measured on the horizontal axis. Actual numbers are given to simplify the explanation, but there is no significance to the particular numbers used in the diagram.

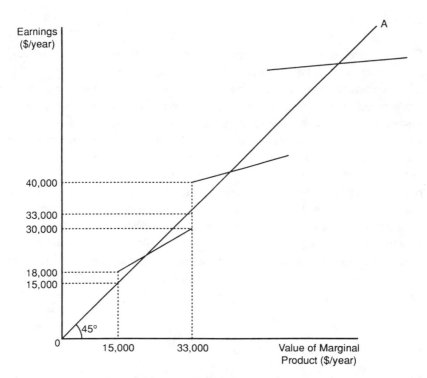

Figure 8–1. A person who has earnings below the 45-degree line accepts a salary less than what she could have earned if she had not been concerned about status.

In a strictly neoclassical world characterized by perfectly competitive markets, each worker earns the value of his or her marginal product. The value of the marginal product is the net contribution to the revenue of the firm made by the last worker hired by the firm. Since, according to neoclassical assumptions, all workers are homogeneous, all workers therefore put an equal amount of effort into the job and all workers performing a particular job have an equal amount of ability with respect to the requirements of that job. Neoclassical theory—using the assumptions of profit maximization, the homogeneity of labor, as well as other assumptions—deduces that each worker will be paid the value of the marginal product of the last worker hired. In other words, if the last worker hired in a firm of 100 employees produces goods that in the course of the year net $33,000 for the firm, $33,000 is the value of the marginal product of the worker and all 100 workers in the firm are paid a wage of $33,000. The word "net" emphasizes that all expenses of the firm are covered, including an ordinary profit for the owners of the firm.[6] In terms of the diagram, this means that the relationship between earnings and the value of the marginal product should be a straight line with a 45-degree angle and starting at the origin, i.e., the ray OA.

Neoclassical theory does not consider status to be a good. On the contrary, it assumes that people are interested only in the absolute amount of profits or the absolute satisfaction they receive from possessing certain goods. But if status is a good, then people are concerned not only with how well they do absolutely but also relatively, that is, compared to other firms or to other people in society. Would a person ever accept a job that pays something less than her marginal product? Yes, if status is important to the person. In the diagram, the three lines that cross the ray OA indicate that some people working at the same firm receive less than the value of their marginal product while other workers at the same firm receive more than the value of their marginal product.

Suppose each line refers to a different type of job. The line closest to the origin pays the least while the job associated with the short line closest to point A pays the most on average. Consider the lowest-paying job, which we imagine to be that of an entry-level cleaner in an office building. In the diagram, the job of cleaner is depicted by the short line closest to the origin. The diagram indicates that the most productive cleaner does $33,000 worth of work per year. She dusts faster, vacuums more thoroughly, polishes more assiduously, etc. If she were only concerned about her absolute well-being, she would want to be paid $33,000, which is what she could earn if she chose a job or a firm which paid her strictly according to the value of her marginal product. (This corresponds to the point on the 45-degree line; her marginal product on the horizontal axis is $33,000, and her earnings on the vertical axis are $33,000.) In fact, because she is concerned with status, she has earnings of $30,000, as indicated by the number on the vertical axis. In effect, she pays $3,000 for the status she enjoys in her cleaning group.

How does she attain status? In her cleaning group she is acknowledged to be the best and most efficient cleaner, and other cleaners look up to her and admire her. The admiration lavished on her is something she finds attractive, so appealing that she forgoes cleaning with some other firm that has a policy of putting all efficient cleaners together. In that environment she would be an ordinary-sized fish in a large pond, but an ordinary-sized fish who earns $33,000, instead of $30,000 at her present job. In her current job, because she is in a pond with fish who are smaller than she is, she is the largest fish and enjoys whatever status accrues to the largest fish.

Note that there is also a least efficient cleaner in her group. The least efficient cleaner performs services worth $15,000. However, according to the graph the worker is actually paid $18,000. The bonus of $3,000 can be considered compensation for working in an environment in which everyone realizes that he is the least productive worker. The inefficient worker could choose to work in a cohort in which everyone is as productive as he is; if he does this, he is paid the value of his marginal product, which is $15,000. By associating with more talented or more dedicated workers, however, the least effective worker increases his earnings by $3,000.

The most efficient worker in the cleaning group also has the option to switch jobs. We pointed out earlier that she could work at a firm that hires only homogeneous workers, i.e., workers who produce the same marginal product, and be paid $33,000, the value of her marginal product. She could also work at the firm indicated by the short line crossing OA in the middle of the graph. Let us assume that this firm steams or foams carpets in large buildings; this may be more technical work, at which she is less experienced and/or adept. In that setting, she is among the least productive in the firm. According to the graph she would nonetheless be paid $40,000, because she would be willing to work side by side with much more productive workers. A decision to remain an entry-level cleaner and earn $30,000 per year means that she enjoys her status at that firm by virtue of her leadership position. As an extraordinary cleaner at a low-level job, she sets the tone, and other workers appreciate the fact that this responsibility falls upon her.

Job selection is only one way in which status enters the economy. The choice of a home, the selection of a community in which a home is to be located, the decision to purchase high-visibility goods rather than other more useful but less noteworthy goods, the choice of insurance coverage, the type of protective devices used on the job, the number of late hours spent on the job, the choice of a name brand (or firm) over a good (or firm) of equal quality without name recognition—all these are instances in which status plays a role.

The desire for status can be powerful and can extend beyond the topography of a person's immediate relationships. Consumers worry not just about their position relative to co-workers, neighbors, colleagues, and friends but also about their overall position in the economy. The larger the number of people in an economy who earn more than person A, the less well-off person A feels, even though, compared to what he was earning only two years ago, person A might be prosperous. The reason is that most people give meaning to the word "prosperous" by comparing their own positions with those of other people in the same economy or other economies. An "objective" observer might declare that person A, who is an American living at some future date and making $50,000 per year, is prosperous. To justify her evaluation the objective observer might use other countries as the standard of comparison. However, if everyone else in America at that time is earning more than $50,000, person A does not enjoy much status within his own country.

When considering status at the macro level, we must be content with general comparisons among people. No one disputes that some people in the economy work harder, are more talented, and are more highly motivated than other workers. Corresponding to these differences, workers earn varying amounts of money during a year. At the macro level, however, economic agents do not have enough information about effort, talent, and motivation to judge whether an overall distribution of income is fair to most, or even some, people in the economy. Their judgment is more impressionistic and relates to groups of people. A common conclusion that many people reach is that, all things considered, some people make too much or too little in a particular economy. As long as this judgment is made at least partially on the basis of a group's ability to pursue the fundamental values, status is worthy of consideration in designing an economy and judging whether the economy conforms to the principles of justice.

Nations also compete with one another. Kennedy (1987) argues that historically the winner in these competitions is, ceteris paribus, not the larger country but the country that grows faster than the other countries with whom it is competing. Many countries are concerned about their world ranking. For these countries what counts is not how fast they are growing in comparison to how fast they have grown in the past but rather how fast they are growing compared to competing countries. Even at the level of nation-states, as long as the concern for status is motivated in part by the desire to pursue the fundamental values more deeply, status and the desire for status have a legitimate role to play in society.

8.2.2 The Economic and Ethical Significance of Status

If agents, even a minority of agents, do not maximize profits and utility, but seek instead to enhance their standing relative to other consumers or producers, this has important consequences on the amount of effort, the determination of efficiency, and the type of equilibrium reached in the economy. In an economy in which status plays a role, the effort expended by workers, managers, and entrepreneurs depends on how their relative standing, micro as well as macro, is affected by their efforts, not on the absolute amount of money they earn. Thus, the profit motive is modified. A second consequence is that a free-market system operating according to the usual assumptions of the Fundamental Theorem but with the modification that consumers and workers are concerned about status is not Pareto efficient. And third, as long as relative position is the *only* factor determining economic decisions for some agents, the economic system does not have a theoretical equilibrium. For a similar reason, actual economic decisions by agents can be significantly influenced by economic decisions made by a small leadership group in the economy.

Before discussing these individual consequences, we examine the question whether it makes sense to assume that people maximize their relative position, an assumption which is an amalgamation of two behavioral characteristics: the neoclassical emphasis on maximization and a concern for relative standing. Let us assume that all consumers agree that a variable z exists according to which status is measured. Economic agent i maximizes the variable z_i, which we assume is the ratio of person i's income to average income in society:

$z_i = y_i / y_{US}$,
   where y_i is the annual income for individual i and
   y_{US} is the average annual income for all U.S. workers

What the reference income (y_{US} in the equation) should be is problematic. For some people, it may be the average income of workers in similar employment; for others it may be the average income in their own town or community; still others will compare their income to the national average. Realistically, different people will decide differently; indeed, each individual may make different comparisons at different times. Economists, however, like to keep things simple. Let us assume that y_{US} is well defined and that everyone tries to maximize z_i

subject to their talents and the time they have available for work. If people's talents are the same and they have the same amount of time available for work, maximizing z_i results in everyone achieving the same value of z_i. This happens because people focus their efforts not on their leisure-time activities but on their performance relative to others.

The above discussion demonstrates that when individuals seek to maximize their relative position in society what they achieve is not great disparity in incomes but equality of income because everyone decides to work as long and as assiduously as anyone else in society. Thus, what makes individual sense does not make collective sense; if it were known that maximizing status led to equality of incomes, people would cease to try to maximize status. Therefore, it is more accurate and consistent to speak of agents' concern about status rather than about maximizing status.[7]

Recall the effects listed above that status has on the way in which the economy functions. The first effect, effort, is the behavioral one and is merely a restatement of the meaning of status. The second effect, efficiency, is on Pareto optimality. The reason why markets are no longer Pareto optimal when agents seek status in society is that agents are willing to pay money for status; consequently, standard utility is not maximized. In Figure 8.1 above, some workers were being paid salaries in excess of the value of their marginal product while others were being paid less. If all agents sought status to the same extent, Pareto efficiency would result, but then one would not observe a distribution of earnings as depicted in Figure 8.1. When we assume that people seek status, we implicitly assume that people are willing to pay different prices to obtain different degrees of status in society, even though they may have identical talents.

The third effect, indeterminacy, concerns the inability of the system to reach an equilibrium unless some influential group in society sets some absolute standard. If people are concerned only about relative position, a group, call it a pacer group that focuses on absolute income or utility, determines the outcome for other participants in the economy since they target their income without respect to the earnings of other people. Suppose, for example, a group of poor people in society is only concerned that they have enough to eat, some clothes, and a roof over their heads; that is, they are not decidedly attracted to middle-class life. Suppose, furthermore, that other groups in society are aware of the concerns of the poor and ratify the concerns in the sense that poor people's desire for adequate food, clothing, and shelter becomes a fixed standard.[8] Satisfaction then for the rest of society is determined by the degree to which their income exceeds that of the poor, which is the pacer group. In this example, if the pacer group has low expectations, these low expectations partially determine the effort made by other members of society. More generally, in a society where position is important, the groups that are uninterested in position and intent only on the absolute level of consumption determine indirectly how much effort those people will expend who are interested in relative position.

Note that the pacer group can exist at any income level in society; it functions in the same way among the rich and middle class as it does among the poor. What distinguishes the pacer group is their concern for the absolute level of satisfaction. Their aspirations may indirectly cause pain to others in society. For example, a group of very wealthy people who have extremely high standards of comfort, beauty, and playfulness is a pacer group that can cause considerable consternation in a status-seeking society. Because groups with lower incomes measure their satisfaction in reference to the extremely wealthy pacer group, most groups when compared with the wealthy fall far short of their goals.

In a status-seeking society, redistributing wealth from the rich to the poor can make people more satisfied, even if the redistribution is not justified by the distribution principle presented in Chapter 6. Given an extremely wealthy pacer group, most people are made better off if the wealthy are made less wealthy or if their wealth is made less conspicuous.

Similar comments about firms seeking absolute levels of profits, and relative levels apply to status-seeking firms. The firm, for example, that tries not to maximize profits but only to improve quality and make reasonable profits becomes the reference group for other firms aspiring to make more profits than other firms.

As long as people are concerned with status or relative position, an important role is played by the group that seeks to achieve an absolute level of income, wealth, or profits. This group may be a particular group of consumers, a type of firm, the government, or more amorphous groups such as social critics, litterateurs, artists, philosophers, or religious leaders; in short, any person or group committed to an absolute standard. Although the group may be small in number, it has an effect proportionately greater than its size suggests if other groups in society gauge their well-being in relation to this group. Suppose that only one group of consumers, group A, takes the pacer group seriously by measuring its satisfaction either in terms of distance from the pacer group or even in terms of the ideals of the pacer group. Individuals in group A make economic decisions that each individual hopes will achieve the desired level of relative satisfaction. But once group A decides and achieves some level of satisfaction, another group, say group B, will start to measure its well-being by the proximity it achieves to group A. This process continues and feedback occurs as A adjusts its decisions to maintain its desired advantage over group B. In a stable process the feedback effects do not overwhelm or reverse the initial effects. Therefore, the pacer group, though small in number, indirectly determines the alignment of other groups in society.

Of course, there is no single pacer group in society. Many groups vie to set the tone for various aspects of economic and cultural life. Although the groups are small and often have adherents who are considered unusual, unorthodox, or even bizarre, much attention is devoted to them in the media. One reason for this attention is that they advocate things that capture the imagination of the populace or are out of the ordinary. Another reason is that pacer groups are attractive precisely because they are committed to some absolute goal rather than a relative one. A third reason is that society realizes, perhaps only vaguely, the ultimate effect that such pacer groups have on economic and social decisions in society, and they want to explore the various dimensions of their fixed target.

The desire for status can motivate people to work harder, but the inability to improve one's status, despite hard work, can also cause people to diminish their productive efforts. It is tempting to propose that the rules for the distribution of goods in society should be so arranged as to maximize the incentives for individuals to work harder at improving their status. But this would be wrong on two counts. First, efficiency, or productivity in this case, is only one principle of justice, as we have seen. Second, improving the status of everyone is an impossible goal, since status involves a comparison with other members of a society. Everyone may *seek* to improve his or her relative standing, and those who strive harder may indeed succeed. However, when everyone strives equally hard, no one can improve his or her relative standing. When some people are more determined than others to improve their status, some people are winners and some are losers because status is a zero-sum game. Ceteris paribus, if everyone has equal ability and everyone strives with the same intensity, whatever improvement in status particular individuals may experience is due to random factors. Neither society nor economists should propose goals that become unattainable once everyone pursues the goals.

The preceding analysis yields important insights for determining the structures of a just society.

1. Contrary to neoclassical assumptions, people are concerned about their relative standing (status) and not merely with maximization of profits or utility.
2. The concern for status is consistent with the pursuit of the fundamental values if it is motivated by admiring envy; it is inconsistent with the pursuit of the fundamental values when it is motivated by selfish envy.
3. For many people a concern for status is partially motivated by admiring envy and partially by selfish envy.
4. The ability to influence one's status in society by effort, training, and education determines the amount of effort expended as well as the training and education undertaken.
5. The role played by status is partially determined by societal attitudes to status; these attitudes are revealed through the institutions and customs of society.
6. For a society in which status is important, the behavior of pacer groups has a disproportionately large effect on other economic agents.

Economic and social institutions in a society committed to the fundamental values must treat status with caution. On the one hand, the legitimate significance of admiring envy as a motive for concern about status must be acknowledged. For this reason an economy should be arranged so that an improvement in a person's status is achievable through effort, education, and training. This is only possible, however, if society promotes an emphasis on the achievement of some absolute levels, since people are bound to be frustrated in the search for status if everyone seeks status by comparing themselves with others. In addition to promoting the pursuit of some absolute goals, society, via its institutional structures and common understandings, should not promote the wholesale desire for status, since much status-seeking is motivated by selfish envy. Rather, society should find ways to accommodate and even foster admiring status at the same time that it frowns upon selfish status. Item 6 underlines the importance of pacer groups and recommends that especially those pacer groups be given advantageous treatment that promote the ethical goals for a society committed to the fundamental values.

8.3 THE PRISONER'S DILEMMA AND STATUS

Many of the assumptions made in the Fundamental Theorem of Welfare Economics are invoked to ensure that economic agents act atomistically. Each agent is assumed to be so small and insignificant, relative to the entire economy, that no agent has a direct effect on any other agent. Although we may imagine people constantly looking over their shoulders at their competitors, in a perfectly competitive society no one actually competes with any other identifiable agent, since other agents are insignificant and imperceptible. In the real world, however, people do interact with one another. They note each other's decisions and sometimes coordinate their plans.[9] Game theorists have studied situations in which agents can be better off if either cooperation or at least the transferral of information were possible.

The most important goal of game theory is to derive optimal strategies, but this goal has proven elusive. The difficulties of formulating and executing the best strategy are clearly illustrated in a problem known as the Prisoner's Dilemma. The Dilemma was originally developed by game theorists to pose the issue of economic cooperation. It can, however, be applied to the neoclassical model and to the phenomenon of status, with admiring envy as a motive. I first present the standard Prisoner's Dilemma and then apply it to the neoclassical model and the issue of status. Finally, I assess what further adjustments to the neoclassical approach are warranted when status is viewed as a pervasive concern for workers and consumers.

8.3.1 The Traditional Prisoner's Dilemma

Suppose that two persons, A and B, have committed crime x together and have been apprehended by the police. The police have not turned up any incriminating evidence against A and B for crime x, although they do have good evidence that they committed some lesser crime. Naturally, the District Attorney (DA) wants to convict A and B of the more serious crime x. A and B are interrogated separately and are not allowed to communicate with each other. A and B both realize that the DA needs a confession from one or both of them if she, the DA, is to get a conviction. They also realize that the DA will offer an incentive to confess to each one separately.

Initially, the DA approaches both criminals and asks them to confess. If they do so, they each receive a sentence of ten years in jail. If they hold out, she then meets with each suspect separately. She offers, as an incentive to confess, to plea bargain for a sentence of one year if the suspect confesses to the crime and implicates his companion. But in this case, one person's confession is costly to the other, who receives a sentence of twelve years. (For simplicity, assume that both the DA and the judge are corrupt and the judge is willing to assign sentences dictated by the DA in return for a small emolument.) If neither confesses, they are each given a two-year sentence, since the DA does have evidence to convict them of a lesser crime. The situation is depicted in Figure 8.2.

Defendant A chooses a strategy by assuming that B has already fixed his strategy. A first assumes that B will not confess. If B does not confess, A's best strategy is to confess, since A will then have to spend only one year in prison. A then assumes that B does confess. Once again, A's best strategy is to confess since A will then only receive 10 years in jail instead of 12 years. B goes through similar reasoning and arrives at the same conclusion that it is better to confess. If the prisoners were allowed to converse and discuss their jointly optimal strategy, they certainly would agree not to confess. Collectively, the best strategy is not to confess. From the individual's point of view, however, it is rational to confess, since that results in less time spent in jail, given the decision made by the other perpetrator.

The Prisoner's Dilemma: Classical Case

		B's Actions	
		Confess	Not Confess
	Confess	A = 10 B = 10	A = 1 B = 12
A's Actions	Not Confess	A = 12 B = 1	A = 2 B = 2

Figure 8–2. The classical Prisoner's Dilemma: each prisoner, acting in his own self-interest, chooses that action which results in the lowest sentence, given the other person's decision.

Figure 8.2 contains particular numbers. Although the individual numbers are not important, the relationship of the numbers to one another is significant. For example, if 9 were used instead of 12, and 4 were put in place of 1 in the figure, the optimal personal as well as collective strategy for A and B would still be not to confess. On the other hand, if instead of 10 the number 0.5 were used, there would be no Prisoner's Dilemma, since both individually and collectively the optimal strategy would be to confess. Inserting 0.5 for 10 is not plausible, however, since it states that the DA gives the criminals a half year in jail if they both confess and one year in jail if only one prisoner confesses. Thus, although the numbers are somewhat arbitrary, they must be chosen to make sense in the particular situation being analyzed. The purpose of the Prisoner's Dilemma is to indicate that some situations result in strategies that are individually optimal or reasonable but collectively suboptimal and perhaps irrational, a point to be explored below.

The primary reason why the prisoner's situation is a dilemma is not that the prisoners are unable to exchange information about their bargaining position or their strategy, but that they cannot trust one another: Even if the prisoners could share information, each prisoner would have reason to doubt that his companion in crime would adhere to his stated strategy. The inability to trust that an acquaintance or even a friend will fulfill his promise is what prevents the criminals from pursuing the collectively optimal strategy. In an economic world in which many decisions are made jointly and implemented jointly, the Prisoner's Dilemma highlights the need for reliable, cooperative behavior.

Cooperation is not a skill one acquires in isolation from other people. As understood here, cooperation is work performed by one person with another person or on behalf of another person to achieve some common goal. The cooperation may be voluntary or contractual. Contractual cooperation, for example, is required by the labor contract or salary agreement under which one is employed, or in a cooperative venture between two firms. If one can rely on people to fulfill their pledges, contractual cooperation is similar to production and consumption in the neoclassical model. An added wrinkle appears when at least two people are required to produce a good since it introduces the possibility that one worker may shirk his responsibility. In a situation where both workers are essential to the production process, the marginal product of labor cannot be defined for each worker, although it can be defined and calculated for the group of (possibly only two) workers. For compensation, the group of workers may be given the value of their marginal product, but since there is no way to determine which member of the group contributes more, inasmuch as all the services are essential to produce the single product, there is an indeterminacy concerning how much individual members of the group are to be paid. Paying a higher salary elicits greater cooperation among group members, if the group can decide how to allocate the increased salary among its members in a fair manner. The difficulty suggested by the Prisoner's Dilemma is that an inability to rely on people to fulfill their contracts prevents individual workers from following the collectively optimal strategy. Instead of "confess" or "not confess" the choice in the workplace is "shirk" or "work hard." Especially in a large organization, shirking is attractive since the shirker is not likely to be caught. However, although shirking may be individually rational, it is not optimal for the group.

The incentive problems discussed here are those encountered in what economists call principal-agent analysis, which addresses the question of how a manager induces a worker, whose productivity on the job cannot be observed directly, to work in an efficient way. Neoclassical economists have answers only for the most simple cases in principal-agent analysis.[10]

Consider a parallel to the Prisoner's Dilemma involving a decision whether to work hard or to shirk on the job at a large firm. In Figure 8.3 an individual worker has a clear incentive to shirk if she only

The Prisoner's Dilemma Applied to Shirking in the Short Run

		B's Actions	
		Shirk	Work Hard
	Shirk	A = 200 B = 200	A = 220 B = 180
A's Actions			
	Work Hard	A = 180 B = 220	A = 200 B = 200

Figure 8–3. If a worker derives psychic benefits from shirking and loses satisfaction when she works hard but another worker shirks, the equilibrium outcome is for both workers to shirk.

considers the short run. The assumption is that in the short run the worker suffers no monetary loss from shirking and that shirking causes some satisfaction to the shirker and dissatisfaction to the person working hard. Figure 8.3 measures the satisfaction that workers receive under the two different regimes of shirking and working hard. (Note that Figure 8.3 measures benefits to economic agents while Figure 8.2 considered losses.) If B shirks, it is in A's interest to shirk, because she gets 200 units of satisfaction for shirking and only 180 for working hard. When B works hard, A also has an incentive to shirk. A realistic example of this situation is someone working in a large firm with a strong union. It is unlikely that the lazy worker will be detected or, if noticed, that she will be disciplined.

In the long-run, the assumption that workers suffer no monetary loss from shirking is untenable. Eventually, as the number of shirkers increases, overall productivity will decline and the amount of money available to pay workers will fall as well, a situation depicted in Figure 8.4. In this case, monetary incentives have been restored, but there is no equilibrium. If one worker shirks, the other will as well because the alternative of working hard yields only 80 units of satisfaction (combined psychic and financial) in the long run. Similarly, if one employee works hard, the other will also be diligent, since both will receive 200 units of benefits. The difficulty is that there is no clear equilibrium. That is, whether the employee works hard or not depends on what the other employee does. Both shirking and working hard are potential

The Prisoner's Dilemma Applied to Shirking in the Long Run

		B's Actions	
		Shirk	Work Hard
	Shirk	A = 100 B = 100	A = 120 B = 80
A's Actions			
	Work Hard	A = 80 B = 120	A = 200 B = 200

Figure 8–4. In the long run there is no equilibrium according to the figures given above. If one person shirks, the other will shirk as well, and if one works hard, the other will have an incentive to work hard.

patterns. This depicts an unstable society of workers in the long run. These results raise an important question: Does the significance of cooperation in the productive sector require incentives beyond individual or group financial reward?

Voluntary cooperation occurs when the work performed is not specified as required in any contract. In this case the work is done for the benefit of the group, even though the persons engaging in cooperative work may receive no tangible benefit, other than knowing that they have improved the performance of the group and have received gratitude from their fellow workers who perceive the contributions made by individual workers. The most unambiguous type of voluntary cooperation is volunteer work performed without remuneration by members of a community to benefit other members of the community. For volunteer work there is no financial remuneration, although the community may esteem and honor the volunteer highly. Voluntary cooperation also occurs in the workplace. Individual efforts, unrewarded by promotions or by an increase in salary, to increase group productivity by assisting others in their tasks are examples of voluntary cooperation. Even in cases when a salary increment is awarded for cooperation, it falls under the category of voluntary cooperation if the person did not cooperate because he or she expected some tangible reward.

Most jobs require some minimum degree of cooperation, although firms do not usually attempt to quantify the amount demanded. When a firm does try to specify the degree of cooperation, the attempt can be called contractual cooperation; to be successful, the distribution of benefits under such an agreement has to be fair if workers are to continue to collaborate. Voluntary cooperation, by contrast, puts a premium on an unselfish contribution to the larger good of the enterprise or community.

Economic activity involving cooperation, although it can be treated in terms of the neoclassical paradigm, prevents the achievement of Pareto optimality by means of the price mechanism because the price is incapable of determining the correct reward for the cooperative worker. Although the price mechanism cannot handle this problem, it is my contention that a well-functioning economy should foster the necessary conditions to allow both types of cooperation to permeate society.

For the most part, neoclassical economists assume that cooperative behavior takes place within individual units but not between units. Thus, family members cooperate with one another, but not with other families; members of one firm work easily with each other to maximize profits, it is assumed, but not with members of another firm and also not with members of a family. Once the possibility of cooperation is introduced into economic behavior, the number of equilibrium solutions increases for any given set of circumstances. For this reason neoclassical economists have focused their efforts on understanding the solution set for games involving limited types of economic cooperation.[11]

8.3.2 The Dilemma Caused by Status and Envy

In the neoclassical model a prisoner's dilemma does not arise, because people maximize their own profits or their own utility without reference to other firms or people. In the real world, however, people keep on eye on decisions taken by people they know.

Suppose individuals A and B initially make independent decisions whether to work 40 hours a week or 80 hours a week, these being the only possible choices. Assume also that we can measure their utility in units that are calibrated identically for individuals A and B. For simplicity, we assume that the individuals have symmetric tastes, although the argument remains valid even if their tastes were dramatically different.

Figure 8.5 shows that both A and B are much happier working 40 hours a week. For each person, working 40 hours a week produces 200 units of satisfaction while working 80 hours a week produces only 100

Prisoner's Dilemma: Neoclassical Self-Interest

		B's Actions	
		40 hours per week	80 hours per week
A's Actions	40 hours per week	A = 200 B = 200	A = 200 B = 100
	80 hours per week	A = 100 B = 200	A = 100 B = 100

Figure 8–5. The Neoclassical Approach to Consumer Choice: In this example there is no dilemma because A's decision has no influence on B's decision and vice versa. Each chooses what is best and both arrive at the best possible outcome for them.

units. The opportunity to enjoy one's leisure counts more heavily than the advantage of having additional income from working overtime. Note in particular that A's satisfaction is independent of what B does; A gets 100 units of satisfaction by working 80 hours a week whether B works 40 hours or 80 hours. B's actions have no influence on the satisfaction which A derives from different strategies for work. The best decision for A and for B is to work 40 hours per week. As long as A's actions are independent of B's and vice versa, the Prisoner's Dilemma cannot occur.

A dilemma appears when A's actions influence B's satisfaction. It is certainly plausible that A's pattern of work and consumption may influence the satisfaction experienced by B. Suppose that, as before, A and B prefer to work 40 hours a week, since with this schedule they do not have to work too hard, have time for their families, and yet earn enough to care for their reasonable needs with some additional money to spare. However, if A works 80 hours a week and B works only 40 hours a week, B feels worse off because she can no longer care for the family in the same style A can afford. When A works 80 hours per week, A's satisfaction jumps from 200 to 800, while B's satisfaction falls from 200 to 50.

In Figure 8.6, A's satisfaction is partially determined by B's actions and vice versa. A and B would prefer to work only 40 hours a week, as long as the other person also works 40 hours a week. However, when one person works 80 hours a week and the other works

Prisoner's Dilemma: Status Counts

		B's Actions	
		40 hours per week	80 hours per week
A's Actions	40 hours per week	A = 200 B = 200	A = 50 B = 800
	80 hours per week	A = 800 B = 50	A = 100 B = 100

Figure 8–6. This example illustrates the role of status in consumer choice. A consumer evaluates her satisfaction in part by considering how well her competitor does. Only when she earns more than the other person does she feel better off.

only 40 hours, envy, presumably a mixture of admiring and selfish envy, becomes operative. The person who works 80 hours earns an income that not only allows a more luxurious lifestyle but, more important, one that is clearly superior to the one enjoyed by the person working 40 hours per week. Other things being equal, people prefer to have more goods rather than less goods; they are willing to work harder for additional goods only when the additional goods place the person in a more advantageous position relative to her rivals. If working 80 hours a week means that a person possesses only those goods that one's neighbor owns, the additional work is not worth it. This is indicated by a utility level of 100 when both people work 80 hours compared with 200 when both work 40 hours per week. On the other hand, the additional work is worth the extra effort if the work enables one person to live a better life, as measured by the possession of material goods, than the other person. Envy also causes a loss in satisfaction for the person who is working 40 hours a week. Although he or she can still afford the same array of goods consumed when both parties were working 40 hours a week, the person now experiences less satisfaction (50 units) because the other person, her rival, can afford a more affluent lifestyle.

When envy enters individual satisfaction in the way indicated by Figure 8.6, the Prisoner's Dilemma appears; there is pressure to make a suboptimal decision from a collective point of view, though rational from an individual perspective. From A's vantage point, it makes sense to work 80 hours per week when B works 40 hours; even if B works 80 hours, A gets more satisfaction by working 80 hours. A similar line of reasoning forces B to conclude that 80 hours per week is optimal for him. Both agents for the same reasons think that 80 hours is the best strategy. If A and B could agree to work only 40 hours per week, both would be more satisfied, but there is no reason to believe that A and B would agree to such an arrangement on their own. However, they might agree if some agency or institution were able to ensure that the "other guy" adhered to the terms of the agreement and if a large number of workers also agreed to work only 40 hours a week. When individuals face a Prisoner's Dilemma, an agency can improve welfare and/or market performance for the participants if the agency can induce a sufficient number of people to commit themselves to the collectively rational course of action. Which agency ought to intervene cannot be decided here, although the principle of subsidiarity indicates that the smaller the agency the better. For example, if a union could force people to comply with a 40-hour-per-week rule, this arrangement can be shown to be more just than government intervention because it accords better with the principle of subsidiarity.

One can easily concoct numbers that force economic agents into a Prisoner's Dilemma. To the extent that envy, whether selfish or admiring, plays a role in an economic agent's evaluation of benefits, the Prisoner's Dilemma is likely to arise. The example above involved two consumers and their selection of work hours per week. However, similar situations can arise when agents compare any aspect of their own economic position with that of others in order to determine how well-off they are.[12]

More general than the problem of the Prisoner's Dilemma is the role played by rankings in society. Whenever ranking is a significant factor, it is unlikely that a person is being paid the value of his or her marginal product and/or that a person is making Pareto optimal purchases. In neoclassical analysis, when each person makes utility-maximizing decisions, the ratio of the marginal utilities for any two goods is equal to the ratio of the prices of those goods. The condition that the wage equal the value of the marginal product and the condition that a person purchase goods so that the ratio of marginal utilities is equated to the price ratio of the goods are necessary requirements for a Pareto-optimal economy and both are particular expressions of the general rule that marginal benefits should equal marginal costs.

The Pareto optimal conditions are violated when ranking plays a role because one individual or group has a perceptible influence on another group. Perfect competition, as we have seen, implies that every economic agent is so small that he/she/it has no perceptible influence on the economy. Agents compete without any individual agent ever directly influencing another agent. The individual assumptions of the Fundamental Theorem are made to guarantee that economic agents are insulated from one another. Once agents have perceptible influences on other agents, different interventions in the economy, such as a prescribing the 40-hour-work week as the norm, are advisable, since they can make the economy more efficient than a laissez-faire approach.

Interpersonal or interfirm comparisons that elevate status to a significant consideration are made for one of three reasons: (1) envy, (2) a societal evaluation of different situations, or (3) some inherent economic advantage. A list of particular areas where problems of status can cause an inefficient allocation of resources, via the Prisoner's

Dilemma or because the usual marginal conditions for Pareto optimality are not fulfilled, suggests several areas in which a rational society should be reluctant to rely on the price mechanism alone.

Selfish envy arises in the context of consumption, especially of goods that signal to other consumers a person's economic standing or rank. As we have seen, it also emerges in a wage context: a person may choose a lower wage for the sake of increased status, working at a firm with a good reputation. Finally, conditions on the job are likely to be affected by envy. Safety features, current nonsalary benefits, deferred benefits (pensions and insurance), perquisites, job titles—all are areas where envy is likely to play a role.

The societal assignment of status affects jobs because society ranks some jobs, such as investment banker, higher than other jobs, such as street cleaning. Personalities also play a role. Stars, whether in entertainment, sports, or politics, are given status by society that is not always related to their economic productivity. Economic report cards, such as balance sheets, income statements, or percentage-of-market share, may influence why a person chooses one company rather than another. Finally, inherent factors make some people or firms better than others. One person or group is often identifiably more productive than another. A person may be a genius; another may have singular entrepreneurial ability; a third may have unusual ability to generate a spirit of cooperation.

In all the circumstances listed above, the unfettered price mechanism is incapable of achieving the conditions for Pareto optimality. Since a broad range of circumstances is covered, any society committed to efficiency as a value must contemplate some intervention. Intervention can be either direct or indirect. Direct intervention means that some agency directly influences the price of a good or service traded in a market. Indirect intervention occurs through common understandings and the behavior prescribed by various institutions in society.

Consider the case of a worker who shirks his responsibilities although his lack of effort cannot be directly observed by the manager. The economist recommends the direct approach: changing the person's compensation package so that he has less of an incentive to shirk. The economist is less inclined to rely on a labor contract stipulating that the person is supposed to work diligently during his hours on the job and more disposed to change the monetary incentives, which alone are operative, according to the economist. The ethical approach, on the other hand, proposes the indirect approach: Teach people that they have a moral obligation to abide by the terms of a contract and teach co-workers to apportion approbation according to how closely a person adheres to ethical standards held by society. The neoclassical economist likely considers the ethical approach nebulous and ineffective. But, in an interesting reversal of perspectives, the ethician considers the economic solution inefficient and impossible to implement. It is inefficient because it undermines the ancient Roman rule that one should keep one's promises, i.e., *pacta servanda sunt* (contracts should be adhered to). Unless this ethical rule exists and is used by society and unless violations are punished in some appropriate manner, the market system itself cannot survive in the long run.

The significance of the Prisoner's Dilemma is not, of course, restricted to situations in which status is involved.[13] Whenever a cooperative arrangement provides a better outcome than an equilibrium resulting from the individual pursuit of self-interest, the Prisoner's Dilemma is the appropriate paradigm. Earlier we referred to common understandings about how people ought to behave in society. From one vantage point, common understandings are rules that, provided most people adhere to them most of the time, generate a cooperative equilibrium that dominates the solution achieved when economic agents pursue their narrow self-interest but are incapable of cooperation. Because common understandings are often not regulated by law and rely instead on support from intermediate institutions in civil society, they are vulnerable to disintegration if free riders operate in sufficient numbers to move from the payoff that is socially optimal to selfish solutions that are socially inferior. The fact that a common understanding is in the process of unraveling does not prove that people are acting more selfishly than earlier. It may simply mean that the factual and cultural situation in which the common understanding arose and thrived has changed to such a degree that the payoff matrix no longer makes cooperation optimal in the manner envisaged by the common understanding.

CHAPTER 9

Conclusion

Economics and ethics are related in the practical world, both because people make ethical decisions about economic matters and because the structure of the economy determines in a significant way the potential decisions which individuals can make. Therefore, as I argued in the introductory chapter, a review of both disciplines is fitting, although for the reasons given there, such an analysis cannot possibly be bipartisan. Any examination of economics without ethical content is vacuous, and any ethical critique of general economics, without reference to a particular tradition, would yield little substance. Therefore, I selected two traditions—one ethical and one economic—and I explored what light each tradition sheds on the other. The economic school chosen was the neoclassical approach, because it is the mainstream; all other economic traditions are deviations from it or challenges to it.

The choice of the natural law tradition as the ethical system was based on its historical popularity in the United States and its congruence with different religious faiths. Jewish, Protestant, and Catholic thinkers have traditionally espoused the natural law approach, and this makes it appealing to a wide American audience. I am also convinced that the natural law approach is better able to respond to fundamental moral dilemmas, including traditional ethical conundrums as well as modern moral problems. At the least, the analysis which utilitarianism and proportionalism offer of happiness or satisfaction is sufficiently simplistic to warrant consideration of a viable alternative. A third reason for focusing on the natural law tradition is that it is instructive to explore what changes must be made in the neoclassical system to accommodate an ethical system which differs radically from utilitarianism, a tradition which appears ethically congruent with the neoclassical approach.

As is apparent from the issues addressed in chapters 3 and 4, the natural law tradition, as articulated in the fundamental values approach, is rich in the principles it proposes and its ability to address specific problems in a consistent manner. Although I chose fairly simple problems for analysis, it is obvious that the natural law approach has sufficient breadth to offer guidance in a wide variety of areas, personal as well as professional. Indeed, the strength of the natural law tradition is that the personal principles can be and have been applied to a variety of institutional settings (economics, medicine, law, politics, etc.).

My expectation is not that every reader has been convinced by the arguments I adduced for the natural law approach. Some may find the concepts alien or an uncomfortable fit; the behavioral prescriptions may be distinctly variant from their own practice, so much so that the system is unappealing. At the end of Chapter 4 I encouraged such individuals to take an approach frequently used by neoclassical economists: Simply assume people behave in a certain way. Transferred to the natural law approach, an equivalent assumption is that a society is committed to the fundamental values in the sense that a large proportion of the population tries to pursue the fundamental values most of the time. If such a society were to exist, how would people behave economically and ethically, and what adjustments would have to be made in the neoclassical paradigm? Of course, for the realism of my model it would not be necessary that every person in every situation pursue the fundamental values, although it is crucial for the realism of the assumption that most people generally seek to realize the fundamental values. Nonetheless, on the theoretical plane, I assume that all people pursue the fundamental values. By making this assumption, I remain on a parallel track with the neoclassical approach, which assumes that all people in every situation are concerned with their own self-interest.

What can be said to a person who genuinely seeks to order his life correctly but who is not convinced by the arguments I presented for the fundamental values? For such a person, the stratagem of *assuming* that people pursue the fundamental values is hardly satisfying. Furthermore, the person may be skeptical about alternatives to the natural law approach. He may have as many difficulties with utilitarian language when thinking about moral issues. What to do? First of all, it may be the case that I cannot convince the individual about the rectitude of the natural law approach because it simply does not fit the experience of some people, at least in these waning years of the twentieth century; utilitarianism may offer a sounder perspective. Although I do not agree with this evaluation, I realize that I can never convince a utilitarian simply by arguing about it.

I have emphasized throughout this analysis that the ethical principles derived here are not Kantian a prioris; they are not derived solely by the use of reason, whether practical or theoretical. Rather, they come from a tradition of inquiry and practice. Seeking the fundamental values in a community precedes reflection upon them. If a person is not persuaded by the fundamental values, one reason may be that he or she has not pursued them consequentially. Alternatively, the young person may seek the fundamental values ardently in her personal life but she has never belonged to a community which attempts to structure itself in such a way as to promote the attainment of the fundamental values by all people. The experience of ethical goodness in a variety of forms must precede an adequate grasp of the nature of those goods. To those who waver in their commitment to the fundamental values but are nonetheless attracted to them, I suggest a period of experimentation in which they try to be faithful to those values in their personal life. If through this process they are convinced that they are becoming more fully human (a realization that comes through the pursuit of practical reasonableness), I recommend that they take the further step of joining some community that as a group attempts to live these values.

9.1 INSTITUTIONS

The personal principles of justice address responsibilities of the individual to herself and to other people in society. Society, however, is richer than the sum of individuals currently living in it. It contains the thoughts and actions of people who have gone before us as well as the anticipated thoughts and actions of those who are yet to come. The accumulated thoughts and actions of deceased members of a society are embodied in common understandings and in the institutions which a society protects and nurtures. These entities are not incidental to the pursuit of the good life. If society has fostered the fundamental values over many years and devised effective ways of promoting them, conventions have arisen to which people are accustomed to adhere.

Persuading people to follow conventions is a difficult task for society, but the chore is much easier when tradition smooths the way. When institutions resolutely pursue the fundamental values, they embody the wisdom of the ages. As became apparent in chapters 7 and 8, people can either be assisted or distracted by others in their pursuit of the fundamental values, and institutions play an important role in modulating these effects. Because institutions take a long time to develop, they are valuable assets that deserve respect and cultivation. Even if the path they use to pursue the fundamental values is not the best possible one, people should not quickly switch to a new road, because decades are required before one convention or practice replaces another.

Traditions, or portions of them, can also inhibit the pursuit of the fundamental values or even promote actions directly contrary to them. In such instances, people should rightly attempt to establish a new convention, more in conformity with the fundamental values. Deciding whether part of a tradition conforms to or violates the fundamental values sometimes requires people with great insight and virtue.[1] Thus, any vital tradition will respect its sages who are committed to the pursuit of the fundamental values. Some people are more perceptive than others, and one important tradition is to listen to wise people even when they speak uncomfortable truths.

Good or tolerable institutions, however, should be protected, not only because they are fragile but also because they often are the result of long years of struggle. The free-market system is anything but "natural," as recent events in Eastern Europe demonstrate. Although most institutions involve arbitrary components that could have been arranged otherwise, this does not render them less important nor does it make adherence to their rules less binding. Institutions and common understandings permit greater expression and more effective pursuit of the fundamental values, at the same time that they constrain the freedom of individuals.

The complexity, centrality, and variability of institutions requires an extension of the personal principles of justice to the social principles of justice, i.e., principles formulated to apply to institutions rather than individuals. The principles of efficiency, subsidiarity, freedom, distribution, impartiality, and relatedness are general guides for all institutions in society. The social principles differ from the personal ones in that the personal principles apply in all circumstances whereas the social ones are supposed to characterize in a general way the structure of society. A particular institution may be designed to support certain principles of justice but not others. For example, law may be focused primarily on impartiality, freedom, and relatedness and not be concerned with one or more of the other principles. Indeed, an institution may play a crucial role in society even though it only supports one social principle of justice and undermines two or three others.[2] Because every society has a plurality of institutions and common understandings, it is not required that each institution individually support each principle of social justice.

Institutions change over time, but certain characteristics of effective institutions (and common understandings) remain constant, such as connectedness. Institutions generate bondings of various intensities among individuals; the stronger the bond, the greater the connectedness of the individuals. Because connectedness implies shared experience and knowledge, it offers the potential for cooperative pursuit of the fundamental values. Those who know certain individuals better than others are in an advantageous position to provide effective help, especially in situations where a person is threatened by some physical evil. The closest bonding occurs in families, although the manner and intensity of interaction within families continue to change, as they have for several centuries. Because bonds of friendship are satisfying in themselves and also allow effective pursuit of the fundamental values, the communities that create those bonds should enjoy a special status. To be sure, any community has a great variety of institutions or collectives that generate close personal bonds. But the most perduring community has been the family; even as it undergoes dramatic changes, it remains the primary locus for the realization of the fundamental values, and for this reason it should enjoy special status in any society. Although the status accorded to the family should be preeminently in its freedom to teach, transmit, and practice the fundamental values, possessing such freedom in a free-market society implies that the economic system should contribute in some way to the status of the family. One explanation why economic status so frequently occupies center stage in public debates is that people realize that in a society increasingly dominated by market transactions family economic status is pivotal for the realization of the fundamental values.

Since the requirements of justice are multiple, how does one decide whether a society is just? A society is just if the great majority of its members act fairly toward one another in most instances. In terms of the fundamental values, this implies that three conditions are fulfilled. First, the distribution of goods, including honors and positions of honor, should be such that all people are enabled to pursue the fundamental values. Second, those who violate the rules of interaction in society, which in one version of the natural law tradition are codified in the personal principles of justice, do not benefit as a result of their actions; offenders are punished in an appropriate manner. And third, society has effective mechanisms both to dissuade people from acting unfairly and to encourage people to promote the common good.

Society achieves goals by establishing institutions that assist individuals and groups.[3] Therefore, in order to decide whether the conditions of fairness are fulfilled, one must examine the primary institutions of a society. An institution is primary if it contributes substantially to satisfying one or more of the three conditions listed above and if it significantly determines the contours of other institutions. If we were to attempt to answer the question whether American society is just, which institutions would we have to examine? Certainly, the free-market system is a primary institution because it plays a pivotal role in the generation and distribution of goods to be used in the pursuit of the fundamental values. Although conceptually distinct, private property is so seamlessly joined to the free-market system that we think of them as a single but primary institution. The free-market system has never appeared without modulating institutions to counteract some of its less desirable outcomes. In particular, the United States and most industrialized nations have redistributive mechanisms—such as income taxes, sales taxes, and inheritance taxes—that modify the outcome of an unimpeded free-market system. Redistributive mechanisms collectively constitute a third primary institution.

Although the free-market system consists mainly of profit-making firms, the nonprofit sector encompasses many people within its fold. Nonprofit organizations are usually established to fulfill some social need and are sustained by contributions from individuals or corporations in the for-profit sector. A complete study of the economy would include nonprofit institutions, which are a species of modulating institutions, to determine whether the nonprofit sector is in some suitably defined sense efficient.[4]

A fourth institution that affects the production and distribution of goods and services is the political system, which among industrialized nations is some variant of the liberal democratic system. When markets break down and private intervention is not forthcoming, the government, which is an instrument of the liberal democratic system, intervenes to effect the distribution of goods.[5]

The liberal democratic system, of course, does more than merely intervene in markets. The system allows and promotes freedom of expression and, to a certain extent, advances the pursuit of the common good. The law and penal system are also primary institutions because they punish, persuade, and educate people. A just society requires formative institutions that instill a commitment to the common good and to the principles of personal justice. Which institution plays the primary function in fulfilling this role is questionable. In earlier times, the family would have been the undisputed institution of education and persuasion. However, because the connectedness in families is looser today, it may be that, despite their many difficulties, schools—elementary and secondary—play the dominant role in generating attitudes of respect for the fundamental values and for all individuals pursuing them.

If we agree that the family is still the primary institution that educates and trains children in the fundamental values, six primary institutions—the free-market system, private property, redistributive mechanisms, the liberal democratic system, law, and the family—must be examined in order to determine whether a society is just. Society is just if these primary institutions support the six social principles of justice.[6] Each of the institutions should be examined to determine which social principles of justice it supports and whether it undermines any of them. But the justice of society as a whole can only be determined by examining all the primary institutions. Nonetheless, it would be disturbing if a primary institution did not support any of the principles of justice. In this case, without rushing to the conclusion that society as a whole is unjust, leaders in society should restructure the particular institution so that it directly promoted at least one of the principles of social justice.[7]

9.2 THE NEOCLASSICAL SYSTEM

In chapters 7 and 8, I began the process of examining the free-market system. My goal was not to determine whether it supports any of the principles of justice but whether neoclassical assumptions about how the free market operates are consistent with the pursuit of the fundamental values and adherence to the personal principles of justice. In the process of this analysis, we uncovered some caveats about the assumptions underlying the free-market system, particularly about self-interest and utility maximization but also concerning conditions that must be fulfilled if production is to be ethically responsible.

Despite the claim of neoclassical economists that the utility framework does not favor any ethical system, careful analysis revealed that the pursuit of the fundamental values, or indeed adherence to any absolute commitment or prohibition, is incompatible with the requirements of the neoclassical structure of indifference curves. Both the fundamental values themselves and a commitment to the common good are problematic for neoclassical economists; one cannot be simultaneously neoclassical and also committed to the pursuit of two or more fundamental values.[8]

A wholesale rejection of the neoclassical approach, however, is equally unwarranted, although some drastic modifications are required. First, if one presumes a commitment to the fundamental values on the part of all people in the economy, then the economic analysis contained in the analysis of indifference curves is convincing and useful in a limited way. The reason is that, provided that the assumptions of the Fundamental Theorem are approximately correct and that the criteria for ethically responsible production and consumption are fulfilled, there is good reason to conclude that the economy is efficient. This is a significant ethical conclusion since efficiency is a moral desideratum in any society. Second, if one assumes a commitment to the fundamental values, the neoclassical assumptions allow a useful formalization of the manner in which people make decisions. In many situations, such as deciding whether or not to purchase a television or whether to buy a domestic or foreign automobile, people act selfishly in the sense that they consider primarily the welfare of their family or of the group with which they most closely identify.

If economists were unable to demonstrate the efficiency of the free-market system, people concerned about justice would have to explore whether the economic system is efficient. Most critics of the free-market system point out its deficiencies and recommend some alteration. However, it is incumbent on someone proposing a change in the free-market system to show how it still generates an efficient outcome after the changes are introduced.

The changes in the free-market system required to make it compatible with a natural law approach to morality in many instances actually strengthen the operation of the system. Thus, promoting a commitment to honesty and knowledge, beauty, friendship, practical reasonableness, and life generates a structure that enables the assumptions of the neoclassical system to prevail in most ordinary circumstances. The remaining two fundamental values appear to have a neutral effect. Playfulness as a value does not support the operation of the free-market system, but neither does it hinder it, and the effect of religion is uncertain. In some societies and at certain times, religion may encourage people to be resigned to their fate rather than work hard to change their situation. At other times, however, religious commitment strengthens people's resolve to pursue the fundamental values; in this way, it helps to inculcate qualities that yield a more productive society.

An important requirement of the free-market system is that people adhere to their contracts. Because most contracts are informal and not subject to review by the judiciary and because in many instances people have an incentive to break informal contracts, the free-market system is vulnerable to abuse for private gain. Therefore, institutions that either directly or indirectly support the conservation of contracts also promote economic efficiency.[9]

The economic relevance of adherence to contracts was highlighted in Chapter 8, where in the context of the Prisoner's Dilemma I noted the difficulty which arises when one person makes his or her commitment to a job dependent upon the attitude taken by co-workers. The short-run equilibrium in such a situation is for workers to shirk, and in the long run the outcome depends on the tradition of workers in the firm. If most employees traditionally work conscientiously, then even those who are inclined to shirk will not do so, if they perceive accurately their long-term self-interest. On the other hand, if workers have historically adopted a casual attitude toward their jobs, even those laborers who are inclined to work assiduously will have an incentive to shirk when they consider the long-term benefits to themselves.

Adherence to contracts covers a broad spectrum, including situations in which contract clauses specify unverifiable behavior. A person with automobile insurance should not drive recklessly simply because she knows that she is "covered." When a firm is exposed to exploitative behavior of this kind the heightened risk is called moral hazard, and economists have explored the best ways for firms to protect themselves from this type of exposure. The core problem is that the firm writes a contract based on a standard pattern of behavior and expects that behavior to remain constant after the agreement is entered into. However, some people "violate" the contract by acting with more abandon than they did before. It appears that the inclination of people to violate a contract clause that cannot be monitored depends partially on their commitment to contracts in general and partially on their attitudes to the behavior to be avoided. By relying on institutions that promote especially the fundamental values related to goods purchased in the marketplace, society can increase the efficiency of its free-market system.

A society with employees who gauge their work commitment by looking over their shoulders at their co-workers can be efficient. As we have seen, what is required is a pacer group of workers in each firm who are committed to consistent, quality work for the full amount of time for which they are hired. Unless a cadre of such individuals exists, managers cannot even calculate the long-run benefits of conscientious work. Even when such a group exists, other workers can and will shirk unless committed workers exert pressure on them to contribute commensurately. One way to promote dedication of this type is to stress the importance of pursuing the fundamental values and making a contribution to the common good in the workplace.

Promoting the common good may have the unintended consequence of undermining the tendency for people to seek their own self-interest, which, if certain conditions are fulfilled, promotes the good of everyone in society. Increasing group awareness may indeed diminish incentives for each individual to care for himself. Therefore, any society that commits itself to the pursuit of the fundamental values must also have institutions that inculcate an ethic of work and fair contribution. If stressing the common good meant only emphasizing the responsibilities of others to care for the less fortunate, there would be a great danger that many people would rely on the goodwill of others for their sustenance. However, as we have seen, the common good means that one has a responsibility to contribute to the production of goods and services useful in the pursuit of the fundamental values. This obligation to contribute is usually fulfilled in a market economy by working in the home or by securing gainful employment.

Rational expectations, which play an important role in the neoclassical system, are conspicuous in this treatment by their absence. Since institutions play an important role in determining personal and societal expectations and since my general argument has been that institutions which promote the pursuit of fundamental values provide an essential context in which neoclassical analysis can be used, it would be inappropriate to consider expectations generated solely by the economic structure. Rational expectations, as defined by neoclassical economists, are those that are generated as a result of most people understanding the manner in which the economic system functions. Defined in this way, "rational" omits consideration of institutions which provide the moral infrastructure for the operation of a free-market system.[10]

Institutions mold people's predispositions to act in certain ways. The latter function is accomplished through peer pressure: When a large number of people behave in ways prescribed by the institution, deviant behavior is more costly. Institutions also provide economic agents with important information, evaluative as well as objective. When a plurality of vibrant institutions convey objective as well as evaluative information, there is a greater likelihood that economic agents will make better decisions. Consider the particular case of the advertising industry, which is often criticized for appealing to the baser instincts of consumers and for disseminating false information. As in the case of moral hazard, this problem would not be acute if consumers had high standards concerning advertising information and if they had sources of information independent of firms selling products. It is conceivable that institutions such as churches, schools, neighborhood organizations, and the media itself could temper whatever adverse effects the advertising industry might generate for society.[11] If institutions train people in the pursuit of knowledge and truth, the existence of some advertisers who embellish or tarnish the truth can be tolerated, since, for the most part, their claims will be rejected by society, following the lead of its more perceptive and morally committed members.

9.3 COMPETING MORAL TRADITIONS

In a pluralistic society, the utilitarian ethic is superficially appealing because it appears to embrace all traditions with either equal fervor or tepidity. In the economic context, utilitarianism welcomes any ethical system and then hides it within the confines of the consumer's utility function. This openness, however, is illusory for a variety of reasons. First, as is argued in Appendix B, the natural law approach cannot be squeezed into the neoclassical utility function without doing violence to its structure and simplicity. Second, utilitarianism is based solely on consequences to the agent, as these are measured by a feeling of satisfaction, well-being, or achievement. I have argued, with the support of MacIntyre, Finnis, and Sen, that using a single measure of satisfaction does not correspond to the lived experience of individuals. Different satisfactions accrue from distinct actions. The well-being that a person achieves by refusing to accept a bribe is not the same as one obtains by eating a hot dog. There is a difference in quality, not just intensity. Finally, utilitarianism's apparent openness is packaged with stringent requirements concerning self-knowledge, even though utilitarianism does not avert to the means by which people arrive at such comprehensive self-understanding. In a utilitarian tradition, people are supposed to be able to calculate in advance the satisfaction they are to receive from a variety of competing goods which are available for purchase or which consumers imagine that they would like to have.[12] It is most unlikely that a person acting solipsisticly can foresee all the particular consequences of using one particular good—new or old—rather than another. A person obtains this information by living in a tradition, e.g., by seeing other people use old goods to pursue the fundamental values or imagining how good people would use new goods. But neoclassical economics does not take seriously the economic (or ethical) functions provided by a tradition, even the utilitarian tradition.

Even if utilitarianism had no logical and moral difficulties associated with it, the absence of competing ethical systems in the marketplace would be cause for concern. Neoclassical economists, in particular, should find the lack of competition among ethical systems distressing, since they are convinced that competition brings out the best in a system. Rather than having all ethical systems fit into the straitjacket of utilitarianism, I imagine that most economists, were it not for their commitment to mathematical tools, would want competing ethical systems, each with its own influence on the manner in which economic exchanges are transacted.

Heated disagreement about particular moral topics may be taken as prima facie evidence of a variety of ethical systems currently competing for allegiance. But, it may also be the case that the controversies take place between competing groups within a single tradition. As I argued in Chapter 4, one of the attractions of the fundamental values approach is that it allows for a diversity of opinion, much of which stems from a lack of agreement concerning the ordering of goods or practices within any single category of the fundamental values. Wide diversity is consistent with general agreement concerning the validity of the fundamental values approach.

Despite this caveat, it is likely that distinct moral traditions influence differentially the thinking of individuals with respect to controversial issues such as abortion, capital punishment, sexual mores, and euthanasia. Any neoclassical economist should greet different ethical systems enthusiastically because they are prominent means by which people secure their satisfaction or well-being. The problem is that neoclassical economists *think* that their model embraces all ethical systems. But this is wishful thinking.

Because traditions are sources for enriching a person's experience, people benefit from living in a tradition as they attempt to live a particular ethical stance consistently. Furthermore, the contributions of a single tradition are often best seen when one tradition is compared with another, not on a theoretical plane but in practice. That is, people will understand and appreciate more fully their own moral commitments if they see them lived out in the quotidian schedule of their lives. It would be helpful, therefore, to see how, for example, a group committed to the natural law approach fulfills its work commitments compared with a group following the utilitarian ethic. Those adhering to the proportionalist ethic may have yet another way in which they address the daily ethical issues confronting people.

Distinct moral traditions with respect to economic practice already exist in many different areas. But they have not been highlighted by neoclassical economists, who assume that preferences can be handled in the same way as moral convictions. According to the neoclassicals, all morality fits into the unitary framework of utilitarianism. The blame for such a simplistic view is not solely with the economists, however, since thinkers within the natural law tradition have not stressed the ways in which its ethical principles influence the economic life of its adherents. At a prescriptive level, this book identifies certain economic practices that are promoted by a commitment to the fundamental values, but more detailed work is necessary, both at the macro and micro level of the economy.

A lived, ethical tradition not only instructs and transmits good (and sometimes bad) ethical practices in an experiential way, but it also offers an outlook on the goods that are necessary to prosper in life. In Chapter 5 I spoke of level 1 goods, which are required for the production of other goods and services, and level 2 goods, which are supposed to enable directly the pursuit of the fundamental values. A lived ethical tradition should steer consumers to those level 2 goods which are effective in helping a person or family attain the fundamental values. At this point in the history of the United States, it is advisable to identify distinct moral traditions and to study economic behavior within each tradition—including perhaps distinct sub-traditions—which remain committed to the fundamental values or to some other ethical tradition. Let us briefly consider two distinct traditions, both of which adhere to the natural law. My descriptions of these groups will be composites of reality and assumption, because groups do not usually identify the ethical system with which they associate, nor do they relate economic behavior to specific moral principles.[13]

Hasidic Jews pursue a life-style that emphasizes hard work, devotion to the family, regular private prayer, and community worship. Although they adhere closely to the Torah, which is divinely revealed, they also believe that the basic tenets of right living are accessible to reason. They do not distinguish clearly the religious foundation for economic decisions from the ethical component. Nonetheless, at least in principle, Hasidic Jews offer a distinct tradition that embraces both economic and noneconomic decision making.

Compare this group with U.S. Roman Catholics who profess to adhere to the teachings of the Catholic Church. The first issue is whether the Roman Catholics follow the natural law. Although the Catholic Church uses this system in the exposition of her moral teaching, many U.S. Catholics use the rhetoric of utilitarianism to explain their moral decisions. But the explanation may be different from the reality. People who profess adherence to utilitarianism may make moral decisions based on the natural law, or they may pay verbal respect to the natural law but decide within the framework of a utilitarian ethic. Nonetheless, if an identifiable, coherent tradition among Roman Catholics does exist, specifying its contours would aid people in making economic decisions and provide an alternative to the otherwise undifferentiated mass of people who follow the utilitarian ethic.

Adherence to an ethical tradition plays an important role in the redistribution of income from the wealthy and middle classes to those in need. In Chapter 6 I noted that if a redistribution of income is to be fair, it must make an accurate assessment of the needs of the poor and the extent to which income, which otherwise would be spent by the middle class and wealthy in the pursuit of the fundamental values, could be more effectively used by the poor for similar pursuits. Hence, two judgments are required: What are the basic needs of the poor, and to what extent should income be taken away from the rich and middle class?

Since standards of living change over time, people perceive poverty differently. Some people and groups are more sensitive to developing disparities between goods available to the poor, on the one hand, and those enjoyed by the rich and middle class, on the other. One function of an ethical tradition is to present its judgment concerning the basic needs of the poor at a particular point in time. The quality of housing, the amount of food and clothing, the quality of health care and education—all those are factors that enter into the determination of the basic needs of the poor. Even if, as a practical matter, society decided to transfer spending power to the poor via a negative income tax, a just transfer requires an evaluation of a minimum acceptable standard, as measured at this point in the development of the economy. The reason for the particularity of the judgment is that society's responsibility is not absolved by a transfer of money to the poor, because the poor, perhaps lacking sufficient knowledge or not having the benefit of a tradition that teaches good consumption patterns, may spend the money foolishly. Society should be structured in such a way that people are encouraged to pursue the fundamental values. This may mean that society provides food stamps and subsidized housing to the poor rather than using a negative income tax.

The more particular the judgment, the more likely it is that people will disagree. One function performed by a tradition is to massage preferences so that society makes reasonable decisions, even when great particularity is required. A tradition offers a way of thinking about the issues and concrete instruction in a way of living. Both aspects assist in the determination of basic goods for the poor.

Similarly, society must judge the extent to which the rich and middle class can be taxed to benefit the poor. Society will be assisted in fulfilling this responsibility if different traditions offer their views. In particular, adherents to the natural law tradition should eschew the simplistic slogan "No more taxes," which emanates from a distaste for taxes. As I noted earlier, taxes are the second stage which society uses to distribute income. The first stage is the free-market system, which makes an initial allocation, after which society determines other needs and levies appropriate taxes. Taxes do not "steal" from anyone; rather, they are the "natural" second step in allocating income so that people can pursue the fundamental values. Adherents of the natural law have to keep one eye on the needs of the poor and another eye on the spending patterns of the middle and upper classes. As long as the basic needs of the poor are not fulfilled and as long as these classes have income that can be used more effectively by the poor, though not in precisely the same way, redistribution is mandated according to the natural law approach that I have presented.

Taxes entail more than redistribution from the well-to-do to the poor. They also imply an approach to public goods such as the environment, the infrastructure, and security. The activities of current consumers should not jeopardize the well-being of future generations by causing irreparable harm to the environment. For this reason, consumers should not waste natural resources nor should they pollute the environment in ways that impose heavy burdens on future generations. Justice implies fairness between as well as within generations. Also, each generation should protect those assets it receives from an earlier generation that are useful in the pursuit of the fundamental values. Roads, bridges, airports—these should be preserved and developed, if sufficient resources are available and if society judges that they will be used effectively in the pursuit of the fundamental values. Furthermore, just as past generations took initiatives to build the infrastructure and extend knowledge, so the current generation should also take appropriate measures to improve the infrastructure, perhaps through amplified communications equipment, and extend knowledge, perhaps through exploration in space or by another innovative program.

In the United States, important decisions such as these are often relegated to the political parties for their recommendations. But, as recent pastoral letters of the U.S. bishops emphasized, one's moral conviction should influence the political stance one takes. Since political parties are not known for their moral astuteness or commitment, groups with a moral commitment should present their views on these subjects and maintain consistency over a period of time so that people can judge whether policies advocated by one tradition better promote the pursuit of the fundamental values.

9.4 MODULATING DESIRES

In the neoclassical system, desires are simply given; they never need to be modulated, i.e., either attenuated or stimulated. I have argued, however, that such an approach is naive both with respect to the individual and with respect to the influence that common understandings and institutions have on groups of people. One conclusion derived in

Chapter 8 is that society should have a mechanism, i.e., an institution, that promotes admiring envy and discourages or otherwise controls selfish envy. These two types of envy may be innate in each individual, but, if so, they are nurtured or discouraged by institutions in society. An influential institution is the free-market system, but other institutions—such as the law, family, the liberal democratic system, and independent churches—are also significant and influence the incidence of admiring and selfish envy.

The natural law does not mean that children "naturally" pursue the fundamental values, though it does mean that they are naturally attracted to life, beauty, knowledge, friendship, playfulness, religion, and practical reasonableness. Such attractions are not sufficient to induce pursuit; children imitate what their parents and elders do or what they see on television and in the movies. If the tradition they are raised in is coherent and convincing in its commitment to the fundamental values, once the children have attained some maturity they may reflect on the pattern of their actions and discover a yearning for the fundamental values. If this portrayal of the process by which one attains insight concerning the fundamental values is correct, then raising a child in a tradition that promotes the fundamental values is crucial. But childhood never ends for someone pursuing the fundamental values since people can always learn new ways to pursue them. For a lifelong learner, the significance of the tradition does not diminish with one's chronological age. Especially in adulthood, one can learn from wise women and men in the tradition or one can make one's own contribution to the tradition, by living in a manner consistent with the tradition or by articulating an insight that enables people of this generation to live the tradition more faithfully.[14]

In Chapter 8 I described two phenomena that arise when people concentrate their efforts on improving their relative position in society: the possibility of low-level equilibria and the importance of pacer groups. If people are concerned about their status relative to others, pacer groups that focus solely on their absolute well-being, as defined within their tradition, exercise a disproportionate influence on others. The reason for their power is that status-conscious people gauge their satisfaction by the extent to which they rise above or fall below the standard achieved by a pacer group. Although I speak as if distance could be measured in terms of a single variable, such as annual income, in fact pacer groups often set styles in distinct areas: modern art and music, clothing, homes, literary criticism, and modes of socializing. The musical group that has an outrageous style, but does not care what other people think, is a pacer group, as is a group that, caring for little else, spends most of its money on the pursuit of the fine arts.

But pacer groups can have an unusual provenance. A pacer group that played a large role in previous centuries was religious orders, both male and female, that led austere lives. By living in a simple, yet healthful way, even today such groups—cleric and lay—offer a standard which others can use to judge whether they are pursuing the fundamental values effectively. To the extent that pacer groups articulate the reasons for their life-style in terms of the fundamental values, they assist many others in the formulation and implementation of a life plan.

Pacer groups are not concerned about status—they ridicule society's obsession about status—but such groups have their biggest impact in a society in which people rearrange their lives to increase their status. As I noted in Chapter 8, the desire to attain status can emerge in many different sectors of the economy, including the workplace. In a society committed to the fundamental values, a person should not be concerned whether her co-worker shirks or not, because her own responsibility is to contribute to the common good, which she does by working hard. On the other hand, every shirker who is not challenged by co-workers contributes in some way to a common understanding that shirking is acceptable. In other words, certain common understandings are threatened by contrary pressures. Those common understandings which promote the common good should be supported and contrary ones should be discouraged. Therefore, a conscientious worker can legitimately be concerned about shirking on the job. Although her tradition may teach her to work hard no matter what others are doing, she may falter and not be able to sustain her conviction in the face of widespread shirking. What she needs is a pacer group that works hard without regard to shirking by others.

The existence of a hardworking pacer group requires that the group remain committed to the common good despite defections on the part of others. Such an attitude runs counter to the self-interestedness propounded as the paradigm by neoclassical economists. If the pacer group remains committed, it accomplishes two worthwhile goals. First, according to the analysis of long-term status in the Prisoner's Dilemma, the pacer gives the shirkers a reason in their own self-interest to work hard. More significantly, the pacer group also molds the attitudes of the shirkers so that they gradually perceive hard work as the accepted norm.

Hard work is but one activity in which status plays a role in the manner analyzed under the Prisoner's Dilemma. Careful work, honesty, and loyalty to the firm are subject to similar analyses. More generally, any activity in which commitment to a fundamental value is questionable is susceptible to abuse, the likelihood of which is diminished by the existence of an identifiable group whose commitment does not waver. I examined the number of hours per week a person is willing to work because a person's commitment to friendship and playfulness is at stake. In a society which maintains a frenetic pace, working to earn money so as to accumulate goods, each individual may conform to a pattern of long work hours, even though each person would prefer shorter hours on the job, less material goods, and more contact with relatives and friends.

Similar dilemmas involving the use of resources arise in other areas related to the fundamental values. Consider, for example, building construction in an urban area. How many resources should be allocated to making a building attractive? By posing the question in this way, I assume that architectural function and beauty do not necessarily coincide in a building. That is, a functional building may be quite unattractive, and a very attractive building may be inefficient. If a society is committed to beauty, people will construct buildings which enhance beauty. Individuals may deviate from this norm—intentionally or by happenstance. But if architectural beauty is appreciated by society, a person or a firm knows that a beautiful building will evoke greater appreciation by a large segment of society. Therefore, even though beautiful buildings cost more, people will build them in order to remain within a well-defined tradition. If, on the other hand, society emphasizes functionality, it places greater importance on efficiency in the production of goods and services than on the creation of a public good such as beauty. In such a society, beautiful buildings will be in short supply, partially because architects are not practiced in ways to enhance the beauty of buildings and partially because the financial benefits to the builder are minimal. Only people or groups with a strong commitment to public beauty will expend the additional funds necessary to create a beautiful building.

A tradition modulates the preferences of individuals and exerts pressure on people to conform to some general norms. Pressure of this type does not violate the principle of freedom, since I have already stressed that one can only experience the fundamental values within some tradition. A tradition that coherently seeks the fundamental values in particular ways forms and informs people belonging to that tradition. The strength of the tradition is the specific practices it employs to promote the positive pursuit of the fundamental values and to avoid actions directly contrary to the fundamental values.[15]

As a final example, consider the incidence of child and wife abuse. In industrialized societies, such behavior is prohibited by law. To the extent that this prohibition is enforced, a tradition develops of protecting women and children in particular. But law and the threat of punishment are usually not potent enough to prevent people from violating the law. Every society uses common understandings that, by means of particular practices, teach men to treat women with respect and train parents to have patience and self-control, especially when dealing with their children. Because child and wife abuse occur in moments of anger or passion, it is unlikely that cognitive information about what a husband or parent is supposed to do will influence the behavior of people in near-crisis situations. Rather, people will behave at the margin of what society considers tolerable, and the range of barely acceptable acts is determined by the normal way in which people interact with one another. In other words, if actions are bad but safely outside a taboo area that people would never consider transgressing, in moments of passion or anger people are liable to perform such actions rather than violate taboos. Each society must determine what taboos it thinks are reasonable and how it wishes to enforce them. But every society, not just primitive ones, needs taboos. Taboos establish danger zones so that a person realizes that he or she is threatened with rejection by society and his closest associates if he violates those taboos. Taboos mold preferences; they also help people to follow those preferences which they know are right and reject those which in their more lucid moments they acknowledge to be warped.

9.5 TEMPERING MAXIMIZATION OF PROFITS AND PERSONAL WELFARE

I have already noted the importance of pacer groups in situations when status plays a role, particularly with respect to work and consumption. But status also influences the way large, prestigious corporations act, even when they do not compete in the same market sector.

If maximizing profits were truly the sole goal of corporate activity, it is likely that many firms would not adhere to the criteria for ethically responsible production. In fact, however, whether they intend to be or not, corporations do more than just maximize profits, or even sales. They subsidize community events, encourage healthy activities for their employees, make funds available to help resolve pressing social problems, and assist employees with personal problems.

Some neoclassical economists are disturbed by the fact that many corporations allocate funds to pursue activities that promote the common good, even though such funds may be better used in other productive activities to increase profits. Such economists would prefer to see firms concentrate on the generation of profits, which are distributed as dividends to shareholders. Then individual shareholders can select those social causes which they think most deserving of financial assistance. If the viewpoint of such economists is a conviction, i.e., more decisive than a mere preference, I claim that they are using an implicit moral structure to arrive at this conclusion. They may respond in two ways: they may insist that their view is a mere preference or they may assert that their opinion is based on important moral principles, such as the principle of freedom and the principle of efficiency. Neither response, however, is convincing.

A mere preference has the weak force of any other preference. Since the total of individual preferences on an individual topic rules supreme in a utilitarian framework, the economist must yield to the wishes of the masses if most people agree with senior management that corporations should commit themselves to the common good by undertaking projects which are at best distantly related to their market activities. It is appropriate for neoclassical economists to point out the consequences of having corporations support some community activities, but, on their own principles, economists should not attempt to change other people's preferences. The natural law tradition requires that institutions mold preferences and convictions, but neoclassicals, if they are true to their tradition, should choose to remain silent.

Alternatively, if a neoclassical economist states that she is morally convinced that her opinion is the correct one, she must adduce a moral argument. I imagine that the economist would stress individual freedom and efficiency, both of which are principles of justice within the natural law tradition. To present a persuasive argument, however, the economist would have to demonstrate that freedom and efficiency are the only two principles of justice—a difficult task unless the economist

has some theoretical or practical basis for this contention. If the economist persists and maintains that freedom and efficiency are the only
significant principles for him or her, one can legitimately ask why his
or her convictions should bind others. In short, the economist must
offer a moral argument and justify it, which is what I have tried to do
in this study.

In my opinion, the more plausible, rational approach is to
acknowledge that moral convictions arise within the context of community and that they can be validated as one community interacts
with another, which has its own moral tradition. As each community
or tradition poses new questions to each other and as each community
tries to remain faithful to its own tradition, people make judgments
about the consistency of each tradition. In this study, I have portrayed
a clash between two traditions—an ethical one and a supposedly
nonethical one. Representing the natural law tradition, I have challenged the utilitarian tradition in this study both to justify its own ethical convictions and to explain why it is that so many institutions in
modern society have characteristics that reveal a commitment to fundamental values. Further study is needed to determine the extent to
which primary institutions support the common good and the social
principles of justice, but we have presented some evidence that the
contours of these institutions can only be explained by a commitment
of many people to fundamental values and the common good.

I have argued also that the primary institutions in modern societies should be explicit and strong in their support of the fundamental
values. Prior to emphasizing the pursuit of profits, corporations and
other institutions should promote the fundamental values by instruction, policy, and action. Of course, support comes through actions, not
primarily through grand statements. Institutions must have specific
practices which they expect to enjoin. After acting in certain ways over
a longer period of time, people may reflect on their experience, and
they might formulate their experience in terms akin to the structure
presented here.

Economic institutions receive some economic benefits by stressing the importance of the common pursuit of the fundamental values.
In all areas in which people seek status and in which the individual
payoffs are structured in the bifurcated manner I described in Chapter
8, the firm will benefit financially by the existence of people who are
committed to the fundamental values. They will also enjoy the rewards

of greater predictability if people consider themselves morally obligated to fulfill their contracts, both the explicit and the implicit.

For any particular firm, however, such benefits may be small. Even if they are nonexistent, people are still called to follow the fundamental values, and institutions should support this commitment, even when institutions may suffer some loss as a result of its emphasis on the fundamental values. Since the economy and other primary institutions exist to enable the pursuit of the fundamental values, every institution in society, including the free-market system, should acknowledge this by granting the pursuit of the fundamental values a lexicographic priority. That is, respect for the fundamental values comes first—in all situations and for every institution. As long as this priority is maintained, the maximization of profits and personal welfare is praiseworthy. This result substantially modifies the neoclassical paradigm, but it appears to be a reasonable response to the challenge offered by the natural law tradition.

Appendix A

Pareto Optimality in a Diagram

Neoclassical economists use a mathematical model to depict consumption and production in a free-market economy. If all the conditions for the Fundamental Theorem of Welfare Economics are fulfilled and if we restrict the number of goods produced and exchanged to two, the mathematical result of the Fundamental Theorem can be depicted in a two-dimensional diagram.

In Figure A.1 the horizontal and vertical axes represent respectively the amounts of clothing and food produced or consumed in a year by the economy of an arbitrary country, which we call the home country. Countries normally trade with one another and one can easily adjust to portray international trade in food and clothing. Since this study deals primarily with the domestic economy of a modern country, the situation of no trade is depicted in the diagram. That is, in the absence of trade, whatever the country produces its population consumes. Each of the axes is calibrated in units of a million. For example, at point A the country is consuming 15 million units of clothing and 25 million units of food. The unit itself may be a ton or a bushel of food and a rack or box of clothing; which particular unit is chosen is not significant for the theorem. Food and clothing in this example are each homogeneous, i.e., there is only one type of food and there is only one type of all-purpose clothing. Although the Fundamental Theorem allows as many different types of food and clothing as there are markets, for each individual market the good is homogeneous. If the good in question is men's suits, then all the men's suits in a particular category are the same (generic suits) and sell for the same price.

The curved line which runs from 52 on the vertical axis to 75 on the horizontal axis is called the production possibilities frontier. It represents all the Pareto efficient points of production in the economy. If,

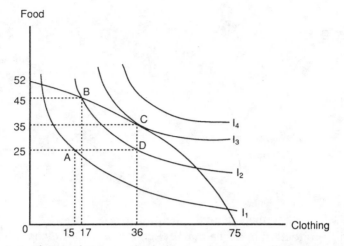

Figure A–1. If no trade is permitted, the country's most efficient point is C.

for example, the economy is producing at point B, no capital or labor is being wasted. Another way of saying this is that if the economy is producing at point B, the only way to increase output of one good is decrease output of another good. If instead of manufacturing 17 units of clothing the economy wanted to generate 36 units of clothing, it could no longer continue to produce 45 units of food; it would have to decrease its food production. In terms of the diagram, one would move from point B along the curved line to the southeast, to point C. To move from one production point to another, one must reassign people and machines in the economy. For simplicity, we assume that there are only two factors of production: labor and capital. If the economy wants to produce more clothing and less food, people and machines have to switch from food production to clothing production.

Capital is an important concept in economics. Unfortunately, it causes confusion because economists frequently use the word in a different way from noneconomists. As used by economists and in this text, capital refers to physical machines or buildings used to produce goods. Most people, however, when they speak of capital, refer to money or stocks or bonds, which economists call financial capital. Without financial capital, physical capital cannot be purchased or produced, and entrepreneurs have to "raise capital," i.e., financial capital, in order to start their business or expand their operations. This means that they have to find investors who will give them money to buy buildings and machines to produce the particular good that the entrepreneur believes consumers are going to want to purchase. Unless otherwise indicated, economists use capital to refer to physical capital, i.e., machines and buildings, not financial capital, and this text adheres to the same usage.

The curved lines which are labeled I_1, I_2, I_3, and I_4 are called community indifference curves. They represent the home economy's preference for clothing relative to food. Each community indifference curve reflects a different level of satisfaction, moving from the lowest, I_1, to the highest, I_4. Although only four indifference curves are drawn on the diagram, there are actually an infinite number of them. If it were possible to measure the level of satisfaction for the community (in fact, it is not possible to develop such a measure for a modern democracy), I_1 might refer to a level of 1,400 and I_4 might be at a level of 3,000. For example, between I_1 and I_2 are community indifference curves corresponding to 2,010, to 2,010.78, etc. For our purposes, however, depicting four community indifference curves suffices.

Consider indifference curve I_2 and look at points B and D. The definition of a community indifference curve is the set of all points that the community, i.e., the consumers in the home country, considers equally desirable in terms of consumption. In other words, consumers do not care whether they are at point B, or point D, or any other point along the curve. They are indifferent to these points because, by definition, each point provides the same level of satisfaction. For example, from the point of view of the consumers, they are just as happy to consume 45 units of food and 17 units of clothing (point B) as they are to consume 25 units of food and 36 units of clothing (point D). Of course, the consumers would prefer to be somewhere on I_3 or I_4, since these represent higher levels of satisfaction. The advantage of moving, say, from I_2 to I_3 is that, compared with point D on I_2, there are many points on I_3 where one has more of both food and clothing. In short, the higher the indifference curve the better off the community is. But if the community moves along the same indifference curve, it is neither worse off nor better off.

Points A and D and many others are inefficient in terms of production because they are "inside" the production possibility frontier. At these points labor and capital are not being used in an efficient manner to generate as many goods as could be produced with the same amount of labor and capital. Remember, the production possibilities frontier (the curved line from 52 on the vertical axis to 75 on the horizontal axis) represents all the efficient points of production. If the home economy is actually producing at A, it must be because resources (capital and labor) are being wasted. There are two possibilities: Either resources are not being used or they are being used inefficiently. When a resource is not used, it is idle. Workers are unemployed or machines are underutilized. Misuse means that the food industry, for example, is using too many machines and not enough workers, and in the clothing industry the reverse situation prevails. Economists say that there is a misallocation of the resources of labor and capital at D, and both A and D are Pareto inefficient points of production.

The usual reason for the misallocation is malfunctioning of the price mechanism. In this model there are four prices because there are four goods: food, clothing, labor, and capital. The corresponding four prices are: the price of food, the price of clothing, the wage rate (the price of a unit of labor), and the price of renting a unit of capital for a year. Like a person, a machine lasts for many years. Since we are looking at what an economy produces in the course of a year, it would not make sense to allocate the entire cost of purchasing a machine to any individual year. After all, at the end of the year, the firm owns the machine and the machine can still generate goods for the following year, in which we have no interest at this point. Because our focus is on a year of economic activity, we think of all machines as being rented for a year, and when we speak of the price of a machine, it is a shorthand expression for the price of renting the machine for a year. Similarly, the wage rate is not the price of "buying a person" but the cost of renting the labor services provided by that person in the course of a year.[1]

When the economy is at point A, the markets are not functioning freely. At point A some capital and some labor are not being used at all. This must be because the prices of labor and capital are too high. In a free-market system, if there is excess labor and capital, then the price of labor and capital should fall. As the wage rate and the price of capital fall, producers hire more capital and more labor. If the market is allowed to function freely, the prices of capital and labor fall just to that level at which the supply of capital equals the demand for capital and the supply of labor equals the demand for labor. There will be no unemployed labor or underutilized capital in the economy. The strength of the competitive market system is that it provides the proper incentives so that resources in the economy are fully utilized. By removing whatever restriction was constraining the market at point A, the economy will start producing at some point along the production possibilities frontier, i.e., the curve stretching from 52 to 75. Assume that the economy moves from point A to point B.

At point B production is efficient, in the sense that all the resources in the economy are being used. At B one cannot produce more clothing without producing less food, nor can one produce more food without producing less clothing. But the entire economy is not yet fully efficient because everyone could still be better off. At B producers produce 45 units of food and 17 units of clothing. If the consumers consume those units, they are on community indifference curve I_2. However, the consumers would much prefer to be at point C. In comparison with point C, the economy at point B is producing too much food and not enough clothing. It must be that the price of food is too high and the price of clothing is too low. In other words, there is some impediment in the goods markets which prevents the markets from adjusting fully. If this impediment is removed, consumers demand more clothing and push the price of clothing up. Because consumers have a fixed amount of money to spend, when they demand more clothing they must also demand less food and, therefore, push the price of food down. Producers who had formerly used capital and labor to produce food will now switch to clothing, because the price of clothing is higher and they can make higher profits (or avoid losses, if they remain in food production) by starting to produce clothing. The net effect is that, if competition prevails in the goods markets, the economy moves to point C.

Consumers would prefer, of course, to be on any point on I_4 rather than point C. The problem is that any point on I_4 is impossible to reach, at least given the production capacity of the economy this year. So, for this year the optimal point is C. C is also called the Pareto optimal point.

How does the Fundamental Theorem relate to the diagram? The Fundamental Theorem says that if there are competitive markets in all goods and factors, the economy will always be at point C, that is, the economy will always produce and consume efficiently. Note that the theorem does not say that everyone in the economy will be well-fed and well-clothed. It merely states that the economy will efficiently produce those goods that are demanded by consumers. It may be because some consumers do not have enough money to demand any food or clothing or because wealthy people prefer clothing to food and spend much more money on clothing than on food that the economy produces too much clothing and is unable to feed the hungry in society. Perhaps the government *ought* to step in and subsidize the food industry or, alternatively, purchase food and clothing, which could be distributed to the poor. That is an *ought*-question, one which can be answered only by applying the ethical principles. "Efficiency within reason" is only one ethical principle, and along with the other principles it must be applied to determine whether an economy is just and how to create a just economy.

Neoclassical Utility and the Fundamental Values: A Mathematical Comparison

The goal of life is to realize the fundamental values. One participates in values through actions, which require resources as well as time. Such claims are in stark contrast to the approach to consumer behavior used by neoclassical economists. Some readers may be familiar with the usual way in which neoclassical economists describe how a consumer decides what goods and how much of each to consume. As in much of modern economics, the favored mode of exposition is mathematics. To clarify the differences between the neoclassical approach and the fundamental values approach, let us first consider the mathematical expressions used by the neoclassical economist to describe a consumer's behavior. I then show what modifications are required to portray the behavior of a person who tries to incorporate the fundamental values into his or her life.

The neoclassical economist assumes that consumer A wishes to maximize his or her satisfaction or utility, which is measured by a utility function, designated by $u^A(...)$. The arguments or variables for the function u^A are the symbols which appear between the parentheses, and they refer to the quantities of goods consumed by person A. The utility function is usually written in the following way:

$$u^A(x_{1t}, x_{2t}, x_{3t}, \ldots, x_{nt}, l_t),$$

where $x_{1t}, x_{2t}, \ldots, x_{nt}$ refer to the quantities of goods $x_{1t}, x_{2t}, x_{3t}, \ldots, x_{nt}$ purchased and consumed by the consumer during the time period t; l_t is the amount of leisure consumed by individual A in time period t.

The utility function applies for some specified period of time, which we assume to be a week. In a week, there are 168 (= $7 \cdot 24$) possible hours of leisure. In the course of a week most consumers spend some time at work and some time in leisure, during which time they consume the goods they have been able to purchase as a result of their employment. Economists place many restrictions on the characteristics of the utility function. For our purposes it is sufficient to single out three important qualities:

1. **More Is Better**: When x_{it} increases, the value of $u^A(...)$ also increases, but at a decreasing rate. In other words, if person A buys another hamburger, he is happier. Suppose we could measure his happiness or satisfaction and assume that he is 50 units happier as a result of the first hamburger he buys. When he purchases a second hamburger during the same week, he is even happier, but his happiness increases by a lesser amount than 50 units, perhaps 42 units. Additional hamburgers always bring additional satisfaction but at a decreasing rate.

2. **Transitivity**: The consumer considers many different bundles of goods. For simplicity, suppose there are three bundles, designated b_1, b_2, and b_3, and each bundle contains different amounts of goods 1 to n and leisure. The property of transitivity requires that if a consumer prefers b_1 to b_2 and also prefers b_2 to b_3, then it must be the case that the person prefers b_1 to b_3.[1]

3. **Self-Interest**: The only goods or services that influence a person's happiness or satisfaction are the goods and services consumed by the person, although the "person" who does the decision-making may be a family or some other small group that acts as if they were a single person. The importance of this requirement is that it does not allow a person to be concerned either with the amount of goods purchased by other people, such as the poor or the wealthy, or the satisfaction or utility of other people, except in those cases when the agent himself can determine the utility of those about whom he is concerned. A person concentrates solely on his or her own welfare.[2]

Although the first assumption is certainly false when a person has an unlimited income, it is not a bad approximation to reality for most people. The second assumption implies that people are never affected by the circumstances of purchasing and consumption. For example, the fact that the merchandise one purchases is produced in South Africa does not influence one's satisfaction, according to this assumption. The third assumption of self-interest is appropriate in many different situations. For example, when consumers have allocated a certain amount of money for clothes or groceries, the choice of particular items does depend on personal preferences. But, given our analysis of the fundamental values and our concern for the common good, the assumption is invalid when deciding how much money ought to be given to charity. The assumption seems realistic for a small number of people all of the time, but for most people it is valid only if certain ethical constraints are not binding. Once we have developed a similar utility model for the essential human goods, we will review again the assumptions of the neoclassical utility function.

If the assumptions are true and if, for simplicity, we suppose that the economy only has two goods, x_1 and x_2, a pictorial representation of the utility function is possible. The curve designated $u^A = 2,500$ in Figure B.1 is called an indifference curve and represents the various combinations of quantities of goods x_1 and x_2 which produce a level of utility of 2,500 for person A. The other curve is a higher indifference

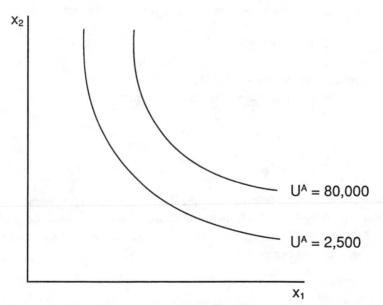

Figure B–1. Each indifference curve indicates a level of satisfaction acquired with goods x_1 and x_2.

curve and indicates a satisfaction of 80,000 units. Of course, there is no reason to believe that person A and person B have the same utility function or that one can compare the satisfaction of A with the satisfaction of B. Person B might have identically shaped curves as person A does but have a different emotional structure. This would be revealed in the utility functions and person B would feel much more intensely about things than does A. Corresponding to A's curve marked $u^A = 2,500$, B might have a curve which looks the same but is marked $u^B = 400,000$. Neoclassical economists admit that they have no way to compare the satisfaction attained by two different individuals.

In order to afford a particular bundle of goods, a consumer must earn a sufficient amount of money during the week. The alternative to leisure is work, at which one earns an hourly wage of w. The total number of work hours is $168 - l_t$. Since the hourly wage is w, total income for the week is $w \cdot (168 - l_t)$, i.e., the wage rate multiplied by the total number of hours worked. The consumer uses this income to purchase the various goods, x_{1t}, x_{2t}, etc., each of which provides satisfaction. Consumer A's expenditures plus the amount of money saved during the period, designated a_t, must equal the total income earned during the period, since we assume that the person does not have accumulated savings to draw upon.[3] The relationship between expenditures and income for a consumer is known as the budget constraint:

$$p_1\, x_{1t} + p_2\, x_{2t} + p_3\, x_{3t} + \ldots + p_n\, x_{nt} + a_t = w \cdot (168 - l_t)$$

The wage rate, w, earned by the person depends on his occupation and the number of hours he works, $168 - l_t$.

The equation can be written more succinctly as:

$$\sum_{i=1}^{n} p_i x_{it} + a_t = w \cdot (168 - l_t)$$

The symbol on the left is mathematical shorthand for indicating that all items numbered i, which extends from 1 to n, should be added together. Expenditures on leisure can be moved to the left-hand side and the equation becomes:

$$\sum_{i=1}^{n} p_i x_{it} + w l_t + a_t = w \cdot 168$$

In this equation, leisure is treated in the same way as any other physical good or service purchased by the consumer, and its price is w, the wage rate. The insight provided in this formulation is that for every hour of leisure one spends one less hour working and one less hour earning a wage of w. Thus, the cost to the consumer of an hour of leisure is w. Therefore, there are really $n + 1$, not just n goods in an economy: the n ordinary goods and services purchased by the consumer and leisure, which is purchased by not working and not receiving a wage. The right-hand side of the equation is the total amount of money which a person could earn in a week in which he or she took no time for leisure, not even to eat or sleep.

Although it is possible to analyze savings and wealth in the above structure, our focus is the purchase and consumption of goods and services within a given week. Therefore, we assume that $a_t = 0$ in each period, i.e., that consumers save nothing and use all their income to purchase goods and services for consumption in that period.

For the sake of comparison, it is useful to express the fundamental values approach in the same basic structure used by neoclassical economists. As has already been pointed out, striving for the essential human goals cannot be reduced to the pursuit of happiness, as if happiness were the hidden essential value lurking behind the fundamental values. Nonetheless, in the interest of accommodating the neoclassical model we can make the herioc assumption that the person is trying to achieve contentment by formulating a coherent life plan which the person realistically expects will lead to the realization of the basic values. In the neoclassical model of economics, the $u^A(\ldots)$ function represents the utility or satisfaction that person A gains by consuming an amount of goods, services, and leisure, which are suggested by the dots between the parentheses. According to the fundamental values approach, the utility function can be written as a function not of goods which are consumed but rather of actions to be performed. Consider the following expressions:

$$u^A(q_t)$$
$$v^A(r_t)$$
$$w^A(s_t)$$

Each one of the arguments represents a different type of action which is evaluated differently:

q_t is the number of good actions (performed each week)
   that realize one or more of the fundamental values;
r_t is the number of mixed actions (performed each week)
   that realize some fundamental values, but which are
   directly contrary to others;
s_t is the number of bad actions (performed each week)
   that are directly contrary to the fundamental values.

For a person adhering to the fundamental values, the three functions u^A, v^A, and w^A are incompatible, for the reasons that were given in the text. One is not allowed to perform an action directly contrary to a fundamental value, no matter how much "satisfaction" it brings to the individual. People do, of course, act directly contrary to the fundamental values. For example, in a moment of weakness they might weigh the benefits of doing something wrong by performing the following calculation. They may assign u^A positive values while v^A and w^A both are given negative values. They may calculate the "benefits" of unethical behavior by adding together the functions u^A, v^A, and w^A. If the number is greater than zero they perform the bad actions, but otherwise they do not. However, if they truly adhere to the fundamental values approach, they will admit at some later point that they deluded themselves by adding together incomparable entities. The only function which bears a partial resemblance to the neoclassical utility function is u^A, and even in this case I will demonstrate that the relationship is distant.

Having a life plan means that one has selected the q, r, and s for the particular point at which one is in life. For ease of exposition, suppose individual A is a "good" person who only chooses q types of actions. The complete set Q of possible actions is large. Each of the actions helps realize the basic human goods in a different way, and each action requires physical resources (goods and services) as well as time for its implementation. For example, if person A wants to participate in knowledge, she can buy a newspaper, enroll in a course at a local university, or travel to Greece to explore the ancient ruins. To realize the value of playfulness, person A can play a game of chess, go to a movie, or go with one's friends to the beach for two weeks. Each action requires goods and services as well as time for its implementation. In a market economy, a person earns money to purchase the goods needed to pursue the fundamental values, and the person must also have sufficient leisure time to use the goods effectively.

Any good person wants to undertake the action that leads to the most intense participation in a basic value, i.e., participation at the highest level of the value. From the selection given above, most people, I imagine, would prefer traveling to Greece to pursue the fundamental value of knowledge and to go to the beach for two weeks in pursuit of playfulness. For most people, however, these possibilities are unrealistic, since time and income limit the types of activities one can undertake in pursuit of the fundamental values. The relationship among physical goods and services, time, and actions is a mathematical one, akin to the production function used in the economics of the firm.

Suppose there is only one activity a person can perform and that the number of times it is performed during the week is designated $q1_t$. To perform this activity one needs goods and services, $x1_t$, and leisure time, $l1_t$. For any given level of activity $q1_t$, one can either use many goods and a little amount of time or one can use a few goods and a lot of time. For example, suppose one intends to participate in the fundamental value of beauty. According to the person's own judgment, she participates in beauty to an equal degree if she purchases a beautiful vase or goes to the country for a walk on a beautiful spring day. Whatever judgment the person makes about the way to participate in a fundamental value, it can be captured in what can be called a fundamental value function:

$$q1_j = F^j(x1_t, l1_t)$$

where j is a number from 1 to 7 and
represents the j-th fundamental value;
$x1_t$ represents a vector of goods and services, i.e.,
$x1_t = (x1_{1t}, x1_{2t}, x1_{3t}, \ldots, x1_{nt})$
devoted to the realization of the j-th fundamental value
by performing act $q1$; and

$$l1_t = \sum_{k=1}^{q1_j} l1_{kt}$$

where $l1_{kt}$ is the amount of leisure time committed to the
realization of the j-th value by performing activity 1.[4]

The function F^j is similar in structure to the neoclassical utility function. A reasonable, if not perfectly accurate, assumption is that as

x_t becomes larger, i.e., as any one of its individual elements increases, $q1_j$ also becomes larger. The greater the participation in the good via repetition of act $q1$ the more resources must be expended. Similarly, as l_t increases, the number of good actions resulting in a realization of the fundamental value is higher, because more time is available to perform the act more carefully. Whether the person undertakes the good actions depends on a disposition of the person's will, a facet not captured in the value function.

In the general model there are n different goods and services in the economy. If one is willing to assume, however, that there are only two goods in the economy, x_1 and l, then it is possible to give a pictorial representation of the value function. The graph in Figure B.2 is practically identical to Figure B.1; the significant difference is in interpretation. The curve marked $q1_3^A = 7$ means that person A is able to perform seven type 1 good actions leading to participation in fundamental value number 3 by using the various combinations of leisure and good x_1. In order to be able to perform 12 actions, the person needs more leisure as well as more of good x_1. Each curve $q1_3^A = 7$ and $q1_3^A = 12$ is an equi-value curve, since the varying resources x_1 and l enable the same number of actions, leading to the same participation in the third fundamental value. Unlike the case for indifference curves,

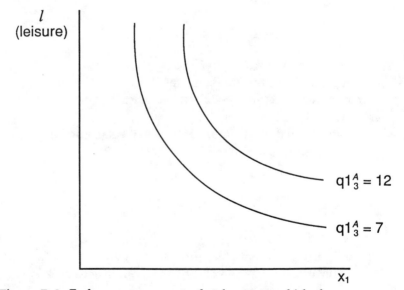

Figure B–2. Each curve represents the degree to which the consumer can achieve the fundamental values through the use of goods x_1 and l.

the equi-value curve does not directly measure the extent to which the person participates in the third fundamental value. It simply reveals the various combinations of goods enabling the person to perform seven good actions of type 1 or level 1. Between the two curves depicted on the diagram lie four other equi-value curves, corresponding to eight, nine, ten, and eleven repetitions of the $q1$ action.

Each good action allows attainment of a basic human goal at a different level. If the actions are ranked, beginning with the action that allows the least participation in the fundamental values ($q1$) and ending with the action allowing the greatest participation (qm_j, where m_j can be extremely large), then a consumer should purchase those goods and services that are expected to allow the highest participation in the fundamental values without violating the budget constraint. Since goods and leisure can be used in a variety of ways to achieve one or more fundamental values, the consumer faces a formidable task of planning. The consumer is supposed to maximize participation in the seven basic values, which are added together by using the weights implicitly assigned by the consumer through the selection of a life plan.[5]

The budget constraint is as binding in the fundamental values approach as it is in the utility-maximizing approach. The graphical difference is that the budget line in the fundamental values approach can be tangent to hundreds of different equi-value curves. Remember that for each fundamental value j there are m_j actions that lead to participation in the particular fundamental value. Even for a single value, the number of possible tangencies to the budget line is high.[6] Assigning weights to the fundamental values creates something similar to the neoclassical utility function, but only for "good" actions. Furthermore, the utility function does not generate the usual shapes of indifference curves. The weighting process twists the equi-value curves so that they no longer have the convex shape depicted in the diagram. Thus, the process of assigning weights for positive actions undertaken in pursuit of the fundamental values preserves the form of the neoclassical utility function. But because the regularity conditions are violated, the "fundamental values" utility function cannot be given a mathematical form similar to that used in neoclassical analysis.

Actions directly contrary to the fundamental values, r (mixed actions) and s (bad actions), also require goods and services for their implementation. Since in any economy some people will act contrary to the fundamental values, they will need goods to perform these actions. The sum total of all the goods and services required for activities q, r, and s is designated x, which is the vector of goods and services $x_t = (x_{1t}, x_{2t}, x_{3t}, \ldots, x_{nt})$ referred to earlier but not aggregated to include all types of actions at various levels.

Because r and s actions are prohibited by the natural law, no calculation of the economic benefits of performing such actions is permitted or valid. Thus, r and s actions are totally incompatible with the neoclassical framework; the framework is not even remotely similar. Actions of the s variety retain a superficial similarity, but the differences are sufficiently dramatic that the neoclassical regularity conditions are not fulfilled for q actions.

In both the neoclassical and the fundamental values model, the budget constraint is identical. The main difference between the two approaches is that the neoclassical objective function is single-valued (utility), while the fundamental values model is multi-valued. Even when the fundamental values approach is reduced to a single-valued function by means of the implicit weighting contained in the life plan of each individual, the equi-value curves, due to the twisting and the nature of the actions taken to pursue the basic goods, do not conform to the regularity conditions imposed by the neoclassical approach. Because of this incompatibility, I abandon the assumption that consumers attempt to maximize utility as understood in the neoclassical model. Instead, I assume that consumers act in the following way:

1. In any given period consumers purchase goods and services that they expect will enable them to pursue their life plan. Each good purchased is capable of being used to pursue a fundamental value.
2. The effectiveness of goods used in pursuing the fundamental values is not known until they have been used.
3. All goods can be used to pursue different fundamental values at a variety of levels and intensities.
4. Even if a consumer makes an incorrect purchase in the sense that the good cannot be used effectively in the manner anticipated, the good can still be used in some other way to achieve a fundamental value.
5. Consumers ought to use whatever goods they have purchased to pursue the fundamental values effectively.

The above model implicitly assumes that the consumer follows a dialectical process in purchasing goods and services. Initial purchases may be "wrong," but the consumer only discovers this after use. Even "wrong" purchases, however, can be used by the consumer to pursue the essential human goals, because goods are fungible and allow for a variety of uses. "Wrong" purchases induce the consumer to modify her future purchases so that the goods purchased in the future are used efficiently in the pursuit of the basic values. One can distinguish two types of uses of a good: efficient and effective. A person uses a good efficiently when he uses it to pursue the fundamental values in the manner anticipated prior to purchase. Effective use means that, although the good is not being used in the way intended prior to purchase, because the good does not have the characteristics one anticipated, the good is nonetheless utilized in some manner to pursue the fundamental values. Effective use of a good indicates some inefficiency, even though goods that are being used effectively are not being wasted. The dialectic process converts effective use of goods and services to efficient use.

In this study I do not attempt to offer a proof that the price mechanism in an economy that is neoclassical on the production side but oriented to the fundamental values on the consumer side achieves the most efficient, or even the most effective, distribution of resources. Instead, I make the following, more modest, but equally unsubstantiated, claim. In an economy in which each consumer uses his own goods and services effectively in the pursuit of the fundamental values, in which producers maximize profits, and in which the other assumptions of the fundamental theorem relating to production and exchange are fulfilled, goods and services will not be wasted.

Notes

NOTES FOR CHAPTER 1

1. This is referred to as the principle of universalizability and is treated extensively in Hare (1952, 1963), who uses it as a rule for eliminating purported ethical maxims. As Lucas shows, Hare's principle is a variation of Kant's famous dictum, "Act only on that maxim through which you can at the same time will that it should become a universal law" (Lucas, 1980, p. 43). MacIntyre (1984, chs. 1–6) demonstrates the inconsistency of the claim called emotivism, which states that all moral principles merely express the private emotions of individuals.

2. The revolution in thinking which occurred during the Enlightenment introduced a caesura between the actions which people actually perform in a community and the actions which they *ought* to undertake. As noted above, MacIntyre (1984, pp. 56–59) shows how an "ought" can be derived from an "is" if functional concepts are included in the premise, as was done by Aristotle and most philosophers prior to the Enlightenment. After describing the transformation in moral thinking that occurred during the Enlightenment, MacIntyre argues that "ought" and "is" cannot be separated, but concedes that most modern moral thinkers require or assume a strict separation of the two concepts.

No argument that uses only facts and logic can ever arrive at a conclusion which validly states what one "ought to do." Similarly, no accumulation of "oughts" can ever produce an "is." However, according to the description of moral experience given in this study, "ought" can never be adequately separated from the "is" of one's own experience. The particular action which ought or ought not be done, according to some moral judgment or rule, depends on whether the factual state of affairs falls under the qualifications included in the "ought"-statement. In an ethical judgment an "is" and an "ought" are joined together to determine an agent of responsibility and an action.

3. Jonsen and Toulmin (1988) present a sympathetic history of casuistry and argue for reconstituting it as a valid form of moral thinking.

4. Jonsen and Toulmin (1988) argue that the method itself contains self-correcting mechanisms which can be relied upon to work as long as the number of thinkers employing this approach is large enough to allow the community of casuists to respond critically to positions tentatively reached by other casuists. See especially chapters 9–11.

Just as ethical principles must be employed deftly when considering a particular ethical problem, economic theory must be applied in a nuanced manner to an actual economy. John Neville Keynes, the father of the famous British economist John Maynard Keynes, distinguished three types of economics: positive economics (economic theory), normative economics (such as the distribution of income), and applied economics. Colander (1992) discusses this distinction and recommends adherence to the tripartite division as a way to make economic thinking more productive. Colander devotes particular attention to applied economics, which is the art of applying theory to reality. Applied economics plays a role analogous to casuistry in ethics.

5. In this text we use the terms ethics and morality (and their cognates) interchangeably, although in common parlance the words have different connotations. Ethics is a system of behavioral norms that appeals to a philosophical system for its justification. It claims to be able to derive its prescriptions from more basic axioms or experiences. Moral reasoning, on the other hand, is often associated with religious thinking; one's morals are derived from one's religious tenets. Despite the linguistic usage, philosophical ethics, on the one hand, and morality in the strict sense of being derived from religious beliefs, on the other hand, are not antithetical. The natural law approach, as developed by various Christian denominations, claims that all its prescriptions can be derived without reference to religious beliefs. Without insisting that ethics and morality are the same, I judge that the words are sufficiently close in meaning and usage that I will use them interchangeably in the text.

6. Hahn, a prominent neoclassical economist, stresses the limited applicability of economic rationality in Hahn (1979, ch. 1).

7. Most introductory texts in economics describe and analyze the complete neoclassical system. A clear presentation of neoclassical microeconomic foundations is given in Salvatore (1986) and McCloskey (1985a). Becker (1976) and Hirshleifer (1985) show how the neoclassical paradigm has been extended to cover a broad range of personal, familial, and social problems. Lucas (1987) gives a justification for the rational expectations approach; he also presents the macroeconomic policy recommendations advocated by rational expectationists. Friedman (1962) presents good, clear arguments on behalf of the market mechanism. Thurow (1983) exposes weaknesses in the rational expectations approach.

8. Baumol and Blinder (1988) offer a persuasive argument for a modern Keynesian approach. Lucas (1981) contrasts the differences between the Keynesian and Monetarist approaches at the macroeconomic level. Akerlof (1982, 1983, 1984) explores the limits of the neoclassical paradigm.

9. See White (1977) for an overview of the Austrian School. For a good description of the institutional approach, see Williamson (1985) who focuses on the centrality of transaction costs in arriving at and monitoring adherence

to contracts. Coase (1992) argues persuasively that transaction costs have been neglected in economic theory and practice. In this article, he explains how transaction costs explain why management is necessary and why economics and law are so closely connected.

10. Bell (1976) highlights the contradictions in the neoclassical and Keynesian systems. Cochran (1974) and Danner (1982) justify an approach that incorporates ethical considerations. Bowles, Gordon, and Weisskopf (1983) present a constructive Marxist and Neo-Keynesian alternative.

11. In recent years, the neoclassicals have spawned an alternative school that adheres to neoclassical tenets only to the extent that empirical investigations support the neoclassical assumptions. The experimental school adjusts assumptions to fit the empirical anomalies. Useful analyses of the approach taken by the experimental school are given by Smith (1990) and Roth (1987).

12. O'Connell (1982) also offers a useful analysis, with attention to the limits of applicability.

Not all neoclassical economists hew strictly to neoclassical norms, and in recent years economists such as Amartya Sen, Robert Frank, and George Akerlof have moved away from some neoclassical assumptions because, in their opinion, neoclassical economists, when dealing with certain problems, have to propose torturous arguments to reconcile neoclassical behavioral assumptions with ordinary observations about the manner in which people act.

NOTES FOR CHAPTER 2

1. Moore (1973) argues that good governments are those that concentrate their efforts on preventing misery. Successful governments focus their activities on preventing harm being done to others, and they avoid the trap of devising positive programs to make their citizens "happy." He notes that one hundred people can more readily agree about what makes people miserable than about what makes them happy. A government can, therefore, be reasonably sure of success if it removes misery-causing institutions from society.

2. Applied economics and applied ethics do not involve any abstraction when the relevant issue is how general rules are to be applied to a specific case. If the application, however, is to a class of cases, some abstraction is involved. Our interest is in ethical theory as it pertains to questions raised by economic theory, and for this reason "ethics" refers to theoretical ethics, unless the context indicates otherwise.

3. There are a variety of ways to introduce altruism into the standard neoclassical utility function. See Malinvaud (1972, pp. 200–29); Andreoni (1989); Collard (1978); Margolis (1971); and Adams (1992).

4. Some might claim that infractions of ethical rules or principles are more numerous than violations of conditions set by neoclassical economists. Although the claim is interesting, evaluating it is difficult, because empirical evidence, in contrast with anecdotal implication, concerning violations either of ethical rules or of economic behavioral conditions is in short supply.

5. This difficulty has been encountered and studied extensively in the income-maintenance experiments conducted in New Jersey, Indiana, and other sites. People were given additional amounts of money each month to determine what effect unearned income would have on their work effort and on other variables. See Killingsworth (1983) for a complete discussion.

6. Whether economists, by theorizing and by estimating empirical relationships, arrive at truth or even try to arrive at the truth is examined by Boland (1982). McCloskey (1983, 1985b, 1990) suggests that economists are not like the empirical scientists they think they are emulating. In fact, the methodology (McCloskey calls it modernism) which is the creed of economists has long ago been abandoned by philosophers. McCloskey argues instead that economists are and ought to be researchers who engage in conversation and use the rhetoric of theory, general examples, and empirical studies to attempt to persuade their colleagues that one economic theory is more convincing than another. Despite McCloskey's philosophical perspective, he does not claim that economists reach the truth, which he regards as uninteresting. Chapter 3 of this study implies that the only justification for conducting research is the expectation that it leads to a greater participation in truth and knowledge. With all due respect to McCloskey, serious conversation is interesting and compelling only because those involved are searching for truth.

7. According to Aristotle, the starting point for reflection concerning what ought to be done is twofold: the practices of a person and what everyone agrees upon as good. See Gadamer (1986, pp. 159–78).

8. Gadamer (1975, pp. 235–341) situates all knowledge in the human sciences within tradition, which creates an acceptable "prejudice." For Gadamer, prejudice is a necessary condition for attaining human understanding.

McCloskey (1990) is equally dismissive of the objective, scientific approach, but he is less explicit about the role of tradition. He asserts that good economics relies upon the traditional rhetorical tetrad: fact, logic, metaphor, and story. As an economic historian, he emphasizes the importance of a historical perspective, and uses history as a story to frame and criticize economic metaphors. But, although he frequently cites bad economic reasoning and locates himself within the tradition of the Chicago School that favors free-market metaphors with much mathematics and statistical inference, in his jaunty, playful style he stops short of saying that economics seeks truth or that truth emerges from within a tradition. He is content to hope that economics reaches an argumentative equilibrium. See especially pp. 150–62.

9. See Boland (1981).

10. See Salvatore (1989, ch. 5).

11. Leamer (1984, pp. 45–59) analyzes various statements of the Heckscher-Ohlin theorem and reviews a variety of methods used to verify both the assumptions of the theorem as well as its predictions.

12. See Akerlof (1982), Cox and Epstein (1989), and Leibenstein (1979).

13. Although ethicians do not attempt to predict what people will do in particular situations, they must make some calculation concerning human behavior in order to determine whether a specific practice or structure is just. In particular, the ethician must consider whether most people are likely to

abide by the rules of the institution without coercion. Since coercion is costly and inhibits freedom, institutions which rely on cooperation rather than coercion are ethically preferred.

14. Lucas (1980, pp. 16–19, 39–44) points out that mathematical arguments, if valid, are always true, whatever the circumstances. Ethical arguments, however, since they are concerned with human affairs, "characteristically contain a suppressed ceteris paribus clause, and hence are perpetually open to a further 'but'" (p. 39). In ethics, the best we can hope for is that we establish premises which are adequate or conclusive, even though objections can always be raised against some ethical position.

15. Rawls (1971, p. 20) describes the end result of this process as reflective equilibrium. In the Rawlsian framework, the expression of the original position must be such that it yields reasonable principles of justice; similarly, one must be able to derive the principles of justice from a description of the original position that is reasonable.

16. Hegel and Marx both developed their own "dialectics." Inasmuch as each of their dialectics involves the resolution of contradicting statements or forces, they are true dialecticians. Since, however, both the Hegelian and the Marxian dialectic subsume many philosophical assertions which are not germane to our analysis, we use the word "dialectics" in the neutral sense of reconciling opposing claims by alternatively adjusting one claim in response to the perceived truth of the opposing claim.

17. For example, suppose one states a principle ("Lying is wrong") and then modifies it because it does not coincide with one's judgment in a particular case ("Lying is wrong except when your spouse telephones you and you don't want to take the call"). Closer examination of the modified principle reveals to the person that there is no reason to distinguish between one's spouse and one's mother or father or any close relative. The principle seems to allow telling mistruths to close relatives. Understandably, the generality of this exception sets ill with the ethician. So she returns to qualify further the already once-qualified statement ("Lying is wrong except in the case when a close relative calls and you don't want to take the call because you are engaged in complicated business that may involve financial loss to the firm"). At this point the ethician should ask herself: "If I have a justifiable reason for not speaking to my close relative, why not state the reason instead of stating the mistruth that I am out of the office?" If this argument is persuasive, one returns again to the original principle, but if arguments can be adduced against offering a reason, one continues to ambulate in dialectical mode in search of some homeostatic equilibrium.

The dialectical process is important because it forces the dialectician to acknowledge explicitly the relative weight she implicitly gives to different values. In this example, the ethician is struggling to assign the proper weight to the following values: knowledge or truth, family, business, right to privacy. An ethician has a responsibility to perform dialectical reasoning in a way which convinces other people, and this is a demanding and lengthy exercise. The issue of lying is not straightforward, and any dialectical conclusion would require detailed treatment in order to convince other people that the conclusion is justified. For the use of the dialectical approach on the topic of lying, see Bok (1978).

18. The goal of the dialectical method is to arrive at insight concerning the true principle guiding behavior in a certain realm of activities. McMullen (1992) notes three different types of logical reasoning: deduction, induction, and retroduction, a term used by the nineteenth- and early twentieth-century American philosopher C.S. Peirce. The term retroduction (or abduction) refers to the leap from discrete facts to a general pattern. Successful use of the dialectical method relies upon retroduction.

19. For an entertaining review of the current dilemma, see McCloskey (1983, 1985b, 1990). McAleer, Pagan, and Volker (1985) present the requirements for an adequate test of an economic model and suggest that the requirements are nearly impossible to fulfill. Sen (1980) says that description in economics is as important as prediction and prescription; furthermore, according to Sen, description requires some insight, which is related to a structure of understanding. That is, description, as well as prediction and theory, not only influences ethical theory but is also influenced by it.

20. The difference between economic justice and business ethics is determined not so much by the manner in which each discipline deals with the nine time-facts but by the level at which economic behavior is examined. Business ethics considers moral decisions from the point of view of a firm or a person operating within a firm or company. The person working in the firm may be the president of the firm, a manager, a worker on the assembly line, a person designing new goods, a salesperson in the field, or any other agent who is paid by the firm to act on behalf of the firm. Each of these persons has duties to the other members of the productive team, as well as to society at large. Consumers are also considered, but primarily in their relationship to firms. The economic questions raised in business ethics are important and can be answered by using the framework of the fundamental values. Because business ethics starts at the level of the firm, however, it considers the institutional structure of the firm in greater detail than is done in economic ethics.

Texts on business ethics usually include some treatment of the broader issues raised in this volume, although the focus remains on the behavior of the firm and of people in the firm. Also, texts in business ethics cite figures and study cases to illustrate ethical conundrums rather than develop principles which provide a coherent approach to ethical problems. See Velasquez (1988); his parallel analysis for my chapters 3 to 7 are (1988, pp. 179–216).

21. Arrow (1963, 1967) demonstrates that usual democratic procedures are inconsistent with reasonable, neoclassical assumptions made about the consistency of people's opinions. It appears that some pressure or leadership is necessary to achieve consistency in a democratic system.

NOTES FOR CHAPTER 3

1. Wolfe (1989, pp. 27–50) documents and critiques the proliferation of the neoclassical approach in related social sciences. In his discussion (p. 35), he approvingly quotes McCloskey, who observes that some of the neoclassicals use a form of rhetoric that introduces moral premises, even though the neoclassicals claim that they do not wish to inject their own moral views.

2. Neoclassical economists, for the most part, acknowledge the inability of the usual model of consumer behavior to pattern the agency of the consumer, but they consider the agency aspect of the person to be a less important motivating factor than the well-being aspect. In various publications, Sen argues forcefully that agency is a significant component of human behavior. See Sen (1980, 1985 ,1987) and Wolfe (1989, p. 218).

3. See Salvatore (1986, pp. 598–99).

4. Sandel (1982, pp. 15–65) shows that the primacy of justice, characteristic of most liberal ethical systems, must be an end in itself, not a means to an end. Hence, the primacy of justice, as opposed to the good, rejects both consequentialism and teleology.

5. For an analysis of the natural law tradition and its rootedness in teleological ethics, see Rhonheimer (1987) and Schüller (1980). Fagothey (1959, pp. 127–44) analyzes the function of right reason in establishing ethical norms.

6. Rawls's contract theory of justice is deontological with respect to the primacy of justice. Similarly, all those people who advocate the primacy of rights are deontologists. Sandel (1982, pp. 1–14, 165–68) refers to the school of rights advocates as deontological liberalism. He distinguishes, however, between their approach to justice, which is deontological, and their approach to the good, which is essentially utilitarian.

7. Since Karl Barth, a number of Protestant theologians have considered natural law thinking antithetical to a Protestant emphasis on sin and the importance of grace. Braaten (1992), however, points out that all the early reformers, with the possible exception of Zwingli, accepted natural law theory and that much of the Protestant distaste for it derives from an identification of natural law with the way in which it was presented by Thomas Aquinas, who lacked an historical, developmental perspective. Braaten, however, notes that natural law theory has developed significantly since the time of Aquinas, who remains but one critical thinker in a long, active tradition of reformulation of the natural law.

8. MacIntyre (1988) presents a critical review of various traditions and argues that the natural law approach, extending from Homer to Aristotle, to Aquinas, and down to the present, is best able to respond to the challenges presented by other ethical systems, including utilitarianism. For the influence of natural law on political thought, especially American political thought, see Sigmund (1971).

9. See Arendt (1958, pp. 153–59). "The perplexity of utilitarianism is that it gets caught in an unending chain of means and ends without ever arriving at some principle which could justify the category of means and end, that is, of utility itself" (p. 154).

10. MacIntyre (1990) argues that the schools of moral philosophy deserve, by reason of their scope and the stature of thinkers who have pursued their main motifs over centuries, to be called traditions and that, despite differing viewpoints on important issues within a single tradition, each school pre-

sents a plausible approach to moral inquiry and life. Each tradition addresses questions or challenges to the other two traditions, some of which are raised by changes in outlook and paradigms of understanding. In MacIntyre's judgment, the natural law tradition has consistently responded most effectively to the challenges presented by rival traditions.

11. In economics a value is a particularly favorable exchange of money, or of some other good, service, or promise, for another good, service, or promise desired or prized by the consumer. Although bartering goods and services for different goods and services occurs in any economy, most transactions involve money in exchange for a good or service. The consumer who purchases a good pays a price for the good which is less than what the consumer theoretically would have been willing to pay. The consumer who gets "good value" is satisfied that a profitable exchange of goods for money has taken place. The judgment that a profitable exchange has taken place requires a prior implicit or explicit calculation on the part of the consumer in which she compares the ticket price of the item with the largest amount of money that she would be willing to pay for the object in the light of the services which it will render to her or to people for whom she cares. This latter price can be considered the "personal price" or the "reservation price" of the consumer. If the personal price is higher than the ticket price and if the consumer has sufficient income, the purchase is made and the consumer is satisfied that he or she has received good value in the exchange.

In philosophy, value is used to designate a different entity, even though a person seeking a philosophical value must, like the consumer, undertake a mental exercise to decide what actions to posit in order to participate in the value.

12. Danner (1982) follows Scheler in the way he categorizes values and considers value to be an immediate intuition of a good accompanied by a feeling that indicates where the good is to be placed in a particular hierarchy. We do not consider the hierarchy of values to be part of an immediate intuition. See also Heilbroner (1988), Margolis (1982), and Lutz and Lux (1988).

13. A value may be both intrinsic, i.e., good in itself, and instrumental, i.e., a means to attain other goods or values. In the text I consider mainly the intrinsic quality of values. Including instrumental values would mean that physical goods and wealth, which are means used to pursue intrinsic values, are treated as values. I prefer to focus, instead, on intrinsic values and refer to physical goods, money, and wealth as means used in the pursuit of intrinsic values.

14. Sen (1987) notes that neoclassical utility may be an inadequate metric for well-being, and that the adoption of goals, values, and commitments may be more significant for economic agents than their well-being.

15. "Phenomenological" in this context simply means that the description provided is an objective one even if some insight and comprehension are required. For some people "phenomenological" implies "factual," but facts are never distinct from the intelligibility of the context in which they are set. See MacIntyre (1984, pp. 204–25).

16. One can extend the list indefinitely by merely changing adjectives that indicate positive qualities to their corresponding cognate nouns. Since the circumstances of life are myriad it is not surprising that the values or virtues corresponding to those circumstances are numerous. For example, many people realize that patience is required in order to participate in the value of friendship. Therefore, patience becomes a desideratum because it leads to the value of friendship. But depending on the circumstances in which a person exercises friendship, it can be labeled tolerance, gentleness, openness, endurance, resignation, equanimity, forbearance, etc. When individual nouns run out, one can describe particular situations in which a response similar to patience is admired and desired. For an interesting and comprehensive discussion of moral values see Everett (1918).

17. Some economists and philosophers object to this approach and dismiss it as sheer introspection. In fact, however, the introspective component is only a device to encourage the reader to review his or her life and consider those components which he or she knows to be important. A person should pick those values which are significant not because he or she has read about them but because he or she has devoted time and energy to the pursuit of those human values. Certainly, other people are among the important human values, but so are less tangible goods such as beauty and knowledge. The realization that these values are fundamental stems from each person's own historical pursuit and continuing pursuit of these values in his or her life. In short, the task is to select from one's personal history those human values which make life meaningful. The claim of the natural law approach as developed in this study is that there are seven fundamental values which are mutually exclusive and inclusive of all the essential human values which people strive to realize in their lives.

18. Bellah et al. (1985) present searing evidence of the difficulty people have in expressing common human values in modern society. They also explore the role which the community plays in fostering values and in allowing them to be expressed publicly. Murray (1960), on the other hand, thinks there is a deep residue of the natural law tradition in American society, in part because the natural law has such profound religious roots in America, since it is historically the preferred approach in most Protestant churches as well as in the Catholic Church. At the time he was writing, he perceived a growing consensus on the dictates of natural law. (He did not, however, formulate the natural law in terms of the fundamental values.)

19. Although I draw on Finnis for the list of values, my development of the principles of personal justice does not parallel his development of the requirements of practical reasonableness (his Ch. 5). My principles of social justice also differ from his approach in chapters 6 and 7 of *Natural Law and Natural Rights*. Grisez (1989) offers an analysis of the relationship between natural law and the fundamental values, and Rhonheimer (1987) explores the meaning of "goals" and identifies how they are specified in the natural law approach.

20. "Religion" may suggest too many irrelevant institutional factors. "Spirituality" is perhaps more appealing to some because a person's spiritual life need not be bound to institutional structures. The difficulty is that "spirituality" might suggest that the value is only concerned with exploring the dimensions of the human psyche and not with some reality above and beyond the human. Despite its shortcomings, "religion" best expresses the reality I seek to describe.

21. Why seven fundamental values and not eight or five? There could be eight or five, depending on how one groups the different components of human experience. Whatever numerical division is chosen, the set of values must possess the properties of mutual exclusivity and completeness. That is, only the taxonomy which allows no overlay between the fundamental values and which is inclusive of all human experience of significant values is the correct one for our purposes. Although each of the fundamental values should be construed broadly and any true value should be able to fit, at least vaguely, in the category of one of the fundamental values, it is important that each fundamental value not overlap with any other fundamental value. Individual actions, of course, can promote one or more fundamental values simultaneously; the fundamental values themselves, however, should remain distinct so that we can speak about the requirements, conflicting at times, of each fundamental value. Many secondary values embrace aspects of two or more fundamental values and, therefore, it may be unclear to which of the fundamental values they best correspond. Another reason why secondary values are secondary is that they are appropriately pursued only in limited circumstances. What distinguishes fundamental values from other values is that the fundamental ones are so basic to what it means to be a human being that a person would not want to act directly against a fundamental value no matter what the circumstances, and that life itself is meaningful only if the person sets as an objective the pursuit of one or more of the fundamental values.

22. See MacIntyre (1984, pp. 61–63) for a discussion of different types of happiness.

23. This modern form of eudaemonism differs essentially from Aristotle. (However, it does represent accurately, according to Sen [1991], the views of Bentham and Mill.) According to Aristotle, happiness is activity in accordance with virtue, and he argued that the highest form of happiness is achieved through intellectual or philosophical activity. For a discussion, see Copleston (1985, I: 332–50).

Aristotle envisions happiness as the consequence of living the ethical life, i.e., of living according to right standards for a human being, which is the highest goal of human endeavors. Therefore, Aristotelian eudaemonism, as well as other classical forms of eudaemonism, incorporates ethical standards not based on happiness, to which a person must adhere. The fundamental values approach is consistent with classical eudaemonism since it claims that true human satisfaction is achieved through the pursuit of the fundamental values. But I reject the simple form of eudaemonism as it is expressed in various utilitarian systems. In the text I argue strongly against the homogeneity of happiness and the legitimacy of making happiness the sole criterion of ethical actions. Notwithstanding such comments, one can validly argue that a common thread is present in all forms of human happiness and that the common thread is the basis for asserting that the ultimate goal of human action is human happiness. Fagothey (1959) provides a useful analysis of the issues.

24. This is a particular example of a larger issue: What is one ethically expected to do in a situation when many other people are acting immorally? To analyze future behavior, economists use the concept of rational expectations, and an analogous concept is appropriate in situations which a large number of agents are acting unethically. The concept of rational moral expectations is examined in a later section.

25. This type of situation is considered later in this section when we treat the reaction principle. Although some action against the terrorist may be taken involving the loss of life, killing the innocent person sought by the terrorist cannot be defended.

26. A thorough review of hierarchies of values is given in McCormick et al. (1978). A traditional moral principle referred to frequently in the literature is the Principle of Double Effect, according to which an act which has a primary effect, which is a physical good, and a secondary effect, which is a physical evil, is morally good if the physical good is proportionately greater than the evil. With the significant restriction that one can only compare physical good and physical evil within the same category of a fundamental value, this principle can be derived from the noncontrary principle.

27. See Schüller (1970), who shows how it is possible to create at least theoretical exceptions to any general moral prohibition or injunction. In a related area, Jonsen and Toulmin (1988, p. 68) argue that the essential nature of the concept of equity in law is to correct the law in those situations where it is too general.

28. In determining the significance or the moral quality of an action, a purely physical description of the action is never adequate. For example, writing one's name is a different action, depending on whether one is signing a treaty, a check, or just doodling. MacIntyre (1962) argues convincingly that in order for actions to be intelligible they must rely upon canons of rationality supported by society.

29. Finnis (1980, pp. 118–24) enunciates this principle but expresses it more generally as the need to show respect for every basic value in every act. I use "action" instead of act, a nontrivial change. For Finnis an act which does not show respect is an act "which *of itself does nothing but damage* or impede a realization or participation of any one or more basic forms of human good." Finnis's formulation suggests that good consequences can never justify the damage done through the act itself. Finnis's articulation of what it means to violate the natural law is either permissive of a wide variety of questionable acts or it is excessively restrictive, depending on one's interpretation. Since most acts enable some participation in a fundamental value, no act is ever purely bad, i.e., "does nothing but damage or impede" realization of basic forms of the human good. On the other hand, if the statement means that no action is allowed which in any way prevents the pursuit of a fundamental value, this renders morally suspect many actions which a wide range of philosophers consider ethically acceptable. I clarify this important ambiguity by endorsing the Principle of Double Effect (see McCormick and Ramsay [1978]) and in so doing I make two distinctions. First, I note the traditional difference between direct and indirect effect, as required by the Principle of Double Effect. Second, I restrict the application of the Principle of Double Effect to a single fundamental value. I justify this stipulation by noting that no fundamental value deserves greater weight than another when contemplating a free decision to act against one of the values. Each fundamental value is a good in itself that is incomparable with other fundamental values. A person can freely choose to pursue one value more intensely than another, but one should never act directly contrary to one value with the specious justification that one is pursuing another fundamental value.

30. Perry (1988, pp. 12–23) criticizes Finnis for claiming that the desire to flourish through the pursuit of the fundamental values (or basic goods) is "self-evident," "unquestionable," or "underived." Perry, instead, stresses the commitment which many people have, de facto, to the fundamental values. Without such a commitment, much of our language about good things in life is without foundation.

31. Finnis (1980, pp. 125–26) says that following one's conscience is a dictate of practical reasonableness. By applying the Principle of Personal Freedom to other people, a person attains an initial understanding of how society in general will respond to various actions performed by individuals.

32. Economists such as Etzioni (1986) and Margolis (1982) recognize that people seek the common good, but in their models they allow the common good to have but a single dimension.

33. For a discussion of the common good see MacIntyre (1984), Finnis (1980, pp. 134–60) and von Nell-Breuning (1980, 1985). Hollenbach (1989) notes a resurgence of interest in the concept and studies the various ways in which the concept of the common good has been used and developed; he argues that the common good is consistent with an emphasis on individual rights, although liberals often set rights in opposition to any conception of the common good that implies content rather than mere procedure or process. Pole (1978) explores the ways in which equality, in its many different meanings and as reflected in federal and state law in the United States, has promoted the common good.

34. Similar to MacIntyre but from a sociological perspective, Wolfe argues persuasively that a full morality can be developed only in community with others: "We make the moral rules that make us; we are, in a word, what we do, and what we do is done together with others" (1989, p. 220).

NOTES FOR CHAPTER 4

1. As a series of organizations, religion has similarities with secular institutions and can be analyzed using neoclassical techniques. Iannaccone (1992) studies the role played by personal sacrifice in helping clubs, cults, and collectives to reduce the amount of free-riding occurring in such groups. He obtains mixed results when he submits his model to an empirical test. This

type of study is useful, but one should not forget that Iannaccone and others do not claim that members of religious institutions are motivated solely by efficiency or economic considerations.

2. The natural law tradition was nurtured by the Judeo-Christian community, and numerous Christian and Jewish philosophers have refined and reformulated it. Nonetheless, in presenting the arguments for the natural law approach, I have used arguments that are persuasive, I think, for people from other religious and nonreligious traditions as well.

3. A person who acts unethically may realize that what she is doing is wrong. However, she hopes and/or deceives herself into thinking that the action, although wrong, will make her happy. It is the focus on short-term happiness and the neglect of the demands of the fundamental values which make the act morally wrong.

4. For an interesting analysis of the relationship among labor, work, and action see Arendt (1958).

5. Sexuality, understood as the proper orientation of one's body and psyche toward members of one's own sex and members of the opposite sex, is a value that is included under the basic good of life. By including the word "proper" in the description, one acknowledges that sexuality can only be defined within a larger context. In this sense, sexuality is a second-order value.

6. Elster (1983) allows fundamental values in his framework but would not consider them normative, either at the individual or collective level.

7. Insofar as the fundamental values are binding on everyone, they are not "values" in the modern understanding of that word. In modern parlance "values" are freely chosen, not imposed on people. In a pluralist society person A chooses sex and violence for his preferred values while person B selects family and loyalty as her preferred values. According to the modern understanding, each person chooses freely and, as long as one is not inclined to act illegally, there are no constraints on the choices which people make. The fundamental values approach, on the other hand, maintains that although values are not imposed in a pluralist society, each person has a moral responsibility to acknowledge the priority of the essential human goals and the demands which they make in his or her life.

8. Conley (1990) presents a carefully justified set of four criteria for public support of the arts in a pluralist society. The four are: formal structure, appropriateness, representativity, and moral sensitivity. Each criterion is partially conditioned by common understandings in society.

9. Fuchs (1989) explores how it is that different cultures and distinct traditions within the same culture rationally propose divergent ethical principles. He notes that practically all societies agree upon ethical values that must be respected when individuals act. For example, people are supposed to be just, merciful, faithful, etc. Individual societies and traditions interpret these requirements in a variety of ways. The result is a plurality of specific ethical principles, although wide uniformity prevails concerning the values human beings are called upon to respect.

10. MacIntyre (1988, pp. 326–48) shows that liberalism, which relies upon the utilitarianism at the basis of neoclassical thinking, is only one tradi-

tion alongside three other traditions. It enjoys no superior vantage point from which it can judge others or establish itself as better than other traditions.

11. The three budget items are interrelated. Basic research may provide a long-term solution for the homeless that is structured with incentives that encourage the homeless to do what they can to care for themselves and that do not encourage more people to become homeless because of the generous benefits they receive. Better public transportation might offer substantial benefits to the homeless. Feedback loops such as these increase the social and moral challenge to legislators.

12. Seligman (1992) presents a potent challenge to my suggestion that society in the latter part of the twentieth century could actually adhere to principles such as the common good. He notes that Locke's idea of civil society included two concepts that are no longer operative in modern society: that God cares for human beings and that passions can be kept under the rule of reason. Though Seligman lacks confidence in the ability of modern society to resurrect the foundational beliefs undergirding civil society, he misrepresents, in my estimation, the degree to which modern members of society have become independent automata. Without trying to respond comprehensively to Seligman's main argument, I observe that the natural law approach antedates by several centuries Locke's treatises on government and that it arises out of a distinctly communitarian—not an individualistic—tradition.

13. In the early part of this century, Pesch (1905–06) undertook an economic study that combined a treatment of the ethical prescriptions contained in natural law theory and economic theory, as it was understood at that time in German-speaking lands. Although I differ from Pesch, my goal is the same as his, that is, to show how the economy can be structured in a way that conforms to a widespread concept of ethics and to show how any individual can behave ethically in a modern economy, even one marred by injustices. The fundamental values approach continues the natural law tradition in an idiom which, I think, is more accessible to the modern mind. Furthermore, the neoclassical theory which I use has the benefit of an additional eighty years of theoretical research and empirical analysis by economists.

14. MacIntyre notes that, prior to the Enlightenment, two important traditions reached a new synthesis in Aquinas. Before Aquinas, one tradition started with Homer and Aristotle, was preserved and developed by Arab and Jewish philosophers, and reached its turning point in Aquinas, and a second one passed from the Bible through Augustine, with assistance from the neoplatonists, and down to Aquinas. The Scottish moral tradition, which adopted Aristotelianism as it was received through the Calvinists, passed it on to Hume, who radicalized it.

15. MacIntyre (1988), chapters 17–20.

16. My claim concerning the cogency of the fundamental values approach can be validated only if the approach I take in this study challenges others to reflect on the issues which I raise and they then confront their own tradition with the same questions. It is my conviction that the other traditions ultimately will acknowledge that the fundamental values approach explains in a more satisfactory manner the moral commitment of people as well as the

way in which people expect just societies to operate. Movement toward such a consensus begins with the reader. If the reader agrees with the various explications of the fundamental values and the four principles of personal justice, his or her agreement is a small, but personally significant, confirmation and reaffirmation of the natural law tradition.

NOTES FOR CHAPTER 5

1. Aristotle, *Nichomachean Ethics* I, 3:1094b, 12–14.

2. Finnis (1980, pp. 111–18) calls this principle "the limited relevance of consequences: efficiency within reason" and says that it is a requirement of practical reasonableness.

3. MacIntyre (1984, pp. 51–61) shows that even our modern society combines factual presentation ("is") with normative implications ("ought"). When desirable skills are discussed—such as what it means to be a sailor—people describe the factual skills as worthy ones. For example, a sailor is someone who adheres to certain standards, as does an airplane pilot or cook.

4. Neoclassical approaches stress efficiency within the family unit. Their approach prevents them from considering ethical considerations or from examining the contribution that the institution of the family makes to society, although they analyze the effect which parental concern has on the quantity and quality of children. See Becker (1976, 1981), Becker and Murphy (1988), and Kotlikoff and Spivak (1981). Goode (1974) notes significant aspects of family life omitted in Becker's studies, and Bergstrom (1989) points out that Becker's well-known "Rotten Kid Theorem" only applies to a restricted class of cases. In particular, he notes that a son can be prodigal and a father can be forgiving.

5. Kohlberg (1969, 1973) delineates the role played by the family as a child moves through the stages of moral development to adult moral judgments.

6. Many modern philosophers and ethical theorists either implicitly or explicitly use the concept of a life plan. See Hittinger (1987, pp. 79–92) for an analysis of the various meanings of "life plan."

7. Nitzan and Paroush (1980) argue that people acquire human capital in order to avoid making mistakes. This may be true, but it presumes some understanding of what a mistake is, in terms of one's life. In the fundamental values approach a mistake is not to seek the fundamental values or to act directly contrary to a fundamental value.

8. In addition to the wage, economists usually list several factors that influence the choice of employment: benefits, working conditions, authority, potential for advancement, pressure, congeniality of fellow employees, etc. "Thrill of the job" is a catchall term for all nonwage related factors that economists list.

9. Lutz and Lux (1988) use Maslow's hierarchy of needs to distinguish between needs, which are primary, and wants, which are secondary. Though not identical to the category of needs identified by Lutz and Lux, my grouping of materials of personal sustenance captures the segment of primary human needs requiring economic resources.

10. The supply of labor and management services depends on the compensation offered. A higher wage, however, does not produce more labor; it merely causes the labor, which already exists, to become effectively present in the marketplace.

11. Society should intervene to prevent construction of the mine if the prices do not reflect the full social costs and benefits of coal production. In these circumstances, the assumptions of the Fundamental Theorem of Welfare Economics (see section 7.1) do not hold, and some intervention is required to promote efficiency.

12. Exceptions usually involve the reaction principle. For example, if all fish become infected with some toxic bacteria so that eating fish is a threat to life, eating chicken would be justified, even though chicken is considered higher on the scale of life than fish.

13. Mackay (1987, pp. 28–31) cites the figure of twenty deaths and also describes the dangers to which the workers were subjected.

14. A project manager does not have to choose the *safest* possible production method without respect to costs. Rather, in order to avoid actions directly contrary to the value of life, the production manager must achieve a degree of safety that approximates the uncertainty faced by people in the ordinary activities of life.

15. The word "society" in this context is used as a generic term to designate whichever group is responsible for making a particular economic decision. According to the principle of subsidiarity the unit selected should be the smallest feasible unit. Since, however, the issue under consideration is the parameters that are appropriate for the economic system as a whole, for the most part "society" refers to the government, rather than to a particular governmental or private institution.

16. Bellah et al. (1991) highlight the significance of institutions, and they note the need for a more positive approach to the role of institutions in American society. Although their concern is mainly with macro-institutions such as the market, government, education, and churches, they identify characteristic attitudes necessary for a society to thrive. They describe democracy as the act of paying attention to common problems and aspirations, and they see in the family paradigmatic qualities that should characterize all macro-institutions in society.

17. Although I have referred to institutions many times throughout the text, I have deferred giving even an informal definition until this time because institutions arise out of common understandings—the topic of this section. The close connection between institutions and expectations (or common understandings) is analyzed by Bellah et al. (1991, pp. 10–12, 287–93). As understood in this text, an institution is a system of common understandings concerning the manner in which people interact effectively in the pursuit of important values. By defining institution in this way, I remain within a long philosophical and sociological tradition that perceives institutions as normative. Bellah et al. offer a comparable definition: "An institution is a pattern of expected action of

individuals or groups enforced by social sanctions, both positive and negative" (p. 10).

18. Culture should be understood in the broad sense in which Geertz (1973) defines it: "[Culture] denotes an historically transmitted pattern of meanings embodied in symbols, a system of inherited conceptions expressed in symbolic forms by means of which men communicate, perpetuate, and develop their knowledge about and attitudes toward life" (p. 89). Geertz quickly notes that the definition requires further specification of "meaning," "symbol," and "conception." In the natural law framework, the fundamental values provide meaning, and common understandings concerning the realization of the fundamental values are both symbols and conceptions.

19. During the Middle Ages and even after the Reformation until the time of the Enlightenment, it was common for the state to impose religious practice on its members. A possible justification is that religion played such an important role in daily life that it was inconceivable how people with different religions could peacefully coexist in the same state or geographical region. The fundamental value of life appeared to be threatened by simultaneous practice of two religions. Since one is not allowed to act against a fundamental value, society sharply curtailed the freedom of religious dissidents. Once peaceful coexistence was perceived as a possibility, the state no longer had any moral justification for imposing a single religion.

20. The example presumes, as is the case, that killing the tribal chief is directly contrary to the fundamental value. The tribe does not share this conviction, but, like any other group in society, the tribe must yield to the judgment of the leadership of all units in society.

21. The reason that opposite colors do not mix is specious for two reasons. First, color does not determine the worth of a person. Second, claiming that people of different color should not mix would prohibit hand holding not just between blacks and whites but between whites and Asians, whites and Native Americans, blacks and Indians, etc. Human experience in the twentieth century rejects such broad prohibitions.

22. Berlin (1969) notes the conflict between negative freedom (human rights) and positive freedom (right to determine by whom one is ruled). Since, in his view, positive freedom is more open to abuse, negative freedom should be given priority. In my view, Berlin does not give sufficient weight to the necessity and usefulness of common understandings to pursue the fundamental values, values which Berlin does not acknowledge as universally binding.

23. This is one of Tawney's main criticisms of capitalism; see Tawney (1948, 1952) and Martin (1985).

24. Moore (1985, p. 104) argues that the inability to develop a working notion of legitimate opposition to prevailing or proposed policies has bedeviled most societies, including modern liberal democracies.

25. John Courtney Murray, a prominent natural law theorist, limited the power of government to four areas, which are necessary for coexistence in a society and which collectively he designates as public order: justice, public peace, public morality, and public prosperity. Only when public order is violated or liable to be violated is the government allowed to intervene. Since the

areas are quite broad, the government has potentially great powers, the exercise of which depends on the situation. See Hollenbach (1988, pp. 12–15, 71–84, 101–104) for an analysis.

26. Most monarchical systems may nonetheless have been unjust because, although the broad structure was reasonable and just, individual institutions in society may have been unjust, and powerful individuals may have consistently acted unjustly.

27. The requirement that people not be forced to relocate is formulated in such a way that both labor and management incur the responsibility to implement the principle. For example, it may be that labor, in its negotiations with management, has a responsibility to contribute money to a fund that provides payments for long-term workers at a particular plant in the event that the plant is closed.

28. Frank (1988, p. 247) makes the practical point that high geographical mobility impairs the ability of people to make credible commitments, which, in turn, decreases the material welfare of society and individuals in society.

NOTES FOR CHAPTER 6

1. Tinari (1987) provides a useful analysis of four concepts of economic equity.

2. Despite the difficulty of identifying a "social minimum," people can agree about trends. Moynihan (1991) justifies positive steps to alleviate poverty among children, especially among African-Americans, by noting that the percentage of children experiencing poverty before reaching the age of 18 has increased substantially over the past twenty-five years. About 80 percent of African-Americans reaching their eighteenth birthday in 1997 will have experienced poverty, according to the federal definition of poverty.

3. Mishan (1980) states that neoclassical theory is almost useless in addressing the needs of the poor in modern, affluent societies.

4. Macpherson (1985, pp. 1–20) claims that this is not a principle of justice for the good reason that it is basically an economic principle (people agree to it out of their own self-interest) and not an ethical one. Macpherson is correct in noting that in order for a rule to be a principle of justice some commitment to the welfare of people other than oneself is necessary. But this concern is not operative for those who choose behind the Rawlsian veil of ignorance.

5. Both Sandel (1982) and Perry (1991) argue that Rawls makes the right (justice) prior to the good. They note that Rawlsian deliberators in the original position are described as having no knowledge of what is good for them; however, they are committed to justice, which is one particular aspect of the good. Perry analyzes Rawls's more recent writings in which Rawls, in response to such criticisms, denies that he wants the right prior to the good. Rather, Rawls adjusts his position to make the right be consonant with the good by allowing any comprehensive system that supports Rawlsian principles of justice—such as the difference principle. Although Rawls intends to make the good prior to the right (justice), Perry remains unconvinced since he notes ambiguities even in Rawls's recent writings concerning this issue.

6. Sandel (1982, pp. 133–74) argues that the "persons" in the original situation are not persons in the ordinary sense of the word because no one in the original position has any sense of what is good in life. Rawlsian persons in the original position are pure selves, separated from any personal knowledge or personal commitment to the good, as they see it. As a result, there is no plurality of persons in the original position but only one person, since all persons are identical. There is no discussion, no disagreement, and no contract, because the Rawlsian persons lack the differentiation required for a discussion, a disagreement, or a contract. The Sandelian critique, which is persuasive, destroys the foundation for the difference principle. The principle itself, however, can be saved and put on a solid foundation, no surprise here, by using the fundamental values approach. The principle of distribution, derived later in this section, incorporates a slightly modified difference principle as one of its components.

Perry (1988) argues in a similar vein: "As I explained, . . . [the effort to imagine a politics that is 'neutral' or 'impartial' among competing conceptions of human good] is a dead-end. The liberal conception of the proper relation of morality/religion to politics/law is impossible to achieve. One's participation in politics and law is and must be based on one's most basic convictions about human good, including one's religious convictions (if one has any religious convictions)" (p. 180). For an expanded treatment, see also Perry (1991).

7. Holcombe (1983) faults Rawls for this omission.

8. According to Sandel (1982), Rawls's notion of the self, as described in the original position, is incompatible with the principles of justice which the self derives.

9. See Frank (1985b) for a good analysis of the role of relative income in determining the structure of economic institutions and markets. Status is an important consideration in determining a just society, and in section 8.2 I present a full analysis of the legitimate role it plays.

10. Neoclassical economists assume that people are selfish, although they do not intend to impugn a person's moral character by this assumption. The neoclassical model suggests an intuitive reason why a person is legitimately concerned about status. Since, according to the neoclassical paradigm, concern for self constitutes the consumer and because the self is partially defined in relation to others, each person compares herself with other people in society. If, on the other hand, the pursuit of fundamental values is the goal of life and if people have sufficient goods to pursue the fundamental values, it is not immediately apparent why people should be interested in how much income other people have.

11. Cooter and Rappoport (1984) argue historically and analytically that the move away from cardinal utility, in which interpersonal comparisons are made, to ordinal utility, which does not allow comparisons between individuals, was not and is not justified.

12. See Rawls (1982) for a discussion of the role of primary goods.

13. Rawls rejects the argument that personal merit is a valid criterion for allocating goods in society. See Sandel (1982, pp. 66–103).

14. See Buchanan (1986, p. 126ff.).

15. Another approach to fairness relying on procedures rather than principles is superfairness. According to Baumol (1986b, p. 15), a superfair distribution is one in which every group prefers the allocation it receives to the share received by other groups. That is, no group envies another group. As will be seen when we analyze envy in Chapter 8, superfair distributions do not occur in society at the macro level. At best they apply in limited situations that already suppose that ethical principles, such as the ones we have enunciated, are binding.

16. Langan (1977) presents a careful analysis of the philosophical and political differences between Rawls and Nozick. Varian (1975) shows that an equitable and efficient solution exists as long as labor is not part of the initial endowment; if it is, one must examine consumption-output bundles in order to arrive at a fair and equitable solution.

17. See Nozick (1974) and Buchanan (1986, pp. 123–39).

18. See Pole (1978, pp. 112–47).

19. The existence of impartial referees or judges assumes that some people who are impervious to bribes can be trained for these positions. It is doubtful that such training can be effective in a society that stresses profit maximization above all else.

20. This consideration constitutes a justification for Rawls's difference principle, but it requires that everyone in society be committed to the fundamental values. If people in the original situation were also committed to the fundamental values, they would have a moral obligation to subscribe to something like the difference principle, in order to protect the fundamental value of life. In this case, however, their support of the difference principle would be based not on preferences but on ethical conviction.

21. MacIntyre (1988, pp. 326–48) illuminates the vacuity of the liberal approach.

22. Etzioni (1987) makes this point. The assumptions of neoclassical economics guarantee that self-interests are automatically compatible with one another; in fact, self-interested individuals are often in conflict and require some harmonization, which is aided by appeals to just behavior.

23. Hampshire (1982) states that only general moral principles are essential to determine a just distribution, while more particular prescriptions depend on the particularities of an individual culture. I agree and present only general moral principles.

24. Despite their many differences, Rawls and Nozick have the same attitude toward utilitarianism: they reject it completely as a method for social analysis. Any individual may choose to be a utilitarian, but for society to be utilitarian implies that social utilitarianism either makes no distinction between individuals or makes arbitrary distinctions. See Sandel (1982, p. 66) and Perry (1988, pp. 57–73).

25. Even these rules cannot be adequately policed and enforced by the authorities, since threat and compulsion are rarely sufficient to gain compliance with rules. Society establishes a mechanism for monitoring compliance and assigns penalties for infractions of the rules, but for the most part it relies on the existence of extra-legal penalties, such as scorn, embarrassment, and

dishonor, which exert pressure on people and institutions to comply with the rules.

26. The veil of ignorance, however, makes the people in the original position more impersonal and less like objective people in the real world. As Wolfe (1989, p. 125) points out, "In a world where people raise children, live in communities, and value friendships, a moral theory that demands rational cognition to the degree that Rawls's does is little help and may well be a burden. It teaches people to distrust what will help them most—their personal attachments to those they know—and value what will help them least—abstract principles that, for all their philosophical brilliance, are a poor guide to the moral dilemmas of everyday life."

27. See National Conference of Catholic Bishops (1986).

28. Sen (1985) points out the difficulty of reconciling a democratic structure with "normal" neoclassical assumptions. He also notes that one way to remove such incompatibilities is for neoclassicals to distinguish between primary goods and other goods which are useful but not necessary for human achievement.

29. See Piderit (1985) for a moral preference for promotion of education and skills among the poor; Schultz (1980) recommends a similar approach.

30. The party in greater need can make no special claim on the other party unless the need is directly related to the disagreement or unless the person in less need has a greater degree of bonding to the person in need than others in society.

31. One requirement which Rawls mentions is that "the judge be immune from all reasonably foreseeable consequences of the judgment" (1951, p. 181). In the fundamental values approach, however, every ethical judgment has consequences for the person, which should be taken into consideration. If, for example, by adjudicating a case in a certain way a judge acts directly contrary to a fundamental value, she is less of a person than before she passed judgment; furthermore, the prior realization of this outcome should influence the decision of the judge to modify her ruling by searching more thoroughly for a legal statute that justifies a decision consonant with the pursuit of the fundamental values.

32. The example assumes that society has specific knowledge about how the woman will react to a change in income-tax rates. As was pointed out in our discussion of redistribution, society should make judgments about redistributing money between groups, not individuals, since society does not know the thoughts and plans of individuals. To make the example more cogent, it should not describe a particular person who gained great wealth honestly but the class of people who earned great wealth honestly.

33. Using data from an extensive case study, Mann (1973) examines the reasons why workers choose to relocate. Not surprisingly, workers in his study considered many quality-of-life factors in deciding whether or not to move to a new city.

34. In subsequent chapters, the social principles of justice are assumed to pertain to modern economies, especially the United States. When applying the rules to a particular modern economy, however, one should be cognizant that it is possible that different common understandings and institutional arrangements in two different modern economies may require two different, and perhaps conflicting, sets of ethical criteria.

NOTES FOR CHAPTER 7

1. The many varieties of capitalism and the degree to which they differ from socialism are given thorough and nuanced treatment in von Nell-Breuning (1986). See also Bell (1976), Heilbroner (1985), Hirschman (1977), and Novak (1982).

2. A society reveals its moral tone in part by specifying types of transactions that are prohibited. Walzer (1983, pp. 95–103) calls these "blocked exchanges" because they limit the types of things that money is allowed to buy.

3. Salvatore (1986, pp. 583–606) gives a lucid graphical presentation of Pareto efficiency and Pareto optimality. An analytically rigorous presentation of the assumptions and proofs of the central theorems of general equilibrium is found in Arrow and Hahn (1971, pp. 16–106), Baumol (1977, pp. 496–569), and Quirk and Saposnik (1968). Duffie and Sonnenschein (1989) present a sympathetic and insightful evaluation of general equilibrium theory and welfare theory.

4. Much productive activity takes place within the home and is not subject to the rules of market interaction. Locay (1990) suggests that firms specialize in the early stages of production while households cover the later stages. The smaller the potential market, the more likely it is that a firm will not only produce the entire good itself but also will introduce multiple product lines.

5. Although more information than less is usually advantageous, under some restricted circumstances more information may create a liability. Dreze (1987) shows how information changes the set of feasible courses of action, and added information may eliminate previously feasible actions. In a complementary way, Camerer, Lowenstein, and Weber (1989) explain that in some circumstances agents are unable to ignore knowledge even though they realize that profits will be higher if they disregard it.

6. Akerlof (1970) launched an investigation of market performance in the presence of heterogeneous quality.

7. In contracts, many clauses are impossible to verify. For example, an automobile insurance policy usually stipulates that the driver not take unnecessary risks. This means that the driver should drive as carefully as she would if she had no insurance. Because the market cannot monitor compliance, it avoids giving complete insurance. The propensity of agents to act differently, usually with more abandon, when they are covered by insurance is called moral hazard by economists (see Arnott and Stiglitz [1991]).

In the work place, employers often find it difficult to verify whether employees work "hard." The difficulties of motivating agents to adhere to a standard established by a "principal," are called agency problems or principal-agent problems. Sappington (1992) reviews research results obtained to date, which have been modest. Germane to our discussion, no significant research, he notes, has been undertaken on principal-agent problems in complex organizations, such as firms or bureaucracies. Only the most straightforward problems between one principal and one agent have been analyzed. Even within this limited framework, Prisoner Dilemma situations involving the potential for cooperation between the principal and agent or between two agents are not considered. See also Lazear (1991) for a similar treatment in the context of labor relations.

8. The text indicates how the condition is violated. Another type of infraction occurs whenever an agent considers how the good enables her to attain a relative advantage over other agents making similar decisions. Prestige or positional goods are purchased by consumers primarily because they communicate to others the relative wealth or sophistication of the owner. Positional goods can be attractive additives—such as jewelry and minks—or they can provide a foundation for further accomplishments—such as education. For a discussion of parents' desire to obtain prestige education for their children see Frank (1992, pp. 162–164) and Mattox (1991).

9. Expressed mathematically, the condition for producers is that the production set be convex; for consumers, the utility function must be quasiconcave.

10. Neoclassical economists try to adhere to as many of these eleven assumptions as possible. Nonetheless, when neoclassical economists can identify an economic reason why the assumptions may not hold, they are willing to consider alternatives. See Mankiw (1990) for a description of topics in which neoclassical economists make nonorthodox assumptions for economic reasons.

11. Instead of earning higher profits, ABC could choose to pay its employees higher wages.

12. See Simon (1957), Hirschman (1970), and Leibenstein (1966, 1980) for useful analyses of organizational slack and "X-inefficiency."

13. If technology is considered a nonrival good, Romer (1990a, 1990b) shows that monopolistic competition determines results but firms invest less in human capital than is necessary to achieve optimal growth. For an analysis of different growth theories, see Ehrlich (1990). Mokyr (1990) argues that, in order to be successful, innovations must be introduced into a receptive environment. Many good innovations have languished because structural elements in society were not prepared to make the necessary changes.

14. See Boland (1981).

15. Gorman and Kehr (1992) review some old evidence and present new data about the extent to which people deviate from profit-maximizing behavior because they want to act fairly. The authors offer a statistical analysis and do not attempt to specify exactly what constitutes fair and unfair activities.

16. As stated in the Fundamental Theorem, profit maximization is a necessary and, together with the other assumptions, sufficient condition for Pareto efficiency. Just because a condition is among the sufficient conditions does not imply that there is a moral obligation to fulfill the condition. If that were true, an efficient society would have to try to banish public goods and externalities from the economy. The correct argument is more nuanced. Individual units

operate efficiently only if their activities are supported by common understandings in society. Workers in firms do not naturally look for ways to produce goods more efficiently and consumers do not naturally spend their money effectively. Both groups are taught how to use resources effectively through a variety of institutions in society. If individual units perform efficiently the function allocated to them by society and if the number and degree of externalities are not significant, then institutions should support the operation of these units with common understandings.

17. Broome (1991) discusses a basic confusion concerning the word "utility." The normal meaning of utility is something that is beneficial for the person, but this is not the way in which it is used by neoclassical economists, for whom utility means preferences, and nothing more. The preferences may be good or bad, helpful or deleterious. By restricting its usage in this way, economists sidestep significant moral issues, some of which are addressed in this text.

18. As is noted in Appendix B, one regularity condition is that more consumption is always better for the consumer. Although no economist thinks this assumption is literally true, most economists use it as a reasonable approximation to most people's attitudes toward consumption. Bellah et al. (1991, pp. 4–9), however, describe the pain experienced by many citizens of the latter twentieth century when they consume goods even as they pass by homeless people or people whose lives are otherwise in complete disarray. Bellah notes "the difficulty of being a good person in the absence of a good society" (p. 4). This is a direct challenge to the third regularity condition that a person's satisfaction is determined solely by his or her own consumption of goods. In a world of crime, drugs, and child abuse, most people would admit that their satisfaction is diminished when they hear of a tragedy—such as child abuse—befalling another person, even though that person may be a perfect stranger.

19. See Cox and Epstein (1989), Chalfont and Alston (1988), Sen (1973, 1974, 1979, 1980, 1987), and Sen and Williams (1982). Conlisk (1989), and Slovic and Lichtenstein (1983) uncover similar anomalies in the more realistic case of uncertainty. Earl (1983) studies alternative approaches to the neoclassical approach; he makes important use of the concept of bounded rationality.

20. Frank (1988, pp. 237–59) presents abundant evidence for altruistic behavior which is inconsistent with "rational" self-interest, but shows how such behavior is "rational" inasmuch as it produces material benefits for individuals.

21. In recent years, the assumptions of utility and profit maximization have been attacked not for their spirit but for their generality. Because people cannot handle all the information available to them, they search for ways to narrow their scope of choices. Within a narrow or bounded scope, maximization is then performed. This phenomenon is called bounded rationality. See Simon (1979), Heiner (1983), and Hirshleifer (1985).

22. Such concerns for the unfortunate can be justified even in a society not committed to the fundamental values by appealing to individual self-interest. That is, if help is not provided, other members of society suffer discomfort because they are required to see others experience pain and squalor.

23. See Arrow (1963, 1967). Salvatore (1986, pp. 589–99) gives a brief but cogent illustration of why a democratic vote can yield inconsistent preferences; useful discussions of voting paradoxes are also found in Baumol (1977, pp. 531–34), Harsanyi (1955), Sen (1970), and Cooter and Rappoport (1984).

24. As before and as a result of the Arrow Impossibility Theorem, we know that no democratic procedure exists for determining the new community indifference curves, which are the curves bending in the opposite direction from the production possibilities frontier. For an analysis of the community indifference curves, see Appendix A.

25. Sen (1987) notes that the neoclassical concepts of self, welfare, and utility allow many nuanced distinctions. Neoclassical utility need not be treated in monolithic fashion; however, accommodating distinctions among satisfaction, means, and ends, for example, dilutes the impact of neoclassical theorems concerning efficiency. See also Frank (1987).

26. Lasch (1991) chronicles the strong tradition of virtuous restraint from the eighteenth century, when thinkers first began to promote desires because they would lead to a general improvement for all people, until the present. This counter-tradition of temperance and moderation is especially strong in the lower-middle-class culture and has been given theoretical substance by a wide variety of thinkers.

27. For a discussion of contestable markets see Baumol (1982c, 1986a), and Baumol, Panzar, and Willig (1982b). Contestable markets do not prevent firms, however, from realizing some monopoly profits, as Shepard (1991) shows.

28. In particular, democratic voting is unlikely to produce an objective evaluation because an economic system needs institutions which require many years to establish and only those people who happen to be living at the current time have the opportunity to vote.

NOTES FOR CHAPTER 8

1. See Hirschman (1977, 1982). While it appears that society is indeed more well ordered in the twentieth century, the order itself is disturbing, since it consigns a majority of the world population to a situation that even wealthy people can only describe as deplorable poverty. See Polanyi (1957) for a similar evaluation of the different "goods" desired by people in earlier ages.

2. In the neoclassical paradigm nothing is said about the head of the firm because the neoclassical paradigm does not allow for a hierarchy within the firm. Only generic categories, such as land, labor, and capital, are analyzed in the neoclassical theory of the firm. CEOs and division managers do not exist in the neoclassical framework. As often happens in economics, a very careful model is outlined, theorems are proved, and then people extend the model informally so that it can apply to aspects of the real world which are not present in the strict, mathematical formulation of the model.

3. Baumol (1982a, 1986b) uses envy as a means to judge whether an allocation is fair; a fair allocation is one in which no one envies another person. According to the fundamental values approach, a fair allocation in Baumol's sense may be unjust, while many unfair allocations in Baumol's sense conform to the principles of justice.

Whenever possible, economists shy away from treating the motives of the consumer and concentrate instead on the goods themselves. If a particular good is desired by most people for its ability to demonstrate the wealth of the owner rather than for its usefulness in performing some activity desirable in itself, economists call it a positional good. Thus, where I speak of type 2 envy, they speak of positional goods.

4. Concerning the economic possibility and plausibility of a nonselfish society see Collard (1978).

5. A thorough as well as entertaining analysis of the question is given in Frank (1985b), upon whom the treatment in this section relies. Figure 8.1 is a variation of the diagrams which Frank presents in chapters 3 and 4. See also Frank (1985a), and Thaler and Shefrin (1981).

6. The word "marginal" is used not to suggest that the worker is marginal in quality, but to indicate that the wages for all are determined by the last worker hired, i.e., by the worker at the margin.

7. Frank (1992, pp. 162–64) shows that parents, in order to enable their children to attend the "best" private schools, work longer hours, and, as a result, have less time to spend with their children. Since "best" is a relative term, the pressure that each parent experiences to outdo the other results in a siutation less than optimal for children as well as parents. This is another instance in which the desire to attain status has unintended, and in this case deleterious, consequences both for society as a whole and for many parents and their children. This evaluation assumes that the advantage of "quality time" spent with children does not outweigh the benefit of an increased amount of "ordinary time" with children, however these special terms are defined.

8. O'Boyle (1990) argues for a standard of poverty that is both relative and absolute while Sawhill (1988) notes that absolute measures of poverty, despite theoretical shortcomings, have achieved broad acceptance.

9. One of the failings of the neoclassical approach is that the firm in the neoclassical model does not require coordination of activities of those acting on behalf of the firm. By assumption, workers, managers, and owners have a common goal and miraculously agree on the means to reach the goal. Coase (1992) criticizes this aspect of the neoclassical model because the very reason for a firm's existence is to reconcile tensions among workers, managers, and owners. If conflicting aspirations were straightforward, the best solution according to the neoclassical doctrine would be to use the price mechanism. In fact, firms use a variety of mechanisms—not merely wages and profits—to foster cooperation among various agents and to render each agent reliable. The successful firm motivates all its employees to act vigorously and jointly on behalf of the firm.

10. See Grossman and Hart (1983), and Hammond (1979).

11. Smale (1980) uses the construct of the Prisoner's Dilemma to analyze games in which decisions are based on the past decisions of agents, but not on

binding agreements. Even for a simple case, he shows that multiple equilibria are possible; therefore, one cannot draw conclusions concerning welfare.

12. Economists have also studied whether Prisoner's Dilemmas are stable when the situation is repeated many times. The results are not promising. One of the easiest strategies for a player to use and an economist to analyze is a tit-for-tat rule according to which person A cooperates if person B cooperated on the previous encounter with the Prisoner's Dilemma. Otherwise, person A acts selfishly and similarly for person B. Sober (1992) shows not only that such a strategy is unstable for any game with a finite number of repetitions but also that it is not stable when the opposing person introduces a completely different strategy. The importance of a commitment by all agents to the common good is that stability becomes more likely. Common understandings or social mores pressure people to act in a cooperative manner.

13. Kavka (1991) argues that internal conflicts in a person confronting a decision may be as frequent and problematic as those involved when two people attempt to coordinate activities in situations characterized by the Prisoner's Dilemma. Opposing preferences within the individual prevent him or her from reaching a decision. If Kavka's analysis is confirmed by other scholars, it points to the importance of a tradition that assists a person in resolving divergent proclivities. In an impressive and comprehensive treatise on agents acting in society, Coleman (1990, pp. 503–28) conceives of the self as containing at least two components: an object self and an acting self, "which is at the service of the object self, attempting to bring it satisfaction" (p. 507). Despite this distinction between the two selves, who nevertheless constitute a unitary actor, Coleman's approach does not capture the aspect of agency stressed by Sen (1987), who rightly claims that much of life consists in a person establishing goals for himself or herself. And although toward the end of his book Coleman presents a sophisticated model of actors (pp. 932–49), he retains a troublesome feature of the neoclassical system by using a utility function with a single dimension of satisfaction.

NOTES FOR CHAPTER 9

1. Wallis (1992) examines MacIntyre's concept of a practice and shows that in the economic sphere the virtues of honesty, justice, and courage are required to sustain the practice of neoclassical economics, which, according to Wallis, is in crisis. To extricate neoclassical economics, neoclassical economists have to listen to other traditions and examine issues that are potentially less rewarding in academe. Also, Bellah et al. (1991, p. 290) uses MacIntyre's concept of practice to justify the value of an institution. According to MacIntyre, practices are both means to a good life and ways of living the good life. Bellah et al. claim that at least a few primary institutions in society are practices. That is, by participating in the institution and paying attention to its goals one lives the good life.

2. Provided institutions generate sufficient adherence by citizens and depending on the array of functions institutions perform, they may create a stable environment that promotes economic productivity. As Leach (1991) demonstrates, even a free market with very neoclassical features may be unstable. In his model agents live at least two generations and have rational expectations about a single asset, but the model does not generate a stable equilibrium.

3. Some institutions are more efficient than others, and some adjust more readily than others to changes in the economic environment. North (1991) shows that productivity is affected by the flexibility of institutions as well as by the sequence of events leading to development. Mokyr (1990) also argues that technological progress is path dependent. Coleman (1982) notes more generally that people interact more frequently with "corporate persons" (institutions or persons who identify with the purposes of the institution) than with "natural persons"; as a result, the concepts of authority and responsibility have been altered, thereby increasing the strain on people and institutions in society.

4. Simon (1991) compares markets with organizations and notes that large bureaucracies are often effective systems for providing services.

5. Drèze and Sen (1989) document the importance of noneconomic institutions in reaching the economic goal of preventing starvation or reducing undernourishment in Third World countries.

6. There is no intrinsic relationship between the six social principles of justice and the six primary institutions. It is merely coincidental that both groups have six components.

7. Recent research by neoclassical economists has begun to acknowledge the role played by institutions in the creation of a favorable economic climate. In an updated version of a Schumpeterian model, Baumol (1990) argues that those societies which direct entrepreneurial talent into innovative rather than rent-seeking activities are more productive. Baumol does not examine, however, the necessary conditions to sustain an institution which promotes innovative activity.

8. Anderson (1990) argues that the market mechanism is appropriate in certain circumstances but not in others. For example, a person insults a friend by not accepting a suitable gift, but one does no harm by rejecting an offer of someone to sell his house. Gift relationships prevail in marriage, friendships, and even some business relationships. She also describes the type of relationships involved in a political community and reasons that market mechanisms, which emphasize "exit" over "loyalty," are inappropriate.

9. Wolfe (1989) laments the lack of "civil society" in the United States, which is a culture that enables and modulates a market system: "The question, then, is not why the market is so strong in America, but why civil society has become so weak. An articulate notion of civil society never developed in the United States because in many ways America already was a civil society and so never needed to develop any theory about how it would work" (p. 77).

10. Davidson (1991) shows that objective probabilities and rational expectations do not constitute a general theory of probability because they do not include the possibility of radical uncertainty. It is my claim that, without institutions committed to fundamental values, radical uncertainty would appear more frequently in economic transactions.

11. Stegeman (1991) shows that firms do not advertise enough if their sole goal is to convey information about the product and its price.

12. In a free-market system, if consumers in sufficient numbers express a demand for a good, it will be produced. Even before it is produced, however, consumers are supposed to know whether they have a need for the good and how much satisfaction they will procure through its use.

13. Notwithstanding Haslett (1990), personal experience is influenced by the community in which one lives and, therefore, by the values pursued by that community.

14. Some writers distinguish between act ethics, duty ethics, and virtue ethics. Virtue ethics emphasizes the distinction between moral rightness (a person undertakes an ethically correct action) and moral goodness (a person has an array of good intentions appropriate for the situation, even if the person posits the ethically incorrect act). As Keenan (1992) shows, virtue ethics offers insights and practical possibilities not available to the other approaches.

The fundamental values approach would be considered by many to be primarily an act ethics. Virtues then are merely helpful means to perform correct acts. An alternative interpretation, which I favor, is that the commitment to the fundamental values promotes the development of virtues. The fundamental values and the four principles of justice provide the taxonomy of virtues that indicates when one virtue should be given greater emphasis than other virtues. Pacer groups are communities that stress the importance of particular values or virtues.

15. Akerlof (1991) urges economists to admit that utilities change in ways that are unanticipated and, sometimes, unrecognized by the agents. In a study of procrastination and obedience, he shows how people combine a confused remembrance of past mistakes and a greater dislike for pain in the present than pain in the future to defer action or to go contrary to the wishes of an authority recognized by the individual.

NOTES FOR APPENDIX A

1. The unit of time chosen is arbitrary. A year is used in the text, but one could just as easily make the time interval a week or a month.

NOTES FOR APPENDIX B

1. For a discussion of plausibility and evidence concerning this assumption see Slovic and Lichtenstein (1983), Conlisk (1989), and Cox and Epstein (1989).

2. Salvatore (1986, pp. 58–93) gives a clear and complete graphical presentation while Malinvaud (1972, pp. 12–42) and Baumol (1977, pp. 179–226) describe the mathematical and economic significance of the assumptions made in the mathematical model. The place of altruism in economic models is discussed by Becker (1981), Bernheim and Stark (1988), Collard (1978), Elster (1983), Kurz (1977), and Lindbeck and Weibull (1988).

3. Borrowing is easily incorporated into the model by allowing a_t to be negative.

4. The symbol $q1_j$ should also have a subscript t, i.e., it should be written as $q1_{jt}$, which indicates that activity one is performed at time interval t to support fundamental value j. Since the focus in this analysis is on the act and not on the time at which the act is performed, I omit the subscript t.

5. Adding the fundamental values together mathematically is possible and necessary for any individual, as long as one only considers good actions, i.e., type q actions. The reason is that, since resources are scarce, the person should allocate resources to the pursuit of the fundamental value on which he or she places greatest emphasis while devoting less resources for the pursuit of other fundamental values. A similar weighting of fundamental values is required for society to determine the good actions it takes collectively to pursue the fundamental values.

6. Because the equi-value curves can only be numbered by the integers, it is possible that no tangencies occur. Even when a tangency does not occur for a given qi_j action, however, there is an optimal combination of goods and services which allows the highest participation in the particular fundamental value.

Bibliography

Adams, Roy D. and Ken McCormick. Fashion Dynamics and the Economic Theory of Clubs. *Review of Social Economy* L (1, Spring): 24–39, 1992.

Akerlof, George A. The Market for "Lemons": Quality Uncertainty and the Market Mechanism. *Quarterly Journal of Economics* 84:488–500, 1970.

Akerlof, George A. The Economic Consequences of Cognitive Dissonance. *American Economic Review* 72:307–19, 1982.

Akerlof, George A. Labor Contracts as Partial Gift Exchange. *Quarterly Journal of Economics* 97:543–69, 1982a.

Akerlof, George A. Loyalty Filters. *American Economic Review* 73:54–63, 1983.

Akerlof, George A. *An Economic Theorist's Book of Tales.* Cambridge: Cambridge University Press, 1984.

Akerlof, George A. Procrastination and Obedience. *American Economic Review* 81:1–19, 1991.

Anderson, Elizabeth. The Ethical Limitations of the Market. *Economics and Philosophy* 6:179–205, 1990.

Andreoni, James. Giving with Impure Altruism: Applications to Charity and Ricardian Equivalence. *Journal of Political Economy* 97:1447–58, 1989.

Arendt, Hannah. *The Human Condition.* Chicago: University of Chicago Press, 1958.

Aristotle. *Nicomachean Ethics*, translated with introduction and notes, by Martin Ostwald. Indianapolis: Bobbs-Merrill Educational Publishing, 1962.

Arnott, Richard, and Joseph E. Stiglitz. Moral Hazard and Nonmarket Institutions: Dysfunctional Crowding Out or Peer Monitoring? *American Economic Review* 81:179–90, 1991.

Arrow, Kenneth J. *Social Choice and Individual Values.* 2nd ed. New Haven: Yale University Press, 1963.

Arrow, Kenneth J. Values and Collective Decision-Making. Chapter 10 In *Philosophy, Politics and Society*, ed. P. Laslett and W. G. Runciman, 215–32. New York: Barnes & Noble, 1967.

Arrow, Kenneth J., and Frank H. Hahn. *General Competitive Analysis.* San Francisco: Holden-Day, 1971.

Baumol, William J. *Economic Theory and Operations Analysis*. 4th ed. Englewood Cliffs, New Jersey: Prentice-Hall, 1977.

Baumol, William J. Applied Fairness Theory and Rationing Policy. *American Economic Review* 72:639–651, 1982a.

Baumol, William J. Contestable Markets: An Uprising in the Theory of Industrial Structure. *American Economic Review* 72:1–15, 1982c.

Baumol, William J. *Microtheory: Applications and Origins*. Cambridge, Massachusetts: MIT Press, 1986a.

Baumol, William J. *Superfairness*. Cambridge, Mass.: MIT Press, 1986b.

Baumol, William J. Entrepreneurship: Productive, Unproductive, and Destructive. *Journal of Political Economy* 98:893–921, 1990.

Baumol, William J., and Alan S. Blinder. *Economics: Microeconomics*. New York: Harcourt Brace Jovanovich, 1988.

Baumol, William J., John C. Panzar, and Robert D. Willig. *Contestable Markets and the Theory of Industry Structure*. New York: Harcourt Brace Jovanovich, 1982b.

Becker, Gary S. *The Economic Approach to Human Behavior*. Chicago: University of Chicago Press, 1976.

Becker, Gary S. Altruism in the Family and Selfishness in the Market Place. *Economica* 48:1–15, 1981.

Becker, Gary S., and Kevin M. Murphy. A Theory of Rational Addiction. *Journal of Political Economy* 96:675–700, 1988.

Bell, Daniel. *The Cultural Contradictions of Capitalism*. New York: Basic Books, 1976.

Bellah, Robert N., Richard Marsden, William M. Sullivan, Ann Swindler, and Stephen M. Tipton. *Habits of the Heart: Individuals and Commitment in American Life*. New York: Harper & Row, 1985.

Bellah, Robert N., Richard Madsen, William M. Sullivan, and Steven M. Tipton. *The Good Society*. New York: Alfred A. Knopf, 1991.

Bergstrom, Theodore C. A Fresh Look at the Rotten Kid Theorem—and Other Household Mysteries. *Journal of Political Economy* 97:1138–59, 1989.

Berlin, Isaiah. *Four Essays on Liberty*. New York: Oxford University Press, 1969.

Bernheim, B. Douglas, and Oded Stark. Altruism Within the Family Reconsidered: Do Nice Guys Finish Last? *American Economic Review* 78:1034–45, 1988.

Bloom, Allan. *The Closing of the American Mind*. New York: Simon and Schuster, 1987.

Bok, Sissela. *Lying: Moral Choice in Public and Private Life*. New York: Random House, 1978.

Boland, Lawrence A. On the Futility of Criticizing the Neoclassical Maximization Hypothesis. *American Economic Review* 71:1031–36, 1981.

Boland, Lawrence A. *The Foundations of Economic Method*. Boston: George Allen & Unwin, 1982.

Bowles, Samuel, David M. Gordon, and Thomas E. Weisskopf. *Beyond the Waste Land: A Democratic Alternative to Economic Decline.* New York: Anchor Press/Doubleday, 1983.

Braaten, Carl E. Protestants and Natural Law. *First Things* I (19 January):20–26, 1992.

Broome, John. "Utility." *Economics and Philosophy* 7:1–12, 1991.

Buchanan, James M. *Liberty, Market and State: Political Economy in the 1980s.* New York: New York University Press, 1986.

Camerer, Colin, George Lowenstein, and Martin Weber. The Curse of Knowledge in Economic Settings: An Experimental Analysis. *Journal of Political Economy* 97:1232–54, 1989.

Chalfont, James A., and Julian M. Alston. Accounting for Changes in Tastes. *Journal of Political Economy* 96:391–410, 1988.

Coase, R. H. The Institutional Structure of Production. *American Economic Review* 82.4:713–19, 1992.

Cochran, Kendall P. Economics as a Moral Science. *Review of Social Economy* 32:186–95, 1974.

Colander, David. The Lost Art of Economics. *Journal of Economic Perspectives* 6.3:191–98, 1992.

Coleman, James S. *The Asymmetric Society.* Syracuse: Syracuse University Press, 1982.

Coleman, James S. *Foundations of Social Theory.* Cambridge, Mass.: Belknap Press of Harvard University Press, 1992.

Collard, David. *Altruism and Economy: A Study in Non-Selfish Economics.* New York: Oxford University Press, 1978.

Conley, S.J., John. Public Art in the Plural City. *America* 162 (23):597–600, 1990.

Conlisk, John. Three Variants on the Allais Example. *American Economic Review* 79:392–403, 1989.

Cooter, Robert, and Peter Rappoport. Were the Ordinalists Wrong About Welfare Economics? *Journal of Economic Literature* XXII: 507–30, 1984.

Copleston, S.J., Frederick. *A History of Philosophy, Greece and Rome.* Vol. I. Garden City, New York: Image Books, 1985.

Cox, James C., and Seth Epstein. Preference Reversals Without the Independence Axiom. *American Economic Review* 79:408–26, 1989.

Danner, Peter L. Personalism, Values and Economic Values. *Review of Social Economy* XL:178–98, 1982.

Davidson, Paul. Is Probability Theory Relevant for Uncertainty? A Post Keynesian Perspective. *Journal of Economic Perspectives* 5:129–43, 1991.

Drèze, Jacques. A Paradox in Information Theory. Chapter 7 In *Essays on Economic Decisions Under Uncertainty,* 105–12. New York: Cambridge University Press, 1987.

Drèze, Jean, and Amartya Sen. *Hunger and Public Action.* Oxford: Clarendon Press, 1989.

Duffie, Darrell, and Hugo Sonnenschein. Arrow and General Equilibrium Theory. *Journal of Economic Literature* XXVII:565–98, 1989.

Earl, Peter. *The Economic Imagination: Towards a Behavioral Analysis of Choice.* New York: M.E. Sharpe, 1983.

Ehrlich, Isaac. The Problem of Development: Introduction. *Journal of Political Economy* 98 (5 Part 2):S1-S11, 1990.

Elster, Jon. *Sour Grapes: Studies in the Subversion of Rationality.* New York: Cambridge University Press, 1983.

Etzioni, Amitai. The Case for a Multiple-Utility Conception. *Economics and Philosophy* 2:159–83, 1986.

Etzioni, Amitai. Toward a Kantian Socio-Economics. *Review of Social Economy* XLV:37–47, 1987.

Etzioni, Amitai. *The Moral Dimension: Toward a New Economics.* New York: Free Press, 1988.

Everett, Walter Goodnow. *Moral Values: A Study of the Principles of Conduct.* New York: Henry Holt and Co, 1918.

Fagothey, S.J., Austin. *Right and Reason: Ethics in Theory and Practice.* 2nd ed. St. Louis: Mosby, 1959.

Finnis, John. *Natural Law and Natural Rights.* Oxford: Clarendon, 1980.

Frank, Robert H. The Demand for Unobservable and Other Nonpositional Goods. *American Economic Review* 75:101–16, 1985a.

Frank, Robert H. *Choosing the Right Pond: Human Behavior and the Quest for Status.* New York: Oxford University Press, 1985b.

Frank, Robert H. If *Homo Economicus* Could Choose His Own Utility Function, Would He Want One with a Conscience? *American Economic Review* 77:593–604, 1987.

Frank, Robert H. *Passions Within Reason: The Strategic Role of the Emotions.* New York: W. W. Norton, 1988.

Frank, Robert H. Melding Sociology and Economics: James Coleman's Foundation of Social Theory. *Journal of Economic Literature* XXX (1 March): 147–70, 1992.

Friedman, Milton. *Capitalism and Freedom.* Chicago: University of Chicago Press, 1962.

Fuchs, S.J., Joseph. Das Absolute in der Moral. *Stimmen der Zeit* 207 (12 Dezember):825–38, 1989.

Gadamer, Hans-Georg. *Truth and Method.* New York: Seabury Press, 1975.

Gadamer, Hans-Georg. *The Idea of the Good in Platonic-Aristotelian Philosophy.* New Haven: Yale University Press, 1986.

Geertz, Clifford. *The Interpretation of Cultures.* New York: Basic Books, 1973.

Goode, William J. Comment: The Economics of Nonmonetary Variables. *Journal of Political Economy* 82:S27–33, 1974.

Gorman, Raymond F. and James B. Kehr. Fairness as a Constraint on Profit Seeking. *American Economic Review* 82(1 March):355–58, 1992.

Grisez, Germain. *Christian Moral Principles*. Vol. 1. (The Way of the Lord Jesus.) Chicago: Franciscan Herald Press, 1983.

Grisez, Germain. A Contemporary Natural-Law Ethics. In *Moral Philosophy: Historical and Contemporary Essays*, ed. William C. Starr and Richard C. Taylor, 125–43. Milwaukee: Marquette University Press, 1989.

Grisez, Germain and Russell Shaw. *Beyond the New Morality*. Indiana: University of Notre Dame Press, Notre Dame, 1980.

Grossman, Sanford J., and Oliver D. Hart. An Analysis of the Principal Agent Problem. *Econometrica* 51:7–46, 1983.

Hahn, Frank. Information Dynamics and Equilibrium. Chapter 5. In: *The Economics of Missing Markets, Information, and Games*. (ed. F. Hahn) Oxford: Clarendon Press, 106–26, 1990.

Hahn, Frank, and Martin Hollis, eds. *Philosophy and Economic Theory*. Oxford: Oxford University Press, 1979.

Hammond, Peter J. Symposium on Incentive Compatibility. *Review of Economic Studies* 46 (2 Symposium):181–203, 1979.

Hampshire, Stuart. Morality and Convention. Chapter 7 In *Utilitarianism and Beyond*, eds. Amartya Sen and Bernard Williams, 145–57. New York: Cambridge University Press, 1982.

Hare, R. M. *The Language of Morals*. Oxford: Clarendon Press, 1952.

Hare, R. M. *Freedom and Reason*. Oxford: Clarendon Press, 1963.

Harsanyi, John. Cardinal Welfare, Individualistic Ethics, and Interpersonal Comparisons of Utility. *Journal of Political Economy* 63:309–21, 1955.

Haslett, D. W. What Is Utility? *Economics and Philosophy* 6:65–94,1990.

Heilbroner, Robert L. *The Nature and Logic of Capitalism*. New York: W. W. Norton, 1985.

Heilbroner, Robert L. *Behind the Veil of Economics: Essays in Worldly Philosophy*. New York: Norton, 1988.

Heiner, Ronald A. The Origin of Predictable Behavior. *American Economic Review* 73:560–95, 1983.

Hirschman, Albert O. *Exit, Voice, and Loyalty*. Cambridge, Mass.: Harvard University Press, 1970.

Hirschman, Albert O. *The Passions and the Interests: Political Arguments for Capitalism before Its Triumph*. Princeton: Princeton University Press, 1977.

Hirschman, Albert O. Rival Interpretations of Market Society: Civilizing, Destructive, or Feeble? *Journal of Economic Literature* XX: 1463–84, 1982.

Hirshleifer, Jack. The Expanding Domain of Economics. *American Economic Review* 75:53–68, 1985.

Hittinger, Russell. *A Critique of the New Natural Law Theory*. Notre Dame, Indiana: University of Notre Dame Press, 1987.

Holcombe, Randall G. Applied Fairness Theory: Comment. *American Economic Review* 73:1153–56, 1983.

Hollenbach, S.J., David. *Justice, Peace, and Human Rights: American Catholic*

Social Ethics in a Pluralistic World. New York: Crossroad, 1988.

Hollenbach, S.J., David. The Common Good Revisited. *Theological Studies* 50: 70–94, 1989.

Iannaccone, Laurence R. Sacrifice and Stigma: Reducing Free-Riding in Cults, Communes, and Other Collectives. *Journal of Political Economy* 100 (2 April):271–91, 1992.

Jonsen, Albert R., and Stephen Toulmin. *The Abuse of Casuistry*. Berkeley: University of California Press, 1988.

Kavka, Gregory S. Is Individual Choice Less Problematic Than Collective Choice? *Economics and Philosophy* 7(2 October):277–83, 1991.

Keenan, S.J., James F. Virtue Ethics: Making a Case as It Comes of Age. *Thought*, 1992.

Kennedy, Paul. *The Rise and Fall of the Great Powers: Economic Change and Military Conflict from 1500 to 2000*. New York: Random House, 1987.

Killingsworth, Mark R. *Labor Supply*. Cambridge: Cambridge University Press, 1983.

Kohlberg, Lawrence L. Stage and Sequence: the Cognitive-Developmental Approach to Socialization. In *Handbook of Socialization: Theory and Research*, ed. D. A. Goslin, 347–480. New York: Rand McNally, 1969.

Kohlberg, Lawrence L. The Claim to Moral Adequacy of a Highest Stage of Moral Judgment. *Journal of Philosophy* LXX:630–46, 1973.

Kotlikoff, Lawrence J., and Avia Spivak. The Family as an Incomplete Annuities Market. *Journal of Political Economy* 89:372–91, 1981.

Kurz, Mordecai. Altruistic Equilibrium. Chapter 8 In *Economic Progress, Private Values, and Public Policy*, eds. B. Balassa and R. Nelson, 177–200. New York: North-Holland, 1977.

Langan, S.J., John P. Rawls, Nozick, and the Search for Social Justice. *Theological Studies* 36:346–58, 1977.

Lasch, Christopher. *The True and Only Heaven: Progress and Its Critics*. New York: W. W. Norton, 1991.

Lazear, Edward P. Labor Economics and the Psychology of Organizations. *Journal of Economic Perspectives* 5:89–100, 1991.

Leach, John. Rational Speculation. *Journal of Political Economy* 99:131–44, 1991.

Leamer, Edward E. *Sources of International Comparative Advantage: Theory and Evidence*. Cambridge, Mass.: MIT Press, 1984.

Leibenstein, Harvey. Allocative Efficiency vs. 'X-Efficiency.' *American Economic Review* 56:392–415, 1966.

Leibenstein, Harvey. A Branch of Economics Is Missing: Micro-Micro Theory. *Journal of Economic Literature* XVII:477–502, 1979.

Leibenstein, Harvey. *Beyond Economic Man*. Cambridge, Mass.: Harvard University Press, 1980.

Lindbeck, Assar, and Joergen W. Weibull. Altruism and Time Consistency: The Economics of Fait Accompli. *Journal of Political Economy* 96:1165–82, 1988.

Locay, Luis. Economic Development and Division of Production Between Households and Markets. *Journal of Political Economy* 98:965–82, 1990.

Lucas, J. R. *On Justice.* Oxford: Clarendon Press, 1980.

Lucas, Robert E., Jr. Tobin and Monetarism: A Review Article. *Journal of Economic Literature* XIX:558–67, 1981.

Lucas, Robert E., Jr. *Models of Business Cycles.* New York: Blackwell, 1987.

Lutz, Mark A., and Kenneth Lux. *Humanistic Economics: The New Challenge.* New York: Bootstrap Press, 1988.

MacIntyre, Alasdair. A Mistake about Causality in Social Science. Chapter 3 In *Philosophy, Politics and Society,* eds. Peter Laslett and W. G. Runciman, 48–70. New York: Barnes and Noble, 1962.

MacIntyre, Alasdair. *After Virtue: A Study in Moral Theory.* 2nd ed. Notre Dame, Indiana: University of Notre Dame, 1984.

MacIntyre, Alasdair. *Whose Justice? Which Rationality?* Notre Dame, Indiana: University of Notre Dame Press, 1988.

MacIntyre, Alasdair. *Three Rival Versions of Moral Inquiry: Encyclopaedia, Genealogy, and Tradition.* Notre Dame: University of Notre Dame, 1990.

Mackay, Donald A. *The Building of Manhattan.* New York: Harper & Row, 1987.

Macpherson, C. B. *The Rise and Fall of Economic Justice and Other Essays.* New York: Oxford University Press, 1985.

Malinvaud, E. *Lectures on Microeconomic Theory.* New York: North-Holland, 1972.

Mankiw, N. Gregory. A Quick Refresher Course in Macroeconomics. *Journal of Economic Literature* XXVIII:1645–60, 1990.

Mann, Michael. *Workers on the Move: the Sociology of Relocation.* Cambridge: Cambridge University Press, 1973.

Margolis, Howard. *Selfishness, Altruism and Rationality: A Theory of Social Choice.* New York: Cambridge University Press, 1982.

Margolis, Joseph. *Values and Conduct.* New York: Oxford University Press, 1971.

Martin, David A. R. H. Tawney's Normative Economic History of Capitalism. *Review of Social Economy* XLIII:84–102, 1985.

Mattox, William R. The Parent Trap. *Policy Review* (55, Winter):6–13, 1991.

McAleer, Michael, Adrian R. Pagan, and Paul A. Volker. What Will Take the Con Out of Econometrics? *American Economic Review* 75:293–307, 1985.

McCloskey, Donald N. The Rhetoric of Economics. *Journal of Economic Literature* XXI:481–517, 1983.

McCloskey, Donald N. *The Applied Theory of Price.* New York: Macmillan, 1985a.

McCloskey, Donald N. *The Rhetoric of Economics.* Madison, Wisconsin: University of Wisconsin Press, 1985b.

McCloskey, Donald N. *If You're So Smart: The Narrative of Economic Expertise.* Chicago: The University of Chicago Press, 1990.

McCormick, S.J., Richard, and Paul Ramsey, eds. *Doing Evil to Achieve Good: Moral Choices in Conflict Situations.* Chicago: Loyola University Press, 1978.

McMullin, Ernan. *The Inference That Makes Science*. Milwaukee: Marquette University Press, 1992.

Mishan, E. J. The New Welfare Economics: An Alternative View. *International Economic Review* 21:691–705, 1980.

Mokyr, Joel. *The Lever of Riches: Technological Creativity and Economic Progress*. New York: Oxford University Press, 1990.

Moore, Barrington, Jr. *Reflections on the Causes of Human Misery and Upon Certain Proposals to Eliminate Them*. Boston: Beacon Press, 1973.

Moore, Barrington, Jr. *Privacy: Studies in Social and Cultural History*. New York: M. E. Sharpe, 1985.

Moynihan, Daniel Patrick. Social Justice in the Next Century. *America* 165 (6):132–37, 1991.

Murray, S.J., John Courtney. *We Hold These Truths: Catholic Reflections on the American Proposition*. New York: Sheed and Ward, 1960.

National Conference of Catholic Bishops. *Economic Justice for All: Pastoral Letter on Catholic Social Teaching and the U.S. Economy*. Washington, D.C.: United States Catholic Conference, 1986.

Nell-Breuning, S.J., Oswald von. *Gerechtigkeit und Freiheit*. Vienna: Europaverlag, 1980.

Nell-Breuning, S.J., Oswald von. *Arbeitet der Mensch zuviel?* Freiburg im Breisgau: Herder, 1985.

Nell-Breuning, S.J., Oswald von. *Kapitalismus—kritisch betrachtet*. Freiburg im Breisgau: Herder, 1986.

The New Encyclopedia Britannica. London: Encyclopedia Britannica Inc.; ninth edition, 1875-1889.

Nietzsche, Friedrich Wilhelm. *A Genealogy of Morals*, translated by William A. Haussmann. New York: Macmillan, 1897, t.p.1907.

Nitzan, Shmuel, and Jacob Paroush. Investment in Human Capital and Social Self-Protection Under Uncertainty. *International Economic Review* 21:547–57, 1980.

North, Douglass C. Institutions. *Journal of Economic Perspectives* 5:97–112, 1991.

Novak, Michael. *The Spirit of Democratic Capitalism*. New York: Simon and Schuster, 1982.

Nozick, Robert. *Anarchy, State and Utopia*. Oxford: Oxford University Press, 1974.

Nozick, Robert. *The Examined Life: Philosophical Meditations*. New York: Simon and Schuster, 1989.

O'Boyle, Edward J. Poverty: A Concept That Is Both Absolute and Relative Because Human Beings Are at Once Individual and Social. *Review of Social Economy* XLVIII:2–17, 1990.

O'Connell, John F. *Welfare Economic Theory*. Boston: Auburn House, 1982.

Perry, Michael J. *Morality, Politics, and Law*. New York: Oxford University, 1988.

Perry, Michael J. *Love and Power: The Role of Religion and Morality in American Politics.* New York: Oxford University Press, 1991.

Pesch, S.J., Heinrich. *Lehrbuch der Nationalökonomie.* Vol. I–V. Freiburg im Breisgau: Herder, 1905–06.

Piderit, S.J., John. *The Role of Economics and Ethical Principles in Determining U.S. Policies Toward Poor Nations. Thought* 60:353–70, 1985.

Polanyi, Karl. Aristotle Discovers the Economy. Chapter V In *Trade and Market in the Early Empires,* eds. Karl Polanyi, Conrad M. Arensberg, and Harry W. Pearson, 64–94. Chicago: Gateway Edition (Regnery), 1957.

Pole, J. R. *The Pursuit of Equality in American History.* Berkeley: University of California Press, 1978.

Quirk, James, and Rubin Saposnik. *Introduction to General Equilibrium Theory and Welfare Economics.* New York: McGraw-Hill, 1968.

Rawls, John. Outline of a Decision Procedure for Ethics. *The Philosophical Review* 60:177–97, 1951.

Rawls, John. *A Theory of Justice.* Cambridge, Mass.: Harvard University Press, 1971.

Rawls, John. Social Unity and Primary Goods. In *Utilitarianism and Beyond,* eds. A. K. Sen and Bernard Williams, 159–85. Cambridge: Cambridge University Press, 1982.

Rhonheimer, Martin. *Natur als Grundlage der Moral: Die personale Struktur des Naturgesetzes bei Thomas von Aquin: Eine Auseinandersetzung mit autonomer und teleologischer Ethik.* Innsbruck, Austria: Tyrolia-Verlag, 1987.

Romer, Paul M. Are Nonconvexities Important for Understanding Growth? *American Economic Review* 80:97–102, 1990a.

Romer, Paul M. Endogenous Technological Change. *Journal of Political Economy* 98 (5.2):S71–S102, 1990b.

Roth, Alvin E., ed. *Laboratory Experimentation in Economics: Six Points of View.* New York: Cambridge University Press, 1987.

Salvatore, Dominick. *Microeconomics: Theory and Applications.* New York: Macmillan, 1986.

Salvatore, Dominick. *International Economics.* New York: Macmillan, 1989.

Sandel, Michael J. *Liberalism and the Limits of Justice.* Cambridge: Cambridge University Press, 1982.

Sappington, David. Incentives in Principal-Agent Relationships. *Journal of Economic Perspectives* 5.2: 45–66, 1992.

Sawhill, Isabel V. Poverty in the U.S.: Why Is It So Persistent? *Journal of Economic Literature* XXVI:1073–119, 1988.

Schüller, S.J., Bruno. Zur Problematik allgemein verbindlicher ethischer Grundsätze. *Theologie und Philosophie* 45:1–23, 1970.

Schüller, S.J., Bruno. *Die Begründung sittlicher Urteile.* Düsseldorf, Germany: Patmos Verlag, 1980.

Schultz, Theodore W. The Economics of Being Poor. *Journal of Political Economy* 88:639–51, 1980.

Scitovsky, Tibor. *The Joyless Economy*. New York: Oxford University Press, 1976.

Seligman, Adam B. *The Idea of Civil Society*. New York: The Free Press, 1992.

Sen, Amartya K. The Impossibility of a Paretian Liberal. *Journal of Political Economy* 78:152–57, 1970.

Sen, Amartya K. Behaviour and the Concept of Preference. *Economica* XL:241–59, 1973.

Sen, Amartya K. Choice Orderings and Morality. In *Practical Reason*, ed. Stephan Korner. New Haven: Yale University Press, 1974.

Sen, Amartya K. Rational Fools: A Critique of the Behavioural Foundations of Economic Theory. Chapter 1 In *Scientific Models and Man*, 1–25. Oxford: Clarendon, 1979.

Sen, Amartya K. Description as Choice. *Oxford Economic Papers* 32:353–69, 1980.

Sen, Amartya K. Social Choice and Justice: A Review Article. *Journal of Economic Literature* XXIII:1764–76, 1985.

Sen, Amartya. *On Ethics and Economics*. Oxford: Blackwell, 1987.

Sen, Amartya K., and Bernard Williams, eds. *Utilitarianism and Beyond*. New York: Cambridge University Press, 1982.

Shepard, Andrea. Price Discrimination and Retail Configuration. *Journal of Political Economy* 99:30–53, 1991.

Sigmund, Paul E. *Natural Law in Political Thought*. Washington, D.C.: University Press of America, 1971.

Simon, Herbert A. *Models of Man*. New York: Wiley, 1957.

Simon, Herbert. Rational Decision Making in Business Organization. *American Economic Review* 69:493–513, 1979.

Simon, Herbert A. Organizations and Markets. *Journal of Economic Perspectives* 5:25–44, 1991.

Slovic, Paul, and Sarah Lichtenstein. Preference Reversals: A Broader Perspective. *American Economic Review* 73:596–605, 1983.

Smale, Steve. The Prisoner's Dilemma and Dynamical Systems Associated to Non-Cooperative Games. *Econometrica* 48:1617–34, 1980.

Smith, Vernon L., ed. *Experimental Economics*. Brookfield, Vermont: Edward Elgar, 1990.

Sober, Elliott. Stable Cooperation in Iterated Prisoners' Dilemma's. *Economics and Philosophy* 8 (1 April):127–40, 1992.

Stegeman, Mark. Advertising in Competitive Markets. *American Economic Review* 81:210–23, 1991.

Tawney, Richard H. *The Acquisitive Society*. New York: Harcourt Brace Jovanovich, 1948.

Tawney, Richard H. *Equality*. London: Allen & Unwin, 1952.

Thaler, Richard H., and H. H. Shefrin. An Economic Theory of Self-Control. *Journal of Political Economy* 89:392–406, 1981.

Thurow, Lester C. *Dangerous Currents*. New York: Random House, 1983.

Tinari, Frank D. Reducing Income Inequality Is Not the Only 'Equitable' Fairness Criterion. *Review of Social Economy* XLV:77–91, 1987.

Varian, Hal R. Distributive Justice, Welfare Economics and the Theory of Fairness. *Philosophy and Public Affairs* 4:223–47, 1975.

Veblen, Thorstein, *The Theory of the Leisure Class*. New York: Penguin Books, 1979, 1899.

Velasquez, Manuel G. *Business Ethics: Concepts and Cases*. 2nd ed. Englewood Cliffs, New Jersey: Prentice Hall, 1988.

Wallis, Joe L. The Relevance for Social Economics of Alasdair MacIntyre's Conception of a Practice. *Review of Social Economy* L(1, Spring):2–23, 1992.

Walzer, Michael. *Spheres of Justice: A Defense of Pluralism and Equality*. New York: Basic Books, 1983.

White, Laurence H. *Methodology of the Austrian School*. New York: Center for Libertarian Studies, 1977.

Williamson, Jeffrey G. Productivity and American Leadership: A Review Article. *Journal of Economic Literature* XXIX:51–68, 1991.

Williamson, Oliver E. *The Economic Institutions of Capitalism*. New York: The Free Press (Macmillan), 1985.

Wolfe, Alan. *Whose Keeper?: Social Science and Moral Obligation*. Berkeley: University of California, 1989.